SCHAUM'S OUTLINE OF

THEORY AND PROBLEMS

of

PROGRAMMING

with

FORTRAN

including STRUCTURED FORTRAN

•

by

SEYMOUR LIPSCHUTZ, Ph.D.
Professor of Mathematics
Temple University

and

ARTHUR POE, Ph.D.
Associate Professor of Computer Science
Temple University

SCHAUM'S OUTLINE SERIES
McGRAW-HILL, INC.
New York St. Louis San Francisco Auckland Bogotá Caracas Lisbon
London Madrid Mexico City Milan Montreal New Delhi
San Juan Singapore Sydney Tokyo Toronto

To our parents,
Florence and Louis
and
Julia Lu and Dison H.F.

0-07-037984-X

15 SH SH 9 8 7 6 5 4

Cover design by Amy E. Becker.

Library of Congress Cataloging in Publication Data

Lipschutz, Seymour.
    Schaum's outline of theory and problems of
programming with Fortran.

    (Schaum's outline series)
    Includes index.
    1. FORTRAN (Computer program language)—Problems,
exercises, etc. I. Poe, Arthur, joint author.
II. Title. III. Title: Theory and problems of
programming with Fortran.
QA76.73.F25L57   001.6′424   77-24492
ISBN 0-07-037984-X

Preface

The second half of the twentieth century may well be called the age of computers. People in almost every field of endeavor—such as engineering, physical sciences, economics, psychology, education, social sciences, medical sciences, law, and business, i.e., wherever data needs to be collected and analyzed with calculations—will have some contact with computers and the languages used to instruct them. One such programming language is called Fortran, short for FORmula TRANslation. This book is designed and written to introduce the Fortran language and to teach problem solving with this language. In addition to presenting the syntax of Fortran, the main aim of the book is to teach the reader how to write clear, efficient Fortran programs by stressing programming techniques as well as good programming practices. All the important principles of standard Fortran are discussed in this book together with the important features of structured Fortran. This book is suitable as a text for an introductory course in Fortran programming, or as a supplement to standard texts in a course in "Introduction to Computer Science".

With its deliberately elementary approach and many graded examples, this book should appeal to a wide audience, and is also particularly suited as an effective self-study guide. Each chapter begins with a clear statement of pertinent definitions and principles together with illustrative and other descriptive material. This is followed by graded sets of solved and supplementary problems. The solved problems serve to illustrate and amplify the material, and the supplementary problems furnish a complete review of the material in the chapter.

The text is divided into twelve chapters. A short discussion of the basic computer operations is given in Chapter 1 by way of simple programs. This gives the reader a glimpse of the Fortran language as well as some feeling for the dynamics involved in Fortran programming. Keypunching instructions and Fortran package arrangement are also discussed in this chapter so that the reader may write and run simple programs as soon as possible. Formal introduction to the Fortran language begins in Chapter 2, where arithmetic expressions and arithmetic assignment statements are presented. Both real and integer arithmetic are also discussed, as well as some pitfalls of computer arithmetic. Chapter 3 is about numerical input/output operations. Both formatted and unformatted features are discussed.

Flowcharting is introduced in Chapter 4 to help the reader set up and visualize problem-solving procedures. More importantly, Chapter 4 discusses the basic Fortran (unstructured) transfer of control statements, including the logical IF statement. Structured control features, including the block IF statement, are discussed in Chapter 12. Similarly, the basic indexed DO loop is presented in Chapter 5, whereas the generalized DO loop and the WHILE- and FOR-structures are treated in Chapter 12. Arrays and subscripted variables are discussed in Chapter 6. To help the reader write complex programs in modules, FUNCTION subprograms and SUBROUTINE subprograms are discussed in Chapter 7.

Programming techniques for searching, sorting, file maintenance, etc. are treated in Chapter 8. Also discussed are numerical computations such as finding zeros of functions and solutions of systems of linear equations. Character information and logical variables, together with their input/output, are treated in Chapter 9. Additional features of input/output, such as G-field and execution-time format, are covered in Chapter 10. Other features of Fortran, such as DOUBLE PRECISION and COMPLEX variables, and COMMON and EQUIVALENCE statements, are presented in Chapter 11. As mentioned earlier, structured Fortran features such as the block IF statement and the generalized DO loop are discussed in Chapter 12. This chapter is compatible with recent changes in standard Fortran and with the WATFOR and WATFIV compilers.

PREFACE

The topics and chapters have been written so that they are as independent as possible from other topics and chapters. This has been done to make the book more flexible, and to provide a more useful book of reference. We have also included an appendix on the internal representation of data in the computer.

We wish to thank many friends and colleagues for invaluable suggestions and critical review of the manuscript. We also wish to express our gratitude to the staff of the McGraw-Hill Schaum's Outline Series, particularly to John Aliano and Ellen LaBarbera, for their unfailing cooperation.

Seymour Lipschutz
Arthur T. Poe

Contents

CONTENTS

Chapter 1

Introduction, Program Organization

1.1 INTRODUCTION

The second half of the twentieth century may well be called the age of computers. These devices and the various "languages" used to instruct them are becoming almost as common as typewriters and slide rules. Essentially, a computer performs three functions:

1. It receives data (input).
2. It processes data by various computations.
3. It emits data (output).

These functions are accomplished by giving the computer a *program* consisting of a sequence of *statements*. (A partial sequence of statements is called a *program segment*.)

The main purpose of this text is to teach the reader to write computer programs using the FORTRAN language. (The word FORTRAN comes from FORmula TRANslation.) This study will formally begin with the next chapter. This chapter will cover certain matters of procedure regarding the punching of Fortran statements on cards and how the Fortran package is arranged for the computer. We will also learn a few facts about computers that may give us a feeling for some of the dynamics involved in Fortran programming. In particular, we will see how a computer executes some simple programs. (In fact, we emphasize that the reader should actually punch one or more of these programs on cards and run them on a computer.)

We close the chapter with an overview of computers and of computer languages. This involves many details which are not absolutely required for many of the subsequent topics in this book. Hence, the reader can skim through this section on a first reading and use it for reference when necessary.

1.2 KEYPUNCHING FORTRAN STATEMENTS

Fortran programs are sometimes first written on Fortran coding sheets. (See Fig. 1-1.) However, once written, they must be given to the computer in some machine-readable form, such as a deck of punched cards, a paper tape, a magnetic tape, or via a typewriter terminal—depending on the input device. We will assume throughout this book that our input device is a card reader, so programs are to be punched on cards. Such a card, pictured in Fig. 1-2(*a*), contains 80 columns and each column can accommodate a single character.

Each statement in a Fortran program must be punched on a separate card. As illustrated in Fig. 1-2(*b*), not all 80 columns of the card are used for the Fortran statement. Specifically, we have the following rules:

1. The actual Fortran statement can only be punched within columns 7 through 72 inclusive.
2. Column 6 is called the continuation column and is reserved for the following purpose. If a Fortran statement is too long for the above-mentioned 66 columns of the

1

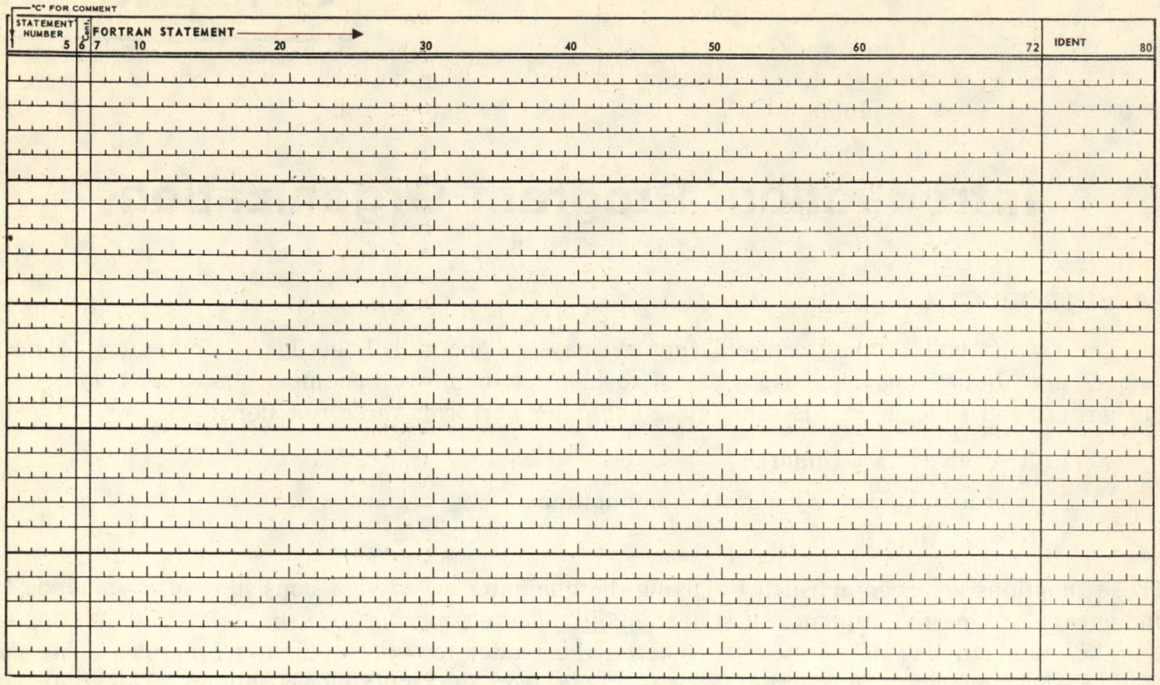

Fig. 1-1 Fortran coding sheet.

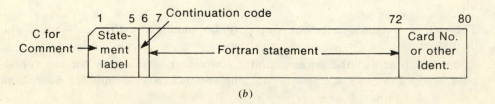

(a)

(b)

Fig. 1-2

card, then it can be continued (within columns 7 through 72) on up to 19 additional cards. In such a case, a "1" (or any symbol other than zero) must be punched in column 6 on each of the additional cards. That is, any symbol (other than zero) punched in column 6 tells the computer that the statement is a continuation of the last statement.

3. Statements can be labeled for reference, and such labels are punched within columns 1 through 5 of the labeled statement. In Fortran, a label is any unsigned positive integer (maximum of five digits) and is called a *statement number*. Clearly, no two different statements can be assigned the same statement number.

4. The content of columns 73 through 80 is ignored by the computer. These columns may be punched for identification, sequencing, or any other purpose.

Comments may be added to a program by punching a "C" in column 1 of the card. The comment itself may be punched anywhere between column 2 and column 80. Comments have no actual bearing on the program. They are usually used to identify a program and for explanation. The computer simply skips a comment and goes on to the next statement. However, the comment will appear on the printout sheet when the program is printed by the computer.

Remark. The reader will notice, when punching cards, that only capital letters are available for the alphabetic characters. The symbols for addition, subtraction, multiplication, and division are written as $+$, $-$, $*$, $/$, respectively. Exponentiation, raising a number to a power, is written as $**$. (These operations are discussed in detail in Chapter 2.) Thus in Fortran,

$$a \cdot b \text{ is written as A} * \text{B}, \qquad \frac{a}{b} \text{ as A/B}, \qquad \text{and} \qquad a^b \text{ as A} ** \text{B}$$

We note that blank spaces in Fortran statements are ignored by the computer, so the reader may insert them for easier reading. For example, we could punch

A**2 + B**2   instead of the equivalent   A**2+B**2

4*I + 6*J   instead of the equivalent   4*I+6*J

and GO TO instead of GOTO.

1.3 FORTRAN PACKAGE

The Fortran program which we write and punch on cards is only one part of a package that we give to the computer when the program is to be executed. This package consists of the following sequence of cards:

1. An ID card. This card usually contains the programmer's name, project, course or account number, priority number, maximum running time, etc.

2. Fortran deck. This deck of cards contains the actual Fortran program.

3. Data deck. This deck of cards, which may be empty, contains the data that is read by the computer.

4. End-of-file card. This card denotes the end of the package.

The above four groups of cards may be separated by one or more control cards, as illustrated in Fig. 1-3. The exact information on the ID card, the end-of-file card, and the control cards will depend upon the particular computing facility to which one has access.

The data deck contains the input data. In punching a data card, we can use the full 80 columns. That is, the rules for punching Fortran statements do not apply here, and none of the columns, e.g., column 6, has any special purpose.

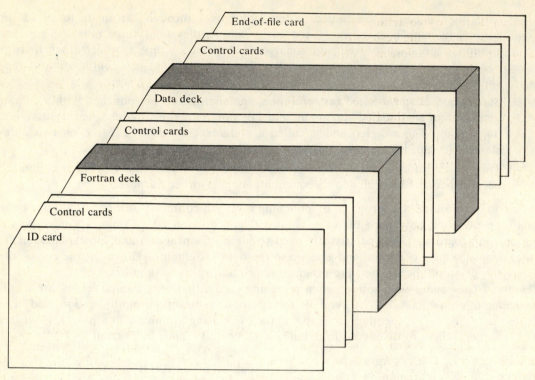

Fig. 1-3 Fortran package.

1.4 STORING NUMBERS

A computer has a memory unit consisting of many *memory cells* (*locations*) for storing data. A number can be assigned to a memory location only if the memory location is given a name. We represent the assignment of a number, say 75, to a memory location called N by

$$N \leftarrow 75$$

More generally,

$$NAME \leftarrow arithmetic\ expression$$

indicates that the value of the arithmetic expression is assigned to a memory location called NAME.

We emphasize that the arrow $\leftarrow$ is universally accepted as "assignment". However, different programming languages represent $\leftarrow$ in different ways.   In Fortran, $\leftarrow$ is represented by

$$=$$

(i.e., the mathematical equal sign).   Thus, the Fortran statement

$$I = 7$$

instructs the computer to assign the number 7 to the memory location named I, and the Fortran statement

$$J = 4 + 5 + 8$$

instructs the computer to:

1. Add the values on the right side of $=$.
2. Store the result, which is 17, in a location named J.

Observe that there are two actions involved here: the evaluation of the expression on the right side of = and the storing of the result in the location given on the left side of =.

An arithmetic expression may also contain the names of storage locations. However, these names must be *defined*, i.e., they are the names of storage locations in which numbers have been stored previously in the same program. The computer evaluates the arithmetic expression by replacing the names by the values stored in these locations.

For example, consider the Fortran statement

$$K = 3*I + 2*J - 24$$

where I and J contain 7 and 17 respectively. (Remember that the star * means multiply in Fortran.) The computer evaluates the arithmetic expression on the right as

$$3 \cdot 7 + 2 \cdot 17 - 24$$

The result, 31, is then stored in a memory location labeled K. Note that the contents of I and J are not literally taken out of locations I and J when the computer evaluates $3*I + 2*J - 24$, but the contents are copied into the arithmetic unit, and I and J still contain the same values.

We illustrate these ideas in our first program.

First Program

We write a program which calculates the sum LS and the product LP of the numbers $I = 24$, $J = 3$, $K = 7$. Figure 1-4(a) is the coding sheet of a Fortran program to carry out these calculations, and Fig. 1-4(b) shows how the program would look if it is punched on a deck of cards.

Observe that each statement is written on a separate line on the coding sheet and is punched on a separate card. We will follow the computer as it reads and executes the program. However, first, here is a brief explanation of several statements in the program:

1. The first card has the letter "C" punched in column 1, so it is a comment card. As noted before, comments have no bearing on the program. When the computer encounters the letter "C" in column 1, it simply prints the comment and proceeds to the next statement.

2. The PRINT statement

    PRINT, I, J, K, LS, LP

    tells the computer to print the current contents of the memory locations I, J, K, LS, and LP in this order. This is an unformatted output statement, and the values will be printed in some predefined format. Formatted and unformatted statements are studied in detail in Chapter 3.

3. The STOP statement tells the computer to stop execution, and the END statement is always the last statement of any program. [See Section 1.7(c) for a further discussion of their differences.]

Program Execution

Line 1. This is a comment since there is a C typed in the first column. As stated earlier, the computer skips this statement and goes on to the next statement.

Line 2. This tells the computer to store the integer 24 in a memory location labeled I:

$$I \leftarrow 24$$

Line 3. $J \leftarrow 3$

Line 4. $K \leftarrow 7$

Line 5. This tells the computer to evaluate the arithmetic expression on the right, by adding

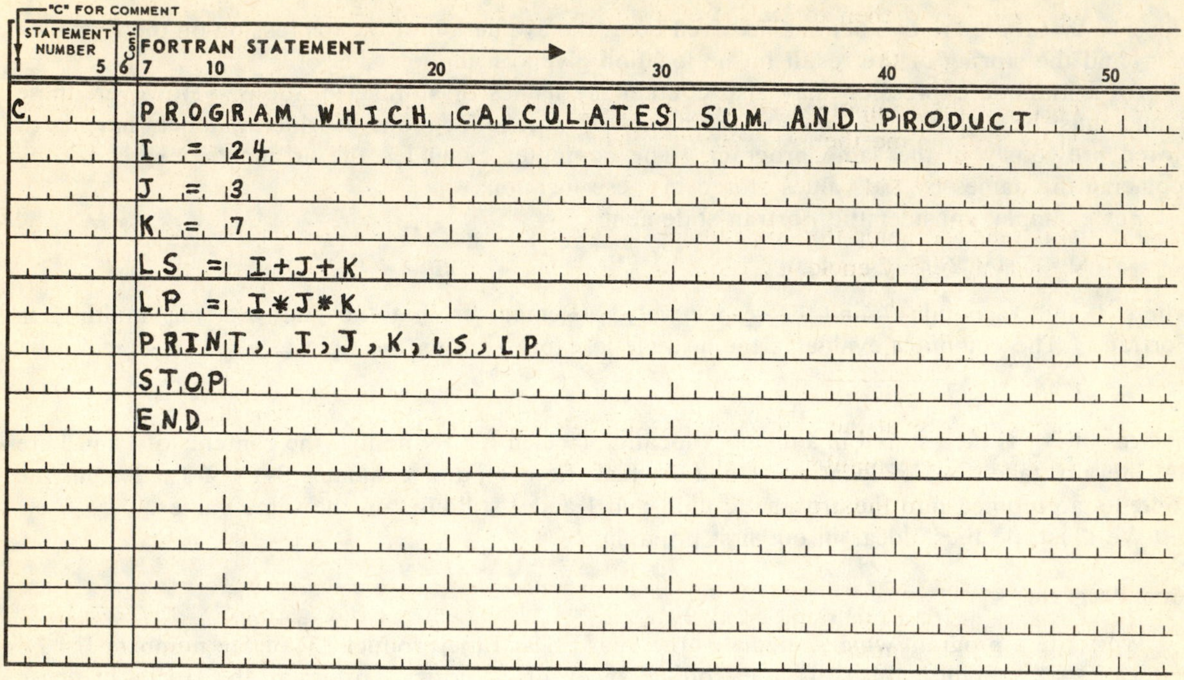

"C" FOR COMMENT

STATEMENT NUMBER	Cont.	FORTRAN STATEMENT ⟶
1 5	6	7 10 20 30 40 50
C		PROGRAM WHICH CALCULATES SUM AND PRODUCT
		I = 24
		J = 3
		K = 7
		LS = I+J+K
		LP = I*J*K
		PRINT, I,J,K,LS,LP
		STOP
		END

(a)

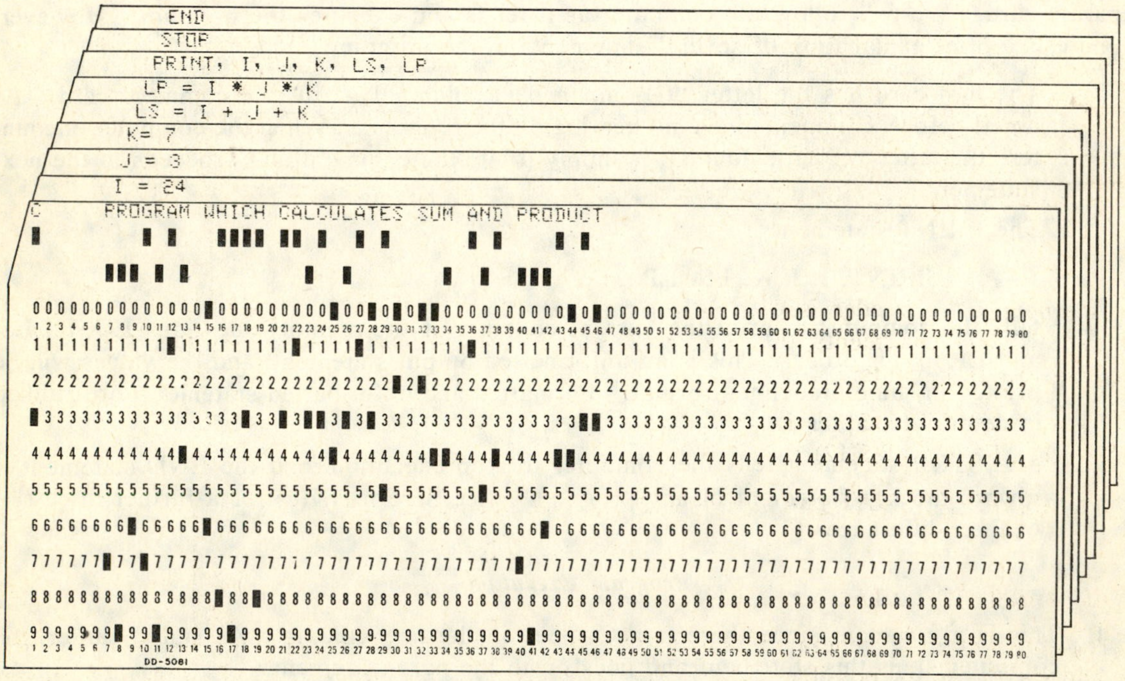

(b)

Fig. 1-4

$24 + 3 + 7$, and then to store the result, which is 34, in a memory location labeled LS:

$$LS \leftarrow 34$$

Line 6. This tells the computer to evaluate the arithmetic expression on the right, by multiplying 24 by 3 by 7, and then to store the result in LP:

$$LP \leftarrow 504$$

Line 7. This tells the computer to print the values stored in I, J, K, LS, LP in that order. We represent this by enclosing the output in a parallelogram as follows:

$$\boxed{24, \quad 3, \quad 7, \quad 34, \quad 504}$$

(See *comment* at the end of the section on this unformatted PRINT statement.)

Line 8. This tells the computer to STOP execution.

Line 9. Every program must be completed with an END statement.

Output

We will assume that our output device is a line printer. The print paper of a line printer is assumed to have 132 columns (print spaces). One normally uses a FORMAT statement to tell the computer where to put the output on the print paper. In this chapter, we use an unformatted PRINT statement, and so there is a preassigned format for the output. The output will appear on one line, as in Fig. 1-5.

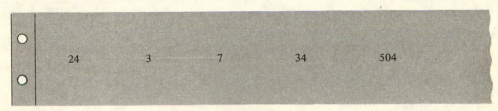

Fig. 1-5

Comment. If a reader is running our program on a computer which does not accept unformatted PRINT statements, then the reader should replace the PRINT statement (line 7) by the following two statements:

```
        WRITE(6, 31) I, J, K, LS, LP
   31   FORMAT(5I12)
```

(Such a WRITE-FORMAT pair will be explained in Chapter 3.)

1.5 READING IN DATA

The above program generated its own data during its execution by explicitly assigning values to I, J, and K. It is also possible for a computer to "read" data from data cards, magnetic tape, or some other input device. Since we assume the use of a card reader, the computer will read data from a deck of cards. (As illustrated in Fig. 1-3, the data deck appears after the Fortran program deck in the Fortran package given to the computer.)

We instruct a computer to acquire data from a data card by means of a READ statement. A typical unformatted READ statement follows:

```
        READ, I, J, K, M, N
```

Observe that the word READ and each variable, except the last, is followed by a comma. This statement instructs the computer to store the first five values in the data deck in locations I, J, K, M, N respectively.

The main advantage of using a READ statement is to make a program more general and independent of the input data. For example, if we had used a READ statement in the above program to read in values for I, J, K, then that program could have been used to find the sum and product of any values of I, J, K, not only the values 24, 3, and 7.

EXAMPLE 1.1

(a) We rewrite the above program except now we will read in values for I, J, K. Specifically, the three statements after the comment are replaced by the one statement

    READ, I, J, K

and a data card is punched, as card A in Fig. 1-6. If the reader does not have access to unformatted input/output, use the two statements

    READ(5, 10) I, J, K
10   FORMAT(3I5)

and punch instead a data card, as card B in Fig. 1-6. The output of this program should be the same as in the first program.

(b) Explain the purpose of the program

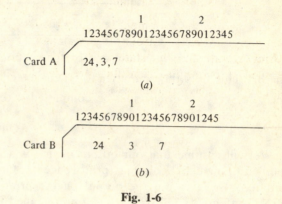

Fig. 1-6

```
READ, A, B, C, D, E
SUM = A + B + C + D + E
PRINT, A, B, C, D, E
PRINT, SUM
STOP
END
```

This program calculates the sum of five numbers. Here there are two PRINT statements. The values of A, B, C, D, E will be printed on one line and their SUM on a second line.

(c) Explain the purpose of the program

```
READ, B, H
AREA = (B*H)/2.0
PRINT, B, H, AREA
STOP
END
```

This program calculates the AREA of a triangle with base B and height H. Here B, H, and AREA are printed on one line.

1.6 MAKING DECISIONS

A computer normally executes the statements of a program one after the other as in the above programs. However, sometimes we want the computer to repeat or skip a portion of a program, i.e., we want the computer to transfer from one point of the program to another. This can be done by the GO TO statement, which has the form

    GO TO n

where n is a *statement number*. This statement tells the computer to transfer control to the statement labeled n; that is, the next statement we want to execute is the one labeled n.

One of the most important features of a computer is its ability to compare values and then make decisions. For example, consider the Fortran statement

    IF(N.LT.300) GO TO 100

(The notation ".LT." is Fortran for "less than".) This IF statement instructs the computer as follows:

> If $n < 300$ is true, then go to execute the statement numbered 100; otherwise continue with the next statement after the IF statement.

In other words, the statement is asking the question, "Is N < 300?". If the answer is yes, then the computer transfers control to the statement labeled 100; if the answer is no, then the computer continues with the next statement.

The following program illustrates these concepts. (Such concepts will be studied in detail in Chapter 4.) The program instructs the computer to print the odd positive integers from 1 through 11 and their squares.

```
C       PROGRAM ODD INTEGERS AND THEIR SQUARES
        N = 1
21      K = N*N
        PRINT, N, K
        N = N + 2
        IF(N.LT.12) GO TO 21
        STOP
        END
```

Before we discuss the program execution, we note that the statement

    N = N + 2

may look puzzling. From Section 1.4 we know, however, that the equal sign = in Fortran does not represent equality but denotes an assignment statement (which involves two actions). The computer first evaluates N + 2 using the current value of N, and then stores this new number in location N. In other words, the statement N = N + 2 says that the new value of N is the present value of N plus 2.

Program Execution

Step

1. Line 1. This is a comment since a C is punched in the first column.
2. Line 2.   N ← 1
3. Line 3. This tells the computer to multiply the value of N times itself, and store the result in K:

        K ← 1

4. Line 4. The values of N and K are printed.

5. Line 5. This tells the computer to add 2 to the current value of N, and store this sum (which is 3) in location N. (The previous value of N is thereby erased.) We represent the

fact that the value 1 in N is erased and the value 3 substituted in its place by

$$N \leftarrow \cancel{1} \; 3$$

6. Line 6.   This asks the following question:

Is N less than 12?

Since N = 3, the answer is yes; that is, the expression in parentheses is true. Hence the computer goes to the statement numbered 21, that is, to line 3 in the program.

7. Line 3.   Square the current value of N and store this result, which is 9, in location K. (Thus, the previous value of K is erased.)

$$K \leftarrow \cancel{1} \; 9$$

8. Line 4.   Print the current values of N and K:

$$\boxed{3, \quad\quad 9}$$

9. Line 5.   The computer adds 2 to the current value of N; hence, we have

$$N \leftarrow \cancel{1} \; \cancel{3} \; 5$$

10. Line 6.   The answer to the question "Is N < 12?" is yes, so the computer returns to the statement numbered 21, that is, to line 3 in the program.

11. Line. 3.   Square the current value of N and store the result, which is 25, in K:

$$K \leftarrow \cancel{1} \; \cancel{9} \; 25$$

12. Line 4.   Print the current values of N and K:

$$\boxed{5, \quad\quad 25}$$

13. Line 5.   The computer increases the value of N by 2:

$$N \leftarrow \cancel{1} \; \cancel{3} \; \cancel{5} \; 7$$

14. Line 6.   Since 7 < 12, the computer returns to line 3.

15. Line 3.   The computer squares N and stores the value in K:

$$K \leftarrow \cancel{1} \; \cancel{9} \; \cancel{25} \; 49$$

16. Line 4.   The computer prints the values of N and K:

$$\boxed{7, \quad\quad 49}$$

17. Line 5.   The computer increases the value of N by 2:

$$N \leftarrow \cancel{1} \; \cancel{3} \; \cancel{5} \; \cancel{7} \; 9$$

18. Line 6.   Since 9 < 12, the computer returns to line 3.

19. Line 3.   The computer squares N and stores this integer in K:

$$K \leftarrow \cancel{1} \; \cancel{9} \; \cancel{25} \; \cancel{49} \; 81$$

20. Line 4.   The computer prints the values of N and K:

$$\boxed{9,\qquad 81}$$

21. Line 5. The value of N is increased by 2:

$$N \leftarrow \cancel{1}\ \cancel{3}\ \cancel{5}\ \cancel{7}\ \cancel{9}\ 11$$

22. Line 6. Since $11 < 12$, the computer returns to line 3.

23. Line 3. The current value of K is replaced by N squared:

$$K \leftarrow \cancel{1}\ \cancel{9}\ \cancel{25}\ \cancel{49}\ \cancel{81}\ 121$$

24. Line 4. The values of N and K are printed:

$$\boxed{11,\qquad 121}$$

25. Line 5. The value of N is increased by 2:

$$N \leftarrow \cancel{1}\ \cancel{3}\ \cancel{5}\ \cancel{7}\ \cancel{9}\ \cancel{11}\ 13$$

26. Line 6. The answer to the question "Is $N < 12$?" is now no; that is, the expression in parentheses is false.   Accordingly, the computer goes on to the next statement in the program.

27. Line 7. This tells the computer to STOP.

Output

Each time a PRINT statement is seen, the computer prints the output on another line.   Hence, each odd number and its square will appear on separate lines, as in Fig. 1-7.

Comment 1.   If line 6 in the program were replaced, say, by

        IF(N.LT.100) GO TO 21

then the computer would print the odd integers and their squares from 1 through 99.

Comment 2.   If a reader is running our program on a computer which does not accept unformatted PRINT statements, then the reader should replace the PRINT statement by the following two statements:

        WRITE(6, 31) N, K
    31 FORMAT(2I15)

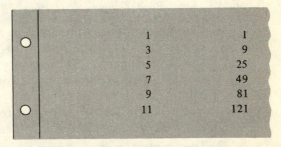

Fig. 1-7

1.7 OVERVIEW OF COMPUTERS AND LANGUAGES

This section gives an overview of computers and of computer languages.   Although the reader can skim through this section on a first reading, there are certain terms and details, e.g., executable and nonexecutable statements, which are required for a clear understanding of subsequent topics.   We have included all the material here for completeness, and readers can use this section for reference when necessary.

(a) Computer Units

A computer consists of five major components: the input unit, the output unit, the memory unit, the control unit, and the arithmetic unit. These units are shown in Fig. 1-8.

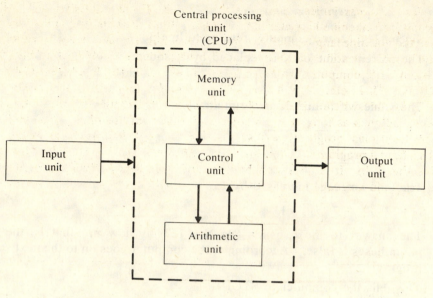

Fig. 1-8

The input and output units consist of devices that permit a computer to receive or exhibit information. They may be card readers, magnetic tapes, paper tape readers, line printers, CRT (cathode ray tube) terminals, or typewriter consoles. Some of these can be used for both input and output.

The three units (the memory unit, the control unit, and the arithmetic unit) make up the so-called *Central Processing Unit* (*CPU*). These three units have the following purpose:

1. The *memory unit* is the component where all data and results are stored. Present-day computers are called *stored-program computers* since programs themselves are also stored in memory. The memory unit consists of many, many cells, each capable of storing a unit of information (word). These cells, electromagnetic in nature, are also called *storage locations* (*variables*). To distinguish cells, they are numbered sequentially. Their numbers are often referred to as *addresses*. For the user, these addresses are given in terms of symbols (names).

2. The *control unit* coordinates all the activities of the various components of the computer. It sends out command and control signals and determines the sequence of the various instructions.

3. The *arithmetic unit* consists of electric circuits that perform the various arithmetic and logic operations.

(b) Hierarchy of Programming Languages

Every computer has its own machine language. Instruction to the computer must be given in this language since this is the only language that a computer actually understands. However, this type of language varies from machine to machine and is a function of the hardware of the computer. Programs written in machine languages are machine dependent, and, hence, are only good for that particular machine.

Machine-language instructions are usually represented by binary numbers, i.e., sequences consisting of 1's and 0's, and programming in machine language is very involved and detailed. Higher up in the ladder (hierarchy) of programming languages are the *assembly languages*. Here the sequences of 1's and 0's are replaced by symbols, so that instructions can be given in symbolic codes called *mnemonics*. An *assembler* program is then needed in the computer to translate assembly language programs into machine-language instructions. Since the structure of the assembly language is very similar to the machine language, programmers must still be concerned with various details, such as indexing and storage locations, in addition to writing a complex sequence of instructions.

Today, we can write computer programs in an "almost English" language, such as FORTRAN, ALGOL, COBOL, PL/I, etc. These are called *compiler languages* and are almost machine independent. Programs written in this type of language can, with possible minor modifications, run on different machines as long as a compiler exists for that machine. A *compiler* is a special program which translates programs written in this type of high-level language into machine language. The original program is called the *source program*, and its translation is called the *object program*. (See Fig. 1-9.) It is important to remember that a high-level language program is first translated into machine-language instructions before the computer actually executes them.

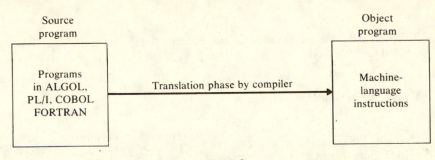

Fig. 1-9

Although compiler languages are less efficient than machine or assembly languages, they do relieve the programmers from the burden of keeping careful details such as storage locations, etc. In addition, they are far easier to learn and use.

As stated earlier, the high-level language we will learn is called Fortran. We will also use the term "computer" in its broad sense, i.e., to include the compiler, line printer, and other accessories.

(*c*) Executable and Nonexecutable Statements

As noted above, our Fortran program will first be handled by a Fortran compiler which translates the program into machine-language instructions. Some of the Fortran statements are meant only to provide the compiler with information, and they will not result in any machine-language instructions. These are called *nonexecutable statements*. In other words, the *executable statements* are those statements which will result in some kind of machine-language instruction.

The STOP statement is an executable statement; its machine-language equivalent stops the computer from executing the next machine-language instruction of the program. On the other hand, the END statement is a nonexecutable statement. It tells the compiler that this is the end of the program, and there are no more Fortran statements to be translated into machine-language instructions. Since the complete Fortran program is translated before any single machine-language instruction is executed, this explains the reason the END statement is always physically the last statement of any Fortran program.

There are many other nonexecutable Fortran statements. We will mention them as we progress through the text.

Solved Problems

1.1 Determine the output of the following program.

```
C     FIRST SOLVED PROGRAM
      J = 1
      K = 3
      L = 2*J + K
      J = 3*J + 2*L
      K = K + 2
      L = J + K + L
      PRINT, J, K, L
      STOP
      END
```

Program Execution

Line 1. The computer skips this statement since it is a comment.

Line 2. The computer stores 1 in a storage location labeled J:

$$J \leftarrow 1$$

Line 3. $\qquad K \leftarrow 3$

Line 4. This tells the computer to calculate 2*J + K, and then to store the result in a storage location labeled L. We have

$$2*J + K = 2 \cdot 1 + 3 = 5$$

Hence, the computer stores 5 in L:

$$L \leftarrow 5$$

Line 5. This tells the computer to calculate 3*J + 2*L using the current values of J and L, and then to substitute this result for the current value of J. We have

$$3*J + 2*L = 3 \cdot 1 + 2 \cdot 5 = 13$$

Hence, the computer erases the current value of J and substitutes 13 in its place. We indicate this by

$$J \leftarrow \cancel{1} \; 13$$

Line 6. This tells the computer to increase the current value of K by 2:

$$K \leftarrow \cancel{3} \; 5$$

Line 7. The computer adds the current values of J, K, and L:

$$J + K + L = 13 + 5 + 5 = 23$$

Then the computer erases the current value of L and substitutes 23 in its place:

$$L \leftarrow \cancel{5} \; 23$$

Line 8. The computer prints the current values of J, K, and L, that is,

$$\boxed{13, \quad 5, \quad 23}$$

Line 9. This tells the computer to STOP.

Output

The output consists of the numbers 13, 5, and 23, which are printed on one line since the PRINT statement was used only once.

1.2   Determine the output of the following program.

```
C       SUM OF SQUARES
        K = 1
        JSUM = 0
   31   JSUM = JSUM + K**2
        K = K + 3
        IF(K.LT.10) GO TO 31
        PRINT, JSUM
        STOP
        END
```

Determine the output if line 6 of the program is replaced by

```
        IF(K.LT.20) GO TO 31
```

Program Execution

Step

1. Line 1.   The computer skips this statement since it is a comment.

2. Line 2. $K \leftarrow 1$

3. Line 3. $JSUM \leftarrow 0$

4. Line 4.   The computer calculates JSUM + K∗∗2 (where K∗∗2 is FORTRAN for K^2) using the current values of JSUM and K:

$$JSUM + K**2 = 0 + 1^2 = 1$$

Then the computer erases 0 in JSUM and substitutes 1 in its place:

$$JSUM \leftarrow \cancel{0} \ 1$$

5. Line 5.   The computer increases the value of K by 3:

$$K \leftarrow \cancel{1} \ 4$$

6. Line 6.   It asks the question:

Is K less than 10?

Since K = 4, the answer is yes; that is, the statement in parentheses is true.   Hence, the computer goes to the statement numbered 31, which is line 4 in the program.

7. Line 4.   It tells the computer to increase the value of JSUM by K^2.   Since K = 4, the computer adds 16 to the current value of JSUM:

$$JSUM \leftarrow \cancel{0} \ \cancel{1} \ 17$$

8. Line 5. $K \leftarrow \cancel{1} \ \cancel{4} \ 7$

9. Line 6.   The computer goes to the statement numbered 31, which is line 4, since

$$K < 10$$

is true.

10. Line 4.   Since K = 7, the computer adds 49 to the current value of JSUM:

$$JSUM \leftarrow \cancel{0} \ \cancel{1} \ \cancel{17} \ 66$$

11. Line 5. $K \leftarrow \cancel{1} \ \cancel{4} \ \cancel{7} \ 10$

12. Line 6.   Since K = 10, the statement

$$K < 10$$

is false; hence, the computer goes to the next statement in the program.

13. **Line 7.** The computer prints the current value of JSUM, which is

14. **Line 8.** This tells the computer to STOP.

Output

The output is only the integer 66, which is the last value of JSUM. Observe that this final value of JSUM is the sum

$$JSUM = 1^2 + 4^2 + 7^2$$

that is, the sum of the squares of the integers in the sequence which begins with 1, increases in steps of 3, and ends just before 10.

In the case where line 6 is replaced by

    IF(K.LT.20) GO TO 31

then the sum will continue until just before 20. That is, the final value of JSUM would be

$$JSUM = 1^2 + 4^2 + 7^2 + 10^2 + 13^2 + 16^2 + 19^2 = 952$$

Thus, in this case, the output would be the integer 952.

1.3   Explain the purpose of each program:

(*a*)   READ, R
       AREA = 3.1416*R*R
       PRINT, R
       PRINT, AREA
       STOP
       END

(*b*)   READ, A, B, C, D
       PROD = A*B*C*D
       PRINT, A, B, C, D
       PRINT, PROD
       STOP
       END

(*a*)   This program calculates the AREA of a circle whose radius R is given.
(*b*)   This program calculates the product PROD of four given numbers A, B, C, and D.

Supplementary Problems

1.4   Find the output of the following program.

```
C      FIRST SUPPLEMENTARY PROGRAM
       I  = 3
       J  = 2
       K  = 2*I + J
       I  = I + 3
       J  = I + 3*J - K
       K  = 2*J + 3*K
       PRINT, I, J, K
       STOP
       END
```

1.5   Determine the output of the following program.

```
C      SECOND SUPPLEMENTARY PROGRAM
       K = 3
       JSUM = 0
 51    JSUM = JSUM + K
       K = K + 4
       IF(K.LT.25) GO TO 51
       PRINT, JSUM
       STOP
       END
```

1.6   Find the output of the following program.

```
C      THIRD SUPPLEMENTARY PROGRAM
       I  = 1
       J  = 2
 71    K  = 2*I + 3*J
       I  = J + K
       J  = I + 2*J
       IF(K.LT.100) GO TO 71
       PRINT, I, J, K
       STOP
       END
```

1.7   Determine the output of the following program.

```
C      FOURTH SUPPLEMENTARY PROGRAM
       I = 1
       PRINT, I
       J = 2
       PRINT, J
 41    K = I + J
       PRINT, K
       I = J
       J = K
       IF(K.LT.99) GO TO 41
       STOP
       END
```

1.8   Find the output of the following program.

```
C       FIFTH SUPPLEMENTARY PROGRAM
        J  = 1
        K = 3
  11    PRINT, J
  12    J = J + 1
        IF(J.LT.K) GO TO 11
        K = K + 3
        IF(J.LT.20) GO TO 12
        STOP
        END
```

Answers to Supplementary Problems

1.4   The integers 6, 4, and 32 are printed on one line.

1.5   The integer 78 is printed.

1.6   The integers 568, 776, and 464 are printed on one line.

1.7   The integers 1, 2, 3, 5, 8, 13, 21, 34, 55, 89, 144 are printed on different lines.

1.8   The computer prints on different lines the numbers from 1 through 20 leaving out multiples of 3, that is, 1, 2, 4, 5, 7, 8, 10, 11, 13, 14, 16, 17, 19, 20.

Chapter 2

Arithmetic Statements

2.1 INTRODUCTION

The first chapter illustrated how a computer reads and executes some simple Fortran programs. Now we will formally study the Fortran language so that we can write programs to solve problems.

The following is a list of the characters used in the Fortran language:

Digits:	0 1 2 3 4 5 6 7 8 9
Alphabetic characters:	A B C D E F G H I J K L M
	N O P Q R S T U V W X Y Z
Symbols:	+ − * / . , ' = $ ( )

There is also a blank space which is recognized as a character. We will sometimes denote the blank character by "$_b$", the letter b written as a subscript. The digits, together with the alphabets, are called *alphanumeric* characters. There are no lowercase letters.

Sometimes one distinguishes the digit 0 (zero) from the letter O (oh) by writing a slash through the letter Ø.

2.2 NUMERICAL CONSTANTS (NUMBERS)

In Fortran, there are two distinct types of numbers, the integers and the reals. Roughly speaking, integers are numbers we use for counting, and reals are numbers we use for measuring. The arithmetic and the representation (both internal and external) of these two types of numbers in Fortran are different. Here we shall discuss only the external representations, forms we write and the computer prints. The internal representations, forms used by the computer to store data in memory, will be discussed in Appendix B.

An *integer* constant, also called a *fixed-point* constant, is any signed or unsigned whole number without a decimal point or any other punctuation. Unsigned numbers are taken to be positive. The maximum length of any integer usually does not exceed 9 digits, although it varies from computer to computer. (Programmers are advised to check with their local computing facilities about those features which are machine dependent.)

EXAMPLE 2.1

The following are acceptable as integer constants:

$$15 \quad -8 \quad 0 \quad 12547 \quad -5286$$

On the other hand, the following are not acceptable as integer constants:

21.0	(contains a decimal point)
−248.	(contains a decimal point)
12,357	(contains a comma)
125000000000	(too large)

In Fortran, a *real* constant, also called a *floating-point* constant, can be written in two different forms: the decimal form and the exponential form. In both forms, there is a finite sequence of digits, together with a decimal point. In fact, it is the decimal point which distinguishes a real constant from an integer constant.

Decimal form. In decimal form, a real constant is written as a signed or unsigned finite sequence of digits, together with a decimal point. There can be no other punctuation. A real number can be written with any number of significant digits; however, the number of significant figures retained by a computer depends upon the word length of a computer. In general, a computer will not retain more than seven or eight significant figures. Again, readers should consult their own computing facilities for such machine-dependent features.

EXAMPLE 2.2

The following are acceptable as real constants:

28.3   −236.0   24.   +.0187   −234.182

The following are not acceptable as real constants:

4,356.2   (contains a comma)

−36   (no decimal point)

Exponential form. Written in exponential form (E-form), a real constant consists of two parts. The first part is a real constant in decimal form (i.e., a signed or unsigned finite sequence of digits with a decimal point). The second part starts with the character E followed by a signed or unsigned integer constant with, at most, two digits. The second part is interpreted as the exponent with base 10. For example,

23.1E−4

is a real constant in E-form which stands for 23.1×10^{-4}. The following are also examples of acceptable real constants in E-form:

24.123E04 $24.123 \times 10^4 = 241230.0$
−5.36E−3 $−5.36 \times 10^{-3} = −0.00536$
2.6E+2 $2.6 \times 10^2 = 260.0$

Whenever we write or input a real number in exponential form, there is no restriction as to where the decimal point is placed. Hence, every real constant in E-form can be written in more than one way. For example,

23.1E−4   2.31E−3   0.0000231E2

all represent the same number and are accepted so by the computer.

One can always represent a real number in *standard exponential form*, i.e., so that the number preceding the character E (called the *mantissa*) lies between

0.1 and 1.0   (or   −0.1 and −1.0)

The computer will, in fact, always print (output) a real number in E-form this way.

As mentioned previously, the number of significant digits retained by a computer is machine dependent. Furthermore, the maximum acceptable exponent (usually limited to at most two digits) is also machine dependent.

Remark. The notion of a real constant in Fortran is different from that in mathematics. In fact, all real numbers in mathematics are approximated by rational numbers in computers.

Although 24.0 and 2.4E1 are different in (external) appearance, they have identical internal representations since they are both real numbers. (See Appendix B.) On the other hand, 24 and 24.0 have different internal representations and are treated differently in Fortran since one denotes an integer constant and the other a real constant. (Mathematically, they represent the same number.)

We have not yet discussed how to instruct the computer to read or to print integers and/or real numbers. These will be discussed in Chapter 3.

2.3 VARIABLE NAMES (NAMES OF STORAGE LOCATIONS)

The term *variable* in computer terminology always means *memory element*. The main characteristics to remember about memory elements are: destructive read-in and nondestructive read-out. That is, if you store information in a memory cell, then the original (previous) content of the cell will be destroyed; but, if you copy information out of (from) a memory cell, then the (original) content in the cell will remain unchanged.

If a memory location (variable) is used to store integer constants, it is called an *integer variable*, and if it is used to store real constants, it is called a *real variable*.

For easy referencing, names are given to memory cells. In general, a variable name is denoted by one to six alphanumeric characters, of which the first must be an alphabetic character. Hence, IAM, A2X3, BAD, DEAN are acceptable variable names, but the following are not:

>   2XY   Did not begin with an alphabetic character.
>
>   A*B6   * is not an alphanumeric character.
>
>   INTEREST   Contains more than six characters.

(Some computers may accept more than six characters for variable names, but most have six as the upper limit.)

Fortran also uses the following implicit rule for variable names: If the first character is one of the six letters I, J, K, L, M, N, then it is an *integer variable name*; but, if the first character is one of the other letters, that is, one of A, . . . , H, O, P, . . . , Z, then it is a *real variable name*. (This rule can be overridden by type declaration statements discussed in the next section.)

EXAMPLE 2.3

The following are acceptable as integer variables,

>   MONEY   NEXT   J4X2   IDIOT

whereas the following are acceptable as real variables,

>   ANSWER   X21   BUM   ENEMY

Remark. Certain words, such as READ, WRITE, PRINT, PAUSE, STOP, END, etc., are part of the Fortran language and hence are not acceptable as variable names by most computers.

2.4 TYPE STATEMENTS—INTEGER, REAL

Sometimes it is not desirable to follow the above, implicit rule for writing variables. For example, one may wish to use the mnemonic (memory aid) INT to denote a real variable for interest rate. To override the implicit rule, Fortran provides us with several explicit type declaration statements. A Fortran statement beginning with the word REAL and followed by a list of variables separated by commas declares these variables to be REAL. Thus,

>   REAL INT

informs the computer that throughout the program, INT will always denote a real variable. Analogously, a Fortran statement beginning with the word INTEGER and followed by a list of variables separated by commas declares the variables to be INTEGER.

These *type statements* provide information to the compiler; hence, they are nonexecutable statements and must appear at the very beginning of the program.   Type statements other than INTEGER and REAL will be introduced in later chapters.

EXAMPLE 2.4

Suppose a program begins with the statements:

        INTEGER A, B, SUM, TIME
        REAL NUMBER, MIN, MAX

then throughout the program A, B, SUM, and TIME will denote integer variables, and NUMBER, MIN, and MAX will denote real variables.

Some programmers feel it is a worthwhile practice to list all variables in type statements regardless of their first letter.   For example, one might write

        REAL NUMBER, MIN, MAX, RATE

even though RATE is real if not explicitly written in a type statement.

2.5   ARITHMETIC OPERATIONS—INTEGER AND REAL ARITHMETICS

Table 2-1 gives the symbols for the five basic arithmetic operations of Fortran.   We emphasize that the algebraic expressions

$$a \cdot b \qquad \frac{a}{b} \qquad a^b$$

are written respectively as A∗B, A/B, A∗∗B.

Table 2-1

Operation	Symbol
Addition	+
Subtraction	−
Multiplication	∗
Division	/
Exponentiation	∗∗

As there are two types of numbers, real and integer, so are there two types of arithmetics, *real arithmetic* and *integer arithmetic*.   These two types of arithmetics are performed differently, so it is very important to have a clear understanding of the difference.

(*a*)   Integer Arithmetic

If the operands are integers, then integer arithmetic is performed to *yield an integer*.   For example, integer arithmetic is used to evaluate

        5 + 3,   5∗3,   and   5 − 3

yielding the integers 8, 15, and 2 respectively.   Integer division in Fortran, say evaluating I/J where I and J are integers, also yields an integer, the integral part of the quotient.   That is, the fractional part of the quotient is deleted (*truncated*) in integer division.   For example,

        5/4 yields 1,   4/5 yields 0,   and   −7/2 yields −3

Thus integer division in Fortran is distinctly different from ordinary division.   However, it can be used to our advantage, as illustrated in Example 2.5.

(*b*) Real Arithmetic

If the operands are real, then real arithmetic is performed to yield a real value. Thus, real arithmetic is used to evaluate

$$5. + 3., \qquad 5.*3., \qquad \text{and} \qquad 5. - 3.$$

yielding the real values 8., 15., and 2. respectively. Division by real arithmetic in Fortran is similar to ordinary division. That is,

$$5./4. \text{ yields } 1.25, \qquad 4./5. \text{ yields } 0.8, \qquad \text{and} \qquad -7./2. \text{ yields } -3.5$$

The most important part of the above discussion is the fact that the type of operand determines the type of arithmetic (or the *mode of operation*), which then yields the same type of resultant. We note that exponentiation is treated differently. Specifically, only positive real values can be raised to real powers, whereas any value, integer or real, can be raised to an integer power. This is discussed further at the end of Section 2.8.

EXAMPLE 2.5

Assuming that the conventional use of parentheses in arithmetic expressions is also acceptable in Fortran, discuss the differences between

$$(a) \quad (N*2)/2 \qquad \text{and} \qquad (b) \quad (N/2)*2$$

Also show how (*b*) can be used to determine if N is even or odd.

The algebraic expressions they represent are

$$\frac{n \cdot 2}{2} \qquad \text{and} \qquad \frac{n}{2} \cdot 2$$

respectively. Mathematically, they are identical. However, under Fortran integer arithmetic, they are not equivalent. Specifically, we have the following:

(*a*) Here N*2 is evaluated first yielding an even integer; hence, (N*2)/2 will always have the value N.

(*b*) Here N/2 is evaluated first, and this yields the integral part of the quotient. Accordingly, if N is even, (N/2)*2 yields N, but if N is odd, (N/2)*2 yields N ± 1. For example, if N = 8, we have

$$(N/2)*2 = 4*2 = 8$$

if N = 11, we have

$$(N/2)*2 = 5*2 = 10$$

and if N = −9, we have

$$(N/2)*2 = -4*2 = -8$$

2.6 ARITHMETIC EXPRESSIONS

One must understand how the computer evaluates arithmetic expressions in order to write them correctly.

The computer evaluates a *parenthesis-free expression* (i.e., an expression or subexpression without parentheses) using the following conventional precedence table:

First precedence: Exponentiation (**)

Second precedence: Multiplication (*) and division (/)

Third precedence: Addition (+) and subtraction (−)

[We will treat unary plus and minus on the same level as binary addition and subtraction; that is, −2.2**2 means −(2.2**2) which yields −4.84.]

Since there are three levels of priority, one can imagine that a computer scans a parenthesis-free arithmetic expression from left to right three times. The first time, it looks for exponentiation; the second time, it looks for multiplication and division; and finally, it looks for addition and subtraction. Since the computer scans from left to right, if two operations are of the same precedence, the leftmost one is performed first.

EXAMPLE 2.6

Consider the expression

A*B + C/D*F**2

The order of execution is indicated in Fig. 2-1(*a*). Equivalently, this order can be written as an inverted tree with operands as nodes, as illustrated in Fig. 2-1(*b*). Observe that the expression represents

$$a \cdot b + \frac{c}{d} \cdot f^2$$

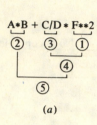

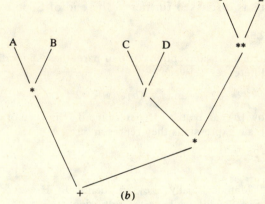

(*a*)

(*b*)

Fig. 2-1

Fortran also permits the use of parentheses in the conventional way. Namely, parentheses have precedence over all arithmetic operations, and the innermost pair of parentheses is treated first.

EXAMPLE 2.7

(*a*) The expression X + Y/(Z*A + B**2) is evaluated as follows:

Thus, the algebraic expression is

$$x + \frac{y}{z \cdot a + b^2}$$

(*b*) The algebraic equation

$$x = [(a + b)^2 + (3c)^3]^{a/b}$$

can be written in Fortran as

X = ((A + B)**2 + (3.0*C)**3)**(A/B)

It is highly advisable to use extra parentheses whenever such use may assure correctness. Furthermore, if an arithmetic expression contains very lengthy and complicated terms, it is always advisable to break it into several smaller statements which are less prone to error. For example, the algebraic equation

$$y = \left[\frac{ab}{c+d} - \frac{g}{5(h+x)} \right]^{1/r}$$

should be represented as:

T1 = A*B/(C + D)
T2 = G/(5.*(H + X))
 Y = (T1 − T2)**(1./R)

Remark. Fortran does not allow two arithmetic operations to appear next to each other. Thus, A* − B must be written as A*(−B).

EXAMPLE 2.8

The following are mathematical expressions and their corresponding Fortran expressions.

	Mathematical	Fortran
(a)	$a + \dfrac{b}{c} + d$	A + B/C + D
(b)	$\dfrac{a+b}{c+d}$	(A + B)/(C + D)
(c)	$a^3 - b^3$	A**3 − B**3
(d)	$\dfrac{ab}{c - d^2}$	A*B/(C − D**2)
(e)	$\dfrac{ab}{c} - d^2$	A*B/C − D**2
(f)	$\dfrac{a}{bc} - d^2$	A/(B*C) − D**2
(g)	$1 + \dfrac{a}{b + \dfrac{1}{c}}$	1. + A/(B + 1./C)

Observe that parentheses must appear in (*f*), but are not needed in (*e*).

2.7 MIXED MODE OF OPERATIONS

As discussed in Section 2.5, when an arithmetic expression is evaluated by the computer, the type of the operands determines the type of arithmetic (mode of operation) that is used. Hence, all variables and constants in any Fortran arithmetic expression must be of the same type, i.e., must be either all real or all integer. Accordingly, if

A + 3

is an expression where one operand A is real and the other integer, one may wonder (1) whether such a *mixed-mode* expression is allowed, and (2) even if it is allowed, what type of arithmetic will be performed.

Some Fortran compilers *do not* allow mixed-mode expressions. In such a case, one must be very careful to avoid mixing two types in one expression. Thus,

A + 3*B	should be written	A + 3.*B
I + 4.0*J	should be written	I + 4*J
B**2 − 4*A*C	should be written	B**2 − 4.*A*C

Raising a real number to an integral power is not considered a mixed mode of operation (see discussion at the end of Section 2.8), so B**2 is permitted and need not be changed to B**2.0. (For the difference between B**2 and B**2.0, see Section 2.8 and also Problem 2.17.)

Most of the larger computers do have compilers which allow mixed-mode expressions. In such a case, whenever the operands of an operation are of two different types, i.e., one integer and the other real, the integer is *first converted* to real and then real arithmetic is performed to yield a real value. This may seem to be a convenience since, then, both integer variables and constants and real variables and constants can appear in one expression; however, programmers should be aware of the hidden pitfalls when both types of variables and constants appear.

EXAMPLE 2.9

(*a*) Assuming mixed-mode arithmetic is allowed, consider the expression

(11./2) + 4.3

Since 11. and 2 are of different types, the integer 2 is converted to 2., and real arithmetic is performed to yield the real number 5.5. Adding the real numbers 5.5 and 4.3, we have 9.8 as the result.

(*b*) Consider the expression

(11/2) + 4.3

The term 11/2 is evaluated first. Since 11 and 2 are integers, 11/2 is evaluated by integer arithmetic, yielding 5 (not 5.5). Since the operands of addition are of different types, the integer 5 is converted to real and added to the real constant 4.3, using real arithmetic, which yields the real number 9.3.

Programmers should also be aware that the above convenience does not come "free". That is, each time an integer value is converted to real, machine time is used. Thus, allowing mixed-mode expressions will increase execution time and will run the danger of greatly reducing the execution efficiency of the program. In addition, programs written with mixed mode will be less portable; i.e., they may not be able to be run on different machines. Lastly, thoughtless use of mixed mode may result in values other than intended, as illustrated implicitly in Example 2.9.

2.8 BUILT-IN MATHEMATICAL FUNCTIONS

The Fortran language has a library of mathematical functions that can be used by a programmer. Some of the more common ones are listed in Table 2-2. A much more extensive list is given in Appendix A.

Table 2-2

Function	Mathematical notation	Fortran
Square root of x	$\sqrt{x}$	SQRT(X)
Absolute value of x	$|x|$	ABS(X)
Exponential of x	e^x	EXP(X)
Sine of x	$\sin x$	SIN(X)
Cosine of x	$\cos x$	COS(X)
Log of x	$\log_{10} x$	ALOG10(X)
Natural log of x	$\log_e x$	ALOG(X)
Convert integer I into real		FLOAT(I)
Truncate real x into integer		IFIX(X)

Although function subprograms will be discussed in detail in Chapter 7, some of the notation and terms will be explained here.   The expression

SQRT(X)

denotes the value that the square root function assigns to X.   The X is called the *argument* of the function, and SQRT is called the *name* of the function.   Observe that each functional name is followed by a pair of parentheses enclosing the argument.

Table 2-2 uses both X and I as arguments of functions.   The X indicates that the argument must be real whereas the I indicates that the argument must be of integer type.   On the other hand, the type of a functional value is determined by the name of the function according to the usual rules for variable names.   For example,

ALOG(X) denotes a real value corresponding to the real argument X

IFIX(X) denotes an integer value corresponding to the real argument X

FLOAT(I) denotes a real value corresponding to the integer argument I

and so on.

The functions FLOAT and IFIX are not usual mathematical functions.   The FLOAT function converts an integer value into its equivalent real value; for example,

FLOAT(4) gives the value 4.0, and FLOAT(-25) gives the value -25.0

The FLOAT function is usually used to avoid the use of mixed-mode arithmetic.   For example, if SUM denotes the sum of N numbers, then one can write

AVE = SUM/FLOAT(N)

to obtain the average AVE of the N numbers.   The IFIX function converts a real value into an integer value by truncation; for example,

IFIX(2.8) gives the value 2   and   IFIX(-3.7) gives the value -3

We emphasize that the IFIX function does not round-off real values to their nearest integer.

The following remarks should be noted:

1. The arguments of the functions need not be single variables.   They may be any arithmetic expression of the required type.   For example, the Fortran translation of

   $$\sqrt{b^2 - 4ac} \quad \text{will be} \quad \text{SQRT(B**2} - 4.*A*C)$$

2. The functions may appear as a part of any arithmetic expression as long as the proper argument is given.   For example, the Fortran translation of

   $$|a - b| + \frac{c}{\sin d} \quad \text{will be} \quad \text{ABS(A} - \text{B)} + \text{C/SIN(D)}$$

3. An argument of a function can call another function.   That is, we can have functions of functions.   For example, the Fortran translation of

   $$\sin \left| \frac{x - y}{x + y} \right| \quad \text{will be} \quad \text{SIN(ABS((X} - \text{Y)/(X} + \text{Y)))}$$

4. For a parenthesis-free arithmetic expression involving built-in library functions, the evaluation of these functions has precedence over the rules discussed in Section 2.6.   For example, the expression

$$\underbrace{\text{ABS}(A - B)}_{\textcircled{1}} + \underbrace{C/\underbrace{\text{SIN}(D)}_{\textcircled{2}}}_{\textcircled{3}}$$
$$\textcircled{4}$$

will be evaluated in the order as indicated. Note that the argument of ABS is an expression; hence, in its evaluation, the precedence rules are again applied.

EXAMPLE 2.10

Following are mathematical expressions and their corresponding Fortran expressions.

	Mathematical	Fortran
(a)	$\dfrac{\sin x}{|y| + \cos z}$	SIN(X)/(ABS(Y) + COS(Z))
(b)	$\dfrac{e^{x+y}}{x + y}$	EXP(X + Y)/(X + Y)
(c)	$e^{|x-y|} + x$	EXP(ABS(X − Y)) + X
(d)	$a + \dfrac{b}{|m - n|}$	A + B/ABS(FLOAT(M − N))

One common mistake made by many beginning programmers is in the writing of the constant π. As π is not a built-in constant, and π is not a character accepted by Fortran, an approximate value of π must be used.   For example, the Fortran expression for

$$\sin(2n\pi + x) \qquad \text{will be} \qquad \text{SIN}(2.*N*3.14 + X)$$

where 3.14 is used for π.   Equivalently, we may assign 3.14 to PI (see Section 2.9), and then write

SIN(2.*N*PI + X)

We end this section with the following subtle, yet important, points concerning exponentiation since they involve the logarithmic function.

1. When a value is raised to a real power as in X**Y, it is evaluated internally as

   $$e^{y \ln (x)}$$

   where ln is the natural logarithmic function, that is, as EXP(Y*ALOG(X)). (See Table 2.2.)   Since the argument for the logarithmic function must be real and positive, only positive real values of X can be raised to real powers.   Programmers should be especially careful about this since the error of raising a negative value to a real power is detected only at execution time.

2. When a number is raised to an integer power as in X**I, it is done by multiplication.   Hence, any value, integer or real, positive or negative, can be raised to an integer power.   (Also, see Problem 2.17.)

3. Mathematically, a^{bc} means $a^{(b^c)}$ which is different from $(a^b)^c$.   However, A**B**C may be treated as (A**B)**C by some compilers, but as A**(B**C) by others.   Hence, we encourage programmers to use parentheses when writing such expressions.   In general, whenever in doubt, it is wise to use parentheses.

2.9 ARITHMETIC ASSIGNMENT STATEMENT

In order for the computer to execute an arithmetic expression, all variables appearing in the expression must have been given values within the program prior to their use; i.e., they must be *defined*. Most computers will give an error message if any variable in an expression is not defined. How does one define a variable, i.e., store a value in memory? A variable is defined either by reading in its value from the data deck (see Chapter 3) or by an arithmetic assignment statement.

Symbolically, we denote storing (assigning) the constant 1.5 in a location called X by

$$X \leftarrow 1.5$$

This is called an *assignment statement*. In Fortran, $\leftarrow$ is represented by =, so $X \leftarrow 1.5$ is written in Fortran as

$$X = 1.5$$

On the other hand, suppose x is already defined, and we wish to compute x^2 and store the value in location Y; that is, $Y \leftarrow x^2$. In Fortran, we write

$$Y = X**2$$

In general, a Fortran *arithmetic assignment statement* has the following form:

Variable name = arithmetic expression

We emphasize that the left-hand side of = must be a single variable name.

It is unfortunate that the symbol = is used for assignment statements in Fortran, since = is conventionally used to mean equality. We strongly suggest that readers remember = as "assignment", "replacement", "copy", etc. In our discussions, we will sometimes use the symbol $\leftarrow$ for assignment rather than its Fortran equivalent = when such use enhances the understanding.

Remark. It is extremely important to know that in an arithmetic assignment statement, two separate actions are taking place:

1. The computation of the arithmetic expression on the right side of =.
2. The assignment of the result of (1) to the storage location on the left side of =.

Therefore, it is acceptable for the two sides of = to be of different types. When the two sides of = have different types, the assignment in the second step includes converting the result of (1) to the same type as the storage location indicated on the left of =. In particular, a real value will be truncated before it is assigned to an integer location.

Many beginning programmers often get confused about mixed-mode expressions and assignment statements with different types on either side. Mixed mode refers to arithmetic expressions in which operands are of different types. Assignment statement refers to the action of storing a value in memory; it is a Fortran instruction and may involve the evaluation of an arithmetic expression. The expression itself is not an instruction. Some compilers do not accept mixed-mode expressions. However, all compilers accept assignment statements with different types on the sides of =.

EXAMPLE 2.11

(*a*) Consider the statement

INCOME = PRIN*(1. + XINT)

The arithmetic expression on the right side of = is of the real type. The result of its computation is first converted into an integer (by dropping its fractional part) before it is stored in INCOME since INCOME is an integer variable. Namely, if PRIN = 100.00 and XINT = 0.0625, then the result of PRIN*(1. + XINT) is 106.25. However, before it is copied into INCOME, the fraction .25 is truncated, and the integer 106 is stored in INCOME.

(*b*) Consider the statement

ASSET = INCOME + LOOT

Here the arithmetic expression is calculated in integer mode and then converted to real type before it is stored in the real location called ASSET.

(*c*) Consider the statement

SUM = SUM + X

As there are two separate actions in the assignment statement, SUM + X is executed first.   Hence, the current values of SUM and X are added.   The result is then stored in SUM again.   Effectively, the statement says:

"The new value of SUM is the result of adding the old value of SUM and X."

Obviously, if = were interpreted as "equality", the given statement SUM = SUM + X would make no sense at all.

2.10 COMPUTER ARITHMETICS

We would be entirely remiss if we did not mention to the reader some of the subtle pitfalls of computer arithmetics.

Since a computer can retain only a particular number of significant figures (because of the finiteness of the word length), all numbers inside the computer are rational numbers.   Thus most numbers, in particular all irrational numbers such as $\sqrt{2}$, π, etc., are not stored with their true value, but with rational approximations.   In fact, many rational numbers with terminating decimal expansions do not have terminating binary expansions; hence they are not stored with their true value.   Accordingly, new problems arise under computer arithmetics.   We shall discuss some of them here.   (See also Problems 2.17 and 2.18.)

(*a*) Conversion Error

Most computers store numbers in their binary form.   Thus, the number 1/2, which is represented in the decimal system by 0.5, is represented in such computers by 0.1.   However, the number 1/10 does not have a finite binary representation:

$$1/10 = 0.0001100110011\ldots\ldots$$

Depending on the length of the *word* (*memory cell*), the conversion error may be negligible.   However, error will propagate as the number of arithmetic operations compounds.

(*b*) Propagation of Round-off Error

For example, let us assume that our computer is a decimal machine which retains only three significant digits.   Then the number 1/3 is stored in the computer as 0.333.

Consider adding 1/3 to itself 10 times.   We have:

```
    .333
+   .333
   ─────
    .666
+   .333
   ─────
    .999
+   .333
   ─────
   1.332
```

At this point in the addition, the computer only retains 1.33 since we are assuming a three-digit machine.   Continuing, we obtain:

$$\begin{array}{r} 1.33 \\ +\ .333 \\ \hline 1.66 \\ +\ .333 \\ \hline 1.99 \\ +\ .333 \\ \hline 2.32 \\ +\ .333 \\ \hline 2.65 \\ +\ .333 \\ \hline 2.98 \\ +\ .333 \\ \hline 3.31 \end{array}$$

Instead of getting the theoretical 3.33, we obtained 3.31, and the error actually propagates rather rapidly. In fact, if you add .333 to itself 300 times in our machine, you only get 90.9 instead of the desired 99.9. Furthermore, if you add .333 to 100, the result will again be 100, and no matter how many times you add .333 to 100, the result will always be 100. Thus, adding .333 to itself successively will eventually only reach 100.

Obviously, something can be done about this particular case, but errors will be propagated if we are not careful about them.

(c) Nonassociativity of Arithmetics

Consider the mathematically equivalent Fortran expressions

$$(A + B) + C \qquad \text{and} \qquad A + (B + C)$$

Suppose the computer is accurate to eight significant places and

$$A = 0.30000000 \qquad B = 87654321. \qquad C = -87654322.$$

Since the computer can only retain eight digits,

$$A + B = 87654321.$$

and A does not affect the result of A + B. Therefore,

$$(A + B) + C = 87654321. - 87654322. = -1.0000000$$

On the other hand, B + C = −1.0000000; hence,

$$A + (B + C) = 0.30000000 - 1.0000000 = -0.70000000$$

There is a 30-percent difference in the result, and this can lead to larger differences if these values are used in other computations; i.e., the round-off error can propagate.

Solved Problems

CONSTANTS

2.1   Write the following as Fortran integer constants:

(a)	34,275	(d)	4.8×10^4	(g)	-7.3
(b)	+275	(e)	$-1,278000$	(h)	12
(c)	-23.0	(f)	2.137×10^2	(i)	-138

(a)	34275	(d)	4800	(g)	Impossible—not an integer
(b)	+275	(e)	-1278000	(h)	12
(c)	-23	(f)	Impossible—not an integer	(i)	-138

2.2   Why are the following unacceptable as Fortran integer constants?

(a)   2,371   (b) -47.0 (c)   28E3   (d)   1234500000

(a)   Contains a comma.
(b)   Contains a decimal point.
(c)   An integer cannot be written in exponential form.
(d)   For most computers, an integer cannot have more than nine characters.

2.3   Write the following as Fortran real constants in the given form and in standard exponential form:

(a)	123	(d)	5.63×10^{-8}	(g)	0.123
(b)	12.3	(e)	$-1,234,000$	(h)	-0.356
(c)	$-3,400$	(f)	0.000347	(i)	3×10^{13}

(a)	123. or .123E3	(d)	5.63E−8 or .563E−7	(g)	0.123 or 0.123E0
(b)	12.3 or .123E2	(e)	$-1234000.$ or $-.1234E7$	(h)	$-.356$ or $-.356E0$
(c)	$-3400.$ or $-.34E4$	(f)	.000347 or .347E−3	(i)	3.E13 or .3E14

We emphasize that a real constant can be written in many different ways in exponential form, but only in one way in standard exponential form, i.e., as a power of 10 times a number between 0.1 and 1.0 or between -0.1 and -1.0.

2.4   Why are the following unacceptable as Fortran real constants?

(a)	3,248.6	(c)	1.6E128	(e)	4E−2
(b)	-13	(d)	E+3	(f)	4.3E3.7

(a)   Contains a comma.
(b)   Missing a decimal point.
(c)   An exponent cannot be more than two digits.
(d)   An exponent cannot appear alone (one can write 0.0E+3).
(e)   The 4 must have a decimal point.
(f)   Most computers only allow integer exponents.

VARIABLES

2.5   Which of the following are unacceptable as integer variables, and why?

(a)	NEXT	(c)	ALPHA	(e)	J + 329	(g)	2I45
(b)	FIRST	(d)	L124	(f)	MACBETH	(h)	N(3)M

    (*a*) Acceptable.
    (*b*) Unacceptable—the first letter is not I, J, K, L, M, or N.
    (*c*) Unacceptable—the first letter is not I, J, K, L, M, or N.
    (*d*) Acceptable.
    (*e*) Unacceptable—the plus (+) sign is not permissible.
    (*f*) Unacceptable—has more than six characters.
    (*g*) Unacceptable—first character must be a letter.
    (*h*) Unacceptable—characters must be letters or digits.

2.6   Which of the following are unacceptable as real constants, and why?

(*a*)	ANSWER	(*c*)	ROOT2	(*e*)	ALTITUDE	(*g*)	STOP
(*b*)	LAMBDA	(*d*)	MAX	(*f*)	4XYZ	(*h*)	X-RAY

    (*a*) Acceptable.
    (*b*) Unacceptable—first letter L reserved for integer variables.
    (*c*) Acceptable.
    (*d*) Unacceptable—first letter M reserved for integer variables.
    (*e*) Unacceptable—has more than six characters.
    (*f*) Unacceptable—first character must be a letter.
    (*g*) Unacceptable—part of Fortran repertoire.
    (*h*) Unacceptable—the hyphen (-) is not a letter or digit.

ARITHMETIC OPERATIONS AND EXPRESSIONS

2.7   Assuming mixed-mode expressions are unacceptable by the computer, determine which of the following are acceptable Fortran expressions and find their values.

(*a*)	2.4 + 3.85	(*c*)	3*4.5	(*e*)	3* + 5	(*g*)	0 + 4.6
(*b*)	12/5	(*d*)	3.**2	(*f*)	4.3 − 7.93	(*h*)	−7/3

    (*a*) 6.25
    (*b*) 2 (the fractional part is truncated in integer division).
    (*c*) Unacceptable—the operands have different types.
    (*d*) 9. (exponents can be integers even though the base is real).
    (*e*) Unacceptable—the operations * and + cannot appear next to each other.
    (*f*) −3.63
    (*g*) Unacceptable—the operands have different types.
    (*h*) −2 (the fractional part is truncated in integer division).

2.8   Assuming mixed-mode arithmetic is acceptable, find the value of each expression:

(*a*)	3 + 4.8*2	(*c*)	2.*6/5	(*e*)	7/(4*2.)	(*g*)	2*(3**2)
(*b*)	5.2 + 12/8	(*d*)	2*6/5	(*f*)	7/(4*2)	(*h*)	2*3**2

    (*a*) Multiplication takes precedence over addition.   Thus,

$$4.8*2 \text{ yields } 9.6 \quad \text{and} \quad 3 + 9.6 \text{ yields } 12.6$$

    (*b*) The integer division 12/8 yields 1, and 5.2 + 1 yields 6.2.
    (*c*) 2.*6 yields the real number 12., and 12./5 yields the real number 2.4.
    (*d*) 2*6 yields the integer 12, and the integer division 12/5 yields 2 as an answer.
    (*e*) 4*2. yields the real number 8., and 7/8. yields 0.875.
    (*f*) 4*2 yields the integer 8, and the integer division 7/8 yields 0 as an answer.
    (*g*) 18
    (*h*) Exponentiation takes precedence over multiplication; hence, we still obtain 18 as in (*g*).

2.9   Write a Fortran expression corresponding to each mathematical expression:

(a) $(x + y)(u + v)$ (d) $a + \dfrac{b}{c^2}$ (f) $\dfrac{x^4}{4!}$

(b) $3(x + y)$

(c) $3xy^2 - 2x^2y$ (e) $\dfrac{a + b}{c \cdot d}$

(a)   (X + Y)*(U + V)   (c)   3.0*X*Y**2 − 2.0*X**2*Y   (e)   (A + B)/(C*D)
(b)   3.0*(X + Y)   (d)   A + B/C**2   (f)   X**4/(4.*3.*2.*1.)

2.10   For each of the following Fortran expressions, find an equivalent expression, i.e., one which does not alter the order of the operations, by deleting superfluous parentheses.

(a)   (A*B)*(C + D)   (c)   (A*B*C)/((X*Y)**2)
(b)   (A*(B**2))/(C*D)   (d)   A*(B*C)

(a)   A*B*(C + D)
(b)   A*B**2/(C*D)
(c)   A*B*C/(X*Y)**2
(d)   A*(B*C); that is, no parentheses can be deleted.   [Although A*B*C, evaluated as (A*B)*C, is mathematically equivalent to A*(B*C), the order of operations is different and so round-off error can lead to different results.   See Section 2.10.]

2.11   Using the mathematical functions in Table 2-2 (page 26), write a Fortran expression corresponding to each mathematical expression:

(a) $\sqrt{a^2 + b^2}$ (c) $\dfrac{1}{|a \cdot b|} + c$

(b) $e^{x+y} - \sin(x + ny)$ (d) $\cos(\log_{10}(a + 3b))$

(a)   SQRT(A**2 + B**2)
(b)   EXP(X + Y) − SIN(X + N*Y)   or
      if the computer does not accept mixed-mode expressions
      EXP(X + Y) − SIN(X + FLOAT(N)*Y)
(c)   1./ABS(A*B) + C
(d)   COS(ALOG10(A + 3.0*B))

2.12   The following are mathematical expressions and incorrect, corresponding Fortran expressions.   Write the correct Fortran expressions.

(a) $\dfrac{a \cdot b}{c \cdot d \cdot e}$,   AB/CDE   (c) $\left(\dfrac{a}{b + c}\right)^2$,   A/(B + C)**2

(b) $\left(\dfrac{x}{y}\right)^{n+1}$,   (X/Y)**N + 1   (d) $\sqrt{\dfrac{a^2}{b + c}}$,   SQRT(A**2/(B + C)

(a)   A*B/(C*D*E)   (b)   (X/Y)**(N + 1)   (c)   (A/(B + C))**2   (d)   SQRT(A**2/(B + C))

ARITHMETIC STATEMENTS

2.13   Consider the following statements:

(a)   A = B + C   (c)   A = A + A   (e)   AB = CD
(b)   B + C = A   (d)   A + B = C + D (f)   A = ABS(A)

Which of the above are unacceptable as Fortran statements?   For those which are acceptable, what implicit condition are we assuming?

Recall that only a variable, i.e., the name of a storage location, can appear on the left side of an equal sign.

(a) Acceptable.
(b) Unacceptable since B + C is not a variable.
(c) Acceptable.
(d) Unacceptable since A + B is not a variable.
(e) Acceptable.
(f) Acceptable.

We are implicitly assuming that all the variables on the right side of any equal sign have been defined, i.e., that numbers are already in the storage locations having these names.

2.14　Suppose A, B, J, and K contain the following values: A = 2.7, B = 3.5, J = 3, and K = −2.　Find the values of X and L after each pair of statements:

(a)　X = A + J*K**2 + B　　(c)　X = K/3*A/2
　　　L = A + J*K**2 + B　　　　　L = K/3*A/2

(b)　X = 5*J/4*K　　　　　(d)　X = ABS(A − J*B)/5
　　　L = 5*J/4.0*K　　　　　　　L = ABS(A − J*B)/5

(a)　Performing exponentiation first, then multiplication, and then addition, the computer evaluates:

$$A + J*K**2 + B = 2.7 + 3(-2)^2 + 3.5 = 2.7 + 12 + 3.5 = 18.2$$

Since X is a real variable, the computer stores 18.2 in X; but since L is an integer variable, the computer stores 18 (that is, the integer part of 18.2) in L.　That is, X = 18.2 and L = 18.

(b)　The computer performs the multiplication and division from left to right:

$$5*J/4*K = 15/4*K = 3*K = -6$$
$$5*J/4.0*K = 15/4.0*K = 3.75*K = -7.5$$

Because of integer division, 15/4 yields 3; but 15/4.0 yields 3.75.　Since X is real, −6 is converted to the real number, −6.0, and then stored in X.　Since L is an integer variable, −7.5 is truncated to −7 and then stored in L.　Thus, X = −6.0 and L = −7.

(c)　Because of integer division, K/3 yields 0.　Hence, X = 0.0 and L = 0.

(d)　ABS(A − J*B)/5 = |2.7 − 3(3.5)|/5 = |−7.8|/5 = 1.56.　So X = 1.56 and L = 1.

2.15　Suppose A and B have the following values: A = 2.5, B = 3.5.　Find the values of A and B as a result of each list of statements:

(a)　A = B　　　(b)　T = A
　　　B = A　　　　　　A = B
　　　　　　　　　　　　B = T

(a)　The statement A = B tells the computer to erase the current value of A and substitute in its place the current value of B; hence,

$$A \leftarrow \cancel{2.5}\ \ 3.5$$

The next statement B = A tells the computer to erase the current value of B and substitute in its place the current value of A; hence,

$$B \leftarrow \cancel{3.5}\ \ 3.5$$

Observe that the value of B has not changed.

(b)　The three statements yield:

$$T \leftarrow 2.5, \qquad A \leftarrow \cancel{2.5}\ \ 3.5, \qquad B \leftarrow \cancel{3.5}\ \ 2.5$$

Observe that the values of A and B have been interchanged by introducing an auxiliary storage location to "hold" the value of one of the variables during the interchange.

2.16 Suppose the variables A, B, and C have already been defined.   Write a Fortran statement which (*a*) doubles the value of A; (*b*) increases the value of B by 4; (*c*) decreases the value of C by the value of A; (*d*) stores in AVE the average value of A, B, and C, that is, the sum of A, B, and C divided by 3; (*e*) stores in DIST the square root of the sum of the squares of A, B, and C, that is, $\sqrt{A^2 + B^2 + C^2}$.

(*a*)   A = 2.0*A   (*c*)   C = C − A   (*e*)   DIST = SQRT(A**2 + B**2 + C**2)
(*b*)   B = B + 4.0   (*d*)   AVE = (A + B + C)/3.0

MISCELLANEOUS PROBLEMS

2.17 Discuss the following three ways of writing x^2 in Fortran:

(*a*)   X*X   (*b*)   X**2   (*c*)   X**2.0

In (*a*), x^2 is written in terms of multiplication and will be so evaluated.   In (*b*), X**2 will be evaluated by multiplication as the result of compiling X**2 into X*X.   In (*c*), the exponent is real, so (*c*) is evaluated as EXP(2.0*ALOG(X)), and X must be positive.   (See Section 2.8.)   Clearly, (*a*) and (*b*) are preferable to (*c*).   In fact, (*c*) may give a slightly different result in view of the round-off errors in evaluating EXP and ALOG.   Furthermore, although (*a*) and (*b*) require the same execution time, (*a*) does not require extra compilation.

2.18 Discuss the following two program segments:

(*a*)   XN = N   (*b*)   AVE = SUM/FLOAT(N)
       AVE = SUM/XN

(Note that both are written to avoid mixed-mode division.)

In (*a*), the integer N is first converted to real, and stored in XN.   Then the average is computed as SUM/XN.   Observe that an extra storage location is required.   On the other hand, (*b*) requires only one statement since we use the function FLOAT in the computation.   Thus, (*b*) seems to be more advantageous than (*a*).   However, if the program is long and N needs to be converted to real many times, then it would be more advantageous to convert N to real once and for all by XN = N, rather than to use FLOAT(N) throughout the program.

Supplementary Problems

CONSTANTS

2.19 Write the following as Fortran integer constants:

(*a*)   2,348   (*d*) 3.1214×10^3 (*g*)   23.51
(*b*) 5.31×10^3 (*e*)   −37.0   (*h*)   1,250,000
(*c*)   −531   (*f*) $21,500 \times 10^{-3}$ (*i*) $57,000.0 \times 10^{-2}$

2.20 Why are the following unacceptable as Fortran integer constants?

(*a*)   2,578   (*b*)   −784.0   (*c*)   37810000000   (*d*)   38E+2

2.21 Write the following as Fortran real constants and also in standard exponential form:

(*a*)   2,345   (*c*)   2,348,500   (*e*)   .00005829
(*b*)   −1.63   (*d*) -7.63×10^{-5} (*f*) 21×10^{18}

2.22   Why are the following unacceptable as Fortran real constants?

  (*a*) −3.6E134   (*c*) 52E−7   (*e*) E21
  (*b*) 2,356.4   (*d*) 256   (*f*) −1,378.0

2.23   Determine which pairs of constants represent the same number:

  (*a*) 43.6   4.36E01   (*d*) 12345   +12345
  (*b*) 543   5.43E+02   (*e*) 0.234E6   234.E4
  (*c*) 0.00004   4.0E − 5   (*f*) 1.00   1.

VARIABLES

2.24   Consider the following list of names. Determine those which are acceptable as either (1) integer variables or (2) real variables. Give the reason that the remaining are not acceptable as variable names.

  (*a*) MORE   (*f*) A567B   (*k*) AMOUNT
  (*b*) LESS   (*g*) RATE   (*l*) A + 567
  (*c*) NEITHER   (*h*) X34.7   (*m*) A12345
  (*d*) AAAAAA   (*i*) GAMMA   (*n*) IN-OUT
  (*e*) 5PQR   (*j*) KAPPA   (*o*) OPERAND

ARITHMETIC OPERATIONS AND EXPRESSIONS

2.25   Assume the computer does not accept mixed-mode arithmetic. Determine which of the following are acceptable Fortran expressions and find their values. Identify errors in unacceptable expressions.

  (*a*) 6.3 + 5.2E3   (*c*) 6.*4   (*e*) 0/3.4   (*g*) 9/ − 4
  (*b*) −18/7   (*d*) 6.**4   (*f*) 6* − 7   (*h*) −4/9

2.26   Assume the computer does accept mixed-mode arithmetic. Find the value of each expression.

  (*a*) 3 − 5*2.5   (*c*) 19/(2*5)   (*e*) −3*2**3   (*g*) (7/3)/(6/5)
  (*b*) 2.8 − 17/5   (*d*) 19/(2.*5)   (*f*) −3*(2**3)   (*h*) 2**2*2/3

2.27   Write a Fortran expression corresponding to each mathematical expression.

  (*a*) $(2x + y)(3z - 4w)$ (*e*) $\left(3 + \dfrac{a}{b}\right)^{m-1}$

  (*b*) $4x^2y - 3xy + 7yz^3$

  (*c*) $\left(\dfrac{a+b}{c+d}\right)^3$ (*f*) $\dfrac{\dfrac{a}{b} + 6}{x - \dfrac{y}{z}}$

  (*d*) $\dfrac{x^5}{5!}$

2.28   For each of the following Fortran expressions, find an equivalent expression, i.e., one which does not alter the order of the operations, by deleting any superfluous parentheses.

  (*a*) (X + Y) + Z   (*c*) A + ((B*C)/D)   (*e*) (X*(Y − Z))*(A**2)
  (*b*) X + (Y + Z)   (*d*) (A + (B**3))/(X*Y)   (*f*) ((A**2) + (B**2)) − (D*(E/F))

2.29 Using the mathematical functions in Table 2-2 (page 26), write a Fortran expression corresponding to each mathematical expression.

(a) $\sqrt{5x^2 + 8y^2}$ (e) $\log_e(x + y)^2$

(b) $\sin(x - 2y) + e^{xy} - |x^2 - y^2|$ (f) $\log_{10}(a - b)^2$

(c) $e^{|a|} - \dfrac{b^2}{|c|}$ (g) $\left|\sqrt{x - y^3} - \dfrac{z^3}{\cos(a + b)}\right|$

(d) $\sqrt{|\cos(a - nb)|}$ (h) $\sqrt{|\sin(a - |b|)|}$

2.30 The following are mathematical expressions and incorrect corresponding Fortran expressions. Write the correct Fortran expressions.

(a) $a + \dfrac{b}{c \cdot d}$ A + B/CD

(b) $\dfrac{x^{n+1}}{y^{n-1}}$ (X**N + 1)/(Y**N − 1)

(c) $\sin(x + n)$ SIN(X + FLOAT(N)

(d) $\log_{10}|a \cdot b|$ LOG(ABS(AB)

ARITHMETIC STATEMENTS

2.31 Which of the following are acceptable as Fortran statements?

(a) X = Y + Z   (d) XY = ZW   (g) ABC = DEF

(b) X + Y = Z   (e) XY = Z*W   (h) ABC = 2DEF

(c) Y + Z = X   (f) X*Y = Z*W   (i) A*B*C = D*E*F

2.32 Suppose X, Y, L, and M contain the following values: X = 3.1, Y = 4.6, L = 2, and M = −3. Find the final values of A and J as a result of each list of statements.

(a) A = X − 2*Y + X/L**2   (d) A = X + 2*Y
    J = X − 2*Y + (X/L)**2   A = 2*A + 4
                                   J = A

(b) A = 8/M + 3*L   (e) J = L + 3*M
    J = 8.0/M − Y   J = J**2 + Y
                                   A = X + J

(c) A = L/M*X/Y   (f) J = SQRT(X*Y)
    J = L/(M + X)*Y   A = J*Y
                                   J = A*M
                                   A = A + ABS(FLOAT(J))

2.33 Assume that X, Y, and Z have been defined. Write an arithmetic statement which accomplishes the following: (a) increases the value of X by 3.2; (b) triples the value of Y; (c) squares the value of Z; (d) stores in PRDT the product of the values of X, Y, and Z; (e) stores in HYP the length of the hypotenuse of a right triangle whose legs have lengths X and Y; (f) stores in AVE the average value of X, Y, and Z.

2.34 Suppose A, B, and C have been defined. Write a program segment which interchanges the values of A, B, and C so that A has B's value, B has C's value, and C has A's value. [Hint: See Problem 2.15(b).]

Answers to Selected Supplementary Problems

2.19   (*a*) 2348   (*b*) 5310   (*c*) −531   (*d*) Impossible   (*e*) −37   (*f*) Impossible
(*g*) Impossible   (*h*) 1250000   (*i*) 570

2.20   (*a*) Contains a comma.
(*b*) Contains a decimal point.
(*c*) For most computers, an integer cannot have more than nine characters.
(*d*) An integer cannot be written in exponential form.

2.21   (*a*) 2345. or 0.2345E4   (*d*) −7.63E−5 or −0.763E−4
(*b*) −1.63 or −0.163E1   (*e*) 0.00005829 or 0.5829E−4
(*c*) 2348500. or 0.23485E7   (*f*) 21.E18 or 0.21E20

2.22   (*a*) An exponent cannot be more than two digits in most computers.
(*b*) Contains a comma.
(*c*) Missing a decimal point.
(*d*) Missing a decimal point.
(*e*) An exponent cannot appear alone.   (One can write 0.0E21.)
(*f*) Contains a comma.

2.23   (*a*) Yes   (*b*) No—one is an integer.   (*c*) Yes   (*d*) Yes   (*e*) No   (*f*) Yes

2.24   (*a*) Integer.   (*b*) Integer.   (*c*) Has more than six characters.   (*d*) Real.   (*e*) Begins
with a digit.   (*f*) Real.   (*g*) Real.   (*h*) The decimal point is not permissible.
(*i*) Real.   (*j*) Integer.   (*k*) Real.   (*l*) The plus sign is not permissible.   (*m*) Real.
(*n*) The hyphen is not permissible.   (*o*) Has more than six characters.

2.25   (*a*) 5206.3   (*b*) −2   (*c*) Unacceptable   (*d*) 1296.   (*e*) Unacceptable
(*f*) Unacceptable since * and − cannot appear next to each other.   (*g*) −2   (*h*) 0

2.26   (*a*) −9.5   (*b*) −0.2   (*c*) 1   (*d*) 1.9   (*e*) −24   (*f*) −24   (*g*) 2   (*h*) 2

2.27   (*a*) (2.*X + Y)*(3.*Z − 4.*W)   (*d*) X**5/(5.*4.*3.*2.*1.)
(*b*) 4.*X**2*Y − 3.*X*Y + 7.*Y*Z**3   (*e*) (3. + A/B)**(M − 1)
(*c*) ((A + B)/(C + D))**3   (*f*) (A/B + 6.)/(X − Y/Z)

2.28   (*a*) X + Y + Z   (*d*) (A + B**3)/(X*Y)
(*b*) X + (Y + Z)   (*e*) X*(Y − Z)*A**2
(*c*) A + B*C/D   (*f*) A**2 + B**2 − D*(E/F)

2.29   (*a*) SQRT(5.*X**2 + 8.*Y**2)
(*b*) SIN(X − 2.*Y) + EXP(X*Y) − ABS(X**2 − Y**2)
(*c*) EXP(ABS(A)) − B**2/ABS(C)
(*d*) SQRT(ABS(COS(A − FLOAT(N)*B)))
(*e*) ALOG((X + Y)**2)
(*f*) ALOG10((A − B)**2)
(*g*) ABS(SQRT(X − Y**3) − Z**3/COS(A + B))
(*h*) SQRT(ABS(SIN(A − ABS(B))))

2.30 (*a*) A + B/(C∗D)   (*c*) SIN(X + FLOAT(N))
     (*b*) (X∗∗(N + 1))/(Y∗∗(N − 1)) or X∗∗(N + 1)/Y∗∗(N − 1)   (*d*) ALOG10(ABS(A∗B))

2.31 (*a*) Yes   (*b*) No   (*c*) No   (*d*) Yes   (*e*) Yes   (*f*) No   (*g*) Yes   (*h*) No
     (*i*) No

2.32 (*a*) A = −5.325, J = −3   (*c*) A = 0.0,   J = 92   (*e*) A = 56.1, J = 53
     (*b*) A = 4.0,   J = −7   (*d*) A = 28.6, J = 28   (*f*) A = 54.8, J = −41

2.33 (*a*) X = X + 3.2
     (*b*) Y = 3.∗Y
     (*c*) Z = Z∗∗2
     (*d*) PRDT = X∗Y∗Z
     (*e*) HYP = SQRT(X∗∗2 + Y∗∗2)
     (*f*) AVE = (X + Y + Z)/3.0

2.34   T = A
           A = B
           B = C
           C = T

Chapter 3

Numerical Input/Output

3.1 INTRODUCTION

In this chapter, we shall see how a computer reads in external data (input) and prints out data (output). This is accomplished by a READ and a WRITE statement respectively. These are called input/output operations or simply I/O operations. As stated before, our input device is assumed to be a card reader, and our output device is a line printer (unless otherwise stated or implied).

A READ statement tells the computer to read in numerical or symbolic information from a deck of cards (the data deck), and a WRITE statement tells the computer to print out information on the printer. Normally, each READ or WRITE statement is accompanied by a FORMAT statement. In input, the FORMAT statement provides the computer with the types of the information and their respective locations within an input record. In output, the FORMAT statement also informs the computer where the information is to be printed. Obviously, the FORMAT statements can be very detailed. However, many computer installations allow so-called *unformatted input/output* features. We shall discuss such unformatted I/O first. (Some texts use the term "format-free" rather than the term "unformatted".)

3.2 UNFORMATTED INPUT/OUTPUT

After reading this section, the reader may proceed to Section 3.10 and the next three chapters before returning to the remainder of this chapter (unless the reader's computing facility does not provide unformatted input/output).

The unformatted I/O discussed here may vary from installation to installation with minor variation. Thus, readers are advised to consult their local facility for exact detail.

A typical unformatted PRINT statement follows:

PRINT, A, B, C, AREA, M, N

Observe that the word PRINT and each variable except the last is followed by a comma. This statement tells the computer to print the values of the variables A, B, C, AREA, M, and N, in that given order. The values will be printed with a preassigned format, and real numbers will *usually* be printed in exponential form. The number of values that can be printed on one line is also predetermined. However, the computer will always begin to print on a new line whenever it encounters a PRINT statement.

A typical unformatted READ statement follows:

READ, A, B, C, LOT, AREA

Observe that the word READ and each variable other than the last is followed by a comma. This statement tells the computer to "read" in five numbers, one for each variable, starting from the card on the top of the data deck. If there are five or more numbers on that card, then the first five are assigned to A, B, C, LOT, AREA respectively, and the card is then discarded. However, if there are fewer than five numbers on the card, then the computer will keep on reading from the data deck until all five numbers are found. That is, the execution of the READ statement is not finished until all the listed variables are assigned values.

Note that a data card is discarded after it is used in reading. Hence, a card not previously read will always be on top of the data deck.

The numbers on the data deck that are read with unformatted input statements should be separated by commas. (Some computer centers allow the numbers to be separated by blank spaces instead of commas.) Real numbers may be punched in either decimal or exponential form. Obviously, the numbers on the card(s) and the corresponding variables should be of the same type.

EXAMPLE 3.1

Suppose a computer executes the following two statements:

        READ, I, J, K
        READ, L, M

and suppose the data cards are punched as follows:

        First data card: 222,76
        Second data card: 38,175,55
        Third data card: 194,58,567

When the computer executes the first READ statement, it assigns 222 and 76 to I and J respectively, and then goes to the next data card and assigns 38 to K. This completes the execution of the first READ statement, and the second data card is discarded—even though the numbers 175 and 55 were not read. When the computer executes the second READ statement, it will read the card on top of the data deck. Then the computer uses the third data card to assign 194 to L and 58 to M. Hence, we have

        I = 222, J = 76, K = 38, L = 194, M = 58

Some computing facilities require that the numbers on the data cards be separated by blank spaces (denoted by subscripted b's) rather than by commas. In such cases, the data cards should be punched as follows:

        First data card: 222$_b$76
        Second data card: 38$_b$175$_b$55
        Third data card: 194$_b$58$_b$567

3.3 INTRODUCTION TO FORMATTED INPUT/OUTPUT

Unformatted (format-free) input/output statements were introduced first so that readers can start writing programs and communicating with the computer as soon as possible. This avoids being held back with the details of writing FORMAT statements. However, as unformatted I/O actually executes with a preassigned format, one really does not have much control as to how information is read and printed. Here we discuss the detail of writing formatted I/O statements. We will limit our discussion to I/O with numerical values. Other types will be treated in a later chapter.

In a large computer installation, many different devices can be used for input and output. For these devices to be distinguished, they are assigned numbers. Table 3-1 shows typical device

Table 3-1

Device	Number
Tape drive	1
Card reader	5
Line printer	6
Card punch	7

numbers. (These numbers were first used in many IBM installations and are still widely used.) In this text, we assume that our input device is a card reader, unit number 5, and our output device is a line printer, unit number 6.

Since our input device is a card reader, our input data will be given to the computer by means of a deck of cards. These cards are identical to the cards on which Fortran statements are punched. However, the rules of punching Fortran statements do not apply here; i.e., the full 80 columns of the data card can be used and no column, e.g., column 6, has any special purpose.

The input is punched into certain blocks of contiguous columns on the data card. Figure 3-1 shows a data card on which four numbers are punched; the first number 24587 is punched within columns 1–8, the second number 193 is punched within columns 9–14, the third number 8.725 is punched within columns 15–22, and the fourth number +43450.75 is punched within columns 23–34. Such blocks of contiguous columns are called *fields*, and the number of columns in a field is called its *field width*. Observe that each number is punched *right-justified* in its field; i.e., the last digit of the number appears in the last column of its field. (Some texts use the term right-adjusted instead of the term right-justified.)

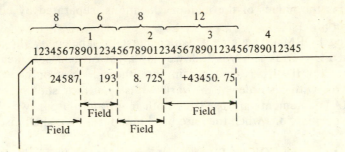

Fig. 3-1 Data card showing fields and field widths.

Suppose we want the above four numbers to be assigned to the variables ID, LOT, RATE, and PRICE, respectively. This is accomplished in Fortran by a READ statement and an accompanying FORMAT statement which could be as follows:

    READ(5, 100) ID, LOT, RATE, PRICE
100   FORMAT(I8, I6, F8.0, F12.0)

Consider the two numbers in parentheses following the word READ. The first number, 5, is the input device number that designates a card reader. (We would write 1 instead of 5 if we wanted to use a tape drive instead of a card reader, e.g., if the input data was stored on a magnetic tape.) The second number 100 specifies the FORMAT statement accompanying this READ statement. (The FORMAT statement provides the necessary type and location information for the variables.) The choice of 100 here is completely arbitrary. The variable names follow next and are listed in the order that their values were punched on the data card.

This order also applies to the four entries in the accompanying FORMAT statement, I8, I6, F8.0, and F12.0. These entries are called *field specifications* (sometimes *field descriptors*) or *format codes*. Each entry contains a letter which denotes the data type, e.g., integer or real, and a number which denotes the field width and, hence, the field location of the corresponding data item. In our case, the first field specification I8 indicates that the first number is an integer and can be found within the first 8 columns of the card. The second specification I6 indicates that the second number is an integer and can be found within the next 6 columns of the card. The third specification F8.0 indicates that the third number is real and can be found within the next 8 columns of the card, and the fourth specification F12.0 indicates that the fourth number is real and can be found within the next 12 columns of the card.

In this example, the field specification of an integer is of the form Iw, and the field specification of a real number is of the form $Fw.0$, where w denotes the field width. We also assume that real numbers are punched in decimal form.

3.4 FORMATTED INPUT AND INPUT FIELD SPECIFICATIONS

The computer reads in data (input) by means of a READ statement and an accompanying FORMAT statement as illustrated in the last section. The general form of such statements follows:

    READ(m, n) variable list
  n   FORMAT(format list)

Specifically, a READ statement begins with the word READ. This is followed by an integer m which specifies the input device number and a statement number n which specifies the FORMAT statement; the m and n are separated by a comma and enclosed in parentheses. The variable list which follows contains the names of the memory locations, separated by commas, in which the input data is to be stored.

The accompanying FORMAT statement, which must be labeled by the statement number n, begins with the word FORMAT. This is followed by a list of field specifications (format codes) separated by commas, and the list is enclosed in parentheses. Not only should the order of the field specifications agree with the order of the variable list, but they should also agree in types.

Although FORMAT statements are used for both input and output, we shall now discuss the meaning of the field specifications when they are used in input. (We shall discuss their meaning in output in Section 3.6.)

The field specifications in a FORMAT statement contain respective field widths $w_1, w_2, \ldots$. In input, they uniquely determine a sequence of fields on a data card as follows: the first field being the first w_1 columns, the second field being the next w_2 columns, and so on. The field widths in the example of the preceding section were 8, 6, 8, and 12 respectively.

Note that when reading with *numerical* field specifications (which will be discussed next), the following two rules apply:

  1. Blank spaces are interpreted as zeros.
  2. Unsigned values are taken to be positive.

It should be emphasized that rule 1 does not hold if nonnumerical field specifications are used.

I-field

The general field specification for reading in an integer is

    Iw

where the character I indicates the integer type, and w is an unsigned integer constant giving the field width.

Since blanks in numerical fields are taken as zeros, it is imperative that an integer be punched

    right-justified

in its field, so that the last digit of the integer appears in the last column of the given field.
Consider the statements

    READ(5, 20) M, N
  20 FORMAT(I3, I5)

These statements tell the computer to read from the data card two integers and store them in M and N respectively. The specification for M is I3 and for N is I5. Since the field widths are 3 and 5 respectively, M is assigned the integer found in columns 1–3, and N is assigned the integer found in columns 4–8.

Suppose the integers 40 and −123 are intended for M and N respectively. Then the data card must be punched as Card A is in Fig. 3-2. On the other hand, if the data card were to be punched as Card B is in Fig. 3-2, then the above READ statement would assign 400 to M and −1230 to N since the blank spaces in columns 3 and 8 are interpreted as zeros.

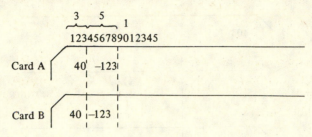

Fig. 3-2

F-field

Real constants in decimal form can be read in using F-fields. The general form is

$$Fw.d$$

The F indicates that the data type is real and the number is written in decimal form, w is an unsigned integer constant denoting the field width, and d is an unsigned integer representing the number of decimal digits. However, *the d is ignored in input* if the number punched in the field has a *decimal point*.

Suppose a number −403.125 is to be read into location A using

```
      READ(5, 20) A
20    FORMAT(F12.4)
```

Since the field width is 12, A will be assigned the number appearing in the first 12 columns of the data card. Then, any one of the first three cards in Fig. 3-3 can be used as the data card.

The value of A did not have to be punched right-justified in its field as was the case for integer constants because the number is in decimal form. Although blank spaces in numerical fields are interpreted as zeros, adding zeros to either of the ends of a number in decimal form does not change its value; for example, −403.125 and −403.12500 have the same value. Hence, as stated earlier, when reading with F-field, as long as the number is punched in decimal form (i.e., contains a decimal point) and lies within the specified field, the integer d in $Fw.d$ will be ignored, and that number will be read in as it appears on the data card. It should be noted that the number of significant figures retained by the computer is a machine-dependent feature.

Many compilers do not require that real constants specified by F-fields be punched with a decimal point in input. In this case, the integer constant d in $Fw.d$ goes into effect. Specifically, if no decimal point is present in the specified field, then the number read will have exactly d decimal digits; a decimal point is embedded between the dth and $(d + 1)$st columns counting leftward from the right end of the field. For example, suppose the above READ-FORMAT pair is used to read card (4) in Fig. 3-3. As there is no decimal point between columns 1 and 12, when reading with the field specification F12.4, a decimal point will be assumed between the 4th and 5th columns from the

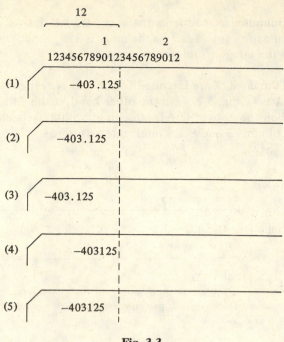

Fig. 3-3

right side of the field, i.e., between columns 9 and 8. Accordingly, the number assigned to A is −40.3125. Similarly, if the same READ-FORMAT pair is used to read card (5) in Fig. 3-3, then the number assigned to A is −4031.25.

The above feature eliminates the need for punching the decimal point in real constants in preparing the data deck. (This clearly will be a timesaving advantage for commercial setups.) However, when this feature is used, the position of the punched number does affect the assigned number. Accordingly, beginning programmers are advised to forgo this feature, i.e., to punch the decimal point when using F-fields.

EXAMPLE 3.2

Suppose the READ-FORMAT pair

        READ(5, 21) A, B
    21 FORMAT(F10.2, F10.2)

is used to read a card punched as follows:

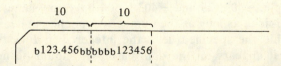

Since the number in columns 1 to 10 contains a decimal point, it is assigned to A as it appears; hence, A will contain 123.456. The second number, in columns 11 to 20, contains no decimal point; hence, it will be read in as 1234.56 and assigned to B.

E-field

Recall, first, that a real constant in exponential form (Section 2.2) consists of two parts; the first part is a real constant in decimal form, and this is followed by the exponential part (the second part) which begins with the character E followed by a signed or unsigned integer constant with at most two digits.

   Real constants in exponential form are read in using E-fields. The general form of the field specification is

   Ew.d

The letter *E* indicates that the data type is real, and the constant is written in exponential form; the *w* is an unsigned integer denoting the field width, and the *d* is an unsigned integer denoting the number of decimal digits.   As in F-field, the *d* is ignored in input if the number is punched with a decimal point.

   Suppose a number $-4.03125E+02$ is to be read into location A using

      READ(5, 30) A
   30   FORMAT(E18.5)

Observe that the field width is 18; so A will be assigned the number appearing in the first 18 columns of the data card.   Thus, any one of the first five cards in Fig. 3-4 can be used as the data

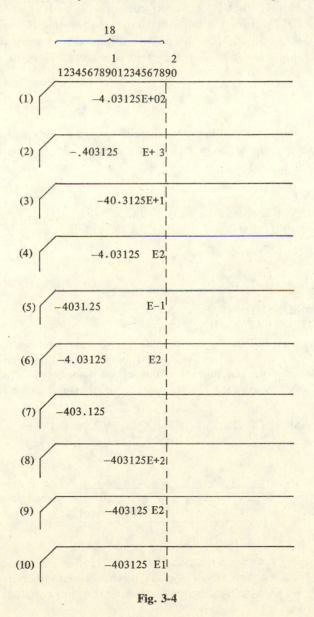

Fig. 3-4

card giving A the value -0.403125×10^3. If the sixth card is used, then $-4.03125E+20$ would be assigned to A since the blank space in column 18 is interpreted as zero. Accordingly, in E-field it is essential that the exponential part be punched right-justified in the field.

If a real constant has a zero exponent (that is, $E + 00$), then the exponent part need not be punched. In other words, if the number is not punched with an exponential part, then the field specification $Ew.d$ is treated in the same way as $Fw.d$. Accordingly, the seventh card in Fig. 3-4 can also be used to assign $-4.03125E+02$ to A. (In view of this flexibility, some programmers prefer to use E-field in input regardless of whether the data cards are punched with exponents.)

As in F-field, the use of a decimal point in input is optional when using the E-field. If no decimal point is present in the specified field (to the left of E), then a decimal point is assumed to be between the d and $d + 1$ columns, counting leftward beginning with the first column to the left of the character E. For example, suppose the above READ-FORMAT pair is used to read card (8) in Fig. 3-4. As there is no decimal point present in columns 1–18, the integer 5 in the field specification E18.5 will cause a decimal point to be embedded between the fifth and sixth columns to the left of the character E, that is, between columns 10 and 11. Accordingly, the number assigned to A is still $-4.03125E+2$. On the other hand, if the same READ-FORMAT pair is used to read card (9) in Fig. 3-4, then $-40.3125E2$ would be assigned to A since a decimal point would be embedded between columns 11 and 12. (Here the character E is in column 17.) Similarly, $-40.3125E1$ would be assigned to A if card (10) is used.

X-field

One can distinguish several constants on the same data card by separating them with one or more blank spaces. These blanks can be "skipped" by using an X-field. Generally speaking, an X-field specification has the form

$$wX$$

The w is an unsigned integer denoting the field width, and the letter X means that the corresponding field of w columns should be *skipped* whether the field contains any information or not.

EXAMPLE 3.3

Suppose a program has the statements

```
     READ(5, 75) ID, AMOUNT, BALANS
  75 FORMAT(I7, 3X, F7.2, 3X, E12.2)
```

and suppose the data card in Fig. 3-5 is read. Observe that the field widths are 7, 3, 7, 3, and 12 respectively. Thus, ID is assigned the integer in the first numerical field (columns 1–7). Columns 8–10 are skipped. AMOUNT is assigned the real number in the second numerical field (columns 11–17). Columns 18–20 are skipped. BALANS is assigned the real number in the third numerical field (columns 21–32). Consequently,

$$ID = 12345, \qquad AMOUNT = 250.25, \qquad BALANS = 402.5 = 40.25E+1$$

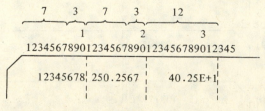

Fig. 3-5

3.5 FORMATTED WRITE STATEMENTS AND CARRIAGE CONTROL

The computer is instructed to output data by means of a WRITE statement and an accompanying FORMAT statement which have the following form:

WRITE(m, n) *variable list*
n FORMAT(format list)

Specifically, the WRITE statement begins with the word WRITE. This is followed by an integer m which specifies the output device number and a statement number n which specifies the accompanying FORMAT statement; the m and n are separated by a comma and enclosed in parentheses. The variables, whose values are to be printed, follow and are separated by commas. We will assume that a line printer is used for printing our output; so in all our examples, the output device number will be $m = 6$. (See Table 3-1.)

The accompanying FORMAT statement must be labeled by the statement number n, and it will have the same form as in input; i.e., it begins with the word FORMAT and is followed by a list of field specifications which are separated by commas and enclosed in parentheses. The meaning of the field specifications in output will be explained in the next section.

Each WRITE-FORMAT pair will generate an output stream (record) of characters. (A blank space is a character and will sometimes be denoted by "$_b$"; that is, a subscripted b.) The first character in an output stream controls the movement of the carriage of the line printer according to the instructions in Table 3-2 and is not printed. Specifically, the computer examines the first

Table 3-2

First character	Instruction	Format entry
b (blank)	Advance one line (normal single spacing)	1X or ` `
0 (zero)	Advance two lines (skip a line, double spacing)	'0'
1	Advance to top of next page	'1'
+	Do not advance	'+'

character of the output stream, performs the carriage control instruction, and then prints the remaining characters in the output stream. For example, the output stream

$_{bbbb}$12345$_{bb}$67.89

tells the computer to advance one line and then print respectively 4 blanks, 12345, 2 blanks, and 67.89; the output stream

0_{bbbb}12345$_{bb}$67.89

tells the computer to advance 2 lines (skip a line) and then print 4 blanks, 12345, 2 blanks, and 67.89; and the output stream

1_{bbbb}12345$_{bb}$67.89

tells the computer to advance to a new page and then print 4 blanks, 12345, 2 blanks, and 67.89.

The FORMAT statement in a WRITE-FORMAT pair tells the computer the types of the output data and where they are to appear in the output stream. Specifically, each value in the variable list in the WRITE statement is assigned a block of spaces (called a *field*) by a corresponding entry in the FORMAT statement.   The numerical value of the variable is always placed

      right-justified

in its field, i.e., so that the number ends in the last space of the field.   We shall illustrate with an example, although the format entries are discussed in detail in the next section.

EXAMPLE 3.4

    Suppose we wanted to print the values of J, K, and L, in this order, where J = 128, K = 72, and L = −179.   This can be accomplished with the following pair of statements.

        WRITE(6, 20) J, K, L
20   FORMAT(I8, I6, I8)

The 6 in the WRITE statement tells the computer that the output device is a line printer, and the 20 says that the values are to be printed according to the FORMAT statement labeled 20.   (The number 20 is chosen arbitrarily.)

    The first three fields in the output stream determined by the WRITE-FORMAT pair contain the following characters:

      bbbbb128   (I8)   The integral value of J is generated right-justified in the first field of width 8; that is, the value of J is padded on the left with 5 blank characters.

      bbbb72   (I6)   The integral value of K is generated right-justified in the next field of width 6.

      bbbb−179   (I8)   The integral value of L is generated right-justified in the next field of width 8.

Accordingly, the output stream contains the following characters:

    Output stream: bbbbb128bbbb72bbbb−179

Furthermore, the output stream tells the computer to advance one line, and then print respectively 4 blanks, 128, 4 blanks, 72, 4 blanks, and −179.   The printed output appears in Fig. 3-6.   Print pages are of various widths, and the one in Fig. 3-6 assumes that there are 132 print columns.

    Summarizing, the computer performs the following steps in a WRITE-FORMAT instruction:

    1. Generates the output stream given rise by the WRITE-FORMAT pair.

    2. Examines the first character and performs the carriage control instruction.

    3. Prints the remaining characters of the output stream.

We note that after the completion of a WRITE instruction, the line printer always stops on the line just printed.   Hence, the first character generated by any succeeding output statement will again be used for carriage control.

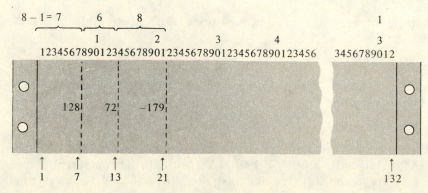

Fig. 3-6

Remark. As a good programming habit, one usually gives an explicit carriage control signal. This is accomplished by choosing one of the entries in Table 3-2 as the first entry of a FORMAT statement. This is discussed and explained in the next section. [Such a habit avoids errors illustrated in Problems 3.12(*b*), 3.32(*f*), and 3.33(*f*)]. Observe that no such explicit carriage control signal was given in the above example, but that the carriage control signal was incorporated in the field specification I8 which gave a field larger than the value of J.

3.6 OUTPUT FIELD SPECIFICATIONS

As discussed previously, the FORMAT statement accompanying a WRITE statement specifies the data types and locations of the information to be printed. In this section, we cover the same types of field specifications that were covered in input:

$$wX, \quad Iw, \quad Fw.d, \quad Ew.d$$

We emphasize that the meaning of these specifications in output may differ from that in input. For one thing, *all numerical constants are printed right-justified in their fields* and padded on the left by blanks. Also, the *d* in *Fw.d* and *Ew.d* always plays a major role in output, whereas the *d* can sometimes be overridden in input.

X-field

To separate several constants on the same line by blank spaces can be achieved by using X-field. The general form of the field specification is

$$wX$$

where *w* denotes the field width. The effect of *wX* is the *generation of w blank spaces in the output stream*.

In particular, if 1X appears as the first entry in a FORMAT statement, then a blank is generated as the first character of the output stream. This blank, used for carriage control, advances the carriage by one line. In other words, FORMAT statements of the form

$$n \quad \text{FORMAT}(1X, \ldots)$$

always lead to normal single spacing. Similarly,

$$n \quad \text{FORMAT}(10X, \ldots)$$

will always mean single spacing with nine-space indentation.

I-field

Integer constants are printed using I-field. The general form of the field specification is

$$Iw$$

where *I* denotes integer type and *w* the field width.

For example, suppose M contains 250, N contains 46, and

        WRITE(6, 10) M, N
10   FORMAT(1X, I6, 3X, I4)

is executed. The entry 1X generates one blank: ᵦ. The entry I6 which corresponds to M generates ᵦᵦᵦ250; that is, the value of M is generated right-justified in the next field of width 6. The entry 3X generates three blanks: ᵦᵦᵦ. The entry I4 which corresponds to N generates ᵦᵦ46; that is, the value of N is generated right-justified in the next field of width 4. Thus, the following output stream is generated:

    Output stream: ᵦᵦᵦᵦ250ᵦᵦᵦᵦᵦ46

Since the first character of the output stream is a blank, which means single spacing, the line printer will advance one line and print the remaining characters:

> Printed characters: $\quad$ bbb250bbbbb46

If insufficient width is provided, i.e., if a numerical value has more characters than its specified field width, some compilers will truncate the value on the left (or right) and print the remaining characters. In the above example, if M contains 54321, then

> bbb250bbb4321

is printed, and no diagnostic message is given. Fortunately, most better-constructed compilers will signal insufficient field width by printing asterisks in the designated field. Using the above example again with M = 54321,

> bbb250bbb****

will be printed. Programmers should be careful that the field width is sufficiently large to accommodate all possible values of the variable.

F-field

Real constants can be printed in decimal form using F-field. The general form of the field specification is

> *Fw.d*

where *F* denotes the data type and *w* the field width. The integer *d* denotes the *number of decimal digits*, and this is always accomplished by rounding off. In other words, *Fw.d* tells the computer to round off the corresponding real number to *d* decimal places, and to print the number right-justified in its field of width *w*.

EXAMPLE 3.5

Suppose ID = 125 and AMOUNT = 450.2462, and

```
      WRITE(6, 27) ID, AMOUNT
27    FORMAT(I8, 3X, F10.2)
```

is executed. Observe that the field specifications contain the field widths 8, 3, and 10 respectively. The field specification I8 which corresponds to ID tells the computer to generate the value of ID right-justified in the first field of width 8 in the output stream, so bbbbb125 is generated. The 3X generates three blanks: bbb. The F10.2 tells the computer to round off the value of A to two decimal places, i.e., to 450.25, and to generate this value right-justified in the next field of width 10, so bbbb450.25 is generated. Thus, the output stream which is generated is:

> Output stream: $\quad$ bbbbb125bbbbbbb450.25

Since the first character is used for carriage control, the output will appear on the print page as in Fig. 3-7.

We emphasize that the number 450.25 occupies six spaces in output since the decimal occupies one printed space.

Fig. 3-7

As with I-field, if insufficient width is provided, i.e., if the numerical value in F-field contains more characters than the field width, then the number may be truncated on the left (or right) or asterisks may be printed.   Thus, when using F-field, care must again be taken that the field width is sufficiently large to accommodate the number.   Specifically, if d is the desired number of decimal digits and n is the number of possible integral digits, then w should at least satisfy $w \geq n + d + 2$. The 2 provides a space for the sign and a space for the decimal point.   For example, if $|X| < 1000$ and we need only two decimal digits, then F7.2 is sufficient: $w = 3 + 2 + 2$, where three spaces are provided for the integral part of X.

Care must also be taken that the number of decimal digits is also sufficiently large.   For example, suppose A contains 0.246E−05, and the field specification is F12.4.   (Real numbers in a computer are stored in scientific form, see Appendix A.)   Then only

    0.0000

is printed since the value of A, which is 0.00000246 in decimal form, will be 0.0000 when it is rounded-off to four decimal places.

E-field

Real constants can be printed in exponential form using E-field.   The general form of the field specification is

Ew.d

where E denotes the data type and w the field width.   The integer d denotes the *number of significant digits* and this is accomplished by rounding off.   Furthermore, in output, real constants are printed in *standard exponential form*, i.e., as constants between 0.1 to 1.0 (or −0.1 to −1.0) together with the appropriate exponent which always contains four characters, E ± XX.   In other words, *Ew.d* tells the computer to round off the corresponding real number to d significant figures and to print the number in standard exponential form right-justified in its field of width w.   (We note that in standard exponential form, the number of significant digits is also equal to the number of decimal digits.)

EXAMPLE 3.6

Suppose A = 251.381 and B = 0.0081626, and suppose

        WRITE(6, 22) A, B
    22 FORMAT(E15.4, E12.3)

is executed.   Since real numbers (in E- or F-form) are stored internally in standard exponential form (see Appendix A), A contains +0.251381E+03, and B contains +0.81626E−02.   The entry E15.4 tells the computer to round-off the value of A to 4 significant figures, that is, 0.2514E+03, and place it right-justified in the first 15 spaces of the output stream.   The entry E12.3 tells the computer to round off the value of B to 3 significant digits, that is, 0.816E−02, and place it right-justified in the next 12 spaces of the output stream.   Consequently, they will appear as shown in Fig. 3-8.

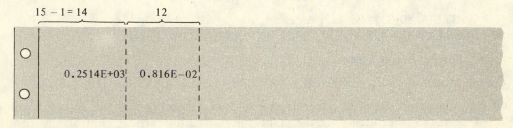

Fig. 3-8

To provide sufficient width to print real numbers in E-form, we calculate w as follows: if d digits of significant figures are desired, then the field width w should satisfy

$$w \geq d + 7$$

This is obtained as follows: four spaces are needed for the exponent E ± XX, one space for the sign, one for the leading zero, and one for the decimal point. Figure 3-9 also illustrates the calculation.

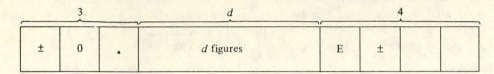

Fig. 3-9

We conclude the Input/Output sections with the following comments:

1. A FORMAT statement may contain many field specifications. The important thing is that the fields are contiguous, i.e., right next to each other.

2. To read in or print out values, the order in which the variables are listed should correspond in a one-to-one fashion with the order of the numerical (or character) field specifications in the corresponding FORMAT statement. They should also agree in types.

3. Each READ or WRITE statement must have an accompanying FORMAT statement. However, a FORMAT statement may accompany (be referenced by) several I/O statements. Furthermore, FORMAT statements are nonexecutable.

3.7   LITERAL FIELD

Suppose we wish to print a heading: POPULATION OF USA. This can be accomplished by *enclosing the message in apostrophes* inside the FORMAT statement as follows:

        WRITE(6, 30)
    30   FORMAT(1X, 'POPULATION OF USA')

When the above WRITE statement is executed, all the characters within the *apostrophes* will be generated. The output stream contains:

    Output stream: ₆POPULATION₆OF₆USA

where the first blank is generated by 1X. Taking care of carriage control, the message POPULATION OF USA is printed.

One may print character messages together with numerical values. Suppose G1 = 84.5, G2 = 78.4, G3 = 94.2, and AVE = 85.7. Then the instructions

        WRITE(6, 80) G1, G2, G3, AVE
    80   FORMAT(6X, 'GRADES', 3F8.1, 4X, 'AVERAGE', F10.1)

generates the following output stream:

    Output stream: bbbbbbGRADESbbbb84.5bbbb78.4bbbb94.2bbbbAVERAGEbbbbbbb85.7

The output will appear on the print paper as in Fig. 3-10. Observe that the entry 6X will cause only 5 = 6 − 1 blanks to be printed since the first blank is used for carriage control. Note also that the messages GRADES and AVERAGE occupy fields of widths 6 and 7 respectively, the number

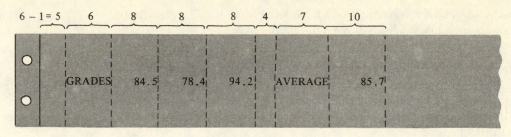

6 − 1 = 5   6   8   8   8   4   7   10

GRADES   84.5   78.4   94.2   AVERAGE   85.7

Fig. 3-10

of characters in the message. (We note that 3F8.1 is an abbreviation of F8.1, F8.1, F8.1. This is covered in Section 3.9.)

One major use of the literal field is for carriage control. Suppose we wanted to print the message POPULATION OF USA on the top of a new page. This can be accomplished with the statements

```
        WRITE(6, 20)
   20   FORMAT('1', 'POPULATION OF USA')
```

The first format entry '1' is the carriage control instruction to go to a new page. Similarly, we would use '0' as the first format entry if we wanted the computer to skip a line before printing POPULATION OF USA, or we would use '+' as the first format entry if we wanted the computer to print on the current line. These entries are listed in their appropriate positions in the third column of Table 3-2 on carriage-control instructions.

3.8 RECORDS, MULTIPLE RECORDS, SLASH

A *record* is a set of data corresponding to variables in an I/O list. The maximum length of a record is limited by the particular I/O device involved: 80 characters for cards, 72 characters for typewriter console, and 132 characters for line printers. Of course, the actual record length given by an I/O instruction is provided by the FORMAT statement.

So far, each of our I/O instructions has transmitted one record of information: each READ-FORMAT pair reads from one input card, and each WRITE-FORMAT pair prints on one output line. However, it is possible to use a single FORMAT statement to define multiple records. Two such ways are discussed next.

Case A

Recall that the execution of a READ/WRITE statement is not completed until all the variables listed are assigned/printed. Suppose

```
        READ(5, 20) A, B, C, D
   20   FORMAT(F8.2, 2X, F15.7)
```

is executed. Note that there are more variables (4) than there are numerical specifications (2). First the variables A, B are read from card 1 in columns 1–8 and 11–25 with specifications F8.2 and E15.7 respectively. Since there are more variables to be read, the same FORMAT statement is used again, but starting a new record, i.e., from another card. Hence, the values for C and D are read from card 2 in columns 1–8 and 11–25 respectively. (See also Section 10.6.)

Similarly, the statements

```
        WRITE(6, 30) A, B, C, D
   30   FORMAT(5X, F8.2, 2X, E14.7)
```

will produce two (2) output streams:

$$\text{bbbbb} + XXXX.XX_{bb} + 0.XXXXXXXE + XX$$
$$\text{bbbbb} + XXXX.XX_{bb} + 0.XXXXXXXE + XX$$

Hence, A, B will be printed on one line according to F8.2 and E14.7 respectively with four-space indentation; and C, D will be printed on the next line in similar fashion.

Remark. In the converse case where there are more field specifications than there are variables, the execution of a READ/WRITE statement is completed once all variables are defined/printed, and, hence, the extra specifications are ignored. For example, if the earlier READ statement is changed to

    READ(5, 20) A, B, C, D, E

then three cards are read and E is assigned the number in columns 1–8 from the third card using F8.2.

Case B

One may also use slashes (/) to define multiple records. Slashes are used in FORMAT statements to indicate the end of records. Thus,

    READ(5, 40) A, B, C, D
40 FORMAT(F10.2, F10.2/E15.7, E15.7)

defines two records; that is, it will read A, B using F10.2 from card 1 and C, D using E15.7 from card 2. Likewise,

    WRITE(6, 50) N, AVE
50 FORMAT('1', 'NUMBER OF STUDENTS =', I3/1X, 'EXAM AVERAGE =', F7.2)

defines two records and will print on top of a new page the following two lines:

    NUMBER OF STUDENTS = XXX
    EXAM AVERAGE = XXX.XX

We emphasize that for each new record in output, the carriage control must be provided. Specifically, the specification 1X following the slash in the above FORMAT statement is the carriage control instruction for the new record.

Consecutive slashes can also appear. However, slashes appearing at the end of a FORMAT statement give a slightly different result than in the middle in input. Specifically:

1. *Output.* When n consecutive slashes appear, then $n - 1$ blank lines are printed. For example,

    WRITE(6, 10) J, K   WRITE(6, 20) J, K
10 FORMAT(1X, I10///1X, I10) and 20 FORMAT(1X, I10///)

will each result in two blank lines appearing between J and K.

2. *Input.* When n consecutive slashes appear in the middle, then $n - 1$ cards are skipped; but, when n consecutive slashes appear at the end, then n cards are skipped. For example,

    READ(6, 30) J, K
30 FORMAT(I10///I10)

will cause J to be read from the first card and K from the fourth card; that is, two cards are skipped. However,

    READ(6, 40) J, K
40 FORMAT(I10///)

will cause J to be read from the first card but K from the fifth card; that is, three cards are skipped.

(See also Problems 3.39 and 3.40.)

3.9 REPETITION FACTOR

Suppose four numbers A, B, C, D are to be read/printed using the same specification F10.2. The FORMAT statement would be

FORMAT(F10.2, F10.2, F10.2, F10.2)

To simplify, a repetition factor 4 can be used:

FORMAT(4F10.2)

These two FORMAT statements have exactly the same meaning.   Similarly,

FORMAT(2I4, 3E15.7)

and

FORMAT(I4, I4, E15.7, E15.7, E15.7)

are the same.

One can also repeat a group of field specifications.   For example,

FORMAT(5X, 2(I5, 3X, F8.2, 2X))

means

FORMAT(5X, I5, 3X, F8.2, 2X, I5, 3X, F8.2, 2X)

and

FORMAT(3(3X, I4), 2(5X, E9.2))

is the same as

FORMAT(3X, I4, 3X, I4, 3X, I4, 5X, E9.2, 5X, E9.2)

These abbreviations allow our FORMAT statements to be much more compact and easier to type.

3.10 SIMPLE, COMPLETE PROGRAM

We have covered sufficient material to write some simple complete programs.   One is written here, and some are given in the solved-problem section.

Suppose the lengths of the sides of a triangle T are a, b, and c.   The perimeter P of T is the sum of these lengths:

$$P = a + b + c$$

The area of T is given by the formula

$$\text{Area} = \sqrt{s(s - a)(s - b)(s - c)}$$

where $s = P/2 = (a + b + c)/2$.

Suppose we want to calculate the perimeter and area of a triangle whose sides have lengths 38.6, 42.4, and 56.1.   We first punch these numbers into a data card using, say, fields of width 10, as in Fig. 3-11.

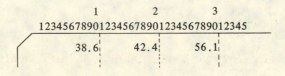

Fig. 3-11

The Fortran program which carries out the above calculations follows:

```
C
C          PROGRAM CALCULATING PERIMETER AND AREA OF A TRIANGLE
C
           READ(5, 11) A, B, C
     11    FORMAT(3F10.1)
           P = A + B + C
           S = P/2.0
           AREA = SQRT(S*(S − A)*(S − B)*(S − C))
           WRITE(6, 12) A, B, C, P, AREA
     12    FORMAT(3(F8.1, 4X), F10.1, 4X, F12.2)
           STOP
           END
```

Program Explanation and Execution

Lines 1–3.   These lines form a comment since a C is punched in the first column.

Lines 4–5.   These lines tell the computer to read in values for A, B, C from the data card using fields of widths 10 each.   Hence, A, B, C are assigned the following values:

$$A \leftarrow 38.6, \qquad B \leftarrow 42.4, \qquad C \leftarrow 56.1$$

Line 6.   The computer adds the values of A, B, and C, which is 137.1, and assigns this value to P:

$$P \leftarrow 137.1$$

Line 7.   The computer assigns P/2 to S:

$$S \leftarrow 68.55$$

Line 8.   The computer evaluates the arithmetic expression on the right, where SQRT means square root, and assigns this value, which is 817.56570 to AREA:

$$AREA \leftarrow 817.56570$$

Lines 9–10.   The computer prints the values of A, B, C, P, and AREA using fields of widths $8 − 1 = 7$, 8, 8, 10, and 12 respectively as in Fig. 3-12.   Observe that these fields are separated by blank fields of width four (4X).   Also observe that P is rounded-off to one decimal place (F10.1), and AREA is rounded-off to two decimal places (F12.2).

Line 11.   This tells the computer to STOP.

Line 12.   The END statement tells the compiler that there are no more statements in the program to be translated.   It will not be in the program at execution time.

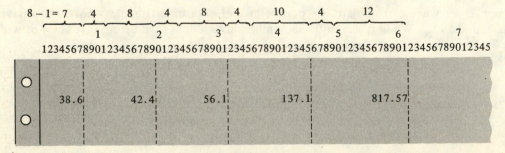

Fig. 3-12

Remark. In the execution of the above program, we indicated that 38.6 was assigned to A. The actual number stored in A is

$$0.38600000E+02$$

since the internal representation of real values is in exponential form with approximately 8–9 significant digits. (See Appendix A.)

Solved Problems

UNFORMATTED INPUT/OUTPUT

3.1   Find errors, if any, in the following unformatted I/O statements:

   (*a*)   READ A, B, X, Y   (*c*)   READ, ID, WAGE, MAX, MIN

   (*b*)   PRINT NUMB, INT, RATE,   (*d*)   PRINT, ROOT, COEF, RANGE,

   (*a*)   There should be a comma after READ.

   (*b*)   There should be a comma after PRINT, but no comma after RATE.

   (*c*)   Correct.

   (*d*)   There should not be a comma after RANGE.

3.2   Suppose three data cards are punched as follows:

        First card: 22.2,3.33,444

       Second card: 555,666,77.77

        Third card: 8.888,9.99

Find the values assigned to the variables if the following is executed:

   (*a*)   READ, A, B   (*b*)   READ, A, B, J, K

       READ, J, K, X, Y   READ, X, Y

   (*a*)   When the computer executes the first READ statement, it assigns 22.2 to A and 3.33 to B. This completes the execution of the first READ statement; so the first card is discarded even though the third value had not been read. When the computer executes the second READ statement, it will read from the card on top of the data deck, the second data card. Hence, it assigns 555 to J, 666 to K, 77.77 to X, and then reads the next card to assign 8.888 to Y. Thus, we obtain:

$$A = 22.2, \quad B = 3.33, \quad J = 555, \quad K = 666, \quad X = 77.77, \quad Y = 8.888$$

   (*b*)   The first READ statement yields:

$$A = 22.2, \quad B = 3.33, \quad J = 444, \quad K = 555$$

The second READ statement yields:

$$X = 8.888, \quad Y = 9.99$$

We note that the second data card is discarded after the execution of the first READ statement, so that the third data card is used for the execution of the second READ statement.

3.3   Suppose the values 123, 456, 7.77, 8.88, and 9.99 are to be assigned to the variables L, M, X, Y, and Z respectively. Write an unformatted READ statement and show how the data should be punched on the data cards if: (*a*) only one data card is used, (*b*) two data cards are used with the integer values on the first card and the real values on the second card.

In each case, we have the READ statement

> READ, L, M, X, Y, Z

The data should be punched as follows:

(a)   First card: 123, 456, 7.77, 8.88, 9.99
(b)   First card: 123, 456
        Second card: 7.77, 8.88, 9.99

3.4   Suppose a data card is punched as follows:

> Data card: 123, 44.4

(a)   Determine the output if the following program segment is executed:

> READ, J, X
> K = J**2
> Y = 3.0*X
> PRINT, J, K, Y

(b)   Explain the difference if the single PRINT statement above is replaced by the two statements:

> PRINT, J, K
> PRINT, Y

(a)   Program execution:

Line 1.   J and X are assigned the values of the data card.   This yields J = 123 and K = 44.4.

Line 2.   K is assigned the square of J; so K ← 15129.

Line 3.   Y is assigned three times the value of X; so Y ← 133.2.

Line 4.   The values of J, K, and Y are printed, with the value of Y in standard exponential form.   Thus, the output will appear as follows:

> 123   15129   0.1332E 03

(b)   Here the values of J and K will appear on one line and the value of K on the second line, so that the output will appear as:

> 123   15129
> 0.1332E 03

FORMATTED INPUT

3.5   Locate errors, if any, in each READ statement and its accompanying FORMAT statement.

(a)   READ(5, 11) A, K, M, Z,   (c)   READ(5, 11), A, B, C, D, J, K, L
        11 FORMAT(F8.0, I15, I10, I15)   11 FORMAT(4F15.2, 3I15)

(b)   READ(5, 11) A, B, J, K, L
        11 FORMAT(3F8.1, 2I8)

(a)   First, there should not be a comma after Z.   Second, the fourth variable in the READ statement is the real variable Z, but its corresponding entry in the FORMAT statement is the integer field specification I15.

(b)   Note first that the FORMAT statement is an abbreviation for

> 11 FORMAT(F8.1, F8.1, F8.1, I8, I8)

Thus, the integer variable J was given a real specification F8.1.

(c)   First, there should not be a comma before A.   Second, the sum of the field widths is 105, which is too large for a data card that has only 80 columns.

3.6 Suppose a data card is punched, as in Fig. 3-13.   Find the values of J, K, and L as a result of each of the following cases:

(*a*)   READ(5, 11) J, K, L   (*c*)   READ(5, 13) J, K, L
     11 FORMAT(I4, I3, I8)   13 FORMAT(2I6, I2)

(*b*)   READ(5, 12) J, K, L
     12 FORMAT(I3, 2X, I6, 3X, I3)

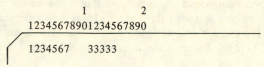

Fig. 3-13

Note first that only integers are read in for the variables since all the numerical field specifications are of the form *Iw*, where *w* is the field width.

(*a*) The field widths are 4, 3, and 8 respectively.   Hence, J is assigned the integer punched in the first 4 columns (columns 1–4), K is assigned the integer punched in the next 3 columns (columns 5–7), and L is assigned the integer punched in the next 8 columns (columns 8–15).   This yields J = 1234, K = 567, L = 33333.

(*b*) The five field specifications instruct the computer as follows:

   I3   Assign to J the integer punched in the first 3 columns (columns 1–3); so 123 is assigned to J.
   2X   Skip the next 2 columns (columns 4–5), even though information is punched in the columns.
   I6   Assign to K the integer punched in the next 6 columns (columns 6–11).   Since blank spaces are interpreted as zeros in numerical fields, 670003 is assigned to K.
   3X   Skip the next 3 columns (columns 12–14).
   I3   Assign to L the integer punched in the next 3 columns (columns 15–17); so 300 is assigned to L.

   Thus, we have J = 123, K = 670003, and L = 300.

(*c*) The 2I6 repeats the I6 twice; i.e., the field specifications are I6, I6, and I2 with field widths 6, 6, and 2 respectively.   This results in J = 123456, K = 700033, and L = 33.

3.7 Suppose a program has the following statements:

      READ(5, 21) A, B
   21 FORMAT(F10.2, F12.3)

Find the values assigned to A and B if (*a*) card A of Fig. 3-14 is read, (*b*) card B of Fig. 3-14 is read.

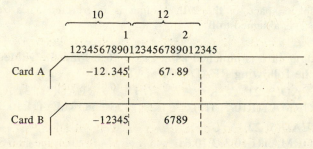

Fig. 3-14

Note first that the field widths are 10 and 12 respectively; hence, A is assigned the real number found in columns 1–10, and B is assigned the real number found in columns 11–22.

(a) Note that since −12.345 is punched in the first field (columns 1–10), it is assigned to A, and since 67.89 is punched in the second field (columns 11–22), it is assigned to B. Since both numbers have decimal points, the 2 in F10.2 and the 3 in F12.3 are ignored.

(b) Note that there is no decimal point punched in the first field (columns 1–10); therefore, the field specification F10.2 will cause a decimal point to be embedded two places from the right side of the field, i.e., between column 8 and column 9. Hence, −123.45 is assigned to A. The number punched in the second field (columns 11–22) also has no decimal point, so the F12.3 will cause a decimal point to be embedded three places from the right side of the field, i.e., between columns 19 and 20. Hence, 678.9 is assigned to B. We emphasize that the position of a number in a field does make a difference if the number is not punched with a decimal point.

3.8 Suppose a program has the following statements:

        READ(5, 22) A, B
    22 FORMAT(E12.4, E15.6)

Find the values assigned to A and B if the data card is (a) card (1) of Fig. 3-15, (b) card (2) of Fig. 3-15.

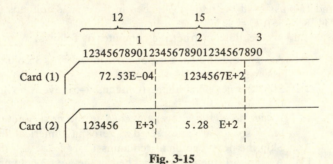

Fig. 3-15

Notice that the field widths are 12 and 15 respectively; hence, A is assigned the real number found in columns 1–12, and B is assigned the real number found in the next 15 columns, i.e., columns 13–27.

(a) Note that 72.53E − 04 is punched in the first field (columns 1–12), and so it is assigned to A. The 4 in the field specification E12.4 is ignored since the number is punched with a decimal point. In the second field (columns 13–27), the number is not punched with a decimal point. Therefore, the 6 in the field specification E15.6 tells the computer to embed a decimal point six places (columns) to the left of the character E, that is, between columns 8 and 9. Hence, 1.234567E + 2 is assigned to B.

(b) Note that there is no decimal point punched in the first field; consequently, the 4 in the field specification E12.4 will cause a decimal point to be embedded between the 4th and 5th columns to the left of the character E, that is, between columns 5 and 6. Hence, 12345.6E + 3 is assigned to A. The number punched in the second field has a decimal point. However, the blank space space in the 27th column is interpreted as a zero. Hence, 5.28E + 20 (not 5.28E + 2) is assigned to B.

3.9 Suppose a data card is punched as in Fig. 3-16. Find the values of the variables as a result of each of the following READ-FORMAT pairs:

(a)   READ(5, 21) A, K   (c)   READ(5, 23) A, B
    21 FORMAT(F10.1, I10)   23 FORMAT(E10.3, E10.4)

(b)   READ(5, 22) A, B
    22 FORMAT(F10.3, F10.6)

```
              1         2
     12345678901234567890123_4
  ⌐
  |
  |       258.34  17963
```

Fig. 3-16

(a) The two field specifications contain field widths 10 and 10 respectively and instruct the computer as follows:

> F10.1 Assign to A the real number punched in the first 10 columns (columns 1–10); hence, A = 258.34. (The 1 in F10.1 is ignored since the number in the field has a decimal point.)
>
> I10   Assign to K the integer punched in the next 10 columns (columns 11–20), where blank spaces are read as zeros; hence, K = 17963000.

(b) As in part (a), we obtain A = 258.34. The second field specification tells the computer to assign to B the real number in columns 11–20. Since there is no decimal point within the field, the 6 in F10.6 tells the computer to embed a decimal point six spaces to the left of the last column (column 20). Hence, we obtain B = 17.963.

(c) Note first that no character E appears on the data card; so the *Ew.d* field specifications are treated the same as the *Fw.d* field specifications. The two field specifications contain field widths 10 and 10 respectively and instruct the computer as follows:

> E10.3 Assign to A the real number punched in the first 10 columns (columns 1–10). Since the field has a decimal point, 258.34 is assigned to A.
>
> E10.4 Assign to B the real number punched in the next 10 columns (columns 11–20). Since there is no decimal point within the field, a decimal point is embedded four spaces to the left of the last column. This gives B = 1796.3.

3.10 Suppose the first three data cards of a data deck are punched as in Fig. 3-17. Find the values of the variables for each of the following cases:

(a)   READ(5, 11) J, A
         READ(5, 11) K, B, L, M
    11   FORMAT(I5, F5.2, I5)

(b)   READ(5, 12) J, K, A, L, B, M
    12   FORMAT(I5/I5, F5.2/I5, F5.2, I5)

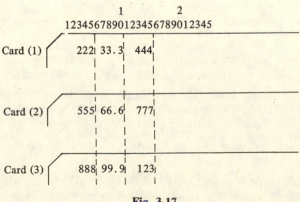

Fig. 3-17

Note first that all field specifications have field widths 5.

(a) Remember that the execution of any READ/WRITE statement is not completed until all variables listed are assigned values/printed. The first READ statement reads from card 1, and the variables J and A are read with field specifications I5 and F5.2 respectively. Hence, J = 222 and A = 33.3. The execution of this READ statement is completed, and card 1 is discarded. The second READ statement also begins reading from the card now on top, namely card 2. As there are more variables (4) than there are field specifications (3), multiple records are read. In this case, two cards are read. The variables K, B, L are read from card 2 using I5, F5.2, I5 respectively, yielding K = 555, B = 66.6, I = 777. The variable M is read from card 3 using I5, yielding M = 888. As all variables are now assigned values, the execution of the second READ statement is now completed, and card 3 is discarded.

(b) As there are two slashes, at least three records (cards) are read. The variable J is read from card 1 with I5, thus J = 222. The variables K, A are read from card 2 with I5 and F5.2 respectively; thus, K = 555 and A = 66.6. Finally, L = 888, B = 99.9, M = 123 from card 3.

FORMATTED OUTPUT

3.11 Locate errors, if any, in each WRITE-FORMAT pair:

(a) WRITE(6, 31), A, B, N (b) WRITE(6, 32) J, Z, K,
31 FORMAT(F10.2, 3X, I8, 5X, I6) 32 FORMAT(1X, I10, 4X, 2F10.3)

(Assume no type statement has changed the types of any of the variables.)

(a) There should not be a comma before the A. The real variable B was given the integer field specification I8.

(b) There should not be a comma after the K. Also, the integer variable K was given the real field specification F10.3.

3.12 Suppose K contains 12345, and the WRITE statement

WRITE(6, 41) K

is executed. Describe the output if the accompanying FORMAT statement is

(a) 41 FORMAT(I10) (c) 41 FORMAT(4X, I3)
(b) 41 FORMAT(4X, I8) (d) 41 FORMAT(I5)

(a) The field specification has field width 10; so the value of K will be printed right-justified in the first $10 - 1 = 9$ columns of the print page, as in Fig. 3-18(a). In other words, the value of K is generated right-justified in the first 10 characters of the output stream, that is, bbbbb12345 is generated; but the first character, a blank, is used for carriage control and is not printed.

(b) The output will appear as in Fig. 3-18(b) since the two field specifications instruct the computer as follows:

4X   Advance a line and print $4 - 1 = 3$ blanks in the first 3 columns of the print page.
I8   Print the value of K right-justified in the next 8 columns (columns 4–11).

In other words, four blanks bbbb and bbb12345 are generated respectively in the output stream, but the first character b is used for carriage control and is not printed.

(c) The field specifications instruct the computer as follows:

4X   Advance one line and print $4 - 1 = 3$ blanks in the first 3 columns of the print page.
I3   Print the value of K right-justified in the next 3 columns (columns 4–6).

Since the field width for K is less than the number of digits in K, either three asterisks *** will be printed as in Fig. 3-18(c), or the value of K is truncated on the left; so only 345 is printed.

(d) The field width of I5 equals the number of digits in K so 12345 is generated in the output stream. However, the first character "1" is used for carriage control and tells the line printer to advance to the top of the next page before printing the remaining four characters in the first $5 - 1 = 4$ columns of the print page, as in Fig. 3-18(d).

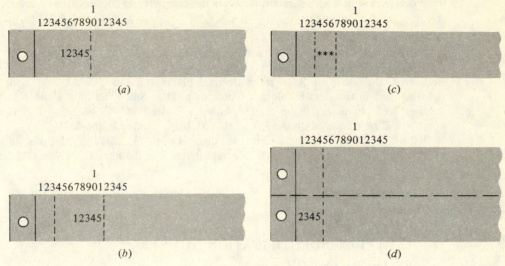

Fig. 3-18

3.13   Suppose A contains 135.2837 and the WRITE statement

WRITE(6, 42) A

is executed.   Describe the output if the accompanying FORMAT statement is:

(a)   42   FORMAT(6X, F10.1)   (c)   42   FORMAT(6X, F6.3)
(b)   42   FORMAT(6X, F12.2)   (d)   42   FORMAT(6X, E15.6)

In each case, the field specification 6X causes the line printer to advance one line and print blanks in the first $6 - 1 = 5$ columns (columns 1–5) of the print page.   The output appears as in Fig.

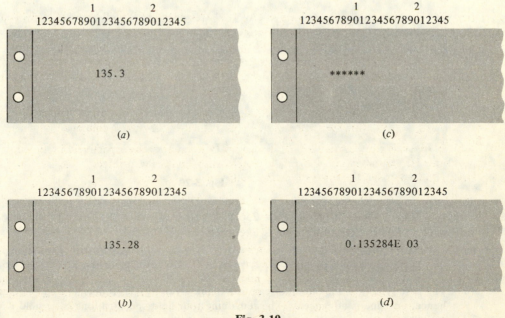

Fig. 3-19

3-19 since the second field specification instructs the computer as follows:

(*a*) Round off the value of A to one decimal place, i.e., to 135.3, and print this number right-justified in the next 10 columns (columns 6–15).

(*b*) Round off the value of A to two decimal places, i.e., to 135.28, and print this number right-justified in the next 12 columns (columns 6–17).

(*c*) Round off the value of A to three decimal places, i.e., to 135.284, and print this number right-justified in the next 6 columns (columns 6–11). Since the field width 6 is less than the number 7 of characters to be printed, either six asterisks will be printed in the field or the number will be truncated on the left so that 35.284 is printed in the field.

(*d*) Round off the value of A to six significant digits, i.e., to 135.284, and print this value in standard exponential form, that is, 0.135284E 03, right-justified in the next 15 columns (columns 6–20).

3.14 Suppose ID = 112233 and WAGE = 275.50. Determine the output for each WRITE-FORMAT pair:

(*a*)   WRITE(6, 11) ID
       11   FORMAT(6X, 'IDENTIFICATION NUMBER', 2X, I8)

(*b*)   WRITE(6, 12) WAGE
       12   FORMAT(6X, 'WEEKLY SALARY $', F8.2)

(*a*) The line printer advances one line and prints blanks in the first 6 − 1 = 5 columns (columns 1–5) of the print page. The entry

                     'IDENTIFICATION NUMBER'

causes the message between the apostrophes to be printed in the next field. Since the message occupies 21 spaces, it will be printed in the next 21 columns (columns 6–26). The 2X causes blanks to be printed in columns 27 and 28. The I8 causes the value of ID to be printed right-justified in the next 8 columns (columns 29–36). See Fig. 3-20(*a*).

(*b*) The output appears as in Fig. 3-20(*b*)

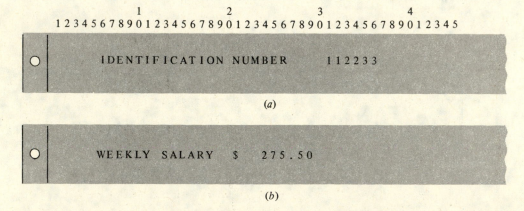

(*a*)

(*b*)

Fig. 3-20

3.15 Suppose ID = 25367, M = 138, A = 256.174, and B = −0.00285293. Find the output if the following WRITE-FORMAT pair is executed:

(*a*)   WRITE(6, 11) ID, M, A, B   (*b*)   WRITE(6, 12) ID, A, B
       11   FORMAT(' ', I10, I6, F8.1, F10.3)   12   FORMAT('1', I10, 2E15.5)

(*a*) The first symbol in the output stream is a blank given by ' '. It acts as a carriage control signal; hence, one line is advanced. The remaining four field specifications have field widths 10, 6, 8, and 10 respectively, and they instruct the computer as follows:

I10   Print the integer value of ID right-justified in the first 10 columns of the print page.

I6   Print the value of M right-justified in the next 6 columns (columns 11–16).

F8.1   Round off the value of A to 1 decimal place, that is, 256.2, and print this real number right-justified in the next 8 columns (columns 17–24).

F10.3   Round off the value of B to 3 decimal places, that is, − 0.003, and print this real number right-justified in the next 10 columns (columns 25–34).

The output appears as in Fig. 3-21(a).

(b) The field specifications instruct the computer as follows:

'1'   Carriage control instruction to advance to a new page.

I10   Print the value of ID right-justified in the first 10 columns of the print page.

E15.5   Round off the value of A to 5 significant figures, that is, 256.17, and print this number in standard exponential form, that is 0.25617E 03, right-justified in the next 15 columns (columns 11–25).

E15.5   Round off the value of B to 5 significant places, that is, −0.0028529, and print this number in standard exponential form, that is, −0.28529E−02, right-justified in the next 15 columns (columns 36–40).

The output appears in Fig. 3-21(b).

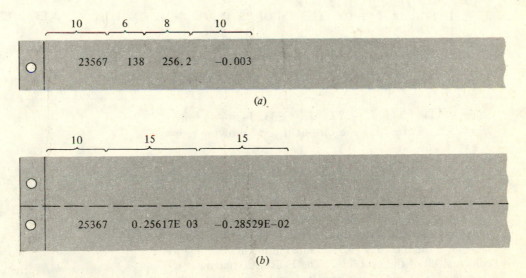

Fig. 3-21

3.16 Suppose the values of J, A, K, and B are to be printed so that each integer is allocated 4 columns, each real number is allocated 8 columns with 3 decimal places, and all values are to be separated by at least 3 spaces.   Find the range of values that can be printed for each variable, and write a WRITE-FORMAT pair which (a) prints the values on one line; (b) prints the values of J and A on one line, and K and B on a second line.

The values of J and K must lie between −999 and 9999, and the values of A and B must lie between −999.999 and 9999.999.

(a)   WRITE(6, 11) J, A, K, B   (b)   WRITE(6, 11) J, A, K, B
    11   FORMAT(1X, I4, 3X, F8.3, 3X, I4, 3X, F8.3)   11   FORMAT(1X, I4, 3X, F8.3)
    or
    11   FORMAT(1X, 2(I4, 3X, F8.3, 3X))

3.17   Suppose J1, J2, and J3 contain three test scores, and K contains their average.

(*a*)   Write a program segment which will print on a new page beginning in column 11 the following:

          TEST SCORES
             XXX
             XXX
             XXX
          AVERAGE
             XXX

where the XXX's denote the values of the test scores and average.

(*b*)   Accomplish the above with only one WRITE statement.)

(*a*)   WRITE(6, 11)
     11   FORMAT('1', 10X, 'TEST SCORES')
         WRITE(6, 12) J1, J2, J3
     12   FORMAT(1X, I17)
         WRITE(6, 13)
     13   FORMAT(13X, 'AVERAGE')
         WRITE(6, 12) K

(*b*)   WRITE(6, 21) J1, J2, J3, K
     21   FORMAT('1', 10X, 'TEST SCORES'/1X, I17/1X, I17/1X, I17/13X, 'AVERAGE'/1X, I17)

     or

     21   FORMAT('1', 10X, 'TEST SCORES'/3(1X, I17/)13X, 'AVERAGE'/1X, I17)

3.18   Suppose J1 = 111, J2 = 222, J3 = 333, J4 = 444, and J5 = 555. Determine the output if the following pair is executed:

         WRITE(6, 15) J1, J2, J3, J4, J5
     15   FORMAT('0', I8/I9)

The computer advances two lines, i.e., skips a line ('0'), and prints J1 in the first 8 columns (I8). The slash / signals the end of the record; so J2 is printed in the first 9 − 1 = 8 columns (I9) of the next line. The FORMAT statement is repeated for J3 and J4 and repeated again for J5. The '0' causes a line to be skipped between J2 and J3 and between J4 and J5. The output will appear as in Fig. 3-22.

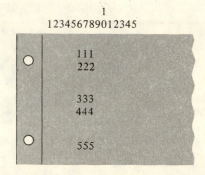

Fig. 3-22

SIMPLE COMPLETE PROGRAMS

3.19   The surface area SUR and volume VOL of a box with dimensions *a*, *b*, *c* is given by

$$SUR = 2(ab + ac + bc) \quad \text{and} \quad VOL = abc$$

Suppose the dimensions of a box are 23.5, 41.3, and 16.2 and are punched on a data card as in Fig. 3-23(*a*). Find the output of the following program:

```
C
C      SURFACE AREA AND VOLUME OF A BOX
C
       READ(5, 61) A, B, C
   61  FORMAT(3F10.2)
       SUR = 2.0(A*B + A*C + B*C)
       VOL = A*B*C
       WRITE(6, 62) A, B, C, SUR, VOL
   62  FORMAT(6X, 'DIMENSIONS OF BOX'/7X, 3(F5.1, 1X)//
    1          6X, 'SURFACE AREA =', F10.1//6X, 'VOLUME =', F16.2)
       STOP
       END
```

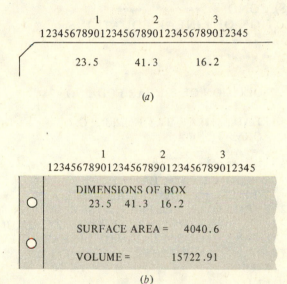

(a)

(b)

Fig. 3-23

Program Execution

The computer reads values for A, B, and C according to the FORMAT statement numbered 61, which is an abbreviation of

        61   FORMAT(F10.2, F10.2, F10.2)

In each case, the field width is 10; so A, B, and C are assigned the numbers punched in columns 1–10, columns 11–20, and columns 21–30, respectively. Thus, A = 23.5, B = 41.3, C = 16.2. (The 2 in F10.2 is ignored since the numbers on the data card already have decimal points.)

The computer calculates 2.0*(A*B + A*C + B*C), which is 4040.62, and assigns this number to SUR, and calculates A*B*C, which is 15722.910, and assigns this number to VOL:

        SUR ← 4040.62,   VOL ← 15722.910

The WRITE-FORMAT pair instructs the computer to print the output as in Fig. 3-23(b). Observe that one slash / causes the printer to advance to the next line, but that two slashes // causes the printer to advance two lines and, hence, skip a line. Also observe that SUR is rounded off to one decimal place (F10.1), and VOL is rounded off to two decimal places (F16.2).

3.20 Assuming $D = a_1b_2 - a_2b_1 \neq 0$, the solution of the linear equations

$$a_1x + b_1y = c_1$$
$$a_2x + b_2y = c_2$$

is given by

$$x = \frac{b_2c_1 - b_1c_2}{a_1b_2 - a_2b_1} \qquad y = \frac{a_1c_2 - a_2c_1}{a_1b_2 - a_2b_1}$$

Write a Fortran program which reads in values for A1, B1, C1 from one data card and A2, B2, C2 from a second data card; calculates the solution pair X, Y; and prints the output so it appears as follows:

```
COEFFICIENTS OF LINEAR EQUATIONS
    FIRST     *****    *****    *****
    SECOND    *****    *****    *****
SOLUTION OF LINEAR EQUATIONS
    X = ********
    Y = ********
```

```
C
C      SOLUTION OF LINEAR EQUATIONS
C
       READ(5, 11) A1, B1, C1, A2, B2, C2
   11  FORMAT(3F10.1)
       D = A1*B2 - A2*B1
       X = (B2*C1 - B1*C2)/D
       Y = (A1*C2 - A2*C1)/D
       WRITE(6, 12) A1, B1, C1, A2, B2, C2, X, Y
   12  FORMAT(11X, 'COEFFICIENTS OF LINEAR EQUATIONS'//15X, 'FIRST',
      1           3X, 3F8.1/15X, 'SECOND', 2X, 3F8.1//
      1           11X, SOLUTION OF LINEAR EQUATIONS'//15X, 'X =',
      1           2X, F12.2/15X, 'Y =', 2X, F12.2)
       STOP
       END
```

Supplementary Problems

UNFORMATTED I/O

3.21 Locate errors, if any, in each unformatted I/O statement:

    (a) READ, FIRST, LAST, NEXT,   (c) READ, INT, LOT, AREA
    (b) PRINT ID, WAGE, RATE,   (d) PRINT, A, B, C, D,

3.22 Suppose the first four data cards of a deck are punched as follows:

    First card: 11, 22, 3.3, 4.4
    Second card: 5.5, 6.6, 77
    Third card: 88, 99, 2.34
    Fourth card: 5.67, 8.90, 123, 456

Find the values assigned to the variables if the following is executed:

    (a) READ, J, K, A, B, C   (b) READ, J, K, A   (c) READ, J, K, A
        READ, L, M, X, Y   READ, B, C, L, M   READ, B, C, L
                           READ, X, Y   READ, M
                                                 READ, X, Y

3.23   Suppose the values 1.1, 2.2, 33, 44, and 55 are to be assigned to the variables A, B, J, K, and L respectively, using the read statement

        READ, A, B, J, K, L

Show how the data should be punched on the data cards if (*a*) only one data card is used, (*b*) two data cards are used with the real values on the first card and the integer values on the second card.

3.24   Suppose two data cards are punched as follows:

        First card: 22.2, 15
        Second card: 25, 35

Find the output if the following program segment is executed:

(*a*) READ, A, J, K   (*c*) READ, A, J, K
     B = A*6.0   B = A*6.0
     PRINT, A, B, J, K   PRINT, A
                                 PRINT, B, J, K

(*b*) READ, A   (*d*) READ, A
     READ, J, K   READ, J, K
     B = A*6.0   B = A*6.0
     PRINT, A, B, J   PRINT, A, J
     PRINT, K   PRINT, B
                                   PRINT, K

FORMATTED INPUT

3.25   Locate errors, if any, in each READ-FORMAT pair:

(*a*)   READ(5, 10), X, Y, L, M,   (*c*)   READ(5, 30) S, T, U, J, K
   10 FORMAT(F8.1, F9.2, 2I12)   30 FORMAT(2F10.3, 3I8)

(*b*)   READ(5, 20) A, L, B, M   (*d*)   READ(5, 40) A, J, B, K, C, L
   20 FORMAT(F10.3, I8)   40 FORMAT(F8.2, I6, F8.3)

3.26   Suppose a data card is punched as in Fig. 3-24, and suppose the following READ statement is executed:

        READ(5, 50) J, K, L, M

Find the values assigned to J, K, L, M if the accompanying FORMAT statement is:

(*a*) 50 FORMAT(I2, I3, I8, I3)   (*c*) 50 FORMAT(2I3, 5X, 2I3)
(*b*) 50 FORMAT(4I4)   (*d*) 50 FORMAT(3I3, 2I4)

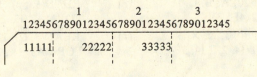

```
                    1         2         3
      123456789012345678901234567890123456789012345
          ┌    11111   22222   33333
          │
```

Fig. 3-24

3.27   Suppose the following READ-FORMAT pair is executed:

        READ(5, 10) A, B, C
   10 FORMAT(F10.2, F10.3, F10.2)

Find the values assigned to A, B, C if the data card is as shown in Fig. 3-25.

1 2 3
12345678901234567890123456789012345
(a) 11.11 −22.22 33.33
(b) 1111 −2222 3333
(c) 1111 −2.222 3333

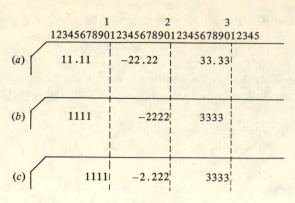

Fig. 3-25

3.28 Suppose the following READ-FORMAT pair is executed:

```
   READ(5, 20) A, B, C
10 FORMAT(E10.2, E10.3, E10.2)
```

Find the values assigned to A, B, C if the data card is as shown in Fig. 3-26.

1 2 3
12345678901234567890123456789012345
(a) −44.4 E+2 5.55 E3 6.66E−04
(b) −444 E+2 555 E3 666E−04
(c) −44.4 E+2 555 6.66
(d) −444E+2 5.55 666 E−04

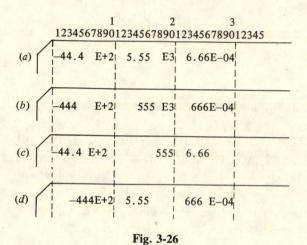

Fig. 3-26

3.29 Suppose a data card is punched as in Fig. 3-27. Find the values assigned to the variables if the following READ-FORMAT pair is executed:

(*a*)
```
   READ(5, 10) I, J, A, B
10 FORMAT(2I5, 2F5.1)
```

(*b*)
```
   READ(5, 20) A, B, C, D
20 FORMAT(4F5.3)
```

(*c*)
```
   READ(5, 30) J, K, X, Y, Z
30 FORMAT(I4, 2X, I4, 3F4.2)
```

(*d*)
```
   READ(5, 40) R, S, T
40 FORMAT(3F4.1)
```

(*e*)
```
   READ(5, 50) J, A, B, L, M
50 FORMAT(I3, 2X, 2F4.1, I3, I4)
```

(*f*)
```
   READ(5, 60) I, J, K, X, Y, Z
60 FORMAT(2X, 3I1, 3X, F4.2, 2F3.1)
```

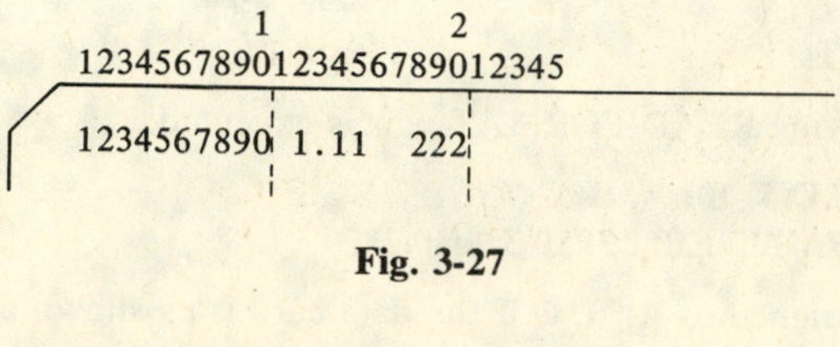

1 2
1234567890123456789012345
1234567890 1.11 222

Fig. 3-27

3.30 Suppose the first three cards of a data deck are punched as in Fig. 3-28.   Find the values assigned to the variables if the following is executed:

(a)   READ(5, 10) J, X
        READ(5, 10) K, Y, L, M
    10 FORMAT(I5, F5.2, I5)

(b)   READ(5, 20) J, A, B, K
        READ(5, 20) L, C
    20 FORMAT(I5, 2F5.2)

(c)   READ(5, 30) J, A, B
        READ(5, 30) K, X, Y, L, M
    30 FORMAT(I5, 2F5.2, I5)

(d)   READ(5, 40) J, X
        READ(5, 40) K, Y, Z
    40 FORMAT(I5, 2F5.2)

(e)   READ(5, 50) J, X, Y, Z, K, L, M
    50 FORMAT(I5, 2F5.2/F5.2/I5, 5X, 2I4)

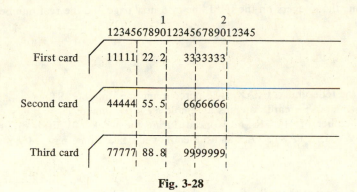

```
                        1         2
              12345678901234567890123456
First card    11111 22.2  3333333
Second card   44444 55.5  6666666
Third card    77777 88.8  9999999
```

Fig. 3-28

FORMATTED OUTPUT

3.31 Locate errors, if any, in each WRITE-FORMAT pair:

(a)   WRITE(6, 10) X, Y, M, N,
    10 FORMAT(1X, 3F8.1, 2I9)

(b)   WRITE(6, 20) A, L, B, M
    20 FORMAT(1X, F9.2, 2(I8, E7.3))

(c)   WRITE(6, 30), S, T, U, J, K
    30 FORMAT(2E12.3, 2(F8.1, 3X, I7))

(d)   WRITE(6, 40) A, J, B, C, K
    40 FORMAT(F7.1, I8, E6.2)

3.32 Suppose J, K, L contain 1111, 2222, 3333, respectively, and

WRITE(6, 50) J, K, L

is executed.   Describe the output if the accompanying FORMAT statement is:

(a) 50 FORMAT(3I10)
(b) 50 FORMAT(1X, I10/2I10)
(c) 50 FORMAT(1X, 'THE NUMBERS ARE', 3I8)
(d) 50 FORMAT(1X, I10)
(e) 50 FORMAT(1X, 2I10)
(f) 50 FORMAT(I4, 7X, I3, 7X, I4)

3.33 Suppose A, B, C contain 111.222, 444.666, 777.888, respectively, and

WRITE(6, 60) A, B, C

is executed.   Describe the output if the accompanying FORMAT statement is:

(a) 60 FORMAT(1X, 3F10.2)
(b) 60 FORMAT(1X, F10.1, 2X, F5.3, 2X, F10.1)
(c) 60 FORMAT('1', E15.5, E15.2, E15.4)
(d) 60 FORMAT(1X, 2E12.4)
(e) 60 FORMAT(1X, F10.2///1X, E10.3///1X, F10.1)
(f) 60 FORMAT(F7.3, 2X, E15.7/F15.1)

3.34   Suppose

WRITE(6, 70) J, K, X, Y

is executed.   Suppose each integer is to be allocated five columns, and each real number is allocated seven columns with two decimal places, and all values are to be separated by at least three spaces.   Find the range of values that can be printed for each variable, and write an accompanying FORMAT statement which:

(*a*) Prints the values on one line.
(*b*) Prints the values on the first line of a new page.
(*c*) Prints the values on the fifth line of a new page.
(*d*) Prints the integers on one line and the real numbers on the next line.
(*e*) Prints each number on a different line.
(*f*) Prints the integers on the third line of a new page and the real numbers on the sixth line.

PROGRAMS

3.35   Suppose the federal tax, FTAX, is 15 percent and the state tax, STAX, is 2.5 percent of the gross pay WAGE.   Suppose a card contains an employee's ID number (nine digits), his hourly RATE of pay, and the number of HOURs he worked during the week.   Write a program which prints the ID, HOUR, WAGE, FTAX, STAX and the employee's take home pay, TPAY.

3.36   Suppose x, y, z are the following functions of t:

$$x = t^3 - 8t + 4, \qquad y = \sin t + \cos 2t, \qquad z = e^{3t+5}$$

Write a program which reads in t and prints t, x, y, z.

3.37   Suppose an automobile starts from rest and has constant acceleration a for t seconds.   The final velocity v and the distance d traveled by the automobile is given by the formulas

$$d = \tfrac{1}{2}at^2 \qquad \text{and} \qquad v = at$$

Write a program which reads in a and t and prints t, d, and v.

3.38   Write a program which reads in the altitude h and the lengths of the two bases b_1 and b_2 of a trapezoid T, and prints h, b_1, b_2, and the area of T.

MISCELLANEOUS PROBLEMS

3.39   Suppose the following READ statement is executed:

READ(5, 10) A, B

Find the number of cards skipped before B is read in if the FORMAT statement is:

(*a*)   10   FORMAT(F10.2/////)
(*b*)   10   FORMAT(F10.2/////F10.2)

[Generally speaking, n cards are skipped if n slashes appear at the end of a FORMAT statement, as in (*a*), but only $n - 1$ cards are skipped if the n slashes appear in the middle of the FORMAT statement, as in (*b*).]

3.40   Suppose the following WRITE statement is executed:

WRITE(5, 20) A, B

Find the number of blank lines before B is printed if the FORMAT statement is:

(*a*)   20   FORMAT(1X, F10.2/////)
(*b*)   20   FORMAT(1X, F10.2/////1X, F10.2)

(Generally speaking, *n* − 1 blank lines are printed whenever *n* slashes appear at the end or at the middle of a FORMAT statement.   Compare with Problem 3.39.)

Answers to Selected Supplementary Problems

3.21   (*a*)   There should not be a comma after NEXT.
            (*b*)   There should be a comma after PRINT but none after RATE.
            (*c*)   No errors.
            (*d*)   There should not be a comma after D.

3.22   (*a*)   11, 22, 3.3, 4.4, 5.5, 88, 99, 2.34, 5.67
            (*b*)   11, 22, 3.3, 5.5, 6.6, 77, 88, 5.67, 8.90
            (*c*)   11, 22, 3.3, 5.5, 6.6, 77, 88, 5.67, 8.90

3.23   (*a*)   Data card: 1.1,2.2,33,44,55
            (*b*)   First card: 1.1,2.2
                     Second card: 33,44,55

3.24   (*a*)   22.2, 133.2, 15, 25 on one line.
            (*b*)   22.2, 133.2, 25 on a line and 35 on the next line.
            (*c*)   22.2 on a line and 133.2, 15, 25 on the next line.
            (*d*)   22.2 and 25 on a line, 133.2 on the next line, and then 35 on the following line.

3.25   (*a*)   There should not be a comma before X nor after M.
            (*b*)   No error.
            (*c*)   The real variable U corresponds to the integer format code I8.
            (*d*)   The FORMAT statement is repeated for K, C, L, but the format codes do not have the correct type.

3.26   (*a*)   11, 111, 222, 220   (*c*)   111, 110, 222, 200
            (*b*)   1111, 1000, 22, 2220   (*d*)   111, 110, 0, 222

3.27   (*a*)   11.11, −22.22, 33.33   (*b*)   11110.00, −2.222, 333.30   (*c*)   11.11, −2.222, 33.33

3.28   (*a*)   −44.4E+2, 5.55E+3, 6.66E−4   (*c*)   −44.4E20, 0.555, 6.66
            (*b*)   −4440.00E2, 5.550E3, 6.66E−4   (*d*)   −4.44E2, 5.55, 66.60E−4

3.29   (*a*)   12345, 67890, 1.11, 22.2   (*c*)   1234, 7890, 1.1, 10.02, 22.00   (*e*)   123, 678.9, 1.0, 110, 222
            (*b*)   12.345, 67.890, 1.11, 0.222   (*d*)   123.4, 567.8, 900.1   (*f*)   3, 4, 5, 90.01, 0.11, 0.2

3.30   (*a*) 11111, 22.2, 44444, 55.5, 66, 77777   (*d*) 11111, 22.2, 44444, 55.5, 0.00
       (*b*) 11111, 22.2, 0.33, 44444, 77777, 88.8   (*e*) 11111, 22.2, 0.33, 444.44, 77777, 9, 9999
       (*c*) 11111, 22.2, 0.33, 44444, 55.5, 0.66, 66666, 77777

3.31   (*a*) There should not be a comma after N. The integer variable M corresponds to the real format code F8.1.
       (*b*) No error.
       (*c*) There should not be a comma before S. The integer variable K corresponds to the real format code F8.1.
       (*d*) No error.

3.32   (*a*) $_{bbbbb}1111_{bbbbbb}2222_{bbbbbb}3333$
       (*b*) $_{bbbbbb}1111$
           $_{bbbbb}2222_{bbbbbb}3333$
       (*c*) THE NUMBERS ARE$_{bbbb}1111_{bbbb}2222_{bbbb}3333.$
       (*d*) The numbers appear on three different lines.
       (*e*) 1111 and 2222 appear on one line and 3333 on the next line.
       (*f*) No explicit carriage-control signal is given. So the first character from "1111" is used for carriage control, and only the remaining three will be printed. Also, the field width for K is insufficient; so either 222 or ∗∗∗ will be printed. Thus, one of the following will appear on the first line of a new page:

            $111_{bbbbbbb}222_{bbbbbbb}3333$ or $111_{bbbbbbb}***_{bbbbbbb}3333$

3.33   (*a*) $_{bbbb}111.22_{bbbb}444.67_{bbbb}777.89$
       (*b*) $_{bbbb}111.2_{bb}*****_{bbbbbbb}777.9$
       (*c*) $_{bbbb}0.11122E\ 03_{bbbbbb}0.44E\ 03_{bbbbb}0.7779E\ 03$ on the first line of a new page.
       (*d*) $_{bb}0.1112E\ 03_{bb}0.4447E\ 03$, and then $_{bb}0.7779E\ 03$ on the next line.
       (*e*) $_{bbbb}111.22$ and then $_{b}0.445E\ 03$ on the fourth line, and then $_{bbbbb}777.9$ on the seventh line.
       (*f*) $11.222_{bbbb}0.4446660E\ 03$ on the first line of a new page, and then $_{bbbbbbbbb}777.9$ on the next line.

3.34   J and K can be printed for values between 99999 and −9999; and X and Y can be printed for values between 9999.99 and −999.99.
       (*a*) FORMAT(1X, 2(I5, 3X), 2(F7.2, 3X))
       (*b*) FORMAT('1', 2(I5, 3X), 2(F7.2, 3X))
       (*c*) FORMAT('1'////1X, 2(I5, 3X), 2(F7.2, 3X))
       (*d*) FORMAT(1X, I5, 3X, I5/1X, F7.2, 3X, F7.2)
       (*e*) FORMAT(1X, I5/1X, I5/1X, F7.2/1X, F7.2)
       (*f*) FORMAT('1'//1X, I5, 3X, I5///1X, F7.2, 3X, F7.2)

3.39   (*a*) 5   (*b*) 4

3.40   (*a*) 4   (*b*) 4

Chapter 4

Transfer of Control.
Flowcharts

4.1 INTRODUCTION

The computer normally executes the instructions of a Fortran program one after the other unless it is instructed otherwise. The order of the execution can be controlled by various instructions. Basically, there are two types of transfer of control: unconditional and conditional. These control statements will be studied mainly in this chapter, Chapter 5, and Chapter 12.

As programs become more complex, a flowchart is most helpful in planning, designing, and structuring a program. A *flowchart* is a graphical representation of an algorithm, i.e., it is a visual picture which gives the steps of an algorithm and also the flow of control between the various steps. (An *algorithm* is a step-by-step method for solving a problem.) In particular, in a flowchart we enclose each operation, instruction, or series of instructions in a box and indicate the flow of control by directed lines between the boxes. Furthermore, different types of operations are indicated by different shaped boxes as illustrated in Fig. 4-1. If a flowchart continues on another page, or if it is difficult to connect two boxes, we use a small labeled circle to represent such a connection.

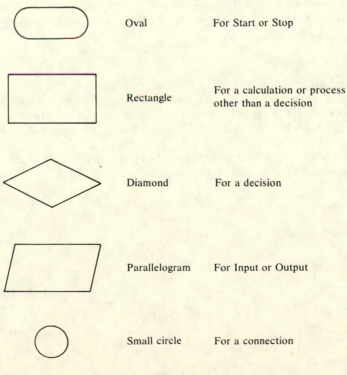

Shape	Name	Use
Oval	Oval	For Start or Stop
Rectangle	Rectangle	For a calculation or process other than a decision
Diamond	Diamond	For a decision
Parallelogram	Parallelogram	For Input or Output
Small circle	Small circle	For a connection

Fig. 4-1

The diamond-shaped box always denotes a decision and, hence, will have two or more lines leaving the box. These lines are labeled with the different decision results, i.e., with "yes" or "no", or with "true" or "false", or with "positive", "negative", or "zero". For example, the question "Is $I \leq 100$?" can appear in a flowchart as shown on the right. (For notational convenience, we will usually omit the question mark.)

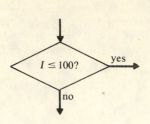

At this point, we will mention once again that the universally accepted symbol for assignment is the arrow $\leftarrow$, but that its Fortran translation is the sign $=$. Since flowcharts are language independent, many Fortran texts prefer using the arrow $\leftarrow$ in their flowcharts. We will generally adopt this policy. For example, to indicate that N is increased by 1, that is, that $N + 1$ is assigned to N, we will usually use

$$\boxed{N \leftarrow N + 1}$$

rather than

$$\boxed{N = N + 1} \quad \text{or} \quad \boxed{\text{Increase N by 1}}$$

We emphasize that all the above are widely used among Fortran texts.

4.2 UNCONDITIONAL TRANSFER

The unconditional transfer of control can be accomplished by writing the statement

$$\text{GO TO } n$$

where n is a statement number. This tells the computer to go, unconditionally, to that part of the program beginning with the statement labeled n. Obviously, the statement labeled n must be executable. (See Section 1.8.)

EXAMPLE 4.1

(*a*) Write a program that generates and prints the positive integers 1, 2, 3, ...

We note that any positive integer can be obtained by adding 1 to its predecessor. Therefore, it is a repeating process, always adding 1 to the present value of an integer. If we denote the present value of an integer by I, then the next integer (its successor) is $I + 1$. As this next integer will again be used to calculate its successor, we assign $I + 1$ to I.

In order to start this process, we initialize the value of I by letting $I = 1$. The flowchart of this program and the Fortran translation of the process are as follows:

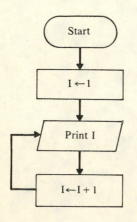

```
        I = 1                  I = 1
   99   PRINT, I          99   WRITE(6, 20) I
        I = I + 1    or   20   FORMAT(1X, I4)
        GO TO 99               I = I + 1
        END                    GO TO 99
                               END
```

(b) A deck of cards is given; each card contains four numbers representing student ID and the scores of three tests.   Write a program to compute, for each card, the average of the three tests.

Again, the process of computing the average of three numbers is repeated.   Therefore, an unconditional transfer is needed.   The flowchart for this process is shown in Fig. 4-2.

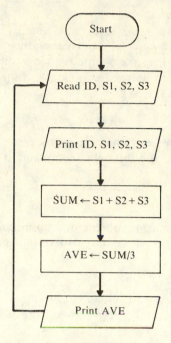

Fig. 4-2

The Fortran program, translated from the flowchart, follows:

```
C
C          PROGRAM TO COMPUTE THE AVERAGE
C          FOR EACH STUDENT
C

      100  READ, ID, S1, S2, S3
           PRINT, ID, S1, S2, S3
           SUM = S1 + S2 + S3
           AVE = SUM/3.0
           PRINT, AVE
           GO TO 100
           END
```

If formatted I/O is used, we have:

```
      100  READ(5, 10) ID, S1, S2, S3
       10  FORMAT(I5, F10.2, F10.2, F10.2)
           WRITE(6, 10) ID, S1, S2, S3
           SUM = S1 + S2 + S3
           AVE = SUM/3.0
           WRITE(6, 20) AVE
       20  FORMAT(1X, 'THE AVERAGE IS', F8.2)
           GO TO 100
           END
```

Note that in each of the two examples above, the process is repeated over and over again without stopping; namely, each program has an *infinite loop*.   Obviously, to terminate the process properly, we need some decision-making instructions.   This leads us to the next section.   We remark here that it is precisely these decision-making abilities that make computers so very powerful.

4.3 CONDITIONAL TRANSFER

Consider again the problem in Example 4.1(a) of generating integers.   Suppose we want only to generate the first 100 positive integers, i.e.; suppose we want the program to terminate after generating the integer 100.   One way to do this is to ask the following question at point A of Fig. 4-3(a).   That is, after executing I = I + 1, ask:

Is the current value of $I \leq 100$?

If yes, repeat the process; otherwise, terminate the process.   In other words, using ordinary English connectives, one wants to give the following command at point A:

IF $I \leq 100$ THEN   repeat the process

ELSE   stop.

This IF ... THEN ... ELSE ... command is represented by a diamond-shaped decision box, as in Fig. 4-3(b).   The flowchart generating the first 100 positive integers is given in Fig. 4-4.

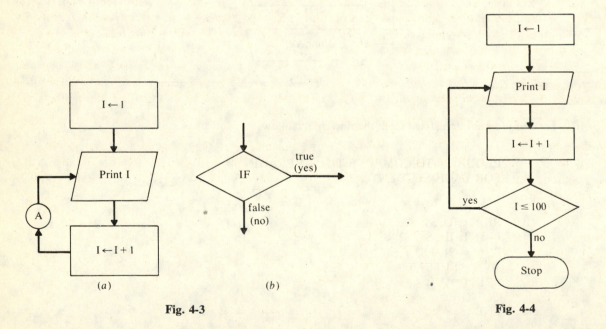

(a)   (b)

Fig. 4-3   **Fig. 4-4**

Consider another example.   Suppose the amount, AMT, of a loan is punched on a card, and suppose the RATE of interest is 7 percent if AMT $\leq$ $10,000, but 6 percent if AMT is greater than $10,000.   We want to write a program segment to calculate the interest, INT.   After reading in AMT, one wants to give the command:

IF   AMT $\leq$ 10,000   THEN   RATE = 0.07
ELSE   RATE = 0.06

Again, we have the IF ... THEN ... ELSE ... connective.   The flowchart for such a program segment appears in Fig. 4-5.

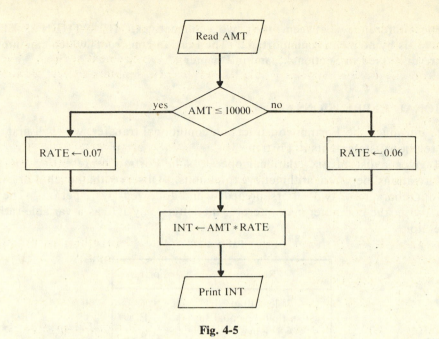

Fig. 4-5

The connective IF . . . THEN . . . ELSE . . . usually assumes that two distinct alternatives can occur, as illustrated in the above two examples.   However, there are situations which require the use of the ENGLISH connective IF . . . THEN . . . .   We show this with a third example.

Suppose the AGE of a man and the number NDEP of his dependents are punched on a card.   We want to calculate his income tax deduction, DEDUCT, which is \$750 per dependent.   However, if the man is 65 or older, then he can claim an extra deduction.   (We assume none of his dependents is 65 or older.)   Thus, we want to give the computer the command:

$$\text{IF AGE} \geq 65 \text{ THEN NDEP} = \text{NDEP} + 1$$

before calculating DEDUCT.   The flowchart for such a program segment appears in Fig. 4-6.

The statement "IF X THEN Y" has the following meaning.   When X is true, execute Y first before continuing to the next statement; when X is false, just continue to the next statement (skipping Y).

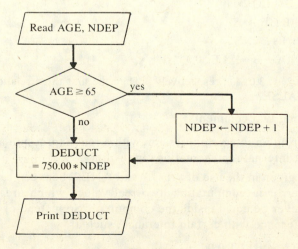

Fig. 4-6

The subtle difference between the two connectives, IF...THEN...ELSE... and IF...THEN..., is by no means unimportant.   The Fortran constructs which can implement these connectives are discussed in Section 4.5 and in Chapter 12.

4.4 RELATIONAL EXPRESSIONS

Before we introduce the Fortran constructs on conditional transfer, we shall first show how to write certain relational statements in Fortran.

Table 4-1 gives a list of six relational operators in Fortran representing the six common mathematical relations between arithmetic expressions.   Observe that each Fortran equivalent consists of four characters, two letters preceded and followed by a period.   The periods are essential; otherwise, the computer may interpret the letters, say LT, as a variable rather than as a relational operator.

Table 4-1

Relation	Fortran
less than	.LT.
less than or equal to	.LE.
equal	.EQ.
not equal	.NE.
greater than	.GT.
greater than or equal to	.GE.

A *relational expression* consists of two arithmetic expressions connected by a *single* relational operator.   Relational expressions are the simplest forms of *logical expressions*.   (More complex logical expressions containing also logical operators will be discussed in Chapter 9.)   At execution time, each logical expression and, hence, each relational expression represents a condition which is either TRUE or FALSE.

EXAMPLE 4.2

The following are mathematical expressions and their equivalent Fortran relational expressions.

$I < J$ I.LT.J

$(A + 3) > B$ (A + 3.0).GT.B

$5I = 2J$ 5*I.EQ.2*J

$B \geq A^2$ B.GE.A**2

$(I + 3) \neq J$ (I + 3).NE.J

$(A + B^3) \leq 50$ (A + B**3).LE.50.0

Suppose I, J, A, B contain 2, 5, 3.0, 4.0, respectively.   Then the first three relational expressions are TRUE and the second three are FALSE.

We make the following two comments:

1. Avoid comparing an integer expression with a real expression as integer and real values have different internal representations in memory.

2. Care must be given in the use of ".EQ." and ".NE." between real numbers.   Because of the inherent error in computation, two real values which are supposed to be equal in theory may never be equal inside the computer.   So instead of using A.EQ.B, one often tests their difference with certain tolerance, such as

       ABS(A − B).LT.0.0001

to compensate for possible round-off errors.

4.5 LOGICAL IF STATEMENT

Conditional transfers may be implemented in many ways in Fortran.   One of them is by use of a logical IF statement whose general form follows:

IF(*logexp*) Statement A

Specifically, a logical IF statement begins with the word IF and is followed by a logical expression *logexp* in parentheses.   (Recall that the logical expression *logexp* is an expression which has the value TRUE or FALSE.   See also Chapter 9.)   The parentheses are then followed by an executable statement Statement A; however, Statement A must not be another IF statement or a DO statement (discussed in Chapter 5).

Examples of logical IF statements follow:

IF(A.LE.B) GO TO 50

IF(L.GE.75) N = N + 1

IF(J.NE.K) WRITE(6, 30) X, Y

Formally speaking, the logical IF statement

IF(*logexp*) Statement A

has the following meaning.   If *logexp* is TRUE, then statement A is executed; otherwise, statement A is skipped.

More precisely, suppose a Fortran segment contains

IF(*logexp*) Statement A
Statement B

where Statement B is the *first executable statement* following the IF statement.   Then the following two possible situations can occur:

1. Statement A is not a GO TO statement.

2. Statement A is a GO TO statement.

Case 1

If Statement A is not a GO TO statement, then the above Fortran segment means the following.   When logexp is TRUE, execute Statement A first and then continue to the next statement, i.e., statement B; and when logexp is FALSE, just continue to the next statement, i.e., Statement B (skipping Statement A).   This situation is shown in Fig. 4-7(*a*).   Note that Statement B is always executed. This chart is equivalent to common usage of the English connective IF . . . THEN . . . discussed in Section 4.3.

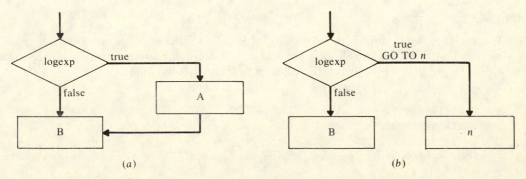

(*a*)   (*b*)

Fig. 4-7

Case 2

Suppose Statement A is a GO TO statement; that is, the above Fortran segment is

    IF(*logexp*) GO TO *n*
    Statement B

This means the following. If *logexp* is TRUE, then the portion of the program starting with the statement labeled *n* is executed; if *logexp* is FALSE, then the portion of the program starting with Statement B is executed. The flowchart appears in Fig. 4-7(*b*). It indicates that two distinct alternatives can occur after the decision, and this is equivalent to the common usage of the connective IF . . . THEN . . . ELSE . . . . Thus, this form of the logical IF statement may be used whenever a command IF . . . THEN . . . ELSE . . . appears in an algorithm. (See also Chapter 12.)

Consider now the flowchart in Fig. 4-5, which calculates the interest, INT, on a loan AMT. Recall that the flowchart came from the command

    IF   AMT $\leq$ 10,000   THEN   RATE = 0.07
                  ELSE   RATE = 0.06

Suppose the Fortran segment

    IF(AMT.LE.10000) RATE = 0.07
    RATE = 0.06

is used to implement the above command. According to Fig. 4-7(*a*) and the discussion on p. 83, RATE = 0.06 will always be executed. But this is not what we want; hence this Fortran segment cannot be used.

In order to bypass RATE = 0.06 when AMT $\leq$ 10,000, we must use a GO TO statement in the logical IF statement as in the following Fortran program.

```
          REAL INT
          READ(5, 10) AMT
    10    FORMAT(F15.2)
          IF(AMT.LE.10000.) GO TO 100
          RATE = 0.06
          GO TO 200
    100   RATE = 0.07
    200   INT = AMT*RATE
          WRITE(6, 20) INT
    20    FORMAT(1X, 'THE INTEREST IS', 2X, F10.2)
          STOP
          END
```

EXAMPLE 4.3

(*a*) We translate into Fortran the flowchart of Fig. 4-4, which prints the first 100 positive integers. Observe that there are two disjoint paths after the decision so that we would expect to use the "IF(*logexp*) GO TO *n*" form of the logical IF statement. The translation follows:

```
          I = 1
    99    WRITE(6, 10) I
    10    FORMAT(1X, I5)
          I = I + 1
          IF(I.LE.100) GO TO 99
          STOP
          END
```

The two statements

> IF(I.LE.100) GO TO 99
> STOP

are the Fortran translation of the command:

> IF $I \leq 100$ THEN   GO TO 99 to repeat the process
>   ELSE   STOP

(*b*)   The Fortran translation of the flowchart of Fig. 4-6, which calculates a person's income tax deduction, DEDUCT, follows:

```
       INTEGER AGE
       READ(5, 10) AGE, NDEP
10     FORMAT(2I15)
       IF(AGE.GE.65) NDEP = NDEP + 1
       DEDUCT = 750.00*FLOAT(N)
       WRITE(6, 20) DEDUCT
20     FORMAT(1X, F12.2)
       STOP
       END
```

Observe the similarity of Fig. 4-7(*b*) and part of Fig. 4-6.   Observe also that we used the library function FLOAT to convert the integer N into a real number so as to avoid mixed-mode arithmetic.

4.6   CONTROLLING A LOOP

Suppose we want to repeat a process (i.e., a set of instructions) say 100 times.   We can do this by using a counter I which counts the number of times the process is repeated.   That is, we initially assign 1 to the counter I, and then each time the process is executed, we increment the counter I by 1.   If the counter I exceeds 100, we terminate the execution of the process.   Figure 4-8 shows a flowchart which accomplishes this task.

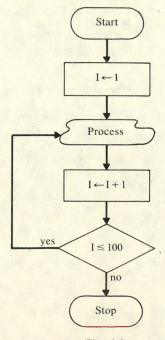

Fig. 4-8

One notes immediately the similarity between Fig. 4-4 and Fig. 4-8. In other words, the controlling mechanism that we used to generate the first 100 positive integers can also be used as the counting process controlling the exit in a loop that is to be repeated 100 times.

EXAMPLE 4.4

Recall Example 4.1(*b*), where we found the average of each student's three grades. Write a program if there are 100 cards in the data deck.

We simply insert the flowchart of Example 4.1(*b*) in the appropriate place in Fig. 4-8 to obtain Fig. 4-9(*a*). The Fortran translation of our program is shown in Fig. 4-9(*b*). Observe that the Fortran translation of a flowchart is generally straightforward.

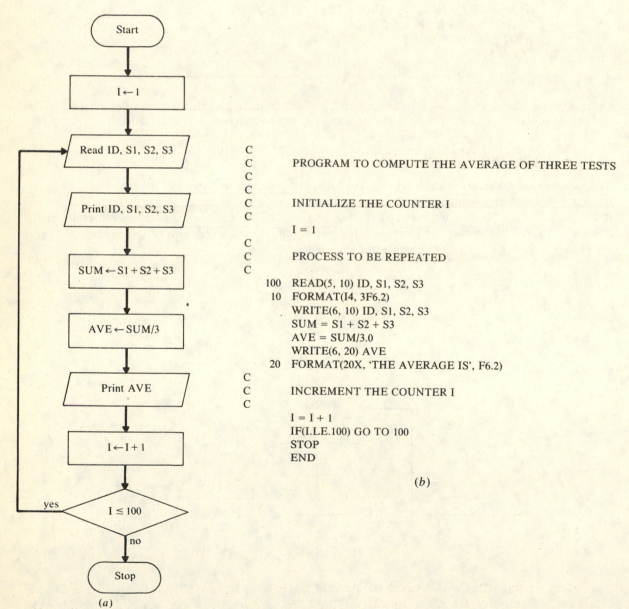

```
C
C       PROGRAM TO COMPUTE THE AVERAGE OF THREE TESTS
C
C
C       INITIALIZE THE COUNTER I
C
        I = 1
C
C       PROCESS TO BE REPEATED
C
100     READ(5, 10) ID, S1, S2, S3
10      FORMAT(I4, 3F6.2)
        WRITE(6, 10) ID, S1, S2, S3
        SUM = S1 + S2 + S3
        AVE = SUM/3.0
        WRITE(6, 20) AVE
20      FORMAT(20X, 'THE AVERAGE IS', F6.2)
C
C       INCREMENT THE COUNTER I
C
        I = I + 1
        IF(I.LE.100) GO TO 100
        STOP
        END
```

(*b*)

(*a*)

Fig. 4-9

EXAMPLE 4.5

Suppose we wish to write a program to read in an integer $N > 2$ and determine if N is a prime number.

Recall that N is a prime number if its only positive divisors are 1 and itself.   For example, 2, 3, 5, 13, 29, and 67 are prime numbers, but 35 is not a prime number since 35 is divisible by 5 and 7.   Clearly, if N is not a prime number, then one of the integers $2, 3, \ldots, N/2$ divides N.   (Compare with Problem 4.48.)

The algorithm we have in mind consists of two parts:

1. Generate the integers $2, 3, \ldots, N/2$.   This can be done as shown in Fig. 4-10.

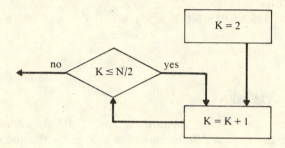

Fig. 4-10

2. For each of the above integers, test if it divides N.   If one of them does, then N is not prime; otherwise, N is prime.

The flowchart of our complete algorithm appears in Fig. 4-11.

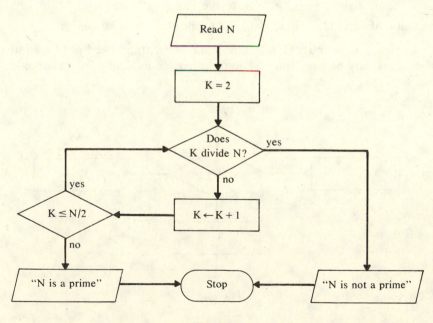

Fig. 4-11

Before we translate the flowchart into Fortran, we have to be able to translate the box "Does K divide N?".   However, from Example 2.9 we know that K divides N if and only if (N/K)∗K has the same value as N.   Thus, we have the program:

```
        READ(5, 20) N
20      FORMAT(I5)
        K = 2
30      IF(N/K*K.EQ.N) GO TO 70
        K = K + 1
        IF(K.LE.N/2) GO TO 30
        WRITE(6, 40) N
40      FORMAT(1X, I5, 1X, 'IS A PRIME')
        STOP
70      WRITE(6, 50) N
50      FORMAT(1X, I5, 1X, 'IS NOT A PRIME')
        STOP
        END
```

4.7 ARITHMETIC IF STATEMENT

Within the Fortran repertoire, there is another type of IF statement called an arithmetic IF statement.   In contrast to the logical IF statement, which tests the logical condition of a logical expression, an *arithmetic IF statement* tests the *sign* of an arithmetic expression.   Depending on whether it is positive, zero, or negative, control can then be transferred to various places.

The form of an arithmetic IF statement is as follows:

IF(*expr*) *l*, *m*, *n*

where *expr* is an arithmetic expression and *l*, *m*, *n* are statement labels.   The statement says:

IF the value of *expr* is negative (<0), go to the statement labeled *l*,

IF the value of *expr* is zero ($=0$), go to the statement labeled *m*,

IF the value of *expr* is positive (>0), go to the statement labeled *n*.

The statements labeled *l*, *m*, *n* must be executable; however, they need not be all distinct, i.e., any two or all of the labels may be the same.   The flowchart equivalent of the arithmetic IF statement is shown in Fig. 4-12.

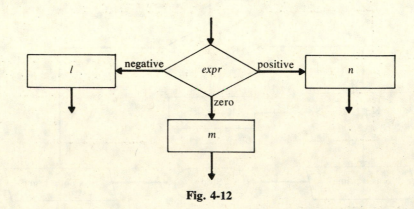

Fig. 4-12

Any arithmetic IF statement can be equivalently executed using one or more GO TO and logical IF statements.   For example,

IF(X − 2.0) 10, 20, 30   and   IF(X − 2.0) 10, 10, 20

are equivalent, respectively to:

IF(X.LT.2.0) GO TO 10		IF(X.LE.2.0) GO TO 10
IF(X.EQ.2.0) GO TO 20	and	GO TO 20
GO TO 30		

Conversely, any logical IF statement can be equivalently executed using arithmetic IF statements. (See Problem 4.5.)   We note that certain specific problems lend themselves naturally to an arithmetic IF statement as seen in the next example.

EXAMPLE 4.6

(a) Suppose the health insurance premium is deducted from an employee's salary according to the following plan:

$$\text{Premium} = \begin{cases} 9.75 & \text{if single} \\ 16.25 & \text{if married without children} \\ 24.50 & \text{if married with children} \end{cases}$$

Suppose TYPE is the integer variable denoting the marital status in codes as follows: 1 being single, 2 being married without children, and 3 being married with children.   Figure 4-13 gives a flowchart of a program segment deducting the premium from an employee's salary, assuming PAY, TYPE, and ID (employee's ID) are given.   Note that TYPE $-$ 2 is negative, zero, or positive according as TYPE equals 1, 2, or 3.   The Fortran translation of Fig. 4-13 follows:

```
        INTEGER TYPE
        REAL NET
        IF(TYPE − 2) 10, 20, 30
   10   NET = PAY − 9.75
        GO TO 75
   20   NET = PAY − 16.25
        GO TO 75
   30   NET = PAY − 24.50
   75   WRITE(6, 40) ID, NET
   40   FORMAT(1X, I5, 3X, F12.2)
```

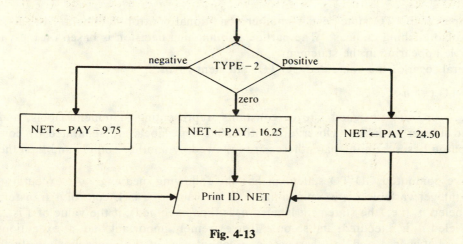

Fig. 4-13

(b) Consider the quadratic equation

$$ax^2 + bx + c = 0$$

where a, b, c are real numbers and $a \neq 0$.   There will be real roots only when the discriminant $D = b^2 - 4ac$ is nonnegative.   The roots are given by

$$\frac{-b \pm \sqrt{b^2 - 4ac}}{2a}$$

Observe that if the discriminant $D = 0$, then we obtain the multiple root $-b/2a$.   Write a Fortran program which computes the real roots of a given set of coefficients A, B, C.

```
      C
      C       COMPUTE THE REAL ROOTS OF A QUADRATIC EQUATION WHERE A
      C          IS NOT ZERO
      C
            READ(5, 11) A, B, C
         11 FORMAT(3F10.2)
            WRITE(6, 12) A, B, C
         12 FORMAT('0', 'THE COEFFICIENTS ARE', 3(2X, F10.2))
            D = B**2 − 4.0*A*C
      C
      C       TEST THE DISCRIMINANT
      C
            IF(D) 22, 33, 44
         22 WRITE(6, 13)
         13 FORMAT(1X, 'THERE ARE NO REAL ROOTS')
            GO TO 10
         33 ROOT = −B/(2.0*A)
            WRITE(6, 14) ROOT, ROOT
         14 FORMAT(1X, 'THERE ARE TWO IDENTICAL ROOTS', 2(3X, F10.2))
            GO TO 10
         44 ROOT1 = (−B + SQRT(D))/(2.0*A)
            ROOT2 = (−B − SQRT(D))/(2.0*A)
            WRITE(6, 15) ROOT1, ROOT2
         15 FORMAT(1X, 'THERE ARE TWO DISTINCT ROOTS', 2(3X, F10.2))
         10 STOP
            END
```

4.8 COMPUTED GO TO STATEMENT

The computed GO TO statement is another conditional control statement.   In fact, it allows any number of branching choices.   The particular branching decision is based on the value of an integer variable appearing in the statement.

The general form of the computed GO TO statement follows:

$$\text{GO TO } (n_1, n_2, \ldots, n_k), \text{ J}$$

Here, $n_1, n_2, \ldots, n_k$ are unsigned integer constants, representing statement labels, and J is an unsubscripted integer variable.   Observe that the statement labels are separated by commas and enclosed in parentheses, and the parentheses are followed by another comma and then the variable name J.

The above computed GO TO statement has the following meaning.   At execution time, the value of the integer variable J is examined first.   If the value of J is 1, control is transferred to the statement labeled n_1 (i.e., the statement labeled n_1 is then executed); if the value of J is 2, then the statement labeled n_2 is executed, and so on.   It is extremely important that, at execution time, the value of J lies between 1 and k; otherwise, one cannot predict the consequence.   In fact, some compilers do not even give an error message.

Suppose, for example, that the following statement is executed:

$$\text{GO TO } (10, 15, 70, 22, 15), \text{ NEW}$$

Then control is transferred to the statement labeled 10, 15, 70, 22, or 15 according as NEW has the value 1, 2, 3, 4, or 5, respectively.   Observe that the statement labels need not be distinct.   We emphasize that at execution time, NEW should be positive and should not exceed 5.

EXAMPLE 4.7

Consider the problem in Example 4.6 where the health insurance premium is deducted according to whether the employee is single (TYPE 1), married without children (TYPE 2), or married with children (TYPE 3). The flowchart and the Fortran program segment using a computed GO TO statement appear in Fig. 4-14.

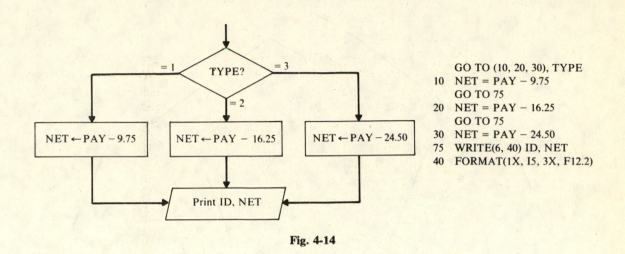

```
     GO TO (10, 20, 30), TYPE
10   NET = PAY − 9.75
     GO TO 75
20   NET = PAY − 16.25
     GO TO 75
30   NET = PAY − 24.50
75   WRITE(6, 40) ID, NET
40   FORMAT(1X, I5, 3X, F12.2)
```

Fig. 4-14

It is easily seen that the computed GO TO statement does not give us any extra problem-solving ability. That is, we can always arrange a sequence of logical IF statements to accomplish the same result as a single computed GO TO statement. For example,

```
IF(MM.EQ.1) GO TO 99
IF(MM.EQ.2) GO TO 88
IF(MM.EQ.3) GO TO 101
IF(MM.EQ.4) GO TO 23
```

is equivalent to

```
GO TO (99, 88, 101, 23), MM
```

However, a set of logical IF statements is less efficient than a single computed GO TO statement, which requires only one step to transfer the control to the desired point. As can be seen, it usually requires less writing.

Remark. There is another type of conditional control statement which allows for multiple branching, the assigned GO TO statement. We shall discuss this statement and the accompanying ASSIGN statement in Chapter 11.

4.9 ALGORITHMS

We shall discuss two programs in this section. The purpose is to show the different stages involved in writing a program—from the inception of an algorithm, to its refinement, and finally to its implementation. The translation of the final flowcharts into Fortran will not be done here, but will be left as exercises (supplementary problems) for the reader.

Suppose a deck of four cards is given and on each card a number is punched. We wish to find the largest of these four numbers. As there are only four numbers, let us read them into memory and call them A, B, C, D. The following algorithm will give us the largest number assuming A, B, C, D are in memory:

1. Compare A and B, and see which is larger.
2. Compare C with the result of 1, and see which is larger.
3. Compare D with the result of 2, and see which is larger.

One direct, intuitive implementation of the above algorithm is illustrated in the flowchart in Fig. 4-15.

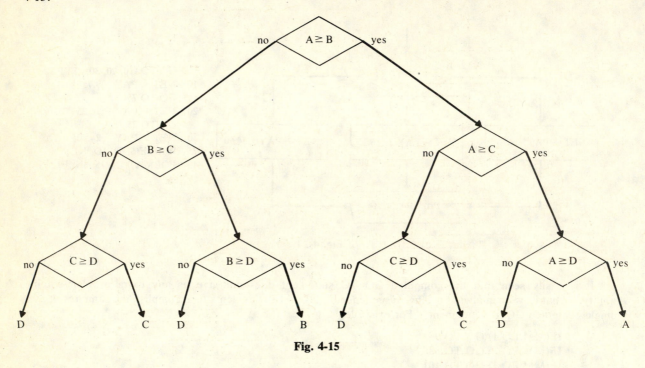

Fig. 4-15

Observe that there are $7 = 1 + 2 + 2^2$ decision boxes in Fig. 4-15.   In fact, the total number of decision boxes in such an algorithm grows exponentially with the number of elements.   Namely, if there were five numbers, there would be $2^3 + 7 = 15$ decision boxes; if there were six numbers, there would be $2^4 + 15 = 31$ decision boxes; and so on.   Obviously, this algorithm is not satisfactory when the number of elements is large.

We refine our algorithm a bit by letting LAR denote the current largest value and using the following four steps:

(0) Assign A to LAR; that is, set LAR = A.

(1) Compare LAR and B, and save the larger in LAR.

(2) Compare LAR and C, and save the larger in LAR.

(3) Compare LAR and D, and save the larger in LAR.

The flowchart of this algorithm is given in Fig. 4-16(a).   Observe that the number of decision boxes is three, and it grows linearly with the number of elements.   That is, for five numbers, there are four decision boxes; and for k numbers, there will be $k - 1$ decision boxes.   Clearly, this algorithm is a great improvement over the preceding algorithm.

One of the most striking things about the flowchart of Fig. 4-16(a) is that a certain group of boxes and information flow is repeated again and again.   This group is exhibited in Fig. 4-16(b) where ? represents an arbitrary element (other than the first).   Accordingly, if we can ensure that the value of ? changes correctly, then we can enclose the boxes in a loop.   This change can be accomplished by reading in the values one at a time using the same name (storage location) each time.   This yields the infinite loop exhibited in Fig. 4-16(c).

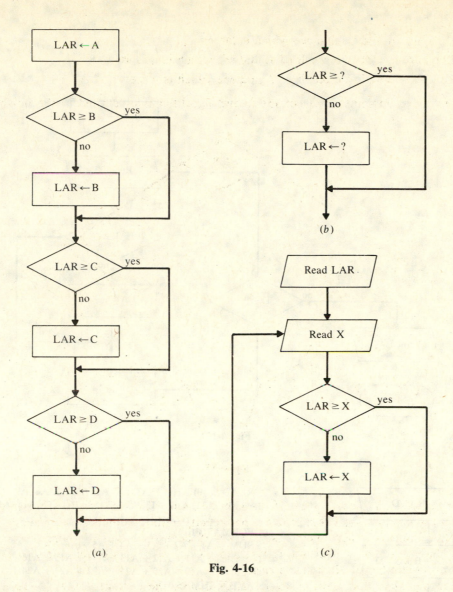

(a)   (b)   (c)

Fig. 4-16

Now suppose there are 100 cards in a given deck.   The flowchart for finding the largest number appears in Fig. 4-17.   (Since LAR is initially assigned the first number, the process is only repeated $100 - 1 = 99$ times.)   The Fortran program for a slightly more general problem appears in Problem 4.13.

We now consider another example.   Suppose a deck of four cards is given, and on each card a number is punched.   We wish to find the average (arithmetic mean) of these numbers.   The most obvious way is to read these numbers into locations, say, A, B, C, D, and then divide their sum by 4.   The flowchart appears in Fig. 4-18(a).

Now suppose the number of cards in the deck is 25 instead of 4.   Using the above scheme, it would require reading in 25 distinct variables, say A1, A2, . . . , A25.   (The numerals 1, 2, . . . , 25 in the variable names play no role other than being distinct symbols.)   Figure 4-18(b) gives the Fortran program which calculates the average of 25 numbers.   Observe that the READ statement and the statement calculating SUM are very long and clearly error-prone.   Furthermore, if there were 100 numbers, this scheme would be completely unmanageable and, in addition, the program would have to be rewritten.   Accordingly, it would be valuable to have a general scheme (algorithm) so that the same program (with possibly minor modification) can be used to calculate the sum of 4 or 25 or 100 numbers.   We shall discuss this next.

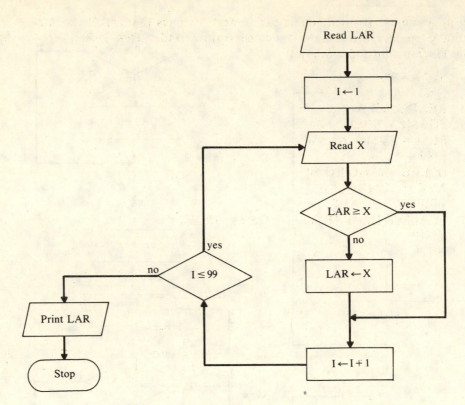

Fig. 4-17

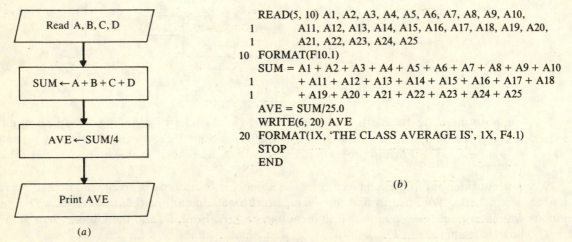

```
    READ(5, 10) A1, A2, A3, A4, A5, A6, A7, A8, A9, A10,
  1           A11, A12, A13, A14, A15, A16, A17, A18, A19, A20,
  1           A21, A22, A23, A24, A25
 10 FORMAT(F10.1)
    SUM = A1 + A2 + A3 + A4 + A5 + A6 + A7 + A8 + A9 + A10
  1           + A11 + A12 + A13 + A14 + A15 + A16 + A17 + A18
  1           + A19 + A20 + A21 + A22 + A23 + A24 + A25
    AVE = SUM/25.0
    WRITE(6, 20) AVE
 20 FORMAT(1X, 'THE CLASS AVERAGE IS', 1X, F4.1)
    STOP
    END
```

(b)

(a)

Fig. 4-18

To calculate $A1 + A2 + A3 + A4 + \cdots$, one may consider it as:

$$((((A1) + A2) + A3) + A4) + \cdots$$

That is, one may begin with SUM = 0 and then add these numbers one at a time to SUM.   In fact, they may be added one at a time as they are read into memory.   This is illustrated in Fig. 4-19(*a*) in an infinite loop.   Now if there are 100 cards in the deck with one number punched on each card, one can set up a counter I which counts the number of times the loop is executed.   We can then stop the adding process after the 100 numbers are added.   This yields the flowchart in Fig. 4-19(*b*).   Its Fortran equivalent follows:

```
     SUM = 0.0
     I = 1
50   READ(5, 10) A
10   FORMAT(F10.2)
     SUM = SUM + A
     I = I + 1
     IF(I.LE.100) GO TO 50
     AVE = SUM/100.0
     WRITE(6, 20) AVE
20   FORMAT(1X, 'THE AVERAGE IS', 1X, F4.1)
     STOP
     END
```

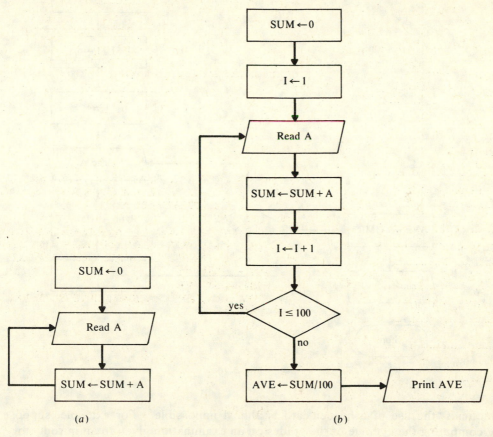

Fig. 4-19

4.10 HEADER CARD AND TRAILER CARD

The programs developed in Section 4.9 have one drawback; namely, they will work properly only if there are exactly 100 cards in the data deck.   If a given deck consists of 76 cards, one has to modify the program—although the same algorithm will work.   Clearly, one wishes to write a program which is independent of the number of cards in the data deck, i.e., that will work for any number of data cards, be it 4 or 100 or 76. We shall discuss two methods by which this is accomplished: (1) the use of a header card and (2) the use of a trailer card.

In the flowchart in Fig. 4-19(*b*), the loop is repeated 100 times in finding the sum of 100 values.   Suppose, on the other hand, we want the loop to be repeated a variable number of times (depending on the particular problem).   We must call this number by a variable name, say N.   To execute the program, with the variable N replacing 100, one must also define the value of N at execution time.   This can be accomplished by punching the number of cards in the deck on a card and placing this card, called a *header card*, on top on the data deck.   We then define N by reading in this number.   The flowchart of this program is given in Fig. 4-20.

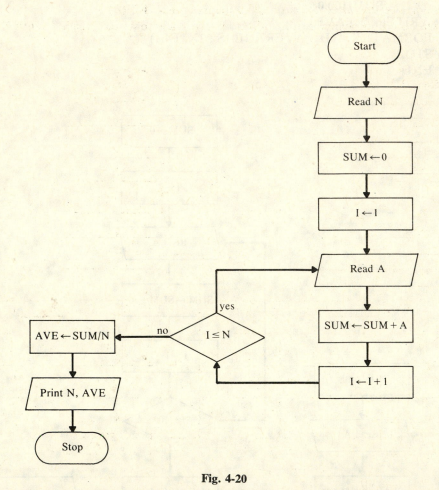

Fig. 4-20

Sometimes, the use of a header card is almost impossible.   For example, suppose we were actually computing the average of the grades on an examination given to an introductory computer programming course with perhaps 200–300 students.   In order to use a header card, someone must count the number of data cards in the deck.   Since there are 200–300 students, there will be 200–300 cards.   Of course, one would rather have the computer do the counting.   This can be accomplished by the use of a trailer card, which we discuss next.

Suppose we are computing the average of grades on an examination as above.   Since a number represents a grade only if it lies between 0 and 100, we may put, at the bottom of the deck, an additional card containing a number outside this range, e.g., a negative number.   This card is called a *trailer card*. When the computer encounters a negative number, it signals the end of the data deck. The flowchart for such a program appears in Fig. 4-21(*a*).

Remark. Observe that in this program, the counter is initialized to zero. The reason for this is that we only want to know the number of positive numbers, but we do not know that a number is positive until the number is tested. Thus, the value of I after I = I + 1 tells which was the last card read, not the card being read.

The above technique works only when we know the range of the numbers. However, a variation of this technique can be used when one has no idea about the data to be manipulated. One could read in an extra value, call it K, and punch a number, say 1, in the field for K on the trailer card. We do not alter any card in the given deck since blanks are read in as zero (in numerical fields). Thus, the computer senses the end of the data deck when K has the value 1. The flowchart of this alternate program appears in Fig. 4-21(*b*).

Lastly, we note that header cards and trailer cards are sometimes called *sentinel cards*.

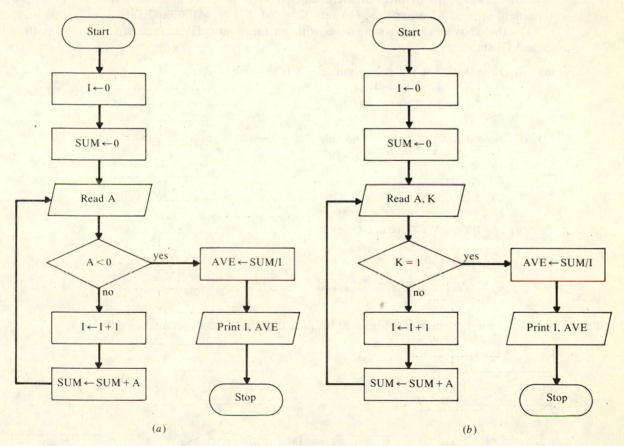

(*a*)   (*b*)

Fig. 4-21

Solved Problems

IF STATEMENTS

4.1   Write the following statements in Fortran:

(*a*)   If X > Y, stop.
(*b*)   If J ≠ K, go to the statement labeled 31.
(*c*)   If $A^2 \leq B + C$, go to the statement labeled 41.
(*d*)   If $A - B \geq X^3$, stop.

(*a*)   IF(X.GT.Y) STOP   (*c*)   IF(A**2.LE.B + C) GO TO 41
(*b*)   IF(J.NE.K) GO TO 31   (*d*)   IF(A − B.GE.X**3) STOP

4.2   Suppose X and Y have been defined.   Write a Fortran statement or Fortran segment which (*a*) transfers control to the statement labeled 41 if $X^2 \leq Y$, and transfers control to the statement labeled 42 otherwise; (*b*) sets K = 0 if X + Y > 100, and sets K = 1 otherwise.

Do the above in two ways, once with an arithmetic IF statement, and once with a logical IF statement.

(*a*)   (*i*)   Note that $X^2 \leq Y$ if and only if $X^2 - Y$ is negative or zero.
                    IF(X**2 − Y) 41, 41, 42

(*ii*)   IF(X**2.LE.Y) GO TO 41
          42 ....

(*b*)   (*i*)   Note that X + Y > 100 if and only if X + Y − 100 is positive.
                    IF(X + Y − 100.0) 20, 20, 10
          10 K = 0
                    GO TO 30
          20 K = 1
          30 ***************************

(*ii*)   IF(X + Y.LE.100.0) GO TO 20
                    K = 0
                    GO TO 30
          20 K = 1
          30 ***************************

4.3   Translate the flowcharts in Fig. 4-22 into Fortran program segments.

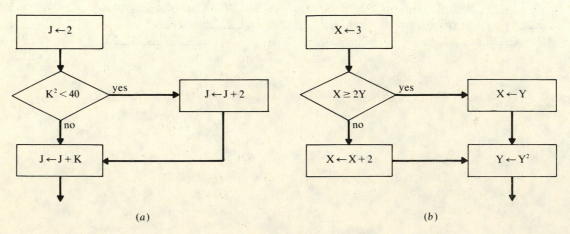

(*a*)   (*b*)

Fig. 4-22

(*a*)   This is equivalent to IF ... THEN ... as discussed in Case (1) of Section 4.5.

> J = 2
> IF(K**2.LT.40) J = J + 2
> J = J + K

(*b*)   This is equivalent to IF ... THEN ... ELSE ... as discussed in Case (2) of Section 4.5.

> X = 3.0
> IF(X.GE.2*Y) GO TO 10
> X = X + 2.0
> GO TO 20
> 10   X = Y
> 20   Y = Y**2

4.4   Suppose T1, T2, and T3 are in memory and denote test scores. Write a Fortran program segment which finds and prints the number of these scores ≥ 90. (A more general problem is given in Problem 4.14.)

We let N denote the number of scores ≥ 90. (Hence, N must equal 0, 1, 2, or 3.)

> N = 0
> IF(T1.GE.90.0) N = N + 1
> IF(T2.GE.90.0) N = N + 1
> IF(T3.GE.90.0) N = N + 1
> WRITE(6, 10) N
> 10   FORMAT(1X, I5)

4.5   Write a Fortran program segment using an arithmetic IF statement which is equivalent to each of the following. (Here S and T are executable statements.)

(*a*)   IF(A.LT.B) S   (*b*)   IF(J.NE.K) S
        T   T

(*a*)   Note A < B if and only if A − B is negative.   (*b*)   Note that J ≠ K if and only if J − K ≠ 0.

> IF(A − B) 10, 20, 20   IF(J − K) 10, 20, 10
> 10   S   10   S
> 20   T   20   T

4.6   Suppose J contains 5 and K contains 10. Find the final value of J after each Fortran program segment:

(*a*)   IF(3*J.LT.K) J = J + 2   (*d*)   IF(4*J − 2*K) 10, 20, 20
        J = J + 3   10   J = K
                                          20   J = J + 1

(*b*)   IF(2*J.EQ.K) J = J + 2   (*e*)   IF(2*K.LE.3*J) GO TO 50
        J = J + 3   J = J + 1
                                               GO TO 60
                                          50   J = K
                                          60   J = J + K

(*c*)   IF(K − J) 10, 20, 10   (*f*)   IF(K.GT.J) GO TO 50
        10   J = K   J = J + 1
        20   J = J + 1   GO TO 60
                                          50   J = K
                                          60   J = J + K

(a) Since $3J < K$ is not true, only $J = J + 3$ is executed; hence, 8 is the final value of J.
(b) Since $2J = K$ is true, first $J = J + 2$ is executed yielding $J = 7$. Then $J = J + 3$ is executed; hence, 10 is the final value of J.
(c) Since $K - J$ is positive, first $J = K$ is executed yielding $J = 10$. Then $J = J + 1$ is executed, which finally yields $J = 11$.
(d) Since $4J - 2K$ is zero, only $J = J + 1$ is executed.   Hence, 6 is the final value of J.
(e) Since $2K \leq 3J$ is false, first $J = J + 1$ is executed yielding $J = 6$. Then $J = J + K$ is executed, which finally yields $J = 16$.
(f) Since $K > J$ is true, first $J = K$ is executed yielding $J = 10$. Then $J = J + K$ is executed, which finally yields $J = 20$.

COMPUTED GO TO STATEMENT

4.7 Find errors, if any, in each computed GO TO statement:

(a) GO TO (5, 8, 4) MARK   (c) GO TO (2, 84, 578), ERIK
(b) GO TO (5, 22, 22, 57), KKK   (d) GO TO (5, 76, 0, 24), J

(a) There must be a comma before MARK.
(b) No errors.
(c) ERIK must be an integer variable.
(d) The zero cannot be a statement label.

4.8 Find the label of the statement to which control is transferred following each Fortran segment:

(a) MARK = 3
     GO TO (23, 47, 16, 94), MARK

(b) J = 2
     J = J + 2
     GO TO (23, 47, 16, 94), J

(c) K = 1
     K = K + 3
     GO TO (23, 16, 94), K

(a) Since MARK = 3, control is transferred to the statement labeled 16, the third number in the list.
(b) J = 4 when the computed GO TO statement is executed; so control is transferred to the statement labeled 94.
(c) K = 4 when the computed GO TO statement is executed. However, there are only three numbers in the list; hence, an error message will be given.

PROGRAMS

4.9 Draw a flowchart and write a program which prints each two-digit odd number N, its square N^2, and its cube N^3 so that different N's appear on different lines.   The program should be written so that the column of N's is headed by NUMBER, the column of N^2's by SQUARE, and the column of N^3's by CUBE.

We let $N = 11$, $J = N^2$, and $K = N^3$.   After incrementing N by 2, we test to see if $N < 100$.   The flowchart is given in Fig. 4-23(a) and the Fortran translation in Fig. 4-23(b).

If we add the following two statements at the beginning of the program,

        WRITE(6, 5)
      5 FORMAT(7X, 'NUMBER', 3X, 'SQUARE', 5X, 'CUBE')

then the output is as shown in Fig. 4-23(c).

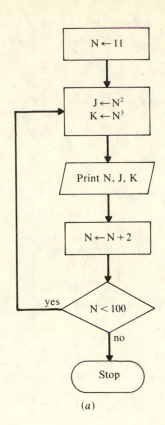

```
      N = 11
10    J = N**2
      K = N**3
      WRITE(6, 20) N, J, K
20    FORMAT(1X, 3I10)
      N = N + 2
      IF(N.LT.100) GO TO 10
      STOP
      END
```

(b)

NUMBER	SQUARE	CUBE
11	121	1331
13	169	2197
15	225	3375
**********	**************	**********
97	9409	912673
99	9801	970299

(a)   (c)

Fig. 4-23

4.10 Draw a flowchart and write a Fortran program which calculates (to five decimal places):

(a) $\dfrac{1}{1} + \dfrac{1}{3} + \dfrac{1}{5} + \cdots + \dfrac{1}{21}$,   (b) $\dfrac{2}{1} \cdot \dfrac{4}{3} \cdot \dfrac{6}{5} \cdot \cdots \cdot \dfrac{22}{21}$

(a) We first set SUM = 0 and then successively add 1/K to SUM for K = 1, 3, 5, . . . , 21. Figure 4-24(a) gives the flowchart. Note that we first set K = 1 and then increase K by 2 each time since the sum only involves odd numbers. Furthermore, we test if K ≤ 21 since we do not want to add anything after adding 1/21. In translating the flowchart into Fortran, we have to write

        1.0/FLOAT(K)

for 1/K since we do not want to do integer division. The program follows:

```
      SUM = 0.0
      K = 1
11    SUM = SUM + 1.0/FLOAT(K)
      K = K + 2
      IF(K.LE.21) GO TO 11
      WRITE(6, 20) SUM
20    FORMAT(1X, 'THE SUM IS', 2X, F8.5)
      STOP
      END
```

(*b*) We first set PRDT = 1 and then successively multiply PRDT by (K + 1)/K for K = 1, 3, . . . , 21. Figure 4-24(*b*) gives the flowchart. Note the similarity with part (*a*). The program follows:

```
        PRDT = 1.0
        K = 1
   13   PRDT = PRDT*FLOAT(K + 1)/FLOAT(K)
        K = K + 2
        IF(K.LE.21) GO TO 13
        WRITE(6, 30) PRDT
   30   FORMAT(1X, 'THE PRODUCT IS', 2X, F8.5)
        STOP
        END
```

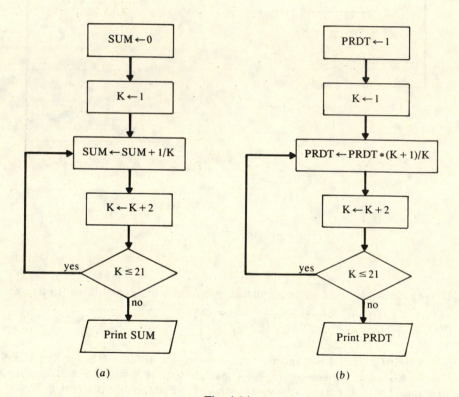

(*a*)   (*b*)

Fig. 4-24

4.11   Suppose an amount of \$2,000.00 is deposited in a savings account in 1977, and suppose the bank pays 6 percent interest on the account compounded annually. Write a program which prints the YEAR and the AMOUNT of the account until 1995.

Each year, AMOUNT is increased by 6 percent. Thus, the assignment

$$AMOUNT \leftarrow AMOUNT + 0.06*AMOUNT$$

is repeated as long as YEAR $\leq$ 1995. The flowchart for the program and its Fortran translation appear in Fig. 4-25.

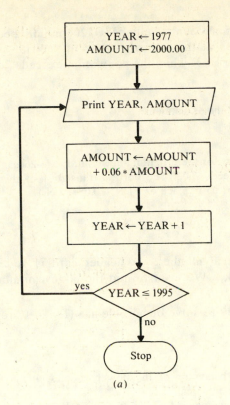

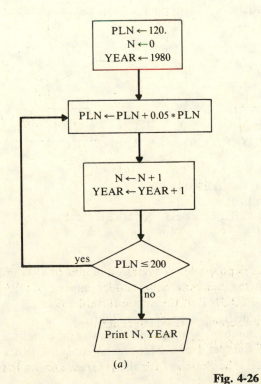

```
INTEGER YEAR
      WRITE(6, 10)
10    FORMAT('1', 6X, 'YEAR', 6X, 'AMOUNT'//)
      YEAR = 1977
      AMOUNT = 2000.00
55    WRITE(6, 20) YEAR, AMOUNT
20    FORMAT(1X, I10, 3X, '$', F8.2)
      AMOUNT = AMOUNT + 0.06*AMOUNT
      YEAR = YEAR + 1
      IF(YEAR.LE.1995) GO TO 55
      STOP
      END
```

(b)

Fig. 4-25

```
INTEGER YEAR
      PLN = 120.0
      N = 0
      YEAR = 1980
100   PLN = PLN + 0.05*PLN
      N = N + 1
      YEAR = YEAR + 1
      IF(PLN.LE.200.) GO TO 100
      WRITE(6, 10) N, YEAR
10    FORMAT(1X, I3, 3X, I4)
      STOP
      END
```

(b)

Fig. 4-26

4.12   Suppose in 1980 the population (PLN) of a country numbers 120 million people, and suppose each year the population increases at the rate of 5 percent. Write a program which finds the number N of years and the YEAR when the population exceeds 200 million people.

Each year PLN increases 5 percent.   Thus, the assignment

$$\text{PLN} \leftarrow \text{PLN} + 0.05*\text{PLN}$$

is repeated as long as PLN $\leq$ 200.   The flowchart for the program appears in Fig. 4-26(a).   Observe that we print N and YEAR only after PLN exceeds 200.   The Fortran translation of the flowchart appears in Fig. 4-26(b).   (One could write PLN*1.05 in place of PLN + 0.05*PLN.)

4.13   Suppose each card in a deck contains a real number. A header card is added which contains the number N of cards in the deck. We want to find the largest number in the deck.

(a)   What changes must be made in Fig. 4-17 to solve our problem.   (Fig. 4-17 refers to a deck with exactly 100 cards.)

(b)   Write the program.

(a)   We need only to insert "Read N" at the beginning of the flowchart, and change I $\leq$ 99 to I $\leq$ N $-$ 1.   Otherwise, the flowchart will be identical.

(b)   The program appears below.   Observe that we needed a type statement declaring LAR to be a REAL variable.

```
      C
      C       PROGRAM FINDING LARGEST NUMBER
      C
              REAL LAR
              READ(5, 10) N
        10    FORMAT(I6)
              READ(5, 20) LAR
              I = 1
       100    READ(5, 20) X
        20    FORMAT(F12.2)
              IF(LAR.GE.X) GO TO 200
              LAR = X
       200    I = I + 1
              IF(I.LE.N − 1) GO TO 100
              WRITE(6, 30) LAR
        30    FORMAT(1X, 'THE LARGEST NUMBER IS', 2X, F12.2)
              STOP
              END
```

4.14   Suppose each card in a deck contains the score of a student on a test. The deck has a trailer card on which a negative number is punched. Draw a flowchart and write the Fortran program which counts the number I of students who took the test and also gives the number N of test scores ≥ 90.

Figure 4-27 is the flowchart. Note that I and N are first initialized to be 0. The Fortran translation follows:

```
C
C         PROGRAM SCORES
C
          I  = 0
          N = 0
  100     READ(5, 10) X
   10     FORMAT(F10.1)
          IF(X.LT.0.0) GO TO 200
          I = I + 1
          IF(X.GE.90.0) N = N + 1
          GO TO 100
  200     WRITE(6, 20) I, N
   20     FORMAT('0', I10, 2X, 'STUDENTS TOOK THE TEST'/
      1       '0', I10, 2X 'SCORED ABOVE 90')
          STOP
          END
```

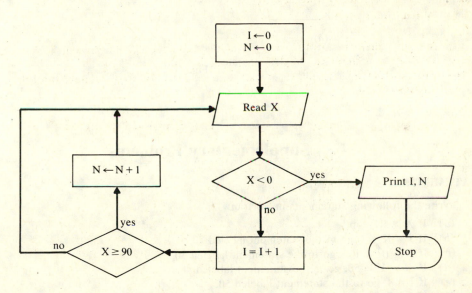

Fig. 4-27

4.15   Consider the equation $y = x^4 - 5x^2 + 7x - 8$. Draw a flowchart and write a Fortran program which calculates y for values of x from -4 to 4 in steps of 0.2. Print x and its corresponding y value on different lines.

First assign -4 to X. After calculating Y and printing X, Y, we increase X by 0.2. We continue to repeat the process as long as $X \le 4$. The flowchart of the algorithm appears in Fig. 4-28(a), and its Fortran translation is shown in Fig. 4-28(b).

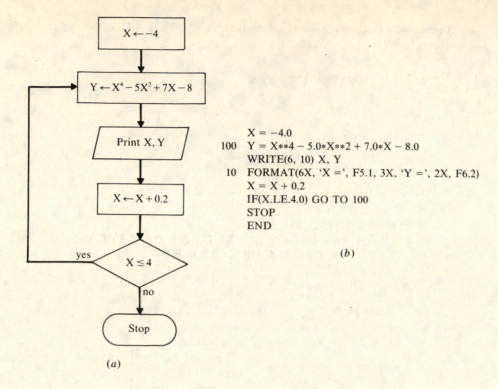

```
        X = -4.0
100     Y = X**4 - 5.0*X**2 + 7.0*X - 8.0
        WRITE(6, 10) X, Y
10      FORMAT(6X, 'X =', F5.1, 3X, 'Y =', 2X, F6.2)
        X = X + 0.2
        IF(X.LE.4.0) GO TO 100
        STOP
        END
```

(b)

(a)

Fig. 4-28

Supplementary Problems

IF STATEMENTS

4.16   Write the following statements in Fortran:

(a)   If $A > B$, stop.

(b)   If $J = K + 3$, go to the statement labeled 20.

(c)   If $A + B^2 < 100$, go to the statement labeled 30.

(d)   If $X - Y \geq 50$, go to the statement labeled 40.

(e)   If $I \neq 4$, go to the statement labeled 50.

(f)   If $J \leq K$, stop.

4.17   Find errors, if any, in each Fortran statement.

(a)   IF(A = B) GO TO 50   (e)   IF(X.LE.100) GO TO K

(b)   IF(X GT Y) STOP   (f)   IF(A − 100) 10, 20, 30,

(c)   IF(B**2 − A*C) STOP   (g)   IF(X.GE.Y) GO TO 55

(d)   IF(X.LT.Y + Z) 10, 15, 20   (h)   IF(INTEREST.LT.AMOUNT STOP

4.18   Do each of the following in two ways, once with logical IF statements and once with arithmetic IF statements.

(a)   Transfers control to the statement labeled 100 if $A + B^2 > 100$, and transfers control to the statement labeled 200 otherwise.

(b)   Sets $K = 1$ if $A - B \leq 100$, and sets $K = 2$ otherwise.

(c)   Transfers control to the statement labeled 10, 20, or 30 according as $J < K$, $J = K$, $J > K$.

4.19   Rewrite the following using arithmetic IF statements.   (Here S and T are executable statements.)

(a)   IF(X.GT.Y) S   (c)   IF(X.LE.Y) S
    T   T

(b)   IF(I.EQ.J) S   (d)   IF(A.GE.B) S
    T   T

4.20   Suppose J and K contain 3 and 5 respectively.   Find the final value of J after each program segment:

(a)   IF(J.GE.K) J = J + 2   (d)   IF(J.LT.K − 1) GO TO 10
       J = J + 2   J = J + 2
                                  10   J = J + K

(b)   IF(5∗J.EQ.3∗K) J = J + 2   (e)   IF(J.GE.K + 1) GO TO 10
       J = J + 2   J = J + 2
                                  10   J = J + K

(c)   IF(J − K) 10, 10, 20   (f)   IF(2∗J − K) 10, 10, 20
   10   J = K   10   J = K
   20   J = J + 2   20   J = J + 2

4.21   Translate each flowchart in Fig. 4-29 into a Fortran program segment.   In each case, find the value of Z if: (a)   A = 2.0, B = 3.0;   (b)   A = 3.0, B = 2.0.

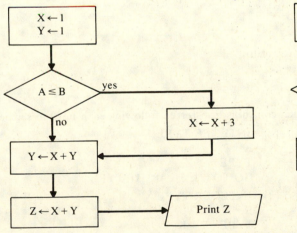
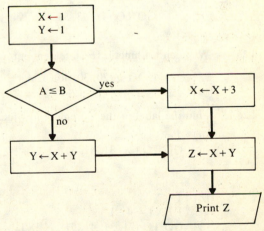

Fig. 4-29

4.22   Translate the flowchart in Fig. 4-30 into a Fortran program segment.   Find the value of Z if:

(a)   A = 2.0, B = 3.0, C = 3.0, D = 2.0   (c)   A = 3.0, B = 2.0, C = 2.0, D = 3.0
(b)   A = 3.0, B = 2.0, C = 3.0, D = 2.0   (d)   A = 2.0, B = 3.0, C = 2.0, D = 3.0

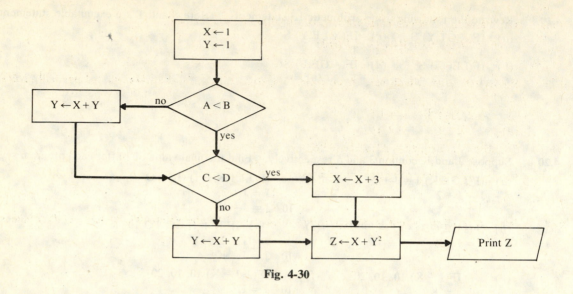

Fig. 4-30

COMPUTED GO TO STATEMENTS

4.23   Find errors, if any, in each computed GO TO statement:

    (*a*)   GO TO (35, 17, 17, 46) JIM
    (*b*)   GO TO (42, 0, 88, 1234), LAST
    (*c*)   GO TO (34, 34, 58, 58, 34), N237K
    (*d*)   GO TO (234, 2345678, 7654), J
    (*e*)   GO TO (34, 82, 56, 77), TOM

4.24   Write a set of logical IF statements equivalent to:

$$\text{GO TO (47, 33, 55, 77), K}$$

4.25   Write an arithmetic IF statement equivalent to:

$$\text{GO TO (20, 30, 40), JIM}$$

4.26   Find the label of the statement to which control is transferred following each Fortran segment:

    (*a*)   J = 3
           GO TO (21, 31, 41, 51), J

    (*c*)   INTEGER TYPE
           K = 2
           TYPE = 2*K
           GO TO (21, 31, 41, 51), TYPE

    (*b*)   I = 2
           NEXT = 4 − I
           GO TO (21, 31, 41, 51), NEXT

    (*d*)   INTEGER TYPE
           K = 3
           TYPE = 2 + K
           GO TO (21, 31, 41, 51), TYPE

PROGRAMS

4.27   Write a program which prints the positive integers from 1 through 300 with three numbers to a line, i.e., so the output looks like

              1   2   3
              4   5   6
           . . . .
         298   299   300

4.28   Write a program which calculates, to two decimal places, the sum

$$1/2 + 2/3 + 3/4 + \cdots + 99/100$$

4.29   Write a program which reads a positive integer $N \geq 10$ and calculates, to two decimal places, the sums

(a) $1 + 1/2 + 1/3 + \cdots + 1/N$
(b) $1 - 1/2 + 1/3 - \cdots \pm 1/N$

Suppose A is defined.   Also calculate

(c) $\dfrac{1}{1+A} + \dfrac{1}{1+2A} + \dfrac{1}{1+3A} + \cdots + \dfrac{1}{1+N \cdot A}$

4.30   Write a program which reads a positive integer $N \geq 10$ and calculates, to five decimal places, the product

$$\frac{1}{1^2} \cdot \frac{3}{2^2} \cdot \frac{5}{3^2} \cdot \cdots \cdot \frac{2N-1}{N^2}$$

4.31   Write a Fortran program to compute the GROSS pay if ID (employee's ID), RATE (hourly rate), and HOUR (number of hours worked in a week) are all in memory, and time and a half is paid overtime (over 40 hours).

4.32   The commission on a clerk's total SALES is as follows:

(a)   If SALES < \$50, then there is no commission.
(b)   If $\$50 \leq$ SALES $\leq \$500$, then commission = 10% of SALES.
(c)   If SALES > \$500, then commission = \$50 + 8% of sales above \$500.

Write a program which reads in the total sales and calculates the commission.

4.33   Suppose an AMOUNT of \$1,000.00 is deposited in a savings account at 7 percent interest compounded annually.

(a)   Write a program which prints the AMOUNT of the account each year for 20 years.
(b)   Write a program to determine the number of years it takes for the account to exceed \$5,000.00.

4.34   Suppose the AMOUNT of deposit, the interest RATE (compounded annually), and the number N of years is read in as data.   Write a program which prints the VALUE of the account each year for N years.   (Test the program with the data in Problem 4.33.)

4.35   The Fibonacci sequence

$$1, 1, 2, 3, 5, 8, 13, 21, \ldots$$

is defined by assuming the first two terms have the value 1, and each term afterward is the sum of the two previous terms:

$$1 + 1 = 2, 1 + 2 = 3, 2 + 3 = 5, 3 + 5 = 8, \ldots$$

(a)   Write a program which prints the Fibonacci sequence not exceeding 10,000.
(b)   Write a program which prints the first 50 terms of the Fibonacci sequence.

4.36   Let J and K be positive integers with $J \leq K$.   The generalized Fibonacci sequence is defined by assuming J is the first term, K is the second term, and each term afterward is the sum of the two previous terms.   Write a program which reads in J and K and prints the first 50 terms of the generalized Fibonacci sequence.

4.37   Each card in a deck contains a positive real number (less than 1000), and the deck has a trailer card.

    (a) Write a program which finds the largest number in the deck. (Compare with Problem 4.13, which uses a header card.)

    (b) Write a program which finds the smallest number in the deck.

    (c) Write a program which finds the second largest number in the deck. (Assume the deck has more than one number.)

4.38   Write a Fortran program which finds the arithmetic mean of N (a positive integer) numbers.

4.39   Translate into Fortran Fig. 4-21(a), which finds the arithmetic mean of a set of nonnegative numbers. The deck has a trailer card with a negative number punched.

4.40   Suppose each card in a deck contains the integer score of a student on a test. (A trailer card is added which contains a negative number.) A test score T is assigned A, B, C, D, or E according as $T \geq 90$, $80 \leq T < 90$, $70 \leq T < 80$, $60 \leq T < 70$ or $T < 60$. Write a program which finds:

    (a) The number I of students who took the test.

    (b) The number of A's, B's, C's, D's, and F's.

    (c) The number of perfect papers, i.e., the number K of 100s. (This generalizes Problem 4.14.)

4.41   Suppose, at present, the populations of countries A and B are 52 and 85 million people respectively. Suppose the rates of population growth for A and B are 6 percent and 4 percent respectively. Write a program which prints the populations (to the nearest thousand) of A and B each year until the population of A exceeds B and finds the number N of years for the population of A to exceed B.

4.42   Redo Problem 4.41, but now the populations and rates of growth of countries A and B, say POPA and POPB and RATEA and RATEB, respectively, are given on data cards. (Test the program with the data in Problem 4.41.)

4.43   (a) Write a program which prints all odd positive integers less than 100 omitting those integers divisible by 7:

$$1, 3, 5, 9, 11, 13, 15, 17, 19, 23, \ldots, 97, 99$$

    (b) Rewrite the preceding program so that there are four numbers to a line, i.e., so that the output looks like

          1   3   5   9
        11   13   17   19
        23   25   27   29
           . . . .

4.44   Write a program which reads a positive integer N, where $10 \leq N \leq 1000$, and then prints, on a new page, the number N and all its divisors so that the output appears as follows (if, say, N = 12):

        DIVISORS OF 12

               1

               2

               3

               4

               6

             12

4.45 For each student in a continuing education class, a card is prepared on which the student's age, sex, class standing, and marital status are indicated.   These are given in codes:

> (*i*)   1 for female, 2 for male
> (*ii*) 1 for freshman, 2 for sophomore, 3 for junior, 4 for senior, 5 for graduate, 6 for nonmatriculated
> (*iii*) 1 for single, 2 for married

A trailer card is used to terminate the deck.   Write a program to calculate the percentages of: (*a*) males, (*b*) females, (*c*) graduate students, (*d*) students over 30.

4.46 For the data in the preceding Problem 4.45, write a program to calculate the percentages of: (*a*) married graduates, (*b*) female upper classmen (juniors and seniors), (*c*) undergraduates over 30.

4.47 Each card in a deck contains three positive numbers A, B, C, and the deck has a trailer card.

> (*a*) Write a program to determine whether A, B, C can form the sides of a triangle.   If yes, compute the perimeter of the triangle; if no, print the message 'NOT A TRIANGLE'.   (Hint: A, B, C can form a triangle if each side is less than the sum of the other two sides, i.e., if $A < B + C$, $B < A + C$, and $C < A + B$.)
> (*b*) Write a program to determine whether A, B, C form the sides of an: (*i*) equilateral triangle (three sides equal), (*ii*) isosceles triangle (two sides equal), (*iii*) right triangle (hypotenuse^2 = side^2 + side^2).

4.48 Example 4.5 gives a program which determines if an integer $N > 2$ is a prime number.   This is done by testing if N is divisible by any of the integers 2, 3,... up to N/2.   Actually, if N is not a prime number, then N has a nontrivial divisor $\leq \sqrt{N}$.

> (*a*) Modify the program so that it only tests if N is divisible by any of the integers 2, 3,..., up to $\sqrt{N}$.
> (*b*) Modify the program so that it only tests if N is divisible by 2 or by any odd integer $\leq \sqrt{N}$.

4.49 Translate the following statement into Fortran:

$$\text{IF} \quad 1 \leq X \leq 2 \quad \text{THEN} \quad K = 1$$
$$\text{ELSE} \quad K = 2$$

(Hint: The condition $1 \leq X \leq 2$ means $1 \leq X$ and $X \leq 2$, and can be implemented by several logical IF statements.)

Answers to Selected Supplementary Problems

4.16 (*a*) IF(A.GT.B) STOP   (*d*) IF(X − Y.GE.50.0) GO TO 40
       (*b*) IF(J.EQ.K + 3) GO TO 20   (*e*) IF(I.NE.4) GO TO 50
       (*c*) IF((A + B**2).LT.100.0) GO TO 30   (*f*) IF(J.LE.K) STOP

4.17 (*a*) .EQ. instead of =.
       (*b*) .GT. instead of GT.
       (*c*) $B^2 − AC$ is not a relational expression.
       (*d*) X.LT.Y + Z is not an arithmetic expression.
       (*e*) 100.0 instead of 100 if X is real.
       (*f*) No error, although A − 100.0 is preferred.

(g)   No error.
(h)   There should be a parenthesis between AMOUNT and STOP; INTEREST has more than six characters; INTEREST and AMOUNT have different types.

4.18   (a)   IF(A + B**2.GT.100.0) GO TO 100   or   IF(A + B**2 − 100.0) 200, 200, 100
            200 ....

(b)   IF(A − B.LE.100.0) GO TO 10   or   IF(A − B − 100.0) 10, 10, 50
            K = 2   50   K = 2
            GO TO 20   GO TO 20
        10 K = 1   10   K = 1
        20 ....   20 ....

(c)   IF(J.LT.K) GO TO 10   or   IF(J − K) 10, 20, 30
      IF(J.EQ.K) GO TO 20
      IF(J.GT.K) GO TO 30

4.19   (a)   IF(X − Y) 20, 20, 10   (c)   IF(X − Y) 10, 10, 20
        10   S   10   S
        20   T   20   T

(b)   IF(I − J) 20, 10, 20   (d)   IF(A − B) 20, 10, 10
        10   S   10   S
        20   T   20   T

4.20   (a) 5   (b) 7   (c) 7   (d) 8   (e) 10   (f) 5

4.21   (a) 9.0 and 5.0   (b) 3.0 and 3.0

4.22   (a) 5.0   (b) 10.0   (c) 8.0   (d) 5.0

4.23   (a)   No comma before JIM.
(b)   0 not permitted.
(c)   No errors.
(d)   2345678 is too large for a statement number.
(e)   TOM should be an integer variable.

4.24   IF(K.EQ.1) GO TO 47
IF(K.EQ.2) GO TO 33
IF(K.EQ.3) GO TO 55
GO TO 77

4.25   IF(JIM − 2) 20, 30, 40

4.26   (a) 41   (b) 31   (c) 51   (d) Error since TYPE contains 5.

Chapter 5

DO Loops

5.1 INTRODUCTION

The transfer of controls discussed in Chapter 4 enabled us to execute a group of instructions repeatedly. Recall that we used a counter I together with an IF statement to exit from the loops discussed in Sections 4.5 and 4.7. This control mechanism of repeating a process N times is illustrated in the flowchart in Fig. 5-1. That is, the counter I is initially set to 1. After each iteration, this counter is incremented by 1, and then the question "I ≤ N?" is asked before the loop is repeated again. The cycling ends once I exceeds N.

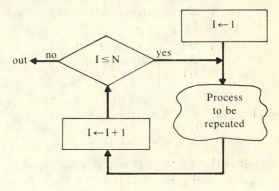

Fig. 5-1

Since repeating a process is fundamental to writing computer programs, it would be extremely useful to have a macrolike command such as: DO ... WHILE $1 \le I \le N$,

```
    DO
        ⎡        ⋮        ⎤
        ⎢ Process to be repeated ⎥    BODY OF DO
        ⎣        ⋮        ⎦
    WHILE 1 ≤ I ≤ N
```

or a macrolike command such as: DO FOR $1 \le I \le N$ ... REPEAT,

```
    DO FOR 1 ≤ I ≤ N
        ⎡        ⋮        ⎤
        ⎢ Process to be repeated ⎥    BODY OF DO
        ⎣        ⋮        ⎦
    REPEAT
```

Unstructured Fortran contains such a type of command—the DO statement. As the DO statement is one of the most powerful constructs of Fortran, this chapter is devoted entirely to the discussion of this macrolike instruction. (By a macrolike instruction, we mean a single instruction which invokes a predetermined list of instructions.)

Structured Fortran, discussed in Chapter 12, contains other types of DO commands.

5.2 CONTINUE STATEMENT

We first introduce a new executable statement, the CONTINUE statement, which simply consists of the word

    CONTINUE

113

The reasons for this statement will be clear later in Section 5.8, but its function is exactly described by its name—continue execution. The CONTINUE statement is also called a *dummy* executable statement since no machine language instruction is generated.

Most compilers allow the free use of the CONTINUE statement anywhere in the program; however, some require that CONTINUE statements be labeled.

5.3 SIMPLE USES OF THE DO STATEMENT

To repeat a process N times, one may use the following frequently used form of the DO statement:

DO 50 I = 1, N

$$\left[\begin{array}{c} \vdots \\ \text{BODY OF DO LOOP} \\ \vdots \end{array}\right.$$

    50   CONTINUE

The above DO-CONTINUE pair instructs the computer to repeatedly execute the statements between DO and CONTINUE (called the *body* of the DO loop). The integer variable I (called the *index variable*) is initially assigned the value 1, and after each iteration, the value of I is increased by 1. The iteration is continued (repeated) as long as I ≤ N. When I > N, the statement following CONTINUE is executed next. (We note that the label of the CONTINUE statement was chosen arbitrarily.)

Remark. For easier reading, one usually indents the body of the DO loop. This does not affect the program since blank spaces in Fortran statements are ignored by the computer.

We emphasize that the exact meaning of the DO statement above is illustrated in the flowchart in Fig. 5-2(*a*). Since a DO statement involves many boxes, we introduce, for convenience, an equivalent macrobox as shown in Fig. 5-2(*b*).

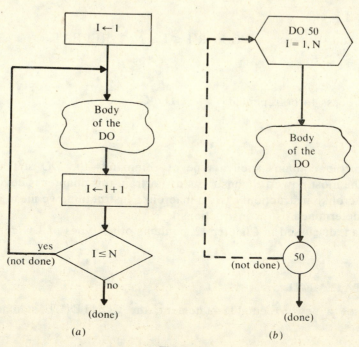

(*a*)   (*b*)

Fig. 5-2

EXAMPLE 5.1

Recall Example 4.4, which computes the average of three test scores for each student in a class of 100 students. (Each student's three test scores and ID number are punched on a data card.)

We rewrite the program using a DO statement. The flowchart of the program and its Fortran translation appear in Fig. 5-3. Observe how clearly the body of the DO loop stands out since it is indented.

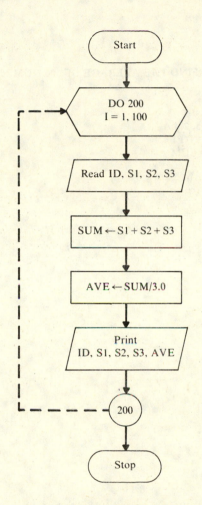

```
        WRITE(6, 5)
    5   FORMAT('1', 3X, 'ID NO.', 4X, 'TEST 1',
    1       4X, 'TEST 2', 4X, 'TEST 3', 3X, 'AVERAGE')
        DO 200 I = 1, 100
            READ(5, 10) ID, S1, S2, S3
   10       FORMAT(5X, I5, 3(4X, F6.2))
            SUM = S1 + S2 + S3
            AVE = SUM/3.0
            WRITE(6, 20) ID, S1, S2, S3, AVE
   20       FORMAT(5X, I5, 4(4X, F6.2))
  200   CONTINUE
        STOP
        END
```

Fig. 5-3

EXAMPLE 5.2

In Section 4.9, we wrote a program to find the average of 100 numbers. We will rewrite this program using the simple version of a DO loop. The flowchart and Fortran translation appear in Fig. 5-4.

Observe that the index I of the DO loop in the above example acts simply as a counter which counts the number of times we proceeded through the loop. Actually, the DO loop is much more powerful in that the value of the index I is also available for computation within the DO loop. This is illustrated in the next example.

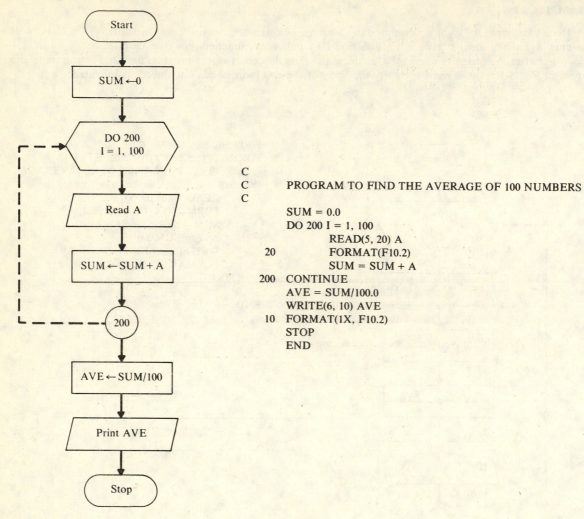

```
C
C        PROGRAM TO FIND THE AVERAGE OF 100 NUMBERS
C
         SUM = 0.0
         DO 200 I = 1, 100
             READ(5, 20) A
   20        FORMAT(F10.2)
             SUM = SUM + A
  200    CONTINUE
         AVE = SUM/100.0
         WRITE(6, 10) AVE
   10    FORMAT(1X, F10.2)
         STOP
         END
```

Fig. 5-4

EXAMPLE 5.3

(*a*) Write a program which prints the first 100 positive integers.   (Compare with Example 4.3.)
The flowchart appears in Fig. 5-5(*a*), and its Fortran translation follows:

```
         DO 500 I = 1, 100
             WRITE(6, 10) I
   10        FORMAT(10X, I3)
  500    CONTINUE
         STOP
         END
```

(*b*) Write a program which finds the sum of the first 30 positive integers.   We wish to compute
$1 + 2 + 3 + \cdots + 30$.   First we set ISUM = 0 and then repeatedly execute

```
         ISUM = ISUM + I
```

for $I = 1, 2, \ldots, 30$ using a DO loop.   The flowchart appears in Fig. 5-5(*b*), and its Fortran translation follows:

```
        ISUM = 0
        DO 700 I = 1, 30
              ISUM = ISUM + I
700     CONTINUE
        WRITE(6, 20) ISUM
 20     FORMAT(10X, I10)
        STOP
        END
```

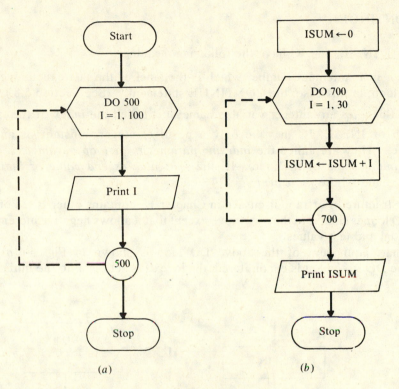

Fig. 5-5

(c) Write a program segment which calculates the product of the first 10 positive integers. The scheme is much like that of (b), except we wish to compute

$$1 \cdot 2 \cdot 3 \cdot \ldots \cdot 10$$

This is done by first setting IPROD = 1 and repeatedly executing

        IPROD = IPROD*I

using a DO loop with index I.   The program segment follows:

```
        IPROD = 1
        DO 100 I = 1, 10
              IPROD = IPROD*I
100     CONTINUE
```

5.4 DO STATEMENT

The DO loop discussed in the preceding section is only a special case. The more general (unstructured) DO loop has the following form:

DO *n* I = IN, IE, IC

$$\begin{bmatrix} \vdots \\ \text{Body of the DO loop} \\ \vdots \end{bmatrix}$$

n CONTINUE

The symbols *n*, I, IN, IE, and IC have the following meaning:

1. The *n* is a statement number which is the label of the last executable statement in the DO loop, in this case, the CONTINUE statement. (See Section 5.8.)

2. The I denotes any integer variable name; it is called the *index* of the loop.

3. Each of IN, IE, IC may be only a positive integer constant or an integer variable name. They are called the *indexing parameters* or *loop parameters*. The IN denotes the *initial value* of the index, IE the *test value* or *end value* or *limiting value* of the index, and IC the *increment*.

Remark. Structured Fortran, discussed in Chapter 12, contains other types of DO loops. One such type of DO loop is similar to the one above except that it allows negative increments and it allows nonpositive initial and test values.

The flowchart equivalent of the above DO loop is shown in Fig. 5-6(*a*). (See also Fig. 5-2.) When the DO statement is encountered, the index I is set equal to the initial value IN. Then

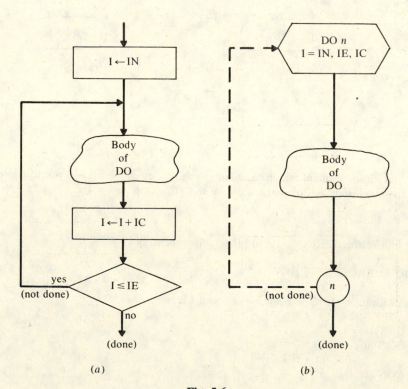

(*a*)   (*b*)

Fig. 5-6

control passes through the body of the DO loop, i.e., from the first statement following the DO statement until the CONTINUE statement.   The index I is now increased by the increment IC, and this new value of I is tested.   If I exceeds the test value IE, then the DO loop is done, and control passes to the first statement following the DO loop (i.e., to the first statement after the CONTINUE statement).   Otherwise the body of the DO loop is executed again; and so on.   The index I has a new value every time the computer proceeds through the DO loop.   Figure 5-6(b) gives the equivalent flowchart using the macrobox for the DO loop.

EXAMPLE 5.4

(a)   Suppose the computer encounters the DO statement:

DO 200 K = 2, 10, 3

The computer can cycle through the DO loop three times, first with K = 2, then with K = 2 + 3 = 5, and thirdly with K = 5 + 3 = 8.   After cycling through three times, K is increased to 8 + 3 = 11, which exceeds the limiting value 10; hence, the computer does not cycle through the DO loop a fourth time.   This shows that the index need not equal the test (limiting) value.

(b)   Suppose we want to print the even integers between 2 and 100, that is, $2, 4, 6, \ldots, 98, 100$.   We initially set IEVEN = 2 and execute IEVEN = IEVEN + 2 repeatedly as long as IEVEN $\leq$ 100.   The flowchart appears in Fig. 5-7(a).   Using a DO loop yields the flowchart in Fig. 5-7(b), and its Fortran translation follows:

```
        DO 200 IEVEN = 2, 100, 2
               WRITE(6, 10) IEVEN
   10          FORMAT(6X, I3)
  200   CONTINUE
```

(c)   Suppose A is in memory.   Compute the products:

   (i) $(1 + A)(1 + 2A)(1 + 3A)\ldots(1 + 10A)$
   (ii) $(1 + A)(1 + 4A)(1 + 7A)\ldots(1 + 19A)$

Like Example 5.3(c), the product (i) can be calculated using a DO loop as follows:

```
        PROD = 1.0
        DO 20 I = 1, 10
              PROD = PROD*(1.0 + FLOAT(I)*A)
   20   CONTINUE
```

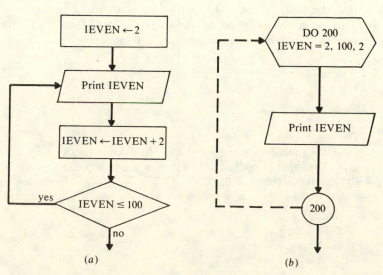

(a)   (b)

Fig. 5-7

With a minor modification, the product (*ii*) can be calculated similarly as follows:

```
      PROD = 1.0
      DO 50 I = 1, 19, 3
         PROD = PROD*(1.0 + FLOAT(I)*A)
   50 CONTINUE
```

5.5 RULES ON THE USE OF THE DO LOOP

The following are a number of rules concerning the above unstructured DO loop.

1. If the increment is 1, it may be omitted entirely.   For example,

    DO 100 I = 1, N, 1

    may be written in the abbreviated form

    DO 100 I = 1, N

2. Each of the indexing parameters IN, IE, IC in any DO statement must be a *positive* integer constant or a single, unsubscripted integer variable assuming a *positive* value.   Thus,

    DO 200 I = 20, 1, −2

    is invalid.   (See Remark on page 118.)

The next two points deserve special attention since they lead to frequent errors.

3. No arithmetic calculation can be performed in the DO statement itself.   Thus,

    DO 300 I = M, K + 3, 2

    is invalid.   However, one can accomplish the same arithmetic calculation by introducing a new variable, say KK, and writing

    KK = K + 3
    DO 300 I = M, KK, 2

4. Although the index I is available for calculations inside the DO loop, it may not be changed within the body of the DO loop.   This is also true for the indexing parameters IN, IE, IC.   In other words, none of the values I, IN, IE, IC can be altered within the DO loop (except by its inherent control mechanism).

EXAMPLE 5.5

(*a*) Consider the DO statement

    DO 200 I = 4, 2, 3

Observe that the initial value IN exceeds the end value IE.   However, the DO loop will be executed once, according to our flowchart.   (For some compilers, such use may cause an error message.)

(*b*) Suppose we wish to print the integers 100, 99, 98, . . . , 1, in this order.   The following program segment, which uses the above unstructured DO loop, is not valid since an increment cannot be negative:

```
      DO 500 I = 100, 1, −1
            WRITE(6, 20) I
   20       FORMAT(1X, I3)
  500 CONTINUE
```

However, it is still possible to write such a program using an unstructured DO loop.   We note first that we can use the statement

      DO 500 I = 1, 100

However, when I is 1, we want to print 100; when I = 2, we want to print 99, and so on.   That is:

        Value of I: 1,   2,   3, ..., 99, 100
   Value to be printed: 100, 99, 98, ...,   2,   1

Letting J denote the value we want printed, observe that $I + J$ is always equal to 101.   Hence $J = 101 - I$.   Thus the following program segment, which uses an unstructured DO loop, accomplishes our task:

```
          DO 500 I = 1, 100
                  J = 101 − I
                  WRITE(6, 20) J
    20            FORMAT(1X, I3)
   500    CONTINUE
```

5.6 EXIT FROM A DO LOOP

There are two ways to get out of any DO loop: (a) normal exit, (b) abnormal exit.   These are discussed below.

(a) Normal Exit

A normal exit takes place when the index I exceeds the test value IE (as indicated in the flowchart in Fig. 5-6(a)).   In such a case, control is transferred to the first executable statement following the DO loop.   One underlying property of the normal exit from a DO loop is that the value of the index I at the time of exit is *not defined* and, hence, should not be used in any further calculations.   All examples discussed so far have normal exits.

(b) Abnormal Exit

It is possible to transfer from the inside to the outside of a DO loop, say by an IF statement in the DO loop, even though the current value of the index I does not exceed the test value IE.   Such an exit will be termed an *abnormal exit*.   One fundamental property of an abnormal exit from a DO loop is that at the time of exit, the current value of the index I is retained (and, hence, can be used in any further calculations or in I/O operations).

The following program skeleton, which uses K for the index of the DO loop, illustrates when the value of the index K is and is not defined.

```
          DO 100 K = 1, 100, 2
                  ***
                  ***
                  IF(X.LT.Y) GO TO 200
                  ***
                  ***
   100    CONTINUE
          ***
          ***          The value of the index K is not defined for these statements.
          ***
          STOP
   200    ***
          ***          The value of the index K is defined for these statements.
          ***
          STOP
```

EXAMPLE 5.6

Write a program which reads in an integer K > 2 and determines if K is a prime number. If not, exhibit a nontrivial divisor of K. (Compare with Example 4.5.)

We have established that if K is not a prime number, then K has a nontrivial divisor ≤K/2. The flowchart and program appear in Fig. 5-8. We note that the loop index is to vary from 2 up to K/2. Since no arithmetic can take place in a DO statement, the statement

$$KK = K/2$$

is used first.

Observe that the DO loop tests each of the integers 2, 3, . . . , KK to see if it divides K. If not, then the loop is continued. Thus, a normal exit takes place when none of the numbers 2, 3, . . . , KK is a divisor of K, and, thus, K is a prime number. On the other hand, any time I divides K, we have an abnormal exit. In that instance, the value of the index I is still defined and, hence,

$$WRITE(6, 20) K, I$$

can be executed.

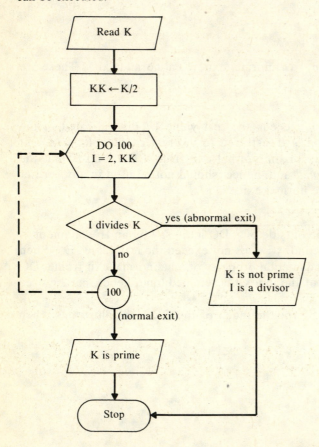

```
        READ(5, 8) K
   8    FORMAT(I10)
        KK = K/2
        DO 100 I = 2, KK
            IF(K.EQ.(K/I)*I) GO TO 50
 100    CONTINUE
        WRITE(6, 10) K
  10    FORMAT(10X, I5, 1X, 'IS A PRIME')
        STOP
  50    WRITE(6, 20) K, I
  20    FORMAT(10X, I5, 1X, 'IS NOT A PRIME'/
   1        10X, I5, 1X, 'IS A DIVISOR')
        STOP
        END
```

Fig. 5-8

5.7 TRANSFER WITHIN AND TO A DO LOOP

One can always transfer from one point in a DO loop to another point in the *same* DO loop, and one can freely jump out of any DO loop. However, it is *not possible* to jump into the middle of a DO loop. That is, the only way to transfer to statements within a DO loop is via the original DO statement. It is important to remember, however, that every time control is transferred to a DO statement, the index of the DO loop is reset at its initial value.

Suppose we want a Fortran program segment using a DO loop which calculates the sum

$$1 + 2 + 3 + 5 + 6 + 7 + 8 + 9 + 10$$

that is, the sum of the first 10 positive integers excluding the integer 4.   Consider the following two program segments:

```
(A)         ISUM = 0
            DO 100 I = 1, 10
                 IF(I.EQ.4) I = I + 1
                 ISUM = ISUM + I
     100    CONTINUE
(B)         ISUM = 0
      50    DO 200 I = 1, 10
                 IF(I.EQ.4) GO TO 50
                 ISUM = ISUM + I
     200    CONTINUE
```

Program A is invalid since the index I in the DO loop is altered.   That is, if the statements

```
IF(I.EQ.4) I = I + 1
ISUM = ISUM + I
```

were not in a DO loop, then 5 would be added to ISUM if I originally contained 4.   However, since we are in the middle of a DO loop here, the statements are not permissible.

In contrast, Program B has a correct use of the DO loop.   However, the logic of the program is not correct.   That is, there is an abnormal exit when I has the value 4, but control is transferred back to the DO statement.   As mentioned before, whenever the DO statement is executed, the index is reset at its initial value which, in this case, is 1.   Accordingly, this program will give an infinite loop computing

$$1 + 2 + 3 + 1 + 2 + 3 + 1 + 2 + 3 + \cdots$$

and so on.

The intention of Program B is to skip ISUM = ISUM + I when I contains 4.   Yet we also want the DO loop to continue its natural course.   This can be accomplished by transferring control to the CONTINUE statement instead of the DO statement.   That is, Program B will compute the required sum if

```
IF(I.EQ.4) GO TO 50
```

were changed to

```
IF(I.EQ.4) GO TO 200
```

This example actually illustrates the main point of the next section—the necessity of the CONTINUE statement.

5.8   NECESSITY OF THE CONTINUE STATEMENT

Actually, the last statement of any DO loop *need not* be the CONTINUE statement, but *must be an executable statement* other than a GO TO statement, or an arithmetic IF statement, or another DO statement.   For example, instead of

```
          ISUM = 0
          DO 200 I = 1, 100
                  ISUM = ISUM + I
200   CONTINUE
```

one may write

```
          ISUM = 0
          DO 200 I = 1, 100
200               ISUM = ISUM + I
```

However, we still advocate the use of the DO-CONTINUE pair as it will prevent the following type of common error:

```
          DO 300 I = 1, 100
                  WRITE(6, 300) I
300               FORMAT(10X, I3)
```

(The error being the use of the nonexecutable FORMAT statement as the last statement in the DO loop. The WRITE statement, instead of the FORMAT statement, should be labeled 300.) Even more important, the DO-CONTINUE pair offers the distinct pedagogical advantage that it standardizes the form of any DO loop, and the CONTINUE statement serves as a delimiter of the DO loop.

On the other hand, there is a situation when one must use a CONTINUE statement. Suppose there is a conditional statement within a DO loop where the two alternatives have nothing in

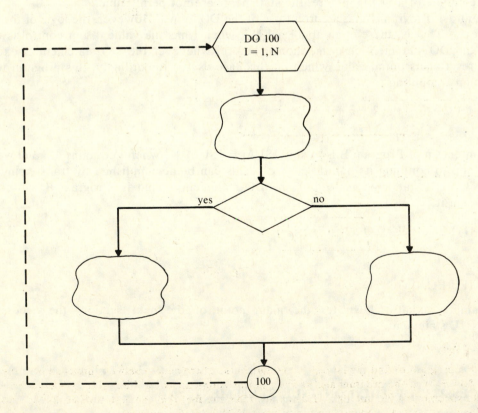

Fig. 5-9

common, as illustrated in Fig. 5-9. A special kind of executable statement is required so that both alternatives can refer to it enabling the DO loop to continue its natural course. The CONTINUE statement was created for that purpose. The corrected program segment B in Section 5.7 is one such example.

EXAMPLE 5.7

A deck of 50 cards is given. On each card, a nonzero number is punched. Write a Fortran program which counts the number of positive numbers and the number of negative numbers.

The flowchart for the program and its Fortran translation appear in Fig. 5-10. Here again one had to use a CONTINUE statement.

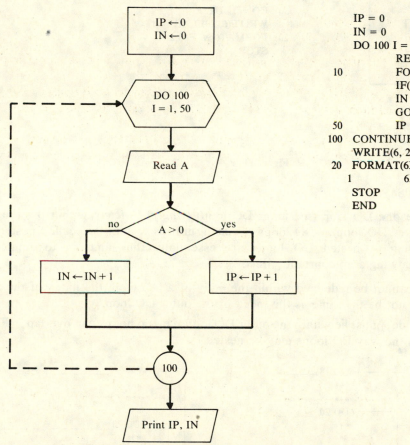

```
          IP = 0
          IN = 0
          DO 100 I = 1, 50
               READ(5, 10) A
  10         FORMAT(F10.2)
               IF(A.GT.0.0) GO TO 50
               IN = IN + 1
               GO TO 100
  50          IP = IP + 1
 100    CONTINUE
          WRITE(6, 20) IP, IN
  20    FORMAT(6X, 'POSITIVE = ', I3/
       1          6X, 'NEGATIVE =', I3)
          STOP
          END
```

Fig. 5-10

EXAMPLE 5.8

Write a program to find the largest of 100 numbers, where each number is punched on a separate card.

The flowchart of the program and its Fortran translation appear in Fig. 5-11. Observe that the end value of the DO statement is 99, not 100. This comes from the fact that the first number is read into LAR before the DO loop is executed. Again, one has to use a CONTINUE statement.

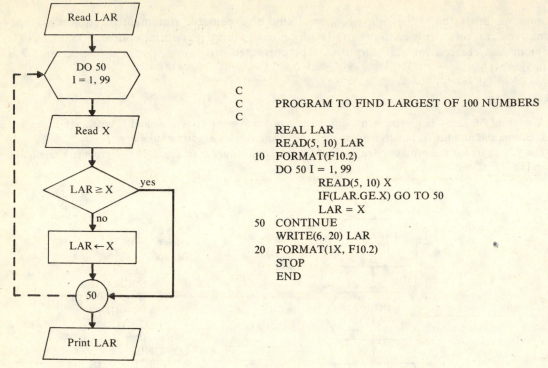

```
C
C          PROGRAM TO FIND LARGEST OF 100 NUMBERS
C
           REAL LAR
           READ(5, 10) LAR
10   FORMAT(F10.2)
     DO 50 I = 1, 99
           READ(5, 10) X
           IF(LAR.GE.X) GO TO 50
           LAR = X
50   CONTINUE
           WRITE(6, 20) LAR
20   FORMAT(1X, F10.2)
           STOP
           END
```

Fig. 5-11

5.9 NESTED DO LOOPS

It is possible to have one DO loop (the inner DO loop) *lying completely* within the range of another DO loop (the outer DO loop). DO loops occurring in this fashion are called nested DO loops. The rules applying to nested DO loops are essentially the same as to single DO loops. However, the following are important points:

1. As the index cannot be redefined within the body of a DO loop, the index of the inner DO loop must not be the same as the index of the outer DO loop.

2. The inner DO loop must lie within the outer DO loop; i.e., no hoops can overlap. Figure 5-12 illustrates the way DO loops may be nested.

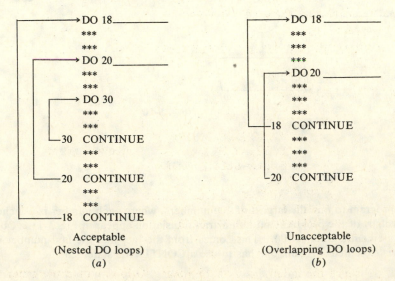

Acceptable
(Nested DO loops)
(a)

Unacceptable
(Overlapping DO loops)
(b)

Fig. 5-12

3. The number of nested DO loops is limited by the compiler.   Transfer of control within nested DO loops can be tricky, but the rules remain the same as with single DO loops.

Lastly, we note that nested DO loops may have the same last statement.   Thus, Fig. 5-13 shows nested DO loops which are acceptable and may be equivalent.

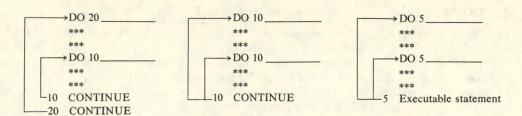

Fig. 5-13

EXAMPLE 5.9

Three (3) tests are given to a class of 25 students.   The student ID numbers and test scores are punched on cards and arranged as in Fig. 5.14.   Write a program to calculate the test average for each student.

We note that the average of three test scores may be calculated by the program segment:

```
        SUM = 0.0
        DO 20 I = 1, 3
                READ(5, 10) SCORE
10              FORMAT(F6.2)
                SUM = SUM + SCORE
20      CONTINUE
        AVE = SUM/3.0
```

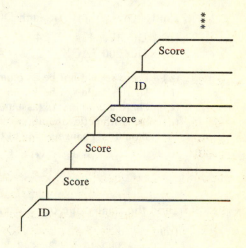

Fig. 5-14

Since we have to compute the average for each of the 25 students, the above segment has to be repeated 25 times.   We enclose the segment in another DO loop as follows:

```
        WRITE(6, 100)
100     FORMAT('1', 4X, 'ID', 9X, 'AVERAGE')
        DO 80 K = 1, 25
                READ(5, 90) ID
90              FORMAT(I10)
                SUM = 0.0
                DO 20 I = 1, 3
                        READ(5, 10) SCORE
10                      FORMAT(F6.2)                    Above segment
                        SUM = SUM + SCORE
20              CONTINUE
                AVE = SUM/3.0
                WRITE(6, 30) ID, AVE
30              FORMAT(1X, I10, 5X, F6.2)
80      CONTINUE
```

Remark.   Observe the indentation of the inner DO loop within the outer DO loop.   Again this is done for easier reading, and it does not affect the execution of the program.

Solved Problems

DO LOOPS

5.1   Determine the number of times and for which values of the index will each DO loop be executed.

   (*a*)   DO 10 K = 1, 11, 3   (*c*)   DO 30 LARGE = 8, 18, 15
   (*b*)   DO 20 JIM = 4, 12   (*d*)   DO 40 M = 7, 4, 2

   (*a*)   The initial value is 1, and the increment is 3.   Hence, the DO loop will be executed for K = 1, for K = 1 + 3 = 4, for K = 4 + 3 = 7, and for K = 7 + 3 = 10.   The next time K is incremented, its value will be greater than the test value 11; so control will be transferred out of the DO loop.   Thus, the DO loop is cycled (executed) four times.
   (*b*)   Since the increment value is missing, the increment is 1.   Hence, the DO loop is executed for JIM = 4, 5, . . . , 12.   Thus, it is executed nine times.
   (*c*)   The DO loop is executed only once for LARGE = 8 since the next value of LARGE is 8 + 15 = 23 which is greater than the test value 18.
   (*d*)   Even though the initial value for M is greater than the test value, the DO loop is still executed once for M = 7 since the testing takes place at the end of the DO loop.   (Some compilers will give an error message.)

5.2   Find errors, if any, in each DO statement:

   (*a*)   DO 100, K = 3, 24, 2   (*c*)   DO 300 JILL = JOHN, JIM
   (*b*)   DO 200 JACK = 5, M, 4,   (*d*)   DO 400 K = 4, 2*M, 3

   (*a*)   There should not be a comma after 100.
   (*b*)   There should not be a comma after 4.
   (*c*)   There are no errors (assuming JOHN and JIM are defined).
   (*d*)   No arithmetic operation can take place in any of the DO loop parameters.   The statement should be changed, say, to the following two statements:

           MM = 2*M
           DO 400 K = 4, MM, 3

5.3   Find the final value of K after each Fortran program segment is executed:

   (*a*)   K = 2   (*c*)   K = 2
               DO 10 I = 3, 8, 2   M = 2
                   K = K + I   DO 40 I = 3, 8, M
        10   CONTINUE   K = K + I
               K = 2*K   40   CONTINUE
                                                          K = 2*K

   (*b*)   K = 2   (*d*)   K = 2
               DO 20 I = 3, 8, 2   DO 50 I = 3, 8, K
                   K = K + I   K = K + I
                   IF(K.GT.6) GO TO 30   50   CONTINUE
        20   CONTINUE   K = 2*K
        30   K = 2*K

   (*a*)   The first statement assigns 2 to K.   The DO loop is then executed as follows:

   (*i*)   First for I = 3.   This yields:

   $$K \leftarrow K + I = 2 + 3 = 5$$

   (*ii*) Then for I = 5.   This yields:

   $$K \leftarrow K + I = 5 + 5 = 10$$

(*iii*) Then for I = 7.   This yields:

$$K \leftarrow K + I = 10 + 7 = 17$$

The next value of I exceeds the test value; so control is transferred to the last statement which doubles the value of K:

$$K \leftarrow 2*K = 2 \cdot 17 = 34$$

Thus, 34 is the final value of K.

(*b*)   The first statement assigns 2 to K, and then the DO loop is executed as follows:

(*i*)   First for I = 3.   This yields:

$$K \leftarrow K + I = 2 + 3 = 5$$

Since K < 6, control is not transferred to the statement labeled 30.

(*ii*) Then for I = 5.   This yields:

$$K \leftarrow K + I = 5 + 5 = 10$$

Since K > 6, control is transferred to the statement labeled 30, that is, the last statement.

The last statement doubles the value of K:

$$K \leftarrow 2*K = 2 \cdot 10 = 20$$

Hence, 20 is the final value of K.

(*c*)   Since M = 2, this is the same program as in (*a*); hence, 34 is the last value of K.

(*d*)   Since K = 2, the DO statement is the same as in (*a*).   However, K is now a parameter, and its value is changed in the program, which is not allowed.   Thus, the program segment cannot be executed.

5.4   Find the final value of K after each Fortran program segment is executed.

(*a*)
```
        K = 2
10  DO 20 I = 3, 8, 2
        IF(I.EQ.5) GO TO 20
        K = K + I
20  CONTINUE
        K = 2*K
```

(*b*)
```
        K = 2
10  DO 20 I = 3, 8, 2
        IF(I.EQ.5) GO TO 10
        K = K + I
20  CONTINUE
        K = 2*K
```

(*a*)   The first statement assigns 2 to K.   Then the DO loop is executed as follows:

(*i*)   First for I = 3.   Since I $\neq$ 5, the statement K = K + I is executed, which yields:

$$K \leftarrow K + I = 2 + 3 = 5$$

(*ii*) Then for I = 5.   Since I = 5, control is transferred to the CONTINUE statement which recycles the DO loop.

(*iii*) Then for I = 7.   Since I $\neq$ 5, the statement K = K + I is executed, which yields:

$$K \leftarrow K + I = 5 + 7 = 12$$

The next value of I exceeds the test value; so control is transferred to the statement following the DO loop, which doubles the value of K.   Hence, 24 is the final value of K.

(*b*)   The first statement assigns 2 to K.   Then the DO loop is executed as follows:

(*i*)   First for I = 3.   Since I $\neq$ 5, the statement K = K + I is executed, which yields:

$$K = K + I = 2 + 3 = 5$$

(*ii*) Then for I = 5.   Since I = 5, control is transferred to the DO statement.

Since control is transferred to the DO statement, the DO loop begins all over again and sets I = 3.   Thus, (*i*) and (*ii*) are repeated over and over again.   This gives an infinite loop, and there is no final value of K.   (We emphasize that if control is transferred to the DO statement, the index is reset at its initial value.)

5.5 Find errors, if any, in each program. The curved arrow represents a transfer of control.

(*a*) C   FIRST PROGRAM
```
              . . . . . . . . . . . . . . . . . .
              . . . . . . . . . . . . . . . . . .  )
              DO 10 I = 1, 25                       )
              . . . . . . . . . . . . . . . . . .  )
              . . . . . . . . . . . . . . . . . .  /
        10    CONTINUE
              . . . . . . . . . . . . . . . . . .
              END
```

(*c*) C   THIRD PROGRAM
```
              DO 10 I = 1, 25
              . . . . . . . . . . . . . . . . . .
              . . . . . . . . . . . . . . . . . .  )
              DO 20 J = 1, 15                       )
              . . . . . . . . . . . . . . . . . .  /
        20    CONTINUE
              . . . . . . . . . . . . . . . . . .
        10    CONTINUE
              . . . . . . . . . . . . . . . . . .
              END
```

(*b*) C   SECOND PROGRAM
```
              . . . . . . . . . . . . . . . . . .
              DO 10 I = 1, 25
              . . . . . . . . . . . . . . . . . .
              DO 20 J = 1, 15
              . . . . . . . . . . . . . . . . . .
        10    CONTINUE                             )
              . . . . . . . . . . . . . . . . . .  )
        20    CONTINUE                             )
              . . . . . . . . . . . . . . . . . .  /
              END
```

(*d*) C   FOURTH PROGRAM
```
              . . . . . . . . . . . . . . . . . .
              DO 10 I = 1, 25
              . . . . . . . . . . . . . . . . . .
              . . . . . . . . . . . . . . . . . .  \
              DO 20 J = 1, 15                       )
              . . . . . . . . . . . . . . . . . .  /
              . . . . . . . . . . . . . . . . . .
        20    CONTINUE
              . . . . . . . . . . . . . . . . . .
        10    CONTINUE
              . . . . . . . . . . . . . . . . . .
              END
```

(*a*) Control cannot be transferred to the middle of a DO loop.
(*b*) The DO loops overlap.
(*c*) Control cannot be transferred from an outer DO loop to inside an inner DO loop.
(*d*) There are no errors. We can transfer from an inner DO loop to an outer DO loop.

PROGRAMS

5.6 Write a program which prints the positive integers from 1 through 300 with three numbers to a line, so that the output looks like

```
      1        2        3
      4        5        6
      . . . . . . . . . . . . . . . .
    298      299      300
```

We want to print I, I + 1, and I + 2 on each line for I = 1, 4, 7, . . . and I $\leq$ 300. Hence, we use a DO loop with index I varying from 1 to 300 with increment 3. The program follows:

```
              DO 100 I = 1, 300, 3
                    J  = I + 1
                    K = I + 2
                    WRITE(6, 10) I, J, K
        10          FORMAT(1X, 3(I5, 3X))
       100    CONTINUE
              END
```

5.7　Write a Fortran program which reads an odd positive integer N and calculates (to three decimal places) the sum:

(*a*)　$1 + 1/2 + 1/3 + \cdots + 1/N$　　(*c*)　$1 - 1/2 + 1/3 - \cdots + 1/N$

(*b*)　$1 + 1/3 + 1/5 + \cdots + 1/N$

(*a*)　First set SUM = 0.0. Then use a DO loop with index $K = 1, 2, \ldots, N$ to add $1/K$ to SUM. The program follows:

```
        READ(5, 10) N
10      FORMAT(I5)
        SUM = 0.0
        DO 100 K = 1, N
                X = FLOAT(K)
                SUM = SUM + 1.0/X
100     CONTINUE
        WRITE(6, 20) N, SUM
20      FORMAT(1X, I5, 3X, F10.3)
        STOP
        END
```

(*b*)　The program is the same as (*a*) except the DO statement should be replaced by

```
DO 100 K = 1, N, 2
```

since only odd values of K are to be used.

(*c*)　The program is the same as (*a*) except that the sixth line should be replaced by

```
SUM = SUM + (-1.0)**(K + 1)/X
```

since the signs are to alternate.

5.8　Suppose an amount of $2000.00 is deposited in a savings account in 1977, and suppose the bank pays 6 percent interest on the account compounded annually. Write a program which prints the YEAR and the AMOUNT of the account until 1995. (Compare with Problem 4.11.)

Recall first that each year the AMOUNT is increased by 6 percent:

AMOUNT ← AMOUNT + 0.06*AMOUNT

(The general formula is

AMOUNT ← AMOUNT + RATE*AMOUNT = AMOUNT(1 + RATE)

where RATE is the rate of interest.)　The program follows:

```
        INTEGER YEAR
        WRITE(6, 10)
10      FORMAT('1', 6X, 'YEAR', 6X, 'AMOUNT'//)
        AMOUNT = 2000.00
        YEAR = 1977
        WRITE(6, 20) YEAR, AMOUNT
20      FORMAT(1X, I10, 3X, '$', F8.2)
        DO 99 YEAR = 1978, 1995
                AMOUNT = AMOUNT + 0.06*AMOUNT
                WRITE(6, 20) YEAR, AMOUNT
99      CONTINUE
        STOP
        END
```

(Observe that we used a DO loop with index YEAR beginning with 1978 since that is the first year that interest is assigned.)

5.9 Assume that a set of data $x_1, x_2, \ldots, x_n$ is punched on cards, one number per card, and the deck contains a header card.

(*a*) Write a program segment to calculate the sums:

$$\text{SUM} = x_1 + x_2 + \cdots + x_n = \sum_{i=1}^{n} x_i$$

$$\text{SUMSQ} = x_1^2 + x_2^2 + \cdots + x_n^2 = \sum_{i=1}^{n} x_i^2$$

[The summation symbol Σ is discussed in Section 8.9(*c*).]

(*b*) The mean, variance, and standard deviation of $x_1, x_2, \ldots, x_n$ are defined by

$$m = \text{mean} = \frac{\sum_{i=1}^{n} x_i}{n}$$

$$\text{variance} = \frac{\sum_{i=1}^{n} (x_i - m)^2}{n}$$

$$\text{standard deviation} = \sqrt{\text{variance}}$$

However, the variance can also be written as

$$\text{variance} = \frac{\sum_{i=1}^{n} x_i^2}{n} - m^2$$

Write a program to calculate the mean, variance, and standard deviation of the data.

(*a*) In the first set, SUM = 0.0 and SUMSQ = 0.0. After reading in N, use a DO loop to read in values for X and also to add X to SUM and X^2 to SUMSQ. The program segment follows:

```
        SUM = 0.0
        SUMSQ = 0.0
        READ(5, 10) N
10      FORMAT(I5)
        DO 100 I = 1, N
            READ(5, 20) X
20          FORMAT(F10.2)
            SUM = SUM + X
            SUMSQ = SUMSQ + X**2
100     CONTINUE
```

(*b*) The second formula for variance enables us to calculate variance at the same time as the mean (without using subscripted variables). We use the above program segment in our program:

```
        REAL MEAN
        SUM = 0.0
        SUMSQ = 0.0
        READ(5, 10) N
10      FORMAT(I5)
        DO 100 I = 1, N
            READ(5, 20) X
20          FORMAT(F10.2)
            SUM = SUM + X
            SUMSQ = SUMSQ + X**2
100     CONTINUE
        XN = FLOAT(N)
        MEAN = SUM/XN
```

```
                    VAR = SUMSQ/XN − MEAN**2
                    SD = SQRT(VAR)
                    WRITE(6, 30) MEAN, VAR, SD
                30  FORMAT(1X, 3(F10.2, 2X))
                    STOP
                    END
```

5.10   One way to calculate depreciation is by the sum-of-digits method.   For example, suppose an automobile costing \$4500.00 is to be depreciated over five years.   The sum-of-the-years-digits SUM in this case is:

$$SUM = 1 + 2 + 3 + 4 + 5 = 15$$

According to this method, 5/15 of \$4500 is depreciated the first year, 4/15 the second year, 3/15 the third year, and so on.   This data can be tabulated as follows:

Year	Depreciation
1	1500.00
2	1200.00
3	900.00
4	600.00
5	300.00

Write a program which accepts a real positive number COST and a positive integer N and prints the depreciation of COST over N years using the sum-of-digits method so that the output appears as above.

We will use the formula that

$$SUM = 1 + 2 + 3 + \cdots + n = n(n + 1)/2$$

Observe that n/SUM of COST is depreciated the first year, $(n − 1)$/SUM the second year, and so on.   In particular, $(n − K + 1)$/SUM of COST is depreciated the Kth year.   In the program, we use a DO loop with index K = 1, 2, ..., N, and the depreciation is calculated using

$$DEP = FLOAT(N − K + 1)/SUM*COST$$

The program follows:

```
        C
        C       PROGRAM USING SUM-OF-DIGITS DEPRECIATION
        C
                READ(5, 10) COST, N
            10  FORMAT(F15.2, I5)
                SUM = N*(N + 1)/2
                WRITE(6, 20)
            20  FORMAT('1', 5X, 'YEAR', 5X, 'DEPRECIATION')
                DO 100 K = 1, N
                    DEP = FLOAT(N − K + 1)/SUM*COST
                    WRITE(6, 30) K, DEP
            30      FORMAT(6X, I3, 6X, F10.2)
           100  CONTINUE
                STOP
                END
```

5.11 (a) Consider the quadratic polynomial $y = 2x^2 - 3x - 5$. Write a Fortran program which finds y for values of x from -4 to 4 in steps of 0.5.

(b) Consider the polynomial

$$z = x^3 - 3xy^2 + 2xy + y - 2y^3$$

Write a Fortran program using nested DO loops which finds z for values of x and y from -4 to 4 in steps of 0.5.

(a) There are 17 values of x, so we will use a DO loop with index $I = 1, 2, \ldots, 17$. The relationship between the index I and x follows:

$$x: \quad -4, \quad -3.5, \quad -3, \quad -2.5, \quad \ldots, \quad 3.5, \quad 4$$
$$I: \quad 1, \quad 2, \quad 3, \quad 4, \quad \ldots, \quad 16, \quad 17$$

Observe that x can be obtained from I using

$$x = -4 + 0.5(I - 1)$$

The program follows:

```
C          PROGRAM QUADRATIC POLYNOMIAL
           DO 100 I = 1, 17
               X = -4.0 + 0.5*FLOAT(I - 1)
               Y = 2.0*X**2 - 3.0*X - 5.0
               WRITE(6, 10) X, Y
    10         FORMAT(1X, F10.3, 3X, F10.3)
   100     CONTINUE
           STOP
           END
```

(b) The program is similar to the one in (a) except that now we have a DO loop for x and also one for y:

```
C          PROGRAM POLYNOMIAL
           DO 200 I = 1, 17
               X = -4.0 + 0.5*FLOAT(I - 1)
               DO 100 J = 1, 17
                   Y = -4.0 + 0.5*FLOAT(J - 1)
                   Z = X**3 - 3.0*X*Y**2 + 2.0*X*Y + Y - 2.0*Y**3
                   WRITE(6, 10) X, Y, Z
    10             FORMAT(1X, 3(3X, F10.2))
   100         CONTINUE
   200     CONTINUE
           STOP
           END
```

5.12 The graph of the equation $x^2 + y^2 = 50$ is a circle C with center at the origin and radius $\sqrt{50}$.

(a) Determine the number of points with positive integer coordinates which lie in the circle.

(b) Determine the number of points with integer coordinates which lie in the circle.

(a) Note first that neither x nor y can exceed 7 since the radius is $\sqrt{50}$. We use nested DO loops, one for x and one for y. We also begin with a counter K initialized at 0, and we do not count those points (x, y) such that $x^2 + y^2 \geq 50$. The program follows. Note that x, y are declared to be integer variables.

```
C          PROGRAM COUNTING POINTS IN CIRCLE
           INTEGER X, Y
           K = 0
           DO 100 X = 1, 7
                   DO 200 Y = 1, 7
                           IF(X**2 + Y**2.GE.50) GO TO 200
                           K = K + 1
200                CONTINUE
100        CONTINUE
           WRITE(6, 10) K
  10       FORMAT(1X, 'THE NUMBER OF POINTS IS', 2X, I5)
           STOP
           END
```

(b) Here we have to test 15 values for x and y, that is, $-7, -6, \ldots, 7$. Hence, we set up a DO loop with index $I = 1, 2, \ldots, 15$ for x, where we let $x = 8 - I$, and a similar DO loop for y. Otherwise, the program is similar to part (a).

```
           INTEGER X, Y
           K = 0
           DO 100 I = 1, 15
                   X = 8 - I
                   DO 200 J = 1, 15
                           Y = 8 - J
                           IF(X**2 + Y**2.GE.50) GO TO 200
                           K = K + 1
200                CONTINUE
100        CONTINUE
           WRITE(6, 10) K
  10       FORMAT(1X, 'THE NUMBER OF POINTS IS', 2X, I5)
           STOP
           END
```

5.13   Find all three-digit prime numbers; that is, find all prime numbers between 100 and 999. (Compare with Example 5.6.)

   None of these prime numbers can be even; therefore, we only consider the odd integers K between 101 and 999 to see if K is prime. Furthermore, if K is not prime, then K must have an odd divisor M between 3 and K/2. Thus, we use a DO loop with index K to generate the possible prime numbers K, and we use a DO loop with index M to generate the possible divisors of a given K. The flowchart and its Fortran translation appear in Fig. 5-15(a) and (b), respectively.

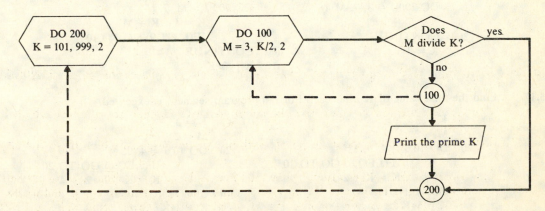

Fig. 5-15(a)

```
C
C          PROGRAM PRINTING PRIME NUMBERS
C
           DO 200 K = 101, 999, 2
               KK = K/2
               DO 100 M = 3, KK, 2
                   IF(K.EQ.(K/M)*M) GO TO 200
100            CONTINUE
               WRITE(6, 10) K
10             FORMAT(1X, I10)
200        CONTINUE
           STOP
           END
```

Fig. 5-15(b)

Supplementary Problems

DO LOOPS

5.14   Determine the number of times and for which values of the index will a DO loop be cycled if its first statement is:

(a) DO 100 L = 2, 15, 3   (c) DO 300 I = 6, 9, 5
(b) DO 200 JOHN = 5, 11   (d) DO 400 J = 8, 5, 4

5.15   Find errors, if any, in each DO statement:

(a) DO 700, LAMB = 1, 14, L,   (c) DO 900 K = I, J, K,
(b) DO 800 J = 7, M**2, 2   (d) DO 1000 LONG = K234, K123, K345

5.16   Find the value of K after each Fortran program segment is executed:

(a)   K = 3   (c)   K = 3
            DO 100 J = 3, 7, 3   M = 2
                K = K + J   DO 300 J = 3, 7, M
      100   CONTINUE   M = M + K
            K = 3*K   300   CONTINUE
                                                 K = 3*K

(b)   K = 3   (d)   K = 3
            M = 2   M = 2
            DO 200 J = 3, 7, M   DO 400 J = M, 7, M
                K = K + J   K = J + K + M
      200   CONTINUE   IF(K.GT.9) GO TO 10
            K = 3*K   400   CONTINUE
                                            10   K = 3*K

5.17   Find the final value of K after each Fortran program segment is executed.

(a)   K = 3   (b)   K = 3
            M = 2   M = 2
       20   DO 10 J = 4, 9, M   20   DO 10 J = 4, 9, M
                IF(J.EQ.6) GO TO 10   IF(J.EQ.6) GO TO 20
                K = K + 2*J   K = K + J**2
       10   CONTINUE   10   CONTINUE
            K = 3*K   K = 3*K
```
```

5.18   Suppose each curved arrow represents a transfer of control.   Find errors in each program.

(a) C   FIRST PROGRAM

         ....
         ....
         DO 100 K = 1, 5   a
         ....
         ....
         ....
    100 CONTINUE   b
         ....
         ....

         END

(b) C   SECOND PROGRAM

         ....
         ....   a
         DO 100 K = 1, 5
         ....
         ....
         ....   b
         DO 100 L = 1, 5
         ....
         ....
         ....
    100 CONTINUE
           c
         ....

         END

(c) C   THIRD PROGRAM

         DO 100 K = 1, 5   a
         ....
         ....
         DO 200 L = 1, 5   b
         ....
         ....
    100 CONTINUE
    200 CONTINUE
         ....

         END

(d) C   FOURTH PROGRAM

         ....   a
         DO 100 K = 1, 5
         ....
         DO 200 L = 1, 5
         ....   b
    200 CONTINUE
         ....
         DO 300 M = 1, 5   c   d
         ....
    300 CONTINUE   e
         ....
    100 CONTINUE
         ....

         END

PROGRAMS

(Many of the problems are the same as those in Chapter 4.   However, now they should be solved using a DO loop rather than using a counter.)

5.19   Write a program which prints each two-digit odd number N, its square N^2, and its cube N^3 so that different N appear on different lines.   (Compare with Problem 4.9.)

5.20   Write a Fortran segment which prints the number 20 twenty times, the number 19 nineteen times, the number 18 eighteen times, and so on.

5.21   Suppose N and K are positive integers in memory with $K < N$.   Write a program segment using a DO statement which prints N, then prints $N - 1$, then prints $N - 2$, and so on down until K is printed.   [Hint: See Example 5.5(b).]

5.22   Given A, B, and N, write a Fortran segment to compute

$$\frac{1}{A} + \frac{1}{A+B} + \frac{1}{A+2B} + \frac{1}{A+3B} + \cdots + \frac{1}{A+NB}$$

5.23   Write a program which reads a positive integer N ≥ 10 and calculates, to five decimal places, the product

$$\frac{1}{1^2} \cdot \frac{3}{2^2} \cdot \frac{5}{3^2} \cdot \ \cdots \ \cdot \frac{2N-1}{N^2}$$

5.24   Write a program which prints all odd positive integers less than 100, omitting those integers divisible by 7:

$$1, 3, 5, 9, 11, 15, 17, 19, 23, \ldots, 97, 99$$

5.25   Suppose the AMOUNT of deposit, the interest RATE (compounded annually), and the number N of years is read in as data.   Write a program which prints the amount in the account each year for N years.   (Compare with Problem 5.8.)

5.26   Suppose $500.00 is deposited *each year* in a savings account which yields 7 percent interest compounded annually.   Write a program which prints the amount in the account each year for 10 years.

5.27   Suppose $500.00 is deposited *every other year* in a savings account which yields 7 percent interest compounded annually.   Write a program which prints the amount in the account each year for 10 years.

5.28   A man borrows $300.00 from a bank at an interest rate of 1.5 percent per month.   He repays $25.00 at the end of each month.   (Thus, at the end of the first month he owes

$$\begin{aligned} \text{AMOUNT} + \text{INTEREST} - \text{REPAYMENT} &= 300 + (1.5\%)(300) - 25 \\ &= 300 + 4.50 - 25 = 279.50 \end{aligned}$$

dollars.)

(*a*)   Write a Fortran program which prints the amount he owes each month for a year.

(*b*)   Write a Fortran program segment which finds the number of months that he must make payments on the loan, and the amount of his last payment.

5.29   Find the number of points with integer coordinates which lie inside the ellipse $2x^2 + 3y^2 = 100$.

5.30   Three positive integers a, b, c, where $a < b < c$, form a Pythagorean triplet if $a^2 + b^2 = c^2$.   For example, 3, 4, 5 form a Pythagorean triplet since $3^2 + 4^2 = 5^2$.   Write a program which finds all Pythagorean triplets a, b, c where a, $b < 25$.

5.31   Suppose each card in a deck contains a real number.   A header card is added which contains the number N of cards in the deck.   Find the largest and smallest values.

5.32   Suppose 25 positive integers are punched on cards, one per card.   Write a program which finds the second largest integer.

5.33   Suppose a deck of cards contains one positive integer per card.   Write a program which finds the largest even integer in the deck, or prints NO EVEN INTEGER if all the integers are odd.   Assume the deck has a header card with the number N of cards in the deck.

5.34   Suppose a deck of cards contains one positive integer per card.   Write a program which finds the number of integers which are even, and the number which are odd.   (Assume the deck has a header card.)

5.35 The constant π can be approximated by:

$$\frac{\pi^2}{6} = 1 + \frac{1}{2^2} + \frac{1}{3^2} + \frac{1}{4^2} + \cdots$$

Write a program which:

(a) Sums the first 1000 terms.
(b) Sums the first 1000 terms in reverse order.

(Question: Is there any difference?)

5.36 Consider the equation $y = x^2 - 4x + 6$. Write a Fortran program which finds y for values of x:

(a) From -5 to 5 in increments of 0.1.
(b) From I to J in increments of $D = 1/N$, where I, J, and N are on a card and $I < J$.

(Each x and its corresponding y value should be on different lines.)

5.37 Consider the equation $z = x^2 - 2xy + 3y^2 - 8x + 3y - 8$. Write a program which finds z for values of x and y, where both x and y range from -3 to 3 with increments of 0.2.

5.38 Modify the preceding Problem 5.37 so that the program also determines the maximum value of z.

5.39 The sine of x (in radians) can be evaluated approximately by summing the first N terms of the series

$$\sin x = x - \frac{x^3}{3!} + \frac{x^5}{5!} - \frac{x^7}{7!} + \cdots$$

(a) Write a program which calculates the sine of 3 radians using the above series and N = 1, 2, 3, ..., 8. Compare each answer with that obtained by using the library function SIN X.
(b) Write a program which accepts a positive integer N and a real value x and evaluates $\sin x$ using the above series.
(c) Write a program which accepts a real value x and evaluates $\sin x$ by summing successive terms of the above series until a term has absolute value less than 10^{-15}.

Answers to Selected Supplementary Problems

5.14 (a) five times: 2, 5, 8, 11, 14　　(b) seven times: 5, 6, 7, 8, 9, 10, 11　(c) once: 6　　(d) once: 8

5.15 (a) There should not be a comma after 700 or after L.
(b) M**2 cannot be used as a parameter.
(c) There should not be a comma after K. The index variable K cannot be one of the parameters.
(d) No error.

5.16 (a) 36　(b) 54　　(c) error since parameter M has been changed　(d) 39

5.17 (a) 81　　(b) Computer never finishes the segment [See Solved Problem 5.4(b)].

5.18 (a) Transfer b is not allowed.
(b) Transfers a and c are not allowed.
(c) The CONTINUE statements should be interchanged.
(d) Transfers a and d are not allowed.

Chapter 6

Arrays, Subscripted Variables

6.1 INTRODUCTION

The variables we have used so far are also called *unsubscripted variables* or *scalar variables*. Each such scalar variable represents a memory cell in which a single value may be stored; e.g., a variable named X could be considered as a box:

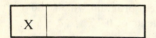

Very frequently, one wishes to use the same name to refer to a list of values having the same common attributes, e.g., the identification numbers of the students in a computer science class, the scores of a final examination, and so on. This is done by the use of arrays or subscripted variables.

In mathematics, one uses a symbol with different subscripts to denote the elements in a given set. For example, $s_1, s_2, \ldots, s_{25}$ may be used to denote the scores of a class of 25 students. Using this subscripted notation, one could then write

$$\sum_{i=1}^{25} s_i = s_1 + s_2 + \cdots + s_{25}$$

for the sum of the scores, and

$$\left(\sum_{i=1}^{25} s_i\right)\Big/ 25$$

for the class average. In other words, the use of subscripts is absolutely necessary in developing concise notation for the algebraic manipulation of the numbers involved.

Subscripts are also used in Fortran, but they have a different appearance. That is, since each Fortran statement must be punched (or typed) on one line, one uses parentheses to enclose subscripts; e.g., one would write $S(1), S(2), \ldots, S(25)$ in Fortran instead of $S_1, S_2, \ldots, S_{25}$. Such sets whose elements are specified by one subscript are called *linear* or *one-dimensional arrays* in Fortran. Analogous sets whose elements are specified by two or more subscripts are called *multidimensional arrays*.

6.2 ONE-DIMENSIONAL ARRAYS

A linear or one-dimensional array with N elements is a list or string of N memory cells, where each cell may store a value. These cells have the same name and are contiguous to each other. Any particular cell in this one-dimensional array is identified by an integer K, its position in the array. (Thus, $1 \le K \le N$.)

For example, suppose ID is a one-dimensional array with 50 elements. Then ID may be pictured as a string of 50 boxes as in Fig. 6-1. Each cell in the array ID is referred to by its name and its position, called *subscript*. Specifically, ID(1) denotes the first element of the array, ID(2) denotes the second element, and so on. Furthermore, if K is defined and $1 \leq K \leq 50$, then ID(K) refers to the Kth element of the array.

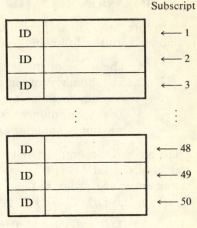

Fig. 6-1

The rules used to name ordinary variables also apply to arrays; i.e., an array name consists of one to six alphanumeric characters with the first character being alphabetic. Also, if the array name begins with the letter I, J, K, L, M, or N, then the array can contain only integers. Likewise, arrays beginning with other letters can contain only reals. Although these conventions can be superseded by a type statement (discussed in Section 6.3), the elements in any array must always be of the *same* type.

Although an element of an array is determined by the array name followed by the appropriate subscript (enclosed in parentheses), each array element can appear in arithmetic expressions just like scalar variables. For example, the following expressions are syntactically correct:

        X = AMOUNT(5) + Q
        PAY(K) = HOUR(K)*40.0
        TAX(6) = 25.75

On the other hand, we cannot use the array names themselves in arithmetic statements. For example, if GRADE is an array and SUM is an ordinary variable, statements such as:

        SUM = GRADE + SUM
        GRADE = SUM + 10.0
        GRADE = GRADE + 20.0

are not allowed. That is, the name GRADE refers to the entire array, while arithmetics involve individual memory locations.

We can also refer to array elements in input/output statements. For example,

        READ(5, 10) X, TAX(3)

will instruct the computer to read in two numbers. The first number is stored in location X, and the second is stored in the third element of the array named TAX. We print out from memory the identification numbers ID(1), ID(2), ..., ID(K), one per line, by using the program segment

            DO 100 I = 1, K
                WRITE(6, 20) ID(I)
        20   FORMAT(11X, I10)
        100 CONTINUE

Although array names alone cannot appear in arithmetic statements, they can appear in input/output statements. This will be discussed later in the chapter.

Remark. The term *subscripted variable* is used by different texts to mean different things. Some texts use subscripted variable to mean the array itself, whereas other texts use subscripted variable to mean an array element. Thus, some texts will say that the array ID above is a subscripted variable, whereas the other texts will say that the elements ID(3), ID(24), etc., are subscripted variables. Many IBM manuals on Fortran do not use the term subscripted variable at all. On the other hand, all texts use the term unsubscripted variable to mean the same thing, ordinary scalar variables.

6.3 DIMENSION STATEMENTS

Before any linear or multidimensional array is used in a program, one must provide the compiler with the following information:

1. The name of the array.
2. The number of subscripts in the array (i.e., whether the array is one-dimensional, two-dimensional, etc.).
3. The total number of memory locations to be allocated or, more specifically, the maximum value of each subscript.

The above is accomplished by the use of the type statement DIMENSION. (As with all type statements, a DIMENSION statement is nonexecutable and must be placed before any executable statement in the program.)

A typical DIMENSION statement is as follows:

DIMENSION AMOUNT(100)

This instructs the compiler that AMOUNT is the *name* of a *linear real array* and that *100* memory locations must be allocated for it.

Instead of listing arrays separately, several arrays may be declared with a single DIMENSION statement. For example,

DIMENSION ID(50), TAX(150)

declares ID to be a linear integer array with 50 elements and TAX to be a linear real array with 150 elements. (The form for multidimensional arrays is similar and will be discussed later.) The order of listing arrays is not important, as long as every variable that is to be subscripted is included in DIMENSION statements. Observe also that there is no comma after the word DIMENSION, but that the different arrays are separated by commas in the DIMENSION statement.

In general, zero or negative subscripts are not allowed. Obviously, one should not use a subscript which is larger than the maximum size specified in the DIMENSION statement. For example, given the above DIMENSION statement, one should not use ID(55) or TAX(182) in the program. One should be particularly careful about this, since many compilers do not check the validity of the subscripts. Consequently, errors of this type may not be detected but will be executed, resulting in erroneous answers.

We mention that the DIMENSION statement allocates the maximum number of memory cells required in an array, even though the programmer may only use parts of the array cells. In general, this overdimensioning may be necessary, but it must be done realistically in terms of the problem itself and its requirements. For example, one may not know the exact number of students taking an exam (e.g., some students may be absent), but one might use

DIMENSION TEST(60)

assuming normal-size classrooms will not seat more than 60. We emphasize that the use of unreasonably large arrays will be costly in terms of running time as well as the overall computing environment.

Remark. We emphasize that memory cells for arrays are allocated by DIMENSION statements during the compilation of the program, not during its execution; hence, the subscript specified in any DIMENSION statement must be an unsigned *integer constant*. (The only exception may be in SUBPROGRAMS; see Chapter 7.) Accordingly, statements of the form

DIMENSION AMOUNT(K)

or

N = 75
DIMENSION SCORE(N)

or

> READ(5, 10) I
> DIMENSION GRADE(I)

are unacceptable.

There is one last point we want to make in this section. Suppose we wish SCORE as the name of a linear array containing at most 50 integers (not real numbers). This can be done by using the type statements

> INTEGER SCORE
> DIMENSION SCORE(50)

However, one can alternately use the single statement

> INTEGER SCORE(50)

as it also provides the necessary information to the compiler. Similarly,

> REAL INVEST(150)

will define INVEST as the name of a linear array of 150 real values. As usual, more than one item of information can appear in such type statements, and such items must be separated by commas.

6.4 ARITHMETIC EXPRESSIONS FOR SUBSCRIPTS

One of the main advantages of using arrays is that the subscripts can themselves be variables. In fact, they may be simple arithmetic expressions limited to one of the following forms:

$$n, \quad K, \quad K + n, \quad n*K, \quad n*K \pm m$$

where n and m are integer constants and K any integer variable. For example, the following are syntactically correct:

$$A(8), \quad A(K), \quad S(K-2), \quad A(3*K), \quad A(4*K-3)$$

On the other hand, the following expressions are normally unacceptable:

A(−4)	(Negative subscripts are not allowed.)
A(0)	(Zero subscripts are not allowed.)
A(K*2)	(Should be written as A(2*K).)
A(K**2)	(Subscript is not one of the above forms.)
A(.TRUE.)	(Subscripts cannot assume logical values (see Section 9.6).)
A(3*M(2))	(Only scalar variables can appear in subscript expressions.)

We note that some modern, large computers do allow any integer-valued arithmetic expressions as subscripts; so the above rules should be modified accordingly.

Although we have only so far discussed one-dimensional arrays, the above rules on subscripts also apply to multidimensional arrays.

6.5 EXAMPLES USING ARRAYS

Suppose an exam is given to a class of no more than 25 students, and the scores are punched on cards, one per card. We are asked to write a Fortran program to:

1. Find the class average, and
2. Count the number of students who scored below the average.

First we discuss the simpler case where exactly 25 students took the exam. (To find the class average, we must first find the grand total of all the scores; hence, we recall the discussion in Section 4.10 for finding the sum of several numbers.)

One way to attack the problem is to use 25 distinct names, say A1, A2, . . . , A25, for the 25 scores. This would lead to very, very long statements which would be subject to error. (See page 94.) In addition, one would require 25 IF statements in order to compare each score with the class average. Furthermore, the program would be completely unmanageable if, say, 100 or more scores were involved. Thus, we look for another way to solve our problem.

The class average can be neatly computed by the flowchart and program segment in Fig. 6-2. (Compare with Fig. 4-17.) However, there is no way to compare any of the scores to the class average since the scores were not placed in memory. Thus, the number of students who scored below the class average cannot be found.

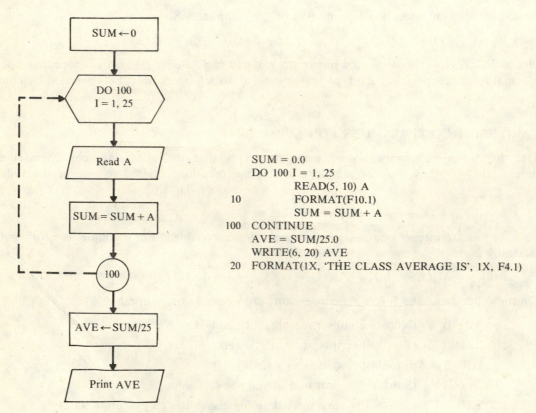

```
           SUM = 0.0
           DO 100 I = 1, 25
                   READ(5, 10) A
     10            FORMAT(F10.1)
                   SUM = SUM + A
    100    CONTINUE
           AVE = SUM/25.0
           WRITE(6, 20) AVE
     20    FORMAT(1X, 'THE CLASS AVERAGE IS', 1X, F4.1)
```

Fig. 6-2

The use of subscripted variables is absolutely necessary if we want to use the above scheme and still be able to compute the number of students who scored below the class average. Specifically, we store the scores in a linear array named SCORE with 25 elements. The flowchart and its Fortran equivalent appear in Fig. 6-3.

Remark. The first WRITE statement in Fig. 6-3 serves two purposes. Besides printing out the scores, it also serves as a check to see if the array SCORE has been read in correctly. This is called an *echo-check*. We note that echo-check is a very helpful tool often used in *debugging*, i.e., finding errors in the program. For complex programs, one often inserts many intermediate WRITE statements showing intermediate results. Errors then can be easily located and identified. After all the *bugs* (errors) are out, one then removes these WRITE statements. (Although the first READ and WRITE statements appear in their own DO loop, it is clear that they could have been combined with the second DO loop into a single loop.)

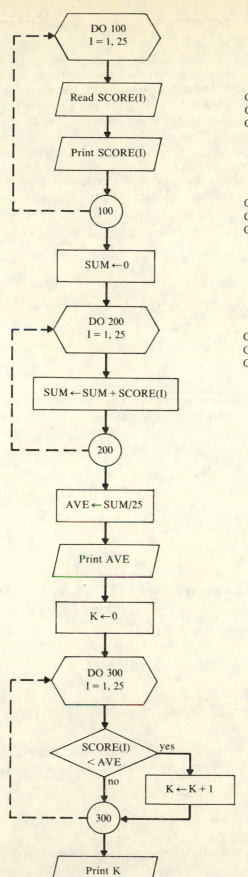

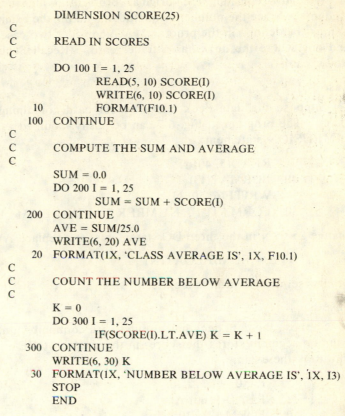

```
          DIMENSION SCORE(25)
C
C         READ IN SCORES
C
          DO 100 I = 1, 25
                READ(5, 10) SCORE(I)
                WRITE(6, 10) SCORE(I)
   10           FORMAT(F10.1)
  100     CONTINUE
C
C         COMPUTE THE SUM AND AVERAGE
C
          SUM = 0.0
          DO 200 I = 1, 25
                SUM = SUM + SCORE(I)
  200     CONTINUE
          AVE = SUM/25.0
          WRITE(6, 20) AVE
   20     FORMAT(1X, 'CLASS AVERAGE IS', 1X, F10.1)
C
C         COUNT THE NUMBER BELOW AVERAGE
C
          K = 0
          DO 300 I = 1, 25
                IF(SCORE(I).LT.AVE) K = K + 1
  300     CONTINUE
          WRITE(6, 30) K
   30     FORMAT(1X, 'NUMBER BELOW AVERAGE IS', 1X, I3)
          STOP
          END
```

Fig. 6-3

We now consider the original problem, which was for a class of no more than 25 students. Since the number N of students taking the exam is needed to compute the class average, N must be defined in the program. We consider two cases, one where the deck has a header card and one where the deck has a trailer card. (Recall Section 4.11 for a discussion of header and trailer cards.)

Case A

Suppose the data deck has a header card containing the number N of students taking the exam. The program in Fig. 6-3 can be easily modified as follows: Insert the following after the DIMENSION statement:

```
      READ(5, 40) N
   40 FORMAT(I3)
      WRITE(6, 50) N
   50 FORMAT('1', 'NUMBER TAKING EXAM IS', 1X, I3)
```

change 25 to N in the three DO statements, and replace AVE = SUM/25.0 by

AVE = SUM/FLOAT(N)

Otherwise, the program is identical.

Case B

Suppose the data deck has a trailer card containing a negative number. The following Fortran program segment stores the scores in the array SCORE and also counts the number N of students who took the exam:

```
        I = 0
   111  READ(5, 60) A
    60  FORMAT(F10.1)
        IF(A.LT.0.0) GO TO 222
        I = I + 1
        SCORE(I) = A
        GO TO 111
   222  N = I
```

This can also be done by the use of a DO loop. We let the index range from 1 to 26 as there could be 25 scores and the trailer card:

```
        DO 500 I = 1, 26
           READ(5, 60) A
    60     FORMAT(F10.1)
           IF(A.LT.0.0) GO TO 222
           SCORE(I) = A
   500  CONTINUE
   222  N = I - 1
```

Observe here that $N = I - 1$ since the index I also counts the trailer card. As there are at most 25 students, there will always be an abnormal exit from the DO loop. Accordingly, the value of I is always defined in statement 222.

We next consider other examples involving arrays.

EXAMPLE 6.1

Suppose A(1), A(2), ..., A(N) are in memory and $N \geq 2$. We wish to find the largest number in the array A.

(a) One method is to find the current value of the largest number as one goes through the array (as discussed in Section 4.10).

```
           XLAR = A(1)
           DO 100 I = 2, N
                    IF(A(I).LE.XLAR) GO TO 100
                    XLAR = A(I)
      100  CONTINUE
```

(*b*) A second method, which will be useful in sorting data, is to find the location L of the largest value, and then A(L) will be the largest value. The algorithm is similar to the one above except now we *remember* the location L of the current largest number rather than the number itself.

```
           L = 1
           DO 200 I = 2, N
                    IF(A(I).LE.A(L)) GO TO 200
                    L = I
      200  CONTINUE
           XLAR = A(L)
```

In the case that we do not know that $N \geq 2$ (i.e., N may equal 1), then the DO statement should be changed so that the index I runs from 1 to N. (Can the reader explain the difference?)

EXAMPLE 6.2

Suppose $A(1), A(2), \ldots, A(N)$ are in memory. Use a DO loop to print $A(N), A(N-1), \ldots, A(2), A(1)$, one per line. [See Example 5.5(*c*).]

As discussed before, the increment of an unstructured DO loop cannot be negative; hence, the following program is not valid:

```
           DO 300 I = N, 1, -1
                    WRITE(6, 10) A(I)
       10           FORMAT(10X, F10.1)
      300  CONTINUE
```

However, as the index I varies from 1 to N, we wish to print $A(N), \ldots, A(1)$. That is, we have:

Value of index I	Element to be printed
1	A(N)
2	A(N − 1)
3	A(N − 2)
...	...
N	A(1)

There is a definite relationship between the index I and the subscript of A; namely, their sum is always $N + 1$. Thus, the following program will print the elements of A in reverse order as required:

```
           DO 300 I = 1, N
                    K = N + 1 - I
                    WRITE(6, 10) A(K)
       10           FORMAT(10X, F10.1)
      300  CONTINUE
```

6.6 MULTIDIMENSIONAL ARRAYS

The linear (one-dimensional) arrays discussed so far have exactly one subscript. Fortran also allows arrays with two and three subscripts. These are called *two-dimensional* and *three-dimensional arrays*, respectively. In fact, some larger computers allow up to seven subscripts. In this section, we shall discuss these multidimensional arrays.

Mathematically speaking, a *matrix* is defined as *a rectangular array of numbers*.   For example,

$$\begin{array}{l} \text{1st row} \\ \text{2nd row} \\ \text{3rd row} \end{array} \begin{pmatrix} a_{11} & a_{12} & a_{13} & a_{14} \\ a_{21} & a_{22} & a_{23} & a_{24} \\ a_{31} & a_{32} & a_{33} & a_{34} \end{pmatrix}$$

$$\begin{array}{cccc} \text{1st} & \text{2nd} & \text{3rd} & \text{4th} \\ \text{col.} & \text{col.} & \text{col.} & \text{col.} \end{array}$$

is a 3 by 4 matrix, i.e., a matrix with three rows (horizontal lines of numbers) and four columns (vertical lines of numbers).   Each element in the matrix is identified by two integers, its subscripts.   The first subscript tells the *row position* of the element, and the second subscript its *column position*.   For example, a_{21} appears in the second row, first column; a_{32} appears in the third row, second column, and so on.   One usually writes 3×4 for "3 by 4".

Analogously, in Fortran a two-dimensional $m \times n$ array is a list of $m \cdot n$ memory cells (elements of the array) in which a particular element is determined by a pair of integers K, L, where $1 \le K \le m$ and $1 \le L \le n$.   The integers K, L are called the *subscripts* of the element; the first subscript K is called the *row* and the second subscript L the *column* of the element.   (Such two-dimensional arrays will also be called *matrix arrays*.)

For example, suppose A is the name of a two-dimensional 3×4 array.   Then A has $3 \cdot 4 = 12$ elements

$$A(1, 1), A(1, 2), A(1, 3), A(1, 4), A(2, 1), A(2, 2), A(2, 3), \dots, A(3, 3), A(3, 4)$$

Observe that each element is designated by the array name followed by its pair of subscripts separated by a comma and enclosed in parentheses.   Although A is usually pictured as a rectangular array as in Fig. 6-4(a), it will actually be represented internally in the computer as a string of 12 memory cells as in Fig. 6-4(b).   Observe that the elements are stored columnwise, so that the first (row) subscript varies first and then the second (column) subscript varies.   This storage order is indicated by arrows as in Fig. 6-4(a).

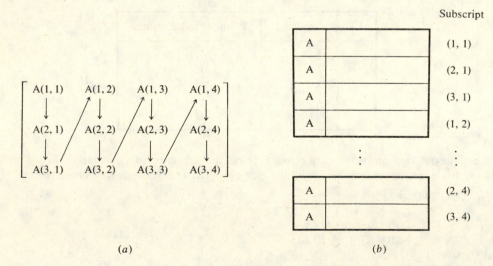

$$(a) \qquad\qquad\qquad\qquad (b)$$

Fig. 6-4

Similarly, a three-dimensional $m \times r \times s$ array is a list of $m \cdot r \cdot s$ memory cells (elements of the array) in which a particular element is determined by three integers J, K, and L (the subscripts), where

$$1 \le J \le m, \qquad 1 \le K \le r, \qquad 1 \le L \le s$$

For example, suppose B is a three-dimensional $2 \times 4 \times 3$ array. Then B has $2 \cdot 4 \cdot 3 = 24$ elements, which appear in Fig. 6-5. Observe that B is pictured as composed of three layers (pages) of 2×4 matrices. We call the first subscript the *row*, the second subscript the *column*, and the third subscript the *page* of the element; for example, B(1, 4, 2) is the element in the first row, fourth column, and second page of B. However, internally B is represented as a string of 24 memory cells listed so that the first subscript varies first (most rapidly), the second subscript second, and so on, as in Fig. 6-6. That is, the elements are listed columnwise from the first page, then columnwise from the second page, and then columnwise from the third page. This storage order is indicated by the arrows in Fig. 6-5.

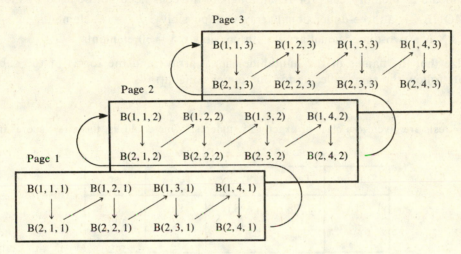

Fig. 6-5

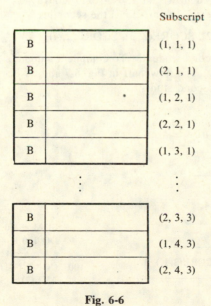

Fig. 6-6

Generally speaking, a p-dimensional $n_1 \times n_2 \times \cdots \times n_p$ array is a list of $n_1 \cdot n_2 \cdot \ldots \cdot n_p$ memory cells (elements of the array) in which a particular element is determined by p integers $K_1, K_2, \ldots K_p$ (the *subscripts*), where

$$1 \leq K_1 \leq n_1, \ 1 \leq K_2 \leq n_2, \ \ldots, \ 1 \leq K_p \leq n_p$$

A particular element is designated by the array name followed by its p subscripts separated by commas and enclosed in parentheses.

Multidimensional arrays must be declared the same way as one-dimensional arrays. For example,

DIMENSION ID(25), MONEY(3, 2, 7), TAX(6, 5)

would inform the compiler that:

1. ID is a one-dimensional array with possibly 25 elements (i.e., the compiler would allocate 25 memory cells for ID although all the cells need not be used by the program);
2. MONEY is a three-dimensional array with possibly $3 \cdot 2 \cdot 7 = 42$ elements;
3. TAX is a two-dimensional array with possibly $6 \cdot 5 = 30$ elements.

We emphasize that the names of the multidimensional arrays and the forms of the subscripts of their elements follow the same rules as for one-dimensional arrays.

EXAMPLE 6.3

Suppose 4 tests are given to a class of exactly 25 students. One could list these test scores in a table as follows:

Student	Test 1	Test 2	Test 3	Test 4
1	78	83	80	87
2	100	100	92	100
⋮	⋮	⋮	⋮	⋮

Suppose these test scores are stored in a real 25×4 matrix array SCORE. That is, SCORE(I, K) gives the Ith student's score on the Kth test. In particular, the second row

SCORE(2, 1), SCORE(2, 2), SCORE(2, 3), SCORE(2, 4)

gives the four test scores for the second student. To compile a student's average, we will let AVE(I) denote the test average for the Ith student. The flowchart in Fig. 6-7 and its Fortran equivalent can be used to find AVE(2), the average grade for the second student.

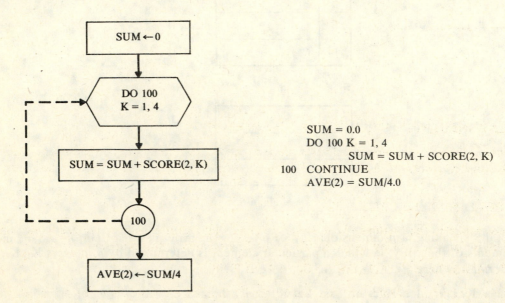

```
        SUM = 0.0
        DO 100 K = 1, 4
              SUM = SUM + SCORE(2, K)
100     CONTINUE
        AVE(2) = SUM/4.0
```

Fig. 6-7

More generally, we can find AVE(I), the test average for the Ith student, by the Fortran segment:

        SUM = 0.0
        DO 100 K = 1, 4
                SUM = SUM + SCORE(I, K)
    100 CONTINUE
        AVE(I) = SUM/4.0

Therefore, to calculate the average for each of the 25 students, we would need a nested DO loop where the outer DO loop runs through each of the 25 students. The flowchart and its Fortran equivalent appear in Fig. 6-8.

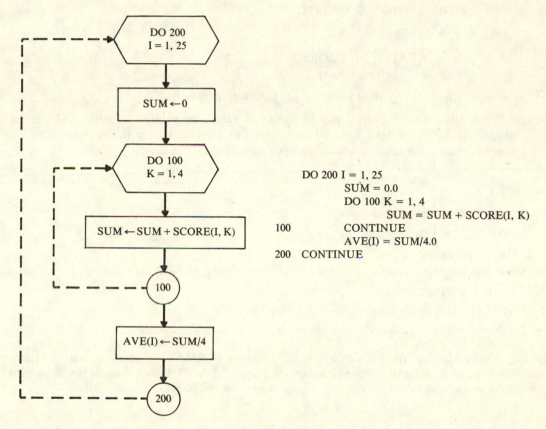

        DO 200 I = 1, 25
                SUM = 0.0
                DO 100 K = 1, 4
                        SUM = SUM + SCORE(I, K)
    100   CONTINUE
                AVE(I) = SUM/4.0
    200 CONTINUE

Fig. 6-8

6.7 ARRAY INPUT/OUTPUT, IMPLIED DO LOOPS

Suppose A and B are linear arrays with four and three elements, respectively. As noted previously, the elements of A and B can appear in I/O statements as ordinary variables. For example,

        READ(5, 10) A(3), B(2), J, X

tells the computer to read values for A(3) and B(2) as well as for J and X. In particular, one can input the entire arrays A, B by listing all the individual elements, for example,

        READ(5, 20) A(1), A(2), A(3), A(4), B(1), B(2), B(3)

Clearly this technique would not be adequate if there were hundreds of elements in the arrays. We shall now discuss other methods for the input/output of arrays.

(*a*) Array Names in I/O Statements

We may read in or print out an *entire* array by using only the array name in an input/output statement.   For example, the above READ statement can be equivalently rewritten as:

READ(5, 20) A, B

However, one must understand clearly the actions resulting from such an I/O instruction:

1. The entire array will be stored or printed; i.e., each and every memory location allocated by the DIMENSION statement will be assigned a value.   Accordingly, if SCORE has been declared an array by

DIMENSION SCORE(35)

then one should not use

READ(5, 30) SCORE
30 FORMAT(5F10.1)

if one only wants to read in 25 values into SCORE.

2. The elements of the array will be assigned values or printed according to the storage order of the array (cf. Figs. 6-1, 6-4, and 6-6), that is, where the first subscript varies most rapidly, the second subscript next, and so on.

EXAMPLE 6.4

Suppose C, D, E are arrays declared by:

DIMENSION C(3), D(2, 3, 2), E(3, 2)

Then the WRITE-FORMAT pair

WRITE(6, 30) C, D, E
30 FORMAT(6X, 4F10.2)

instructs the computer to print a total of

$$3 + 2 \cdot 3 \cdot 2 + 3 \cdot 2 = 21$$

values; 3 from the array C, 12 from D, and 6 from E.   Since the FORMAT statement has only four numerical field specifications, four numbers will be printed on each line, and the FORMAT statement will be used over and over again until all the values are printed.   Thus, the output will appear as in Fig. 6-9.

$C(1)$	$C(2)$	$C(3)$	$D(1, 1, 1)$
$D(2, 1, 1)$	$D(1, 2, 1)$	$D(2, 2, 1)$	$D(1, 3, 1)$
$D(2, 3, 1)$	$D(1, 1, 2)$	$D(2, 1, 2)$	$D(1, 2, 2)$
$D(2, 2, 2)$	$D(1, 3, 2)$	$D(2, 3, 2)$	$E(1, 1)$
$E(2, 1)$	$E(3, 1)$	$E(1, 2)$	$E(2, 2)$
$E(3, 2)$			

Fig. 6-9

We note that if a different FORMAT statement is used in the above example, say

30 FORMAT(6X, 6F10.2)

then the output will contain six numbers on a line.   However, the order of the numbers is not changed by the different FORMAT statement.

(*b*) Implied DO loops

Suppose we want only to store or print part of an array, or suppose we do not want to store or print an array in its prescribed storage order.   One could possibly do this using a DO loop.   For example, suppose AMOUNT is a linear array with possibly 100 elements.   Then the DO loop

```
        DO 100 I = 11, N, 1
              READ(5, 10) AMOUNT(I)
   100   CONTINUE
```

tells the computer to read in values for AMOUNT(11), AMOUNT(12), up to and including AMOUNT(N), where N is previously defined and N ≤ 100.   We can accomplish the same thing by the READ statement

        READ(5, 20) (AMOUNT(I), I = 11, N, 1)

The expression

        (AMOUNT(I), I = 11, N, 1)

is called an *implied DO loop* since it causes a looping action to take place within the READ statement.   The notation

        I = 11, N, 1

has the same meaning here as it has in the DO loop; that is, 11 is the initial value of I, N is the test value, and 1 is the increment.

We note that the implied DO loop is much more versatile than the DO loop.   Specifically, each time the READ statement is encountered in the above DO loop, another data card must be read regardless of how the FORMAT statement labeled 10 is specified.   Accordingly, the input values must each be put on a separate card.   On the other hand, in the implied DO loop, only one READ statement is encountered, so that the input can be put on one or more cards depending on the FORMAT statement.

The general form of an implied DO loop of an I/O statement follows:

        (VN(I), I = IN, IE, IC)

Here:

VN	Array name	IE	End or test value of I
I	Index	IC	Increment
IN	Initial value of I		

We note that each of IN, IE, and IC can be a positive integer constant or an integer variable.   Also, if 1 is used for IC, then it can be omitted.   We emphasize that the outer parentheses and the comma before the index are absolutely necessary when using the implied DO loop.

The index I may be used to control more than one array.   For example,

        READ(5, 30) (A(K), B(3, K), C(K, K, 2), K = 2, 9, 3)

tells the computer to cycle through the variable list first with K = 2, then K = 5, and lastly K = 8.   Hence, the READ statement is equivalent to

        READ(5, 30) A(2), B(3, 2), C(2, 2, 2), A(5), B(3, 5), C(5, 5, 2),
      1   A(8), B(3, 8), C(8, 8, 2)

In general, the variables in an implied DO loop need not be subscripted nor involve the counter.

EXAMPLE 6.5

(*a*)   Suppose X is a linear array with 100 elements already stored in memory.   We can output the array one item a line by:

```
        DO 100 I = 1, 100              or        WRITE(5, 20) (X(I), I = 1, 100)
            WRITE(5, 10) X(I)               20    FORMAT(2X, F8.2)
  10            FORMAT(2X, F8.2)
 100    CONTINUE
```

We can output the array four items a line by

```
        DO 100 I = 1, 100, 4
            WRITE(5, 10) X(I), X(I + 1), X(I + 2), X(I + 3)
  10            FORMAT(4(2X, F8.2))
 100    CONTINUE
```

or

```
        WRITE(5, 20) (X(I), I = 1, 100)
  20    FORMAT(4(2X, F8.2))
```

Thus, we see the versatility of the implied DO loop over the DO loop for I/O operations.

(*b*)   Consider the WRITE-FORMAT pair:

```
        WRITE(6, 40) (A(I), B, X(3), Y(I, I), I = 1, 8, 3)
  40    FORMAT(6(2X, F8.2))
```

The DO loop inside the WRITE statement is executed three times, first with $I = 1$, then $I = 4$, and finally with $I = 7$.   Hence, the WRITE statement is equivalent to:

```
        WRITE(6, 40) A(1), B, X(3), Y(1, 1), A(4), B, X(3),
  1                  Y(4, 4), A(7), B, X(3), Y(7, 7)
```

Observe that B and X(3) appear three times.   The FORMAT statement will cause the numbers to be printed six to a line, so that the output appears as follows:

```
    A(1)        B           X(3)        Y(1, 1)     A(4)        B
    X(3)        Y(4, 4)     A(7)        B           X(3)        Y(7, 7)
```

(*c*)   The program segment

```
        WRITE(6, 50) (I, X(I), I = 1, 3)
  50    FORMAT(1X, 'A(', I1, ') = ', F10.2)
```

will print

```
        A(1) = XXXXXXX.XX
        A(2) = XXXXXXX.XX
        A(3) = XXXXXXX.XX
```

(*c*)   Nested Implied DO loops

The implied DO loop described above can be generalized to control multidimensional arrays.   (This generalization is analogous to nested DO loops.)   Suppose, for example, that F has been declared a 3×2 array and the program contains the statement

```
        READ(5, 10) ((F(I, J), J = 1, 2), I = 1, 3)
```

The outside index I is analogous to the index of an outer DO loop, and the inside index J is analogous to the index of an inner DO loop.   That is, the inner implied DO loop is executed for each value of the index of the outer implied DO loop.   Thus, the READ statement is equivalent to

```
        READ(5, 10) (F(1, J), J = 1, 2), (F(2, J), J = 1, 2), (F(3, J), J = 1, 2)
```

which is equivalent to

```
        READ(5, 10) F(1, 1), F(1, 2), F(2, 1), F(2, 2), F(3, 1), F(3, 2)
```

Observe that the above READ statement reads values into F row by row.   On the other hand, the statement

$$\text{READ}(5, 20)\ ((F(I, J), I = 1, 3), J = 1, 2)$$

(where the indices I and J have been interchanged) is equivalent to

$$\text{READ}(5, 20)\ F(1, 1), F(2, 1), F(3, 1), F(1, 2), F(2, 2), F(3, 2)$$

and, in this case, values are read into F columnwise.

Nested implied DO loops can have more complex combinations and can also appear in WRITE statements.

EXAMPLE 6.6

(a)   Consider the statement

$$\text{WRITE}(6, 11)\ ((B(L, M), L = 2, 10, 2), M = 1, 11, 3)$$

First the inner DO loop $(B(L, M), L = 2, 10, 2)$ is executed with $M = 1$, then $M = 4$, then $M = 7$, and lastly $M = 10$.   Thus, the statement is equivalent to

$$\text{WRITE}(6, 11)\ (B(L, 1), L = 2, 10, 2), (B(L, 4), L = 2, 10, 2),$$
$$1 \qquad\qquad\quad (B(L, 7), L = 2, 10, 2), (B(L, 10), L = 2, 10, 2)$$

which is equivalent to

$$\text{WRITE}(6, 11)\ B(2, 1), B(4, 1), B(6, 1), B(8, 1), B(10, 1), B(2, 4), B(4, 4),$$
$$1 \qquad\qquad B(6, 4), B(8, 4), B(10, 4), B(2, 7), B(4, 7), B(6, 7), B(8, 7),$$
$$1 \qquad\qquad B(10, 7), B(2, 10), B(4, 10), B(6, 10), B(8, 10), B(10, 10)$$

Observe that the second subscript M in $B(L, M)$ appears in the outer DO loop, whereas the first subscript I in $F(I, J)$ appears in the outer DO loop in the preceding example.

(b)   Suppose B is a $4 \times 5 \times 3$ array, and suppose we want to print the values of B rowwise from the first page, then rowwise from the second page, and lastly rowwise from the third page.   This can be done with the WRITE-FORMAT pair:

$$\text{WRITE}(6, 50)\ (((B(K1, K2, K3), K2 = 1, 5), K1 = 1, 4), K3 = 1, 3)$$
$$50 \quad \text{FORMAT}(5(2X, F8.2))$$

In fact, the FORMAT statement will only allow five numbers to be printed on a line, so that the different rows of B will appear on different rows on the print page.

6.8   PROGRAMMING TECHNIQUE EXAMPLE

Given any problem, there may be many different ways (algorithms) to formulate and solve the problem.   Some are better than others; i.e., some may require less memory and/or less operations.   Chapter 8 is devoted to various programming techniques.   Here, we consider a simple problem which will illustrate the subtleties that can arise in its solution.

Suppose we want to move the elements $A(1), A(2), \ldots, A(N)$ in an array down the list by one position:

$$A(1) \quad A(2) \quad A(3) \quad \ldots \quad A(N - 1) \quad A(N)$$

that is, so that $A(2)$ contains the old $A(1)$, $A(3)$ contains the old $A(2)$, and so on.

The intuitive thing to do is to first assign $A(1)$ to $A(2)$, then $A(2)$ to $A(3)$, and so on until we assign $A(N)$ to $A(N + 1)$.   This could be done by the DO loop

$$\text{DO } 100\ I = 1, N$$
$$A(I + 1) = A(I)$$
$$100 \quad \text{CONTINUE}$$

However, this procedure *will not work*. The reason is that the first assignment of A(1) to A(2) erased the original value of A(2), so that the subsequent assignment of A(2) to A(3) will store the original value of A(1) in A(3). In fact, by the above procedure the original value of A(1) will be assigned to all the locations A(2), A(3), . . . , A(N + 1).

One way to correct the above procedure is to temporarily save the original values of A in other locations. This can be done by using another array, say B. Specifically, we use a DO loop to assign A(I) to B(I + 1), and then another DO loop to transfer the elements back to A by assigning B(I + 1) to A(I + 1). However, this means we have to use twice as many memory cells as in A just to move the elements of A down one position; i.e., if A contained 1000 memory cells, then we would need another 1000 memory cells for B.

Another way requires only two additional memory cells. Namely, we first save A(2) in a temporary location, TEMPA, before assigning A(1) to A(2), and then we save A(3) in a temporary storage location, TEMPB, before assigning TEMPA to A(3):

$$\begin{aligned}
\text{TEMPA} &\leftarrow \text{A(2)} \\
\text{A(2)} &\leftarrow \text{A(1)} \\
\text{TEMPB} &\leftarrow \text{A(3)} \\
\text{A(3)} &\leftarrow \text{TEMPA}
\end{aligned}$$

Observe that A(3) now contains the original A(2). We then use TEMPA again to save A(4) before assigning TEMPB to A(4), and so on. The above can be accomplished by a DO loop. Although only two additional memory cells are used, the algorithm does require $2N - 1$ assignments.

Actually, the best way requires no extra memory and only N assignments. First, one simply moves A(N) to A(N + 1), then A(N − 1) to A(N), and so on. That is, we give the following sequence of instructions

$$\begin{aligned}
\text{A(N + 1)} &\leftarrow \text{A(N)} \\
\text{A(N)} &\leftarrow \text{A(N − 1)} \\
&\;\;\vdots \\
\text{A(2)} &\leftarrow \text{A(1)}
\end{aligned}$$

The Fortran equivalent is given below:

```
        DO 100 J = 1, N          or simply      DO 100 J = 1, N
            K = N + 1 − J                            A(N − J + 2) = A(N − J + 1)
            A(K + 1) = A(K)              100   CONTINUE
    100 CONTINUE
```

(See Example 6.2 for the reason that the new variable K is introduced.)

Solved Problems

ARRAYS

6.1   Determine the number of elements in arrays A, B, and K according to the DIMENSION statement

        DIMENSION A(25), B(3, 8, 4), K(7, 5)

A has 25 elements.
B has $3 \cdot 8 \cdot 4 = 96$ elements.
C has $7 \cdot 5 = 35$ elements.

6.2   Find the number of elements in an array X defined by:

$$\text{DIMENSION } X(2, 4, 3)$$

Describe the output if the following pair is executed:

WRITE(6, 10) X
10   FORMAT(6(2X, F12.2))

X has $2\cdot4\cdot3 = 24$ elements.   They will be printed in their storage order, i.e., so that the first (row) subscript varies most rapidly, the second (column) subscript next, and the third (page) subscript last.   Also, there will be six numbers to a line.   Thus, the output will appear as follows:

X(1, 1, 1)	X(2, 1, 1)	X(1, 2, 1)	X(2, 2, 1)	X(1, 3, 1)	X(2, 3, 1)
X(1, 4, 1)	X(2, 4, 1)	X(1, 1, 2)	X(2, 1, 2)	X(1, 2, 2)	X(2, 2, 2)
X(1, 3, 2)	X(2, 3, 2)	X(1, 4, 2)	X(2, 4, 2)	X(1, 1, 3)	X(2, 1, 3)
X(1, 2, 3)	X(2, 2, 3)	X(1, 3, 3)	X(2, 3, 3)	X(1, 4, 3)	X(2, 4, 3)

6.3   Suppose N and a linear array A with N elements are in memory.   Write a Fortran program segment which:

(*a*)   Calculates the sum of the squares:

$$\text{SUM} = A_1^2 + A_2^2 + \cdots + A_n^2$$

(*b*)   Calculates the product

$$\text{PROD} = (1 - A_1)(1 - A_2)\ldots(1 - A_N)$$

(*a*)   First set SUM = 0.0 before performing the summation:

```
      SUM = 0.0
      DO 100 K = 1, N
          SUM = SUM + A(K)**2
100   CONTINUE
```

(*b*)   First set PROD = 1.0 before performing the multiplication.   (This is analogous to setting SUM = 0.0 in (*a*).)

```
      PROD = 1.0
      DO 100 K = 1, N
          PROD = PROD*(1.0 − A(K))
100   CONTINUE
```

6.4   Find the output in the following program:

```
      INTEGER A(10)
      DO 100 I = 1, 10, 2
          A(I) = 2*I − 3
          A(I + 1) = I**2 − 5
100   CONTINUE
      DO 200 I = 2, 10, 3
          A(I) = A(I + 2) − A(I)
200   CONTINUE
      WRITE(6, 10) A
10    FORMAT(1X, 5I8)
      STOP
      END
```

The first statement declares A to be an integer linear array with 10 elements.   The first DO loop is executed:

(*i*)   First for I = 1.   This yields A(I) = −1 and A(2) = −4.
(*ii*)   Then for I = 3.   This yields A(3) = 3 and A(4) = 4.
(*iii*) Then for I = 5.   This yields A(5) = 7 and A(6) = 20.
(*iv*)   Then for I = 7.   This yields A(7) = 11 and A(8) = 44.
(*v*)   Lastly for I = 9.   This yields A(9) = 15 and A(10) = 76.

The second DO loop is executed:

(*i*)   First for I = 2.   This changes the value of A(2) as follows:

$$A(2) \leftarrow A(4) - A(2) = 4 - (-4) = 8$$

(*ii*)   Then for I = 5.   This changes the value of A(5) as follows:

$$A(5) \leftarrow A(7) - A(5) = 11 - 7 = 4$$

(*iii*) Lastly for I = 8.   This changes the value of A(8) as follows:

$$A(8) \leftarrow A(10) - A(8) = 76 - 44 = 32$$

The WRITE-FORMAT pair prints the values of A with five integers on a line in fields with width 8.   Hence, the output will appear as follows:

```
    −1      8      3      4      4
    20     11     32     15     76
```

6.5   Suppose N and a linear array A with N elements are in memory locations.   Write a Fortran program segment which:

(*a*)   Interchanges the values of A_1 and A_2, interchanges the values of A_3 and A_4, and so on.   (Here we assume that N is even.)

(*b*)   Cyclically permutes the values of A so that A_1 contains the original value of A_2, A_2 contains the original value of A_3, and so on, with A_N containing the original value of A_1.

(*a*)   Recall first that we interchange the values of variables X and Y by using a temporary storage location T as follows:

$$T = X$$
$$X = Y$$
$$Y = T$$

Thus, we have the program segment:

```
        DO 100 K = 1, N, 2
            T = A(K)
            A(K) = A(K + 1)
            A(K + 1) = T
100     CONTINUE
```

(*b*)   First, we temporarily store A_1 in T; then, we let $A_1 = A_2$, $A_2 = A_3, \ldots, A_{N-1} = A_N$; and then finally, let $A_N = T$.   Thus, we have:

```
        T = A(1)
        NN = N − 1
        DO 100 K = 1, NN
            A(K) = A(K + 1)
100     CONTINUE
        A(N) = T
```

Observe again that we use the statement NN = N − 1 since we cannot use N − 1 as a parameter.

PROGRAMS

6.6   Consider a set of numbers $x_1, x_2, \ldots, x_n$. The arithmetic mean $\bar{x}$, the variance, and the standard deviation σ are defined by:

$$\bar{x} = (x_1 + x_2 + \cdots + x_n)/n = \left(\sum_{k=1}^{n} x_k\right)\Big/ n$$

$$\text{variance} = \frac{\sum_{k=1}^{n} (x_k - \bar{x})^2}{n}$$

$$\sigma = \sqrt{\text{variance}}$$

Suppose N numbers are stored in a linear array A. Write a Fortran program segment which will store the mean, variance, and standard deviation of the numbers in AVE, VAR, and SD respectively. (Compare with Problem 5.9 where the second formula for variance had to be used.)

The program segment follows:

```
            SUM1 = 0.0
            DO 100 K = 1, N
                  SUM1 = SUM1 + A(K)
      100   CONTINUE
            AVE = SUM1/FLOAT(N)
            SUM2 = 0.0
            DO 200 K = 1, N
                  SUM2 = SUM2 + (A(K) − AVE)**2
      200   CONTINUE
            VAR = SUM2/FLOAT(N)
            SD = SQRT(VAR)
```

6.7   A department store chain has 6 stores, and each store has the same 10 departments. The weekly sales of the chain are stored in a 6 × 10 array SALES. [Here SALES(I, J) denotes the weekly sales in the Ith store in the Jth department.] Write a Fortran program segment which:

(a) Prints the total weekly sales of each store.
(b) Prints the total weekly sales of each department.
(c) Prints the total weekly sales of the chain.

We assume that STORE and DEPT have been declared linear arrays by

        DIMENSION STORE(6), DEPT(10)

(a) We sum up the sales for a given I, after initially setting STORE(I) = 0.

```
            WRITE(6, 10)
      10    FORMAT('1', 5X, 'STORE', 5X, 'SALES'//)
            DO 99 I = 1, 6
                  STORE(I) = 0.0
                  DO 88 J = 1, 10
                        STORE(I) = STORE(I) + SALES(I, J)
      88          CONTINUE
                  WRITE(6, 20) I, STORE(I)
      20          FORMAT(6X, I3, 5X, F9.2)
      99    CONTINUE
```

(*b*)   We sum up the sales for a given J after initially setting DEPT(J) = 0.

```
            WRITE(6, 30)
     30     FORMAT('0', 2X, 'DEPARTMENT', 3X, 'SALES'//)
            DO 77 J = 1, 10
                  DEPT(J) = 0.0
                  DO 66 I = 1, 6
                        DEPT(J) = DEPT(J) + SALES(I, J)
     66           CONTINUE
                  WRITE(6, 40) J, DEPT(J)
     40           FORMAT(3X, I5, 5X, F9.2)
     77     CONTINUE
```

(*c*)   We can sum up the values stored in the array SALES, or in STORE, or in DEPT (or in each of the three for a check of the results). We do it for the array STORE.

```
            CHAIN = 0.0
            DO 55 K = 1, 6
                  CHAIN = CHAIN + STORE(K)
     55     CONTINUE
            WRITE(6, 50) CHAIN
     50     FORMAT('0', 'TOTAL WEEKLY SALES'/6X, F9.2)
```

6.8   Print the first 50 terms of the Fibonacci sequence so that there are five numbers on a line.

Recall that the Fibonacci sequence is

$$1, 1, 2, 3, 5, 8, 13, 21, \ldots$$

that is, the first two terms are 1, and each other term is obtained by adding the two preceding terms:

$$2 = 1 + 1, \quad 3 = 1 + 2, \quad 5 = 2 + 3, \quad 8 = 3 + 5, \ldots$$

Thus, we let

$$J(1) = 1, \quad J(2) = 1, \quad \text{and} \quad J(I) = J(I - 2) + J(I - 1)$$

for $I > 2$. The program follows:

```
            DIMENSION J(50)
            J(1) = 1
            J(2) = 1
            DO 100 I = 3, 50
                  J(I) = J(I - 2) + J(I - 1)
    100     CONTINUE
            WRITE(6, 10)
     10     FORMAT('1', 15X, 'FIBONACCI SEQUENCE'//)
            WRITE(6, 20) J
     20     FORMAT(1X, 5(3X, I6))
            STOP
            END
```

Observe that there are only five numerical specifications in the FORMAT statement labeled 20, so that only five numbers are printed on each line.

6.9   (*a*)   Suppose B is a linear array with M elements. Write a program segment to find the location J such that B(J) contains the largest absolute value in B. (See Example 6.1.)

         (*b*)   Suppose A is an M × N matrix array already in memory. Write a Fortran program segment which:

(*i*) finds the position J so that J contains the largest absolute value in the first column, and

(*ii*) interchanges the first row with the Jth row.

(Hence, A(1, 1) will contain the largest absolute value in the first column.)

(*a*) We set J = 1 and BIG = ABS(B(1)) and then compare BIG with the other elements of B. If BIG is less than ABS(B(K)), then we set BIG = ABS(B(K)) and change J to K. The program follows:

```
         J = 1
         BIG = ABS(B(1))
         DO 100 K = 1, M
                IF(BIG.GE.ABS(B(K))) go to 100
                BIG = ABS(B(K))
                J = K
100  CONTINUE
```

The index K is initially set to 1 to take care of the possibility that M may be 1.

(*b*) The program segment has two parts: (*i*) First find J. (*ii*) If J ≠ 1, then interchange the first and Jth rows.

```
C
C        FIND THE POSITION J WITH LARGEST ABSOLUTE VALUE
C
         J = 1
         BIG = ABS(A(1,1))
         DO 100 K = 1, M
                IF(BIG.GE.ABS(A(K,1)))GO TO 100
                BIG = ABS(A(K,1))
                J = K
100  CONTINUE
         IF(J.EQ.1) GO TO 500
C
C        INTERCHANGE THE FIRST AND JTH ROWS
C
         DO 200 L = 1, N
                TEMP = A(1, L)
                A(1, L) = A(J, L)
                A(J, L) = TEMP
200  CONTINUE
500  ********************************************
```

Observe the similarity between the first part of the program segment and part (*a*).

6.10 Write a program segment which inserts an element D in the Kth position of the array A(1), A(2), . . . , A(N).

Before we assign D to A(K), we must move the array segment A(K), A(K + 1), . . . , A(N) down one position. This is done by starting at the end of the array, i.e., by first assigning A(N) to A(N + 1), then A(N − 1) to A(N), and so on until A(K) to A(K + 1). (See Section 6.8.) Observe first that N − K + 1 elements must be moved, not N − K, since we are also moving A(K). We use a DO loop with index J = 1, 2, . . . , N − K + 1. The relationship between the index J and the action follows:

Value of J	Action
1	A(N + 1) ← A(N)
2	A(N) ← A(N − 1)
3	A(N − 1) ← A(N − 2)
...	....
N − K + 1	A(K + 1) ← A(K)

The program segment follows:

```
      NN = N - K + 1                 or simply       NN = N - K + 1
      DO 100 J = 1, NN                               DO 100 J = 1, NN
         L = N - J + 1                                  A(N - J + 2) = A(N - J + 1)
         A(L + 1) = A(L)                         100 CONTINUE
  100 CONTINUE                                       A(K) = D
      A(K) = D
```

6.11 (*Linear Search*) Given an array A(1), A(2), . . . , A(N), and an element D, write a program segment which finds the location L of D when D is in the array, or sets L = 0 when D is not in the array.

Given no other information about the array A, the most intuitive way to solve the problem is to compare D with each of the elements of A; that is, we test if D = A(1), then test if D = A(2), and so on. This method is called *linear search* or *sequential search* since it searches for D by testing it one by one with the elements of A. (Other methods of searching are discussed in Chapter 8.) Clearly it takes at most N comparisons to locate D, and it always takes N comparisons when D is not in the array. Figure 6-10 shows the flowchart for the algorithm and its Fortran translation.

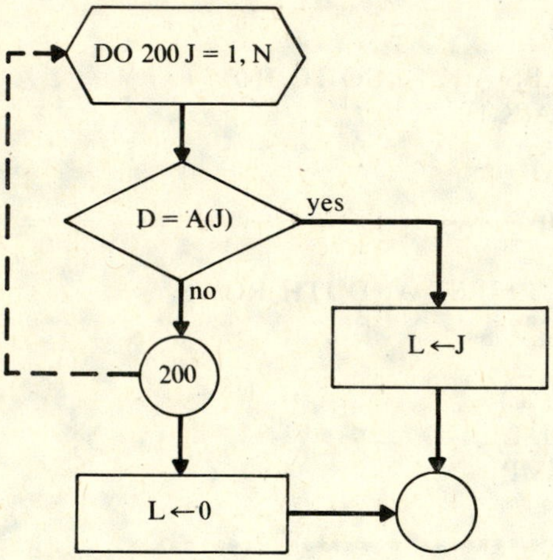


```
      DO 200 J = 1, N
         IF(D.EQ.A(J)) GO TO 300
  200 CONTINUE
      L = 0
      GO TO 400
  300 L = J
  400
       .
       .
       .
```

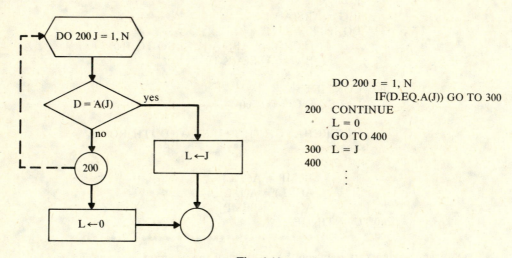

Fig. 6-10

6.12 (*Sorting*) An array is said to be *sorted* if its elements are arranged in some order. Write a program segment which sorts the array A(1), A(2), . . . , A(N) so that its elements are in increasing order.

We sort A by the algorithm known as "Bubble Sort". (Other methods of sorting are discussed in Chapter 8.) We first compare A(1) and A(2) and arrange them in the desired order, i.e., so that A(1) < A(2). Then we compare A(2) and A(3) and arrange them so that A(2) < A(3). Then we compare A(3) and A(4) and arrange them so that A(3) < A(4). This is continued until A(N − 1) < A(N). While "sweeping through" the elements, the largest element is "bubbled up" to the Nth position.

The above process is repeated for the elements A(1), A(2), . . . , A(N − 1). After sweeping through these elements, the second largest element is bubbled up to the N − 1st position, and so on. After N − 1 sweeps, the array A will be sorted in increasing order.

We state the algorithm formally:

Step 1.   For $L = 1, 2, \ldots, N - 1$, compare $A(L)$ with $A(L + 1)$ and order them so that $A(L) < A(L + 1)$.

Step 2.   For $L = 1, 2, \ldots, N - 2$, compare $A(L)$ with $A(L + 1)$ and order them so that $A(L) < A(L + 1)$.

$\vdots$

Step $N - 1$.   For $L = 1$, compare $A(L)$ with $A(L + 1)$ and order them so that $A(L) < A(L + 1)$.

Observe that the action in each step is identical. Hence, we can have a DO loop controlled by an index K with $K = 1, 2, \ldots, N - 1$ (corresponding to the $N - 1$ steps), and within this DO loop we have an inner DO loop with index $L = 1, 2, \ldots, N - K$. Figure 6-11 shows the flowchart for the algorithm and its Fortran translation.

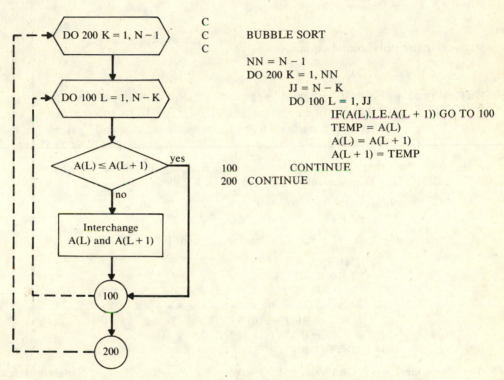

```
C
C        BUBBLE SORT
C
         NN = N - 1
         DO 200 K = 1, NN
            JJ = N - K
            DO 100 L = 1, JJ
               IF(A(L).LE.A(L + 1)) GO TO 100
               TEMP = A(L)
               A(L) = A(L + 1)
               A(L + 1) = TEMP
100         CONTINUE
200      CONTINUE
```

Fig. 6-11

6.13   Write a program which accepts 25 different positive integers, $N_1, N_2, \ldots, N_{25}$, and prints, on separate lines, each pair of the integers which add up to 75. (Remark: If 25 and 50 are two of the integers, then we want 25, 50 printed, or 50, 25 printed, but not both.)

First we compare N_1 with each of $N_2, N_3, \ldots, N_{25}$ to see if

$$N_1 + N_K = 75$$

where $K > 1$. Then we compare N_2 with each of $N_3, N_4, \ldots, N_{25}$ to see if

$$N_2 + N_K = 75$$

where $K > 2$, and so on. In other words, for $J = 1, 2, \ldots, 24$, we check to see if

$$N_J + N_K = 75$$

for $K > J$. This can be done with nested DO loops as follows:

```
            DIMENSION N(25)
            READ(5, 10) N
      10    FORMAT(5I5)
            DO 100 J = 1, 24
                  JJ = J + 1
                  DO 200 K = JJ, 25
                        IF(N(J) + N(K).NE.75) GO TO 200
                        WRITE(6, 20) N(J), N(K)
      20          FORMAT(1X, I5, 3X, I5)
      200         CONTINUE
      100   CONTINUE
            STOP
            END
```

6.14   Consider the polynomial equation

$$y = 2x^4 - 5x^3 + 6x^2 - 8x + 9$$

(a) Write a Fortran program segment which stores and prints y for $x = -10$, $-9, \ldots, 10$, that is, for integer values of x from -10 to 10.

(b) Write a Fortran program segment which stores and prints y for $x = -N$, $-N + 1, \ldots, N$, where N is read is as data.   (Assume $0 < N \le 25$.)

(a) Note that there are 21 values of X. Hence, we use a DO loop with index $K = 1, 2, \ldots, 21$.   The relationship between X and K follows:

```
Value of X:     -10,  -9,  -8,  ...,   9,  10
Value of K:       1,   2,   3,  ...,  20,  21
```

Observe that $X = -11 + K$.   The program segment follows:

```
            DIMENSION Y(21)
            DO 100 K = 1, 21
                  X = -11 + K
                  Y(K) = (((2.*X - 5.)*X + 6.)*X - 8.)*X + 9.
                  WRITE(6, 10) X, Y(K)
      10          FORMAT(1X, F5.1, 2X, F8.1)
      100   CONTINUE
```

(b) Now there are $2N + 1$ values of X.   (Note that $2N + 1 \le 51$ since $N \le 25$.)   Hence, we use a DO loop with index $K = 1, 2, \ldots, 2N + 1$.   Here X and K are related by $X = -N - 1 + K$.

```
            DIMENSION Y(51)
            READ(5, 20) N
      20    FORMAT(I5)
            NN = 2*N + 1
            DO 88 K = 1, NN
                  X = -N - 1 + K
                  Y(K) = (((2.*X - 5.)*X + 6.)*X - 8.)*X + 9.
                  WRITE(6, 30) X, Y(K)
      30          FORMAT(1X, F5.1, 2X, F8.1)
      88    CONTINUE
```

Observe that we used Horner's formula to calculate Y.   (See Section 8.6.)

6.15   (*Frequency Distribution*)   A deck with 200 cards contains one positive integer K per card, where $K \le 25$.   Write a program which prints the positive integers from 1 to 25 and the number of times each of the integers occurs in the deck.

The algorithm we use is as follows.   We declare N to be a linear array with 25 elements, and we let N(K) denote the number of times the value K has appeared.   Specifically, we initially set each $N(K) = 0$, and whenever the value K appears, we increase $N(K)$ by one.   For example, we initially set $N(8) = 0$, and if $K = 8$ occurs 14 times, then $N(8) = 14$ after all the cards are read.   The program follows:

```
              DIMENSION N(25)
       C
       C      SET EACH N(K) = 0
       C
              DO 100 K = 1, 25
                   N(K) = 0
       100    CONTINUE
       C
       C      READ AND COUNT THE NUMBERS
       C
              DO 200 J = 1, 200
                   READ(5, 10) K
         10        FORMAT(I5)
                   N(K) = N(K) + 1
       200    CONTINUE
       C
       C      PRINT THE DISTRIBUTION
       C
              DO 300 K = 1, 25
                   WRITE(6, 20) K, N(K)
         20        FORMAT(6X, 2(I4, 5X))
       300    CONTINUE
              STOP
              END
```

6.16 Consider a linear array A with N elements.   The first difference DA of A is obtained by subtracting each element, except the last, from the next element in the array:

$$DA(K) = A(K + 1) - A(K)$$

(where $K \leq N - 1$).   Note that DA has $N - 1$ elements.   The second difference D2A of A is defined as the first difference of DA, and so on.

Suppose A is in memory.   Write a program segment which finds the first DA, the second D2A, and the third D3A differences of the sequence A:

$$2, 8, -3, 5, 9, -4, 8, 0, -8, 16$$

and then prints A, DA, D2A, and D3A.

The differences can be shown to be:

2	8	−3	5	9	−4	8	0	−8	16
	6	−11	8	4	−13	12	−8	−8	24
		−17	19	−4	−17	25	−20	0	32
			36	−23	−13	42	−45	20	32

That is, the second row of numbers is the first difference, the third row is the second difference, and the last row is the third difference.

The program follows:

```
C
C          FIND THE FIRST DIFFERENCE
C
           N = N − 1
           DO 100 K = 1, N
                DA(K) = A(K + 1) − A(K)
   100  CONTINUE
C
C          FIND THE SECOND DIFFERENCE
C
           N = N − 1
           DO 200 K = 1, N
                D2A(K) = DA(K + 1) − DA(K)
   200  CONTINUE
C
C          FIND THE THIRD DIFFERENCE
C
           N = N − 1
           DO 300 K = 1, N
                D3A(K) = D2A(K + 1) − D2A(K)
   300  CONTINUE
C
C          PRINT OUT THE ARRAYS
C
           WRITE(6, 10) A
           WRITE(6, 10) DA
           WRITE(6, 10) D2A
           WRITE(6, 10) D3A
    10  FORMAT(1X, 10(2X, F8.2))
```

If the arrays DA, D2A, D3A are not needed later in the program, one could use nested DO loops.

IMPLIED DO LOOPS

6.17 Rewrite each implied DO loop statement so there are no errors.

(a) READ(5, 10), (A(K) K = 1, 20)
(b) WRITE(6, 20), A(I, I), S, B(I), I = 1, N, 3
(c) READ(5, 30) (A(J), J = 1, 7), B, (C(K), K = 1, M, L)
(d) WRITE(6, 40) (A(L, K + 3), K = 1, 7), L = 1, 5)

(a) READ(5, 10) (A(K), K = 1, 20)
(b) WRITE(6, 20) ((A(I, I), S, B(I)), I = 1, N, 3)
(c) No errors.
(d) We cannot use K + 3 as a parameter; but, we can write:

```
           KK = K + 3
           WRITE(6, 40) ((A(L, KK), KK = 4, 10), L = 1, 5)
```

6.18 Describe the output if each WRITE-FORMAT pair is executed:

(a)   WRITE(6, 10) (A(K), K = 2, 25, 3)
     10 FORMAT(1X, 5(3X, F10.2))

(b)   WRITE(6, 10) (A(L), B, C(3, L), L = 1, 8, 2)
     10 FORMAT(1X, 5(3X, F10.2))

(c)   WRITE(6, 10) (B(J), J = 1, 4), (B(K), K = 3, 10, 4)
     10 FORMAT(1X, 5(3X, F10.2))

(a) Note that 2 is the initial value of K, 3 the increment, and 25 the limit value.   Hence, A(2), A(5),
     A(8), A(11), A(14), A(17), A(20), and A(23) are printed five numbers to a line.   Therefore, the
     output appears as:

         A(2)   A(5)   A(8)   A(11)   A(14)
         A(17)   A(20)   A(23)

(b) Note the computer executes the implied DO loop first with L = 1, then L = 3, then L = 5, and
     finally L = 7.   Hence, A(1), B, C(3, 1), A(3), B, C(3, 3), A(5), B, C(3, 5), A(7), B, and C(3, 7) are
     printed five numbers to a line:

         A(1)   B   C(3, 1)   A(3)   B
         C(3, 3)   A(5)   B   C(3, 5)   A(7)
         B   C(3, 7)

(c)   B(1)   B(2)   B(3)   B(4)   B(3)
         B(7)

6.19   Describe the output if the following is executed:

        WRITE(6, 20) ((A(J, K), J = 2, 8, 3), K = 1, 4)
     20 FORMAT(IX, 5(3X, F10.2)

The inner implied DO gives: A(2, K), A(5, K), A(8, K).   Thus, for K = 1, 2, 3, 4, there will be a
total of 12 values to be printed five to a line.   Therefore, the output appears as follows:

         A(2, 1)   A(5, 1)   A(8, 1)   A(2, 2)   A(5, 2)
         A(8, 2)   A(2, 3)   A(5, 3)   A(8, 3)   A(2, 4)
         A(5, 4)   A(8, 4)

6.20   An $N \times N$ matrix array A is in memory.   Write a Fortran program segment which prints
the elements of A above the diagonal, i.e., the elements A(I, J) for which $I < J$.

We want to print the elements:

$$A_{12} \quad A_{13} \quad A_{14} \quad \cdots \quad A_{1N}$$
$$A_{23} \quad A_{24} \quad \cdots \quad A_{2N}$$
$$\cdots\cdots\cdots\cdots$$
$$A_{N-1,N}$$

The first subscript I denotes the row of the element and, hence, will vary from 1 to $N - 1$.   The
second subscript J denotes the column and, hence, will vary from $I + 1$ to N.   We cannot use the
nested implied DO loop

        WRITE(6, 10) ((A(I, J), J = I + 1, N), I = 1, N - 1)

since $I + 1$ and $N - 1$ cannot be parameters.   However, we can use a DO loop together with an
implied DO loop:

           NN = N - 1
           DO 100 I = 1, NN
               K = I + 1
               WRITE(6, 10) (A(I, J), J = K, N)
        10   FORMAT(1X, 8(3X, F10.2))
       100 CONTINUE

Supplementary Problems

ARRAYS

6.21   Find errors, if any, with each DIMENSION statement:

   (*a*)   DIMENSION, J(8), INTEREST(5, 10),
   (*b*)   DIMENSION A(4, 0, 3), B(6) C(9, 4)
   (*c*)   DIMENSION, A(M, N) XYZ(4, −8, 7)

6.22   Determine the number of elements in arrays NAME, ID, X, Y according to the statement

       DIMENSION NAME(5, 300), ID(3, 5, 2), X(50), Y(4, 8)

6.23   Using the array ID in the preceding Problem 6.22, describe the output if the following pair is executed:

       WRITE(6, 10) ID
   10   FORMAT(1X, 8I8)

6.24   Using the array Y in Problem 6.22, write a WRITE-FORMAT pair which will print the four rows of Y on the first four rows of a print page respectively.

6.25   Find the output for each program segment:

   (*a*)   DIMENSION ID(5)   (*b*)   INTEGER X(6)

```
(a)      DIMENSION ID(5)            (b)      INTEGER X(6)
         DO 100 K = 1, 5                     DO 100 K = 1, 6, 2
              ID(K) = 2*K                         X(K) = 3*K
    100   CONTINUE                                X(K + 1) = K + 2
         ID(2) = ID(2) + ID(3)          100  CONTINUE
         ID(5) = ID(5) − ID(4)              DO 200 J = 1, 6, 3
         WRITE(6, 10) ID                         X(J) = X(J) + X(J + 1)
     10  FORMAT(1X, 5I8)                200  CONTINUE
                                            IF(X(2).LT.7) X(2) = X(3)
                                            WRITE(6, 20) X
                                         20 FORMAT(1X, 6I8)
```

6.26   Suppose a linear array A with N elements is in memory.   Write a program segment which:

   (*a*)   Interchanges A_1 and A_2 only if A_1 is larger than A_2, interchanges A_3 and A_4 only if A_3 is larger than A_4, and so on.   (Here we assume N is even.)
   (*b*)   Cyclically permutes the values of A so that A_2 contains the original value A_1, A_3 contains the original value A_2, and so on, with A_1 containing the original value A_N.

IMPLIED DO LOOPS

6.27   Describe the output if the WRITE-FORMAT pair is executed:

   (*a*)   WRITE(6, 10) (A(N), N = 4, 28, 5)
       10   FORMAT(1X, 3F15.2)

   (*b*)   WRITE(6, 20) (J(L), K, N(3, L), L = 2, 13, 3)
       20   FORMAT(1X, 4I10)

6.28   Describe the output if the WRITE-FORMAT pair is executed:

    (*a*)   WRITE(6, 30) (A(M), M = 1, 5), X, (B(N), N = 1, 7, 3)
           30   FORMAT(1X, 4F15.2)

    (*b*)   WRITE(6, 40) ((A(M, N), M = 1, 5), N = 1, 7, 3)
           40   FORMAT(1X, 4F15.2)

    (*c*)   WRITE(6, 50) ((A(M, N), N = 1, 7, 3), M = 1, 5)
           50   FORMAT(1X, 4F15.2)

PROGRAMS

6.29   A class of 35 students takes an exam on which scores range from 0 to 100. Write a Fortran program which finds: (*a*) the average score; (*b*) the number of students who failed, i.e., scored below 60; and (*c*) the number of students with perfect papers, i.e., scored 100.

6.30   A student takes seven tests (on which scores range from 0 to 100), and his final grade is the average of the six highest test scores. Assuming the seven test scores are punched on a data card, write a Fortran program segment which finds the student's final grade. (Hint: Subtract the smallest score from the SUM of the seven scores.)

6.31   Each year for 10 years a man invests money in a savings account that earns 7 percent interest compounded annually. Suppose a card contains 10 numbers denoting, respectively, his investment each year. Write a program which prints the amount in his account each year for 20 years. (Note that no additional investment is made in the last 10 years.)

6.32   A department store chain has 6 stores, and each store has the same 12 departments. The weekly sales of the chain are stored in a $6 \times 12 \times 7$ array SALES such that SALES(I, J, K) denotes the sales in the Ith store, in the Jth department, on the Kth day. Write a Fortran program segment which:

    (*a*) Prints the total weekly sales of each store.
    (*b*) Prints the total weekly sales of each department.
    (*c*) Prints the total weekly sales of the chain.

(Compare with Problem 6.7.)

6.33   A department store chain has 14 stores (numbered from 1 to 14) and each store has the same 8 departments. Each week, each store submits a data card to the central office on which the store number is punched in columns 1–3, and then 8 numbers are punched representing the weekly sales in each department. Write a Fortran program segment which:

    (*a*) Reads the data into an array SALES such that SALES(I, J) contains the weekly sales in the Ith store in the Jth department. (Assume the data cards are not arranged in any special order.)
    (*b*) Prints the total sales of each store.
    (*c*) Prints the number of the store with the maximum sales.

6.34   Given positive integers I and J, the generalized Fibonacci sequence is defined by

$$\text{JFIB}(1) = I, \quad \text{JFIB}(2) = J, \quad \text{and} \quad \text{JFIB}(K) = \text{JFIB}(K - 2) + \text{JFIB}(K - 1)$$

for K > 2. (See Problem 6.8.) Write a program which reads I and J and prints the first 30 terms of the sequence so that there are three numbers to a line.

6.35   Write a Fortran program which:

(*a*)   Accepts 25 positive integers and decides if any two of the integers add up to 15.

(*b*)   Accepts 25 positive integers and finds the second smallest and the second largest.

(*c*)   Accepts 25 positive integers and finds the largest even integer, or prints THERE ARE NO EVEN INTEGERS.

(*d*)   Accepts 25 positive integers and counts the number of them which are even and the number which are odd.

6.36   College Entrance Examination Board scores of 450 students are punched on cards, one per card. (Such scores range from 200 to 800.) Write a program which finds the number of scores between 200 and 300, between 300 and 400, and so on.

6.37   Write a program which reads the coefficients $a_1, a_2, \ldots, a_{n+1}$ of the polynomial

$$p(x) = a_1 x^n + a_2 x^{n+1} + \cdots + a_n x + a_{n+1}$$

stores them in a linear array COEF, and prints the values of $p(x)$ for $x = -5, -4.5, -4, \ldots, 4.5, 5$, that is, for x from -5 to 5 with steps of 0.5. Use Horner's method to evaluate $p(x)$; that is,

$$p(x) = ((\ldots ((a_1 x + a_2)x + a_3)x + \cdots + a_{n-1})x + a_n)x + a_{n+1}$$

6.38   (*Set Theory*) Suppose JSET and KSET are linear arrays each of which contain distinct positive integers.

(*a*)   Write a program segment which stores in INTER the intersection of JSET and KSET, that is, those elements in both JSET and KSET.

(*b*)   Write a program segment which stores in JUNION the union of JSET and KSET, that is, those elements in JSET or KSET (or both).

6.39   The inventory of a TV appliance warehouse is stored in memory in two integer linear arrays ID and AMOUNT as follows. Each entry of ID gives the model number (six-digit number) of a TV, and the corresponding entry in AMOUNT gives the number of TV's of that model in the warehouse. Each incoming or outgoing shipment order submits a deck of data cards (with a trailer card) on which the model number is punched in columns 1–8, and the quantity of the item shipped is punched in columns 11–20. (The number is positive if the shipment is incoming and negative if it is outgoing.) Write a program which updates the inventory after each shipping order. It should also print

INSUFFICIENT QUANTITY MODEL NUMBER XXXXXX

if the outgoing order of an item exceeds the number in stock.

6.40   An $N \times N$ matrix array A is in memory.

(*a*)   Write a program which sums the elements above the main diagonal, i.e., those elements A(I, J) such that $I < J$.

(*b*)   Write a program which sums the elements below the main diagonal, i.e., those elements A(I, J) such that $I > J$.

6.41   (*Bowling*) A linear array A contains the number of pins hit in each roll. Write a program segment which stores in an array B the score after each frame. Hence, B(10) gives the final score. Test the program with the following data:

(*a*)   4, 5, 10, 10, 6, 4, 7, 3, 8, 0, 7, 3, 10, 8, 1, 10, 7, 2

(*b*)   6, 4, 7, 2, 10, 7, 3, 10, 5, 4, 3, 0, 10, 10, 8, 2, 7

6.42   (*Sieve Method*)   Write a program which prints the prime numbers less than 400 as follows.

(*a*)   Let A be a linear array with 400 elements.

(*b*)   Store K in A(K); that is, let A(1) = 1, A(2) = 2, . . . , A(400) = 400.

(*c*)   Print A(2) and then set all multiples of 2 equal to 0.

(*d*)   Print the next nonzero element in the array, which is A(3), and then set all multiples of 3 equal to 0.

(*e*)   Continue the above process as long as A(K) $\leq 20 = \sqrt{400}$.

(*f*)   When A(K) > 20, print all the nonzero elements of A.

Answers to Selected Supplementary Problems

6.21   (*a*)   There should not be a comma after DIMENSION, nor at the end.

(*b*)   There should be a comma after B(6).   Also 0 cannot be a subscript.

(*c*)   There should not be a comma after DIMENSION; there should be a comma before XYZ; M, N, and −8 cannot be subscripts.

6.22   1500, 30, 50, 32

6.23   Since only the array name appears, ID will be printed in storage order; that is, ID will be printed columnwise from the first page and then columnwise from the second page with eight elements on a line.

6.24   WRITE(6, 20) ((Y(I, J), J = 1, 8), I = 1, 4)

   20   FORMAT('1', 8F15.2/1X, 8F15.2/1X, 8F15.2/1X, 8F15.2)

6.25   (*a*)   The integers 2, 10, 6, 8, 2 are printed right-justified in fields of width 8.

(*b*)   The integers 6, 9, 9, 20, 15, 7 are printed in fields of width 8.

6.26   (*a*)   DO 99 K = 1, N, 2   (*b*)   T = A(N)

                IF(A(K).LE.A(K + 1)) GO TO 99   NN = N − 1

                T = A(K)   DO 88 K = 1, NN

                A(K) = A(K + 1)   A(N − K + 1) = A(N − K)

                A(K + 1) = T   88 CONTINUE

         99 CONTINUE   A(1) = T

6.27   (*a*)   A(4), A(9), A(14) on one line and A(19), A(24) on the next.

(*b*)   J(2), K, N(3, 2), J(5) on one line; K, N(3, 5), J(8), K on the next line; and N(3, 8), J(11), K, N(3, 11) on the third line.

6.28   (*a*)   A(1), A(2), A(3), A(4) on one line; A(5), X, B(1), B(4) on the next line; and B(7) on the third line.

(*b*)   A(1, 1), A(2, 1), A(3, 1), A(4, 1) on one line; A(5, 1), A(1, 4), A(2, 4), A(3, 4) on the next line; A(4, 4), A(5, 4), A(1, 7), A(2, 7) on the third line; and A(3, 7), A(4, 7), A(5, 7) on the fourth line.

(*c*)   A(1, 1), A(1, 4), A(1, 7), A(2, 1) on one line; A(2, 4), A(2, 7), A(3, 1), A(3, 4) on the next line; A(3, 7), A(4, 1), A(4, 4), A(4, 7) on the third line; and A(5, 1), A(5, 4), A(5, 7) on the fourth line.

Chapter 7

Functions and Subroutines

7.1 INTRODUCTION

As programs become more and more complex and involved, several immediate problems arise:

1. Algorithms for solving more complex problems become more difficult and, hence, harder to design.

2. Even if an algorithm is known, its Fortran implementation becomes more difficult because the size of the program is longer.

3. As programs become longer and more complex, debugging becomes more difficult. Longer programs are naturally more prone to errors, and mistakes will be harder to isolate.

4. More and more documentation is required to make the program more understandable for people who will read and use the program.

5. Similar tasks may be required in several parts of a program. If they are implemented individually, they make the complex problem even more confusing.

These problems may be alleviated by the use of subprograms. A *subprogram* is a complete and independent program which can be used (or: invoked or called) by the main program or other subprograms. A subprogram receives values (called *arguments*) from a calling (originating) program, performs calculations, and then sends back (RETURNs) the result or results to the calling program.

In Chapter 2, we discussed some library functions such as ABS, SQRT, EXP, ALOG, etc. These functions are actually subprograms. They were written and incorporated into the Fortran repertoire because they are used in many, many situations. Instead of having each user write these subprograms, Fortran compilers provide these built-in library functions as a convenience. Obviously, the Fortran library cannot contain all functions or subprograms used in all application areas. However, it is possible for users to write their own subprograms whenever such a need is desirable. This chapter is devoted to the discussion of preparing and using such subprograms.

Recall the arrangement of the Fortran package as shown in Fig. 1-3 in Section 1.3. The Fortran deck should consist of the main program, together with all the subprograms. Usually one places the main program first and subprograms afterward. This is illustrated in Fig. 7-1 where the Fortran deck has two subprograms.

Subprograms fall into two basic categories: FUNCTION subprograms and SUBROUTINE subprograms. The similarities and differences of these two types of subprograms will be examined in the next few sections. Although both types of subprograms may receive one or more values from the calling program, the FUNCTION subprogram usually sends back only one result, whereas the SUBROUTINE usually sends back more than one result.

172

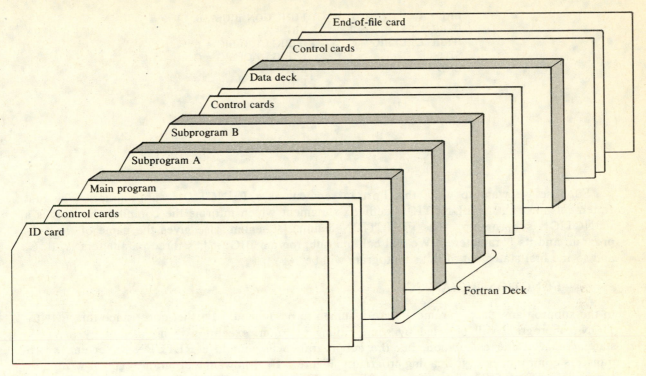

Fig. 7-1   Fortran package.

7.2   FUNCTION SUBPROGRAMS

We note that each of the library functions, ABS, SQRT, SIN, ALOG, etc., computes a value whenever the proper argument is given.   Suppose, for example,

SQRT(A**2 + B**2)

appears in an arithmetic expression.   When it is executed, the computer:

1. Calls the subprogram SQRT.

2. Calculates the real value $A^2 + B^2$ and uses this value for the argument in the subprogram.

3. The subprogram calculates the square root of the given argument (which is $A^2 + B^2$) and assigns this real value to the variable SQRT in the subprogram.

4. Sends the value of SQRT in the subprogram back to the calling program, and this value is then substituted for SQRT(A**2 + B**2).

Observe that this subprogram has a value associated with its name SQRT.   Subprograms of this kind are called FUNCTION subprograms.

We now give two examples of FUNCTION subprograms.   We will refer to them later when we list rules for writing subprograms.

First Subprogram

Consider the problem of finding the largest of three numbers A, B, and C.   Assuming A, B, and C are in memory and BIG is the real variable to be used for storing the largest value, Fig. 7-2(*a*) gives a Fortran segment which terminates after calculating BIG.

```
BIG = A                              FUNCTION BIG(A, B, C)
IF(BIG.LT.B) BIG = B                 BIG = A
IF(BIG.LT.C) BIG = C                 IF(BIG.LT.B) BIG = B
STOP                                 IF(BIG.LT.C) BIG = C
END                                  RETURN
                                     END
```

         (a)   (b)

Fig. 7-2

Suppose we want to write this Fortran segment as a FUNCTION subprogram. The first statement must be the FUNCTION defining statement which informs the compiler that this is a FUNCTION subprogram. The FUNCTION defining statement also gives the name of the subprogram and its parameters. We will call our subprogram BIG; it has three parameters A, B, C, and so the first statement of the subprogram will be

    FUNCTION BIG(A, B, C)

In the subprogram, these parameters are assumed to be defined. Furthermore, since this FUNCTION subprogram will be used by some calling program, execution is not halted by a STOP statement after the calculation, but the subprogram will contain a RETURN statement which transfers control back to the calling program. Figure 7-2(b) shows the program segment written as a complete FUNCTION subprogram. Observe the similarity of the subprogram and the Fortran segment Fig. 7-2(a).

Second Subprogram

The function $k!$ (k factorial) is defined by

$$k! = \begin{cases} 1 \cdot 2 \cdot 3 \cdot \ldots \cdot (k-1) \cdot k, & \text{if } k \geq 1 \\ 1 & \text{if } k = 0 \end{cases}$$

For example, $0! = 1$, $1! = 1$, $4! = 1 \cdot 2 \cdot 3 \cdot 4 = 24$, and $6! = 1 \cdot 2 \cdot 3 \cdot 4 \cdot 5 \cdot 6 = 720$.

Consider the problem of calculating $k!$ for any nonnegative integer k. Assuming k is in memory and IFACT is the integer variable to be used for storing $k!$, Fig. 7-3(a) gives a Fortran segment which terminates after calculating IFACT. On the other hand, Fig. 7-3(b) shows how IFACT can be obtained from a FUNCTION subprogram. Observe that there are two RETURN statements corresponding to the two STOP statements.

```
                                     C       FUNCTION IFACT(K)
                                     C
       IFACT = 1                     C       COMPUTES K FACTORIAL
       IF(K.EQ.0) STOP               C
       DO 10 J = 1, K                        IFACT = 1
           IFACT = IFACT*J                   IF(K.EQ.0) RETURN
    10 CONTINUE                              DO 10 J = 1, K
       STOP                                      IFACT = IFACT*J
       END                           10      CONTINUE
                                             RETURN
                                             END
```

         (a)   (b)

Fig. 7-3

We now summarize the main points in writing FUNCTION subprograms:

1. The first statement of the subprogram must be the FUNCTION defining statement which has the following form:

    FUNCTION NAME(param1, param2, . . . , param$n$)

    That is, the word FUNCTION is followed by the NAME of the function, and the NAME is followed by the parameters which are separated by commas and enclosed in parentheses. These parameters must be nonsubscripted variable names (or array names, see Section 7.6), and to the subprogram they are assumed to be already defined.

2. Naming a FUNCTION subprogram must follow the usual rules for variable names; i.e., it must contain one to six alphanumeric characters with the first character being an alphabet. The NAME of the FUNCTION subprogram (without its parameters) must also be defined in some manner in the subprogram (i.e., it should appear either on the left side of an assignment statement or in an input statement) before any RETURN statement is executed. (Thus naming a FUNCTION subprogram should also follow the type convention for variable names.)

3. A subprogram is a complete and independent program:

    (*a*) It is *complete* because it contains the necessary type declarations (such as, INTEGER, REAL, DIMENSION, etc.), use of library functions and other subprograms, and the END statement.

    (*b*) It is *independent* because all variable names (except the parameters) and all statement labels used are local to the subprogram and unknown outside. Thus, the same variable names and statement numbers may be used in different subprograms and calling programs.

4. The only communication between a calling program and a subprogram is through the parameters. (See Section 7.3.)

5. Every FUNCTION subprogram must contain at least one parameter and one RETURN statement which transfers control back to the calling program.

7.3 CALLING FUNCTION SUBPROGRAMS

A FUNCTION subprogram is *invoked* (or: *called*) in the same way as any library function. Namely, in those places where one wants the function value, one writes

    NAME(arg1, arg2, . . . , arg$n$)

That is, one writes the NAME of the function followed by suitable expressions for its arguments, which are separated by commas and enclosed in parentheses.

The names of the arguments in the calling statement need not be the same as the corresponding parameters in the FUNCTION defining statement. In fact, like library functions, the arguments may be constants, single variables, arithmetic expressions, or even the names of library functions or other subprograms. The most important thing to remember is that the arguments must agree in a one-to-one manner with the *order* and the *data type* of the corresponding parameters in the FUNCTION defining statement. For example, consider the FUNCTION subprogram BIG mentioned earlier whose defining statement is

    FUNCTION BIG(A, B, C)

Observe that it requires three real arguments to call BIG, so that the following statements are all syntactically correct:

    GRADE = BIG(T1, T2, T3)
    GRADE = FINAL/3.0 + (2.0/3.0)*BIG(T1, 60.0, SQRT(A))
    GRADE = 0.5*(FINAL + BIG(S(I, 1), S(I, 2), Z(I))

The following illustrates the one-to-one correspondence between the arguments of the second statement and the parameters of the subprogram:

Argument list: T1,   60.0,   SQRT(A)
                   ↓   ↓   ↓
Parameter list: A,   B,   C

There is one subtle point that must be understood when using subprograms. The parameters used in the FUNCTION defining statement are called *dummy variables* because no storage locations are actually established for them. Specifically, the addresses of the corresponding arguments in the calling program are used in the execution of the subprogram. For example, in the calling statement

GRADE = BIG(T1 + T2, C, 60.0)

the addresses of the arguments T1 + T2, C, 60.0 will be used in place of the parameters A, B, C in the execution of the subprogram BIG.

Remark. Observe that we use the term *parameters* for the variables in the subprogram appearing in the defining statement and the term *arguments* for the corresponding values in the calling program.

EXAMPLE 7.1

(a) The binomial coefficient $\binom{n}{i}$ for nonnegative integers n and i (where $i \leq n$) is defined by

$$\binom{n}{i} = \frac{n!}{(n-i)!\,i!}; \text{ for example, } \binom{8}{3} = \frac{8!}{5!3!} = \frac{1 \cdot 2 \cdot 3 \cdot 4 \cdot 5 \cdot 6 \cdot 7 \cdot 8}{1 \cdot 2 \cdot 3 \cdot 4 \cdot 5 \cdot 1 \cdot 2 \cdot 3} = \frac{6 \cdot 7 \cdot 8}{1 \cdot 2 \cdot 3} = 56$$

Write a program which accepts nonnegative integers N and I (where I ≤ N) and prints the value $\binom{N}{I}$.

Using the subprogram IFACT of the preceding section, the following Fortran program gives us the required binomial coefficient.

```
C       PROGRAM CALCULATING BINOMIAL COEFFICIENT
        INTEGER UP, DOWN
        READ(5, 10) N, I
10      FORMAT(2I8)
        UP = IFACT(N)
        DOWN = IFACT(N − I)*IFACT(I)
        IBINQ = UP/DOWN
        WRITE(6, 20) N, I, IBINQ
20      FORMAT(6X, 'N = ', I5, 5X, 'I = ', I5, 5X,
     1          'BINOMIAL COEFF = ', I8)
        STOP
        END
```

Observe that the use of the subprogram makes the main program simple and clear. On the other hand, if $n!$, $(n - i)!$ and $i!$ were computed separately in the main program, the program would be long, less comprehensible, and more error prone. Observe also that IBINQ can be calculated by one statement:

IBINQ = IFACT(N)/(IFACT(N − I)*IFACT(I))

However, longer and more complex expressions are more error prone. It is usually advisable to break down complex expressions into several simpler ones when writing.

Remark. We ignore the fact that $n!$ may cause overflow for larger n. Other ways of computing $\binom{n}{i}$ will be discussed later.

(*b*) Suppose three hourly exams and one final were given to a class of 25 students.   These scores, together with the students' ID numbers, are punched on cards—one per student.   The numerical grade for the course is computed as the average of the final exam and the highest of the three hourly exams.

The following program, which uses the subprogram BIG, calculates each student's numerical grade:

```
        WRITE(6, 10)
    10  FORMAT('1', 4X, 'ID', 6X, 'SCORE 1', 2X, 'SCORE 2',
      1          2X, 'SCORE 3', 6X, 'FINAL', 5X, 'GRADE')
        DO 500 I = 1, 25
            READ(5, 20) ID, T1, T2, T3, FINAL
            GRADE = 0.5*(FINAL + BIG(T1, T2, T3))
            WRITE(6, 30) ID, T1, T2, T3, FINAL, GRADE
   500  CONTINUE
    20  FORMAT(I10, 4(F6.2, 4X))
    30  FORMAT(1X, I6, 5(3X, F6.2))
        STOP
        END
```

Remark.   Any subprogram can call any other subprogram, but not itself.   More generally, the calling programs cannot form a cycle; e.g., one cannot have the situation where:

Subprogram A calls subprogram B,

subprogram B calls subprogram C,

subprogram C calls subprogram D, and

subprogram D calls subprogram A.

One way to guarantee that this does not happen is to place a subprogram before any other subprogram that it invokes; e.g., if subprograms X and Y call subprogram Z, then Z is placed after X and Y in the Fortran deck.

7.4   FUNCTION SUBPROGRAMS COMPUTING SEVERAL VALUES

So far, all our FUNCTION subprograms have computed one value, and this value was assigned to the NAME of the function in the subprogram.   Question: Can a FUNCTION subprogram compute several values?   The answer is "Yes" (although the SUBROUTINE subprogram discussed in Section 7.7 is usually used in such a situation).

Recall that the only communication between a calling program and a subprogram is via the arguments and parameters.   Accordingly, whenever a FUNCTION subprogram is used to compute several values, one value is assigned to the NAME of the function and the others must be assigned to dummy parameters (which are also transmitted to the calling program).

EXAMPLE 7.2

Suppose we want to write a FUNCTION subprogram which will compute the largest and the sum of three numbers A, B, C.   We call the program BBB, where BBB is used to store the largest value.   This subprogram will be similar to the subprogram BIG in Fig. 7-2, except BBB must have a fourth parameter, say SUM, which will be used to transfer the sum of A, B, and C to the calling program.   Such a program BBB follows:

```
        FUNCTION BBB(A, B, C, SUM)
        SUM = A + B + C
        BBB = A
        IF(BBB.LT.B) BBB = B
        IF(BBB.LT.C) BBB = C
        RETURN
        END
```

Suppose the calling program has the statement

$$\text{RESULT} = \text{BBB}(X, Y, Z, \text{TOTAL})$$

After this statement is executed, RESULT will contain the largest of the numbers, X, Y, Z, and TOTAL will contain the sum.   TOTAL will then be available for computation.   For example, if

$$\text{AVE} = \text{TOTAL}/3.0$$

is executed some time later, then AVE will contain the average of X, Y, Z.

7.5 ARRAYS AND FUNCTION SUBPROGRAMS, VARIABLE DIMENSION

One can also use an array as a parameter of a FUNCTION subprogram.   In such a case, its corresponding argument in the calling statement must also be an array.   However, the array in the subprogram must still be declared by a DIMENSION statement in the subprogram.   Furthermore, its dimensions cannot exceed those of its corresponding argument.

Figure 7-4(a) is a subprogram BIGG which finds the largest element for a given linear array A of 25 elements, and Fig. 7-4(b) is a typical calling program.

```
      FUNCTION BIGG(A)                        DIMENSION X(25)
      DIMENSION A(25)                         REAL LARGE
      BIGG = A(1)                             READ(5, 10) X
      DO 10 K = 2, 25                  10     FORMAT(5(F8.2, 2X))
         IF(BIGG.LT.A(K)) BIGG = A(K)         LARGE = BIGG(X)
   10 CONTINUE                                WRITE(6, 20) LARGE
      RETURN                           20     FORMAT('0', 'LARGEST VALUE IS', 2X, F8.2)
      END                                     STOP
                                              END

              (a)                                       (b)
```

Fig. 7-4

The above subprogram BIGG will find the largest element in a linear array with exactly 25 elements, which obviously limits its use.   To allow more generality, Fortran permits us to use *variable dimensions* (i.e., adjustable dimensions) in subprograms.   This we discuss next.

Variable Dimension.   Recall that in any program the subscript of an array name in a DIMENSION statement must be an integer constant and cannot be a variable.   This is not entirely true if the DIMENSION statement appears in a subprogram.   Specifically, suppose a DIMENSION statement in a subprogram declares a variable A to be an array and A is a parameter of the subprogram.   Then a subscript of A in the DIMENSION statement may be an integer variable provided that the variable is also a parameter of the subprogram.   This is illustrated in the following FUNCTION subprogram which will find the largest element of an array A with N elements.

```
      FUNCTION BIGMM(A, N)
      DIMENSION A(N)
      BIGMM = A(1)
      DO 10 K = 1, N
         IF(BIGMM.LT.A(K)) BIGMM = A(K)
   10 CONTINUE
      RETURN
      END
```

We emphasize that the use of the variable dimension is allowed only in subprograms, i.e., never in the main program.

   Remark. The value of a parameter N used in a variable DIMENSION statement in a subprogram should not exceed the actual dimension size of the corresponding array in the calling program.

EXAMPLE 7.3

   (*a*)   Write a FUNCTION subprogram which calculates the sum of the elements in a linear array with N elements.   Here A and N are parameters:

```
        FUNCTION SUM(A, N)
        DIMENSION A(N)
        SUM = 0.0
        DO 99 K = 1, N
             SUM = SUM + A(K)
     99 CONTINUE
        RETURN
        END
```

   (*b*)   Suppose X and Y are linear arrays in memory declared by

```
        DIMENSION X(100), Y(200)
```

Use (*a*) to find the averages:

$$(X_1 + X_2 + \cdots + X_{25})/25$$
$$(Y_1 + Y_2 + \cdots + Y_M)/M$$

We have:

```
        AVEX = SUM(X, 25)/25.0
        AVEY = SUM(Y, M)/FLOAT(M)
```

(We assume $M \leq 200$.)

7.6   ARITHMETIC STATEMENT FUNCTIONS

   Suppose we want to evaluate the quadratic function

$$g(x) = x^2 - 5x + 2$$

for $x = 1, 2, \ldots, 20$.   Using a FUNCTION program, we have:

Calling Program	Subprogram
DO 100 J = 1, 20	FUNCTION G(X)
VALUE = G(FLOAT(J))	G = X*X − 5.0*X + 2.0
WRITE(6, 10) J, VALUE	RETURN
100 CONTINUE	END
10 FORMAT(1X, I3, 3X, F8.2)	
STOP	
END	

Observe that this FUNCTION subprogram consists of a single arithmetic statement (besides the FUNCTION defining statement and the RETURN and END statements).   We may simplify this kind of FUNCTION subprogram by simply writing the statement

```
        G(X) = X*X − 5.0*X + 2.0
```

at the beginning of the calling program as follows:

```
C
C        DEFINE THE FUNCTION G
C
         G(X) = X*X − 5.0*X + 2.0
C
C        COMPUTE FUNCTIONAL VALUES
C
         DO 100 J = 1, 20
                 VALUE = G(FLOAT(J))
                 WRITE(6, 10) J, VALUE
100      CONTINUE
10       FORMAT(1X, I3, 3X, F8.2)
         STOP
         END
```

This function G is called an *arithmetic statement function.*

Rules for statement functions follow:

1. A statement function is declared using the following form:

$$\text{NAME}(param1, param2, \ldots, paramn) = \underline{\text{arithmetic expression}}$$

The parameters must be single nonsubscripted variables, and the arithmetic expression must not contain any subscripted variables. However, the arithmetic expression may contain library functions, FUNCTION subprograms, and other statement functions (provided they are defined earlier). Although some compilers allow the defining statement to appear anywhere in the program prior to its use, many compilers require that it be placed at the beginning of the program after any type or declaration statements, but before any executable statements.

2. Naming the function and its parameters follows the same rules as for FUNCTION subprograms. The parameters are, as in FUNCTION subprograms, dummy variables, and no storage locations are assigned. Thus, they are local to the statement.

3. The rules for calling statement functions are also the same for FUNCTION subprograms. That is, in those places in the program where one wants the function value, one simply writes the name of the function statement with suitable arguments. The arguments may be any arithmetic expressions as long as they agree in a one-to-one manner with the order and type of the parameters in the defining statement. For example, assuming the above function statement G(X) has been defined in the program, one can write

$$AVE = (G(A + SQRT(B)) + DEP)/2.0$$

where AVE is to be the average of DEP and G evaluated at A + SQRT(B). Here A + SQRT(B) is the argument, and it corresponds to the parameter X in the statement function.

4. An important point is that a statement function is internal to the program (or subprogram) in which it appears; hence, it may not be called by any other program.

Since a statement function is internal to its program, it has a degree of freedom which FUNCTION subprograms do not have. Namely, variables which do not appear in the parameter list can appear in the statement. For example, the following is a syntactically correct arithmetic statement function:

$$F(X, Y) = A*X**2 + B*X*Y + C*Y**2$$

In this case, the X and Y are dummy variables; hence, one can use X and Y as variable names elsewhere in the program.   However, the A, B, C are not dummy variables since they are not in the parameter list, and so they will be assumed to be defined when the function is called.   For example,

F(1.0, 2.0)

will calculate the function for the current values of A, B, C.

EXAMPLE 7.4

A deck of N cards is given, each with three real numbers punched on it.   They are the coefficients A, B, C of the quadratic equation

$$F(X) = AX^2 + BX + C$$

Write a Fortran program to evaluate, for each triplet A, B, C, the function values for $X = -5, -4, \ldots, 5$.

Observe that there are 11 values of X.   We will use a DO loop with index $I = 1, 2, \ldots, 11$.   The relationship between the index I and the values of X can be exhibited as follows:

I: 1,   2,   3,   4,   5, 6, 7, 8, 9, 10, 11
X: −5,   −4,   −3,   −2,   −1, 0, 1, 2, 3,   4,   5

Observe that X and I are related by $I - X = 6$.   Hence

$$X = -6 + I$$

The required program follows:

```
      C
      C         EXAMPLE USING STATEMENT FUNCTION
      C
                F(X) = A*X*X + B*X + C
                READ(5, 5) N
        5       FORMAT(I3)
                DO 100 J = 1, N
                    READ(5, 10) A, B, C
        10          FORMAT(3F5.1)
                    WRITE(6, 15) A, B, C
        15          FORMAT('1', 'A = ', F5.1/1X, 'B = ', F5.1/1X, 'C = ', F5.1)
      C
      C             EVALUATING THE FUNCTION
      C
                    DO 200 I = 1, 11
                        Y = F(-6.0 + FLOAT(I))
                        WRITE(6, 20) I, Y
        200         CONTINUE
        20          FORMAT(1X, 3I, 2X, F8.2)
        100     CONTINUE
                STOP
                END
```

7.7 SUBROUTINES

There is another type of subprogram called a SUBROUTINE subprogram.   Recall first that the name of a FUNCTION subprogram is always assigned a value in the subprogram.   This is not true for SUBROUTINE subprograms.   Aside from this difference and its implications, the rules and restrictions governing the writing of SUBROUTINE subprograms are analogous to those of FUNCTION subprograms.   We note that one generally uses a SUBROUTINE rather than a FUNCTION subprogram when one has several values to calculate.   Furthermore, besides computing values, one uses SUBROUTINE subprograms to perform tasks (e.g., interchanging elements, etc.).

Like FUNCTION subprograms, SUBROUTINE subprograms must first be so declared, using the defining statement SUBROUTINE. The declaration has the following general form:

SUBROUTINE NAME(param1, param2, . . . , param*n*)

Since the NAME of the subroutine is not assigned a value in the subprogram, the question of type does not occur. (However, names of subroutines still cannot exceed six characters.)

Like any subprogram, a SUBROUTINE is also a complete and independent program. Hence, it may contain all the characteristics of any program: type declarations, DIMENSION statements, other FUNCTION and/or SUBROUTINE subprograms, the END statement, and so on. Furthermore, communication between a calling program and the SUBROUTINE subprogram is only transmitted through the parameters; hence, variable names (other than the parameters) and statement labels in the SUBROUTINE are all local to that subprogram. (The way a SUBROUTINE is called and the way the values are transmitted through the parameters is discussed later in the section.)

We now give two examples of SUBROUTINE subprograms. The first will perform a task, and the second will compute values.

1. Assuming X and Y are defined, the following program segment interchanges the values in X and Y:

T = X
X = Y
Y = T

We can write a SUBROUTINE subprogram named INTCHG to perform the exchange:

SUBROUTINE INTCHG(X, Y)
T = X
X = Y
Y = T
RETURN
END

Observe first that the name INTCHG is not assigned a value in the subprogram. (Thus, starting the name with the letter I is immaterial.) Assuming the interchanged values will be later used in the calling program, we have the RETURN statement which transfers control back to the calling program.

2. Consider again the problem of writing a subprogram which calculates the largest and the sum of three numbers A, B, C. This can be done with a SUBROUTINE subprogram where we use the arguments to transmit the computed values back to the calling program. Such a SUBROUTINE follows:

SUBROUTINE LARGE(A, B, C, BIG, SUM)
SUM = A + B + C
BIG = A
IF(BIG.LT.B) BIG = B
IF(BIG.LT.C) BIG = C
RETURN
END

Observe the similarity and difference between this subprogram and the FUNCTION subprogram in Example 7.2. The name LARGE here has no value; hence, BIG, the largest of A, B, C, must be listed as a parameter so that it can be transmitted back to the calling program.

How are SUBROUTINE subprograms invoked? As just mentioned, unlike a FUNCTION subprogram, the name of a SUBROUTINE subprogram does not have a value; therefore, a new kind of statement—the CALL statement—is required. The following calling statement invokes (calls) the subroutine INTCHG

> CALL INTCHG(A(3), T)

The net effect of this statement in the calling program is that the values of A(3) and T are interchanged.

We note that after INTCHG is invoked, the addresses of A(3) and T are transferred to the subprogram and are substituted for the dummy variables X and Y there. The fact that the name T in the calling program is also used as a name in the subroutine INTCHG does not cause any complications because the variable T in the SUBROUTINE is local to that subprogram, and only the address of the calling argument T (not the name T) is used in the execution of the SUB-ROUTINE.

The following calling statement is also syntactically correct:

> CALL LARGE(U + V, W − SQRT(V), U*U, T, S)

The net effect of this statement in the calling program is that S will contain the sum of U + V, W − SQRT(V), and U*U; and T will contain the largest of the three values.

We emphasize again, as in the case of FUNCTION subprograms, that the arguments in the calling statement must agree in a one-to-one manner with the order and the type of the parameters in the defining SUBROUTINE statement. We illustrate this fact using the above CALL statement:

Argument list:	U + V,	W − SQRT(V),	U*U,	T,	S
	↓	↓	↓	↓	↓
Parameter list:	A,	B,	C,	BIG,	SUM

EXAMPLE 7.5

Suppose A is a linear array containing at most N elements. Write a SUBROUTINE subprogram which:

1. Finds the largest value among the first K elements,

> A(1), A(2), . . . , A(K).

2. Computes the sum of the first K elements,

> A(1) + A(2) + · · · + A(K)

The following subroutine SEEK accomplishes the above:

```
          SUBROUTINE SEEK(A, N, K, HIGH, SUM)
          DIMENSION A(N)
          SUM = 0.0
          HIGH = A(1)
          DO 100 J = 1, K
               SUM = SUM + A(J)
               IF(HIGH.LT.A(J)) HIGH = A(J)
100   CONTINUE
          RETURN
          END
```

As seen in the above example, array names can be used as parameters in a SUBROUTINE subprogram (providing they also appear in a DIMENSION statement in the subprogram), and they can have variable dimension. That is, the rules governing arrays in SUBROUTINE subprograms are similar to those for FUNCTION subprograms.

EXAMPLE 7.6

Suppose an array A with N elements is stored in ascending order; namely, $A(1) \leq A(2) \leq \cdots \leq A(N)$. Write a SUBROUTINE subprogram to rearrange the array elements in descending order, that is, $A(1) \geq A(2) \geq \cdots \geq A(N)$.

We obviously can sort the array in descending order. However, this would be very inefficient since we know that A is in ascending order. One simple way to accomplish our task is to invert the array; that is, to interchange $A(1)$ and $A(N)$, to interchange $A(2)$ and $A(N-1)$, and so on. We call this subroutine INVERT, and it calls the subroutine INTCHG:

```
        SUBROUTINE INVERT(A, N)
        DIMENSION A(N)
        NN = N/2
        K = N + 1
        DO 20 I = 1, NN
                CALL INTCHG(A(I), A(K - I))
    20  CONTINUE
        RETURN
        END
```

(Observe the DO statement. Can the reader tell the reason the DO loop goes only to N/2 rather than to N?)

The employment of subprograms chops a big, complex problem into smaller program units. Each smaller unit will be simpler to implement and debug. Furthermore, the smaller program units can also be done by different people in a team. Accordingly, a big programming task can be done in parallel rather than in sequential order.

7.8 SUBROUTINE VERSUS FUNCTION

Generally speaking, FUNCTION subprograms are used to compute a single value, while SUBROUTINE subprograms are used to compute several values or to perform tasks (e.g., interchanging two values). We note that anything done by a FUNCTION subprogram can also be accomplished by a SUBROUTINE subprogram. Conversely, most of the tasks performed by SUBROUTINE subprograms can also be done by FUNCTION subprograms. For example, we write a FUNCTION subprogram to interchange the values of X and Y:

```
        FUNCTION EXCHG(X, Y)
        T = X
        X = Y
        Y = T
        EXCHG = 0.0
        RETURN
        END
```

Observe that the name of the FUNCTION is arbitrarily assigned a value since it must be defined in the subprogram. Since communication is via the parameters, the values of X and Y will be interchanged in the main program. However, the setup is rather artificial and unnatural. Listed are the main differences between a SUBROUTINE and a FUNCTION subprogram:

1. No value is associated with the NAME of a SUBROUTINE, while the NAME of a FUNCTION subprogram must have a value, numerical or logical. Hence, the NAME of a FUNCTION subprogram must follow the type convention, and it must be defined in the subprogram.

2. A SUBROUTINE may be invoked only by a special calling statement—the CALL statement. The NAME of a FUNCTION subprogram may be used in the same way as library functions, i.e., in arithmetic statements, etc.

3. A FUNCTION subprogram must have at least one argument, while a SUBROUTINE need not have any. (See Problem 7.11.)

4. Since a FUNCTION subprogram computes at least one value, it must contain a RETURN statement. A SUBROUTINE subprogram need not contain a return statement. (See Problem 7.13.)

Solved Problems

SUBPROGRAMS

7.1 Find errors, if any, in each of the following subprogram defining statements:

   (*a*) FUNCTION, NEXT(A, B + C, X)   (*c*) SUBROUTINE NEW(X, Y(3), Z)
   (*b*) FUNCTION GRADE A, B, C   (*d*) SUBROUTINE(U, V, W)

   (*a*) There should be no comma after FUNCTION. Also B + C cannot be a parameter.
   (*b*) The parameters A, B, C should be enclosed in parentheses.
   (*c*) The subscripted variable Y(3) cannot be a parameter in a subprogram defining statement.
   (*d*) The subroutine has no name.

7.2 Find errors, if any, in each segment:

   (*a*) FUNCTION XXX(A, N, K)   (*b*) SUBROUTINE YYY(A, N, K)
          DIMENSION A(N, N + 1), B(K)   DIMENSION A(J, K), B(N)

   (*a*) The arithmetic expression N + 1 cannot appear in the DIMENSION statement.
   (*b*) The variable J cannot appear in the DIMENSION statement since it is not one of the parameters.

7.3 Find errors, if any, in each subprogram:

   (*a*) FUNCTION ADD(X, Y, Z)   (*b*) SUBROUTINE AAA(X, Y, Z)
          Z = X + Y   Z = X + Y
          RETURN   RETURN
          END   END

   (*a*) The name of the function ADD must be assigned a value in the subprogram, and it hasn't been.
   (*b*) There are no errors. (The name of a subprogram is not assigned a value.)

7.4 Define a statement function to calculate $R = \sqrt{u^2 + v^2 + w^2}$ and use it to calculate

$$A = \frac{x}{\sqrt{x^2 + y^2 + z^2}}, \qquad B = \sqrt{x^4 + y^4 + z^4}, \qquad C = \sqrt{4x^2 + 9y^2 + 4z^2}$$

we observe that $x^4 = (x^2)^2$, $4x^2 = (2x)^2$, and so on.

```
R(U, V, W) = SQRT(U*U + V*V + W*W)
A = X/R(X, Y, Z)
B = R(X*X, Y*Y, Z*Z)
C = R(2.0*X, 3.0*Y, 2.0*Z)
```

7.5 Find the output of the following programs which use statement functions:

(a)
```
      JF(M) = M**2 − 3*M + 4
      K = 2
      L = JF(K + 2)
      M = JF(L − 3*K) + K
      WRITE(6, 10) K, L, M
10    FORMAT(1X, 3(I10, 2X))
      STOP
      END
```

(b)
```
      F(X, Y) = A*X + B*Y
      X = 2.0
      Y = 3.0
      A = 4.0
      B = 5.0
      C = F(6.0, 7.0)
      WRITE(6, 10) C
10    FORMAT(1X, F10.2)
      STOP
      END
```

(a) The first line defines the function $JF(M) = M^2 − 3M + 4$. The second line assigns 2 to K. By lines three and four:

$$L \leftarrow JF(2 + 2) = JF(4) = 4^2 − 3 \cdot 4 + 4 = 8$$
$$M \leftarrow JF(8 − 3 \cdot 2) + 2 = JF(2) + 2 = (2^2 − 3 \cdot 2 + 4) + 2 = 4$$

Hence, 2, 8, and 4 will be printed on a line, each in a field of width 10.

(b) By lines two to five X, Y, A, B are assigned 2, 3, 4, 5 respectively. Recall that the X, Y in F(X, Y) are dummy variables and have no relation to the values of X and Y in the program. Specifically, in evaluating C by line six, we substitute 6 for X and 7 for Y in F(X, Y), using the values of A and B in the program. Thus,

$$C \leftarrow 4 \cdot 6 + 5 \cdot 7 = 59$$

Consequently, 59.00 will be printed right-justified in the first 10 columns of the print page.

7.6 Suppose the following subprograms are given:

```
FUNCTION SUM(X, Y, Z)        SUBROUTINE ADD(X, Y, Z, TOTAL)
SUM = X + Y + Z              Y = X + Y
Y = X + Y                    Z = Y + Z
Z = Y + Z                    X = Z + X
X = Z + X                    TOTAL = X + Y + Z
RETURN                       RETURN
END                          END
```

Find the output of the program segment:

```
      A = 1.0
      B = 2.0
      C = 3.0
      AMOUNT = SUM(A, B, C)
      CALL ADD(A, B, C, GT)
      WRITE(6, 10) A, B, C, AMOUNT, GT
10    FORMAT(1X, 5(F4.1, 2X))
```

After line 4 is executed, A = 7.0, B = 3.0, C = 6.0, and AMOUNT = 6.0. After line 5 is executed, A = 23.0, B = 10.0, C = 16.0, and GT = 49.0. Hence the output consists of 23.0, 10.0, 16.0, 6.0, and 49.0.

PROGRAMS

7.7 Write a SUBROUTINE subprogram which calculates the new monthly balance of a checking account, say in the form

```
BANK(BAL, DEP, M, CK, N)
```

where

   BAL denotes the monthly balance of the checking account,

   DEP is an array listing the M deposits for the month,

   CK is an array listing payments on N checks during the month.

Assume there is a service charge, SC, which is $1.00 per month and 5¢ for each check and 2¢ for each deposit.   Also assume DEP and CK never exceed 100 elements.

   We simply add the deposits and subtract the checks and service charge.   However, one must also consider the case where M and/or N are zero.   The subprogram follows:

```
        SUBROUTINE BANK(BAL, DEP, M, CK, N)
        DIMENSION DEP(100), CK(100)
        IF(M.EQ.0) GO TO 10
        DO 100 K = 1, M
            BAL = BAL + DEP(K)
100     CONTINUE
10      IF(N.EQ.0) GO TO 20
        DO 200 K = 1, N
            BAL = BAL − CK(K)
200     CONTINUE
20      SC = 1.00 + M*0.02 + N*0.05
        BAL = BAL − SC
        RETURN
        END
```

7.8   Write a SUBROUTINE subprogram which does not have any (*a*) argument, (*b*) RETURN statement.

   (*a*)   The following is a SUBROUTINE subprogram without any argument:

```
        SUBROUTINE NEW
        WRITE(6, 10)
10      FORMAT(1X, 'NEW DEPOSITOR')
        RETURN
        END
```

   The statement

   CALL NEW

in a calling program will have the effect of printing the message

   NEW DEPOSITOR

   (*b*)   A SUBROUTINE subprogram does not need to return to the calling program.   Specifically, if we replace the RETURN statement in any SUBROUTINE subprogram by the STOP statement, the execution of the Fortran program will be terminated by the SUBROUTINE.   For example, if RETURN is replaced by STOP in (*a*), the program will stop after NEW DEPOSITOR is printed.

7.9   Suppose A, B, C, D are linear arrays stored in memory with 100, 50, 75, and 200 elements respectively.   Suppose L and K are also in memory and $5 \leq L \leq 75$ and $L < K \leq 200$. Write a Fortran segment to calculate:

1. $A_{15} + A_{17} + A_{19} + \cdots + A_{77}$ 3. $C_2 + C_5 + C_8 + \cdots + C_L$

2. $B_{22} + B_{23} + B_{24} + \cdots + B_{36}$ 4. $D_L + D_{L+1} + D_{L+2} + \cdots + D_K$

Observe that each of the calculations involves finding the sum of terms in a linear array. Rather than do each of the calculations in the program, we write a function subprogram called SUM to calculate $X_{IN} + X_{IN+IC} + \cdots + X_{IT}$, where X is a linear array with N elements, IN the initial subscript, IC the increment, and IT the terminal subscript. The subprogram and Fortran segment follow.

Subprogram	*Fortran Segment*
FUNCTION SUM(X, N, IN, IT, IC)	T1 = SUM(A, 100, 15, 77, 2)
DIMENSION X(N)	T2 = SUM(B, 50, 22, 36, 1)
SUM = 0.0	T3 = SUM(C, 75, 2, L, 3)
DO 20 I = IN, IT, IC	T4 = SUM(D, 200, L, K, 1)
SUM = SUM + X(I)	
20 CONTINUE	
RETURN	
END	

7.10 Suppose X, Y are linear arrays each with N elements. Write a program segment to compute

$$\frac{\sqrt{x_1^2 + x_2^2 + \cdots + x_n^2} \cdot \sqrt{y_1^2 + y_2^2 + \cdots + y_n^2}}{\sqrt{x_1 y_1 + x_2 y_2 + \cdots + x_n y_n}}$$

using a FUNCTION subprogram INNPRO which calculates $a_1 b_1 + a_2 b_2 + \cdots + a_n b_n$

Subprogram	*Fortran Segment*
REAL FUNCTION INNPRO(A, B, N)	UP1 = SQRT(INNPRO(X, X, N))
DIMENSION A(N), B(N)	UP2 = SQRT(INNPRO(Y, Y, N))
INNPRO = 0.0	DOWN = SQRT(INNPRO(X, Y, N))
DO 100 K = 1, N	ANGLE = UP1*UP2/DOWN
INNPRO = INNPRO + A(K)*B(K)	
100 CONTINUE	
RETURN	
END	

(Observe the type declaration since INNPRO is to be real.)

7.11 Write a SUBROUTINE subprogram which prints a two-dimensional array row by row (assuming the array does not have more than 13 columns). The program will have adjustable dimension.

```
      SUBROUTINE PRINT(A, M, N)
      DIMENSION A(M, N)
      DO 100 J = 1, M
          WRITE(6, 10) (A(J, K), K = 1, N)
   10     FORMAT(1X, 13(2X, F8.2))
  100 CONTINUE
      RETURN
      END
```

7.12 Suppose an N × L matrix A is in memory. Write the following SUBROUTINE subprograms:

(*a*)   SUBROUTINE FIND(A, N, L, K, J)

which finds row J such that A(J, K) contains the largest absolute value among A(K, K), A(K + 1, K), ..., A(N, K). (See Problem 6.9.)

(*b*)   SUBROUTINE CHANGE(A, N, L, K, J)

which interchanges the elements of the Kth row of A with the corresponding elements of the Jth row.   (See Problem 6.9.)

(*c*)   SUBROUTINE ROWMUL(A, N, L, K, J, D)

which adds D times the Kth row to the Jth row.   (These SUBROUTINE subprograms are used in the solution of linear equations by Gauss elimination, which is treated in Chapter 8.)

(*a*)
```
        SUBROUTINE FIND(A, N, L, K, J)
        DIMENSION A(N, L)
        J = K
        KK = K + 1
        DO 100 I = KK, N
            IF(ABS(A(J, K)).LT.ABS(A(I, K))) J = I
100     CONTINUE
        RETURN
        END
```

(*b*)
```
        SUBROUTINE CHANGE(A, N, L, K, J)
        DIMENSION A(N, L)
        IF(J.EQ.K) RETURN
        DO 100 I = 1, L
            T = A(K, I)
            A(K, I) = A(J, I)
            A(J, I) = T
100     CONTINUE
        RETURN
        END
```

Observe that we allowed for the possibility that J = K and, in that case, we would not have to go through the DO loop.

(*c*)
```
        SUBROUTINE ROWMUL(A, N, L, K, J, D)
        DIMENSION A(N, L)
        DO 100 I = 1, L
            A(J, I) = A(J, I) + D*A(K, I)
100     CONTINUE
        RETURN
        END
```

Supplementary Problems

SUBPROGRAMS

7.13   Find errors, if any, in each subprogram defining statement:

   (*a*) FUNCTION, ORDER(A, B, 2∗X),   (*c*) SUBROUTINE SEEK(A, B, X, M (K), Z),
   (*b*) FUNCTION(I, J, K)   (*d*) SUBROUTINE LOOK(K, J(4), L, M)

7.14   Find errors, if any, in each Fortran segment:

   (*a*) FUNCTION BANK(A, B, N, K)   (*b*) SUBROUTINE LOOK(X, M, N, Z)
          DIMENSION A(N, N − 1), C(K), B(200)   DIMENSION X(M), Y(M, K), Z(N)

7.15   Find errors, if any, in each subprogram:

   (*a*) FUNCTION DEP(X, Y, N)   (*b*) REAL SUBROUTINE LOOK(X, Y, Z)
          Z = X + FLOAT(N)   Z = X + Y
          Y = X − N∗Z   RETURN
          RETURN   END
          END

7.16   Find the output of the program:

                    JG(K) = K∗∗2 + L∗K + M
                    K = 3
                    L = 4
                    M = 5
                    I = JG(6)
                    J = JG(L)
                    WRITE(6, 10) I, J
              10   FORMAT(1X, 2I10)
                    STOP
                    END

7.17   (*a*) Write a FUNCTION subprogram ADD(M, N) which calculates the sum of the N consecutive
                integers beginning with M; namely,

                    M + (M + 1) + (M + 2) + ⋯ + (M + N − 1)

                For example, MM = ADD(5, 4) will store 5 + 6 + 7 + 8 = 26 in MM.
         (*b*) Find the output of the following program which uses the above FUNCTION subprogram:

              C   PROGRAM USING FUNCTION SUBPROGRAM
                       I = 1
                       J = 2
                       K = 3∗I + 2∗J
                       I = ADD(J, K − 3)
                       J = ADD(I − 1, J + 1)
                       K = ADD(K, K − 3)
                       WRITE(6, 10) I, J, K
              10   FORMAT(1X, 3I10)
                       STOP
                       END

7.18   (*a*) Write a SUBROUTINE subprogram SUB(J, K, JSUM, JPROD, JDIFF) such that JSUM,
                JPROD, and JDIFF give the sum J + K, the product J∗K, and the difference J − K, respectively.
         (*b*) Find the output of the following program which uses the above subprogram:

```
C       PROGRAM USING SUBROUTINE SUBPROGRAM
        J  = 3
        K = 2
        CALL SUB(J, K, L, M, N)
        CALL SUB(L + M, 3*N, J, N, M)
        WRITE(6, 10) J, K, L, M, N
   10   FORMAT(1X, 5(I5, 2X))
        STOP
        END
```

7.19   Write a real FUNCTION subprogram ADDS(J, K) which calculates the sum

$$1/J + 1/(J + 1) + 1/(J + 2) + \cdots + 1/K$$

when $J \leq K$ but sets ADDS = 0.0 when $J > K$.   Find the output of the program:

```
        I  = 2
        J  = 4
        K = 3
        X = ADDS(I, J)
        Y = ADDS(J, K)
        Z = ADDS(J, 5)
        WRITE(6, 30) X, Y, Z
   30   FORMAT(1X, 3F12.2)
        STOP
        END
```

7.20   Write a program segment to calculate:

$$A = x^2 + y^2 - 25$$
$$B = 4x^2 + 9y^2 - z^2$$
$$C = \sqrt{x^2 + y^2 - 36}$$

(Hint: Use the arithmetic statement function $F(r, s, t) = r^2 + s^2 - t^2$.)

PROGRAMS

7.21   Given an array $A_1, A_2, \ldots, A_N$ of N elements, the arithmetic mean is defined as

$$(A_1 + A_2 + \cdots + A_N)/N$$

and the geometric mean is defined as

$$\sqrt[N]{A_1 \cdot A_2 \cdot \ldots \cdot A_N}$$

(a)   Write a SUBROUTINE subprogram to calculate the arithmetic and geometric means.
(b)   Write a FUNCTION subprogram to calculate the arithmetic and geometric means.

7.22   Suppose C is an $N \times N$ matrix array.   Write a FUNCTION subprogram which finds the product of the diagonal elements C(1, 1), C(2, 2), . . . , C(N, N) of C.

7.23   Suppose B is an $M \times N$ matrix array.

(a)   Write a FUNCTION subprogram which finds the largest element in B.
(b)   Write a FUNCTION subprogram which finds the element of B with largest absolute value.
(c)   Write a FUNCTION subprogram which finds the sum of the elements of B.

7.24 Four examinations are given in a class of exactly 25 students. Each student's test scores are punched on a card together with his/her student ID. The grade for the course is computed as the average of the best three exams. Write a program to compute the grades for the students. (Hint: One way to compute the sum of the best three scores is to subtract the lowest score from the sum of all four scores. Hence, write a FUNCTION subprogram to find the lowest score, and then use this subprogram in writing the main program.)

7.25 Write a SUBROUTINE subprogram in the form

STAT(A, N, SUM, AVE, VAR, SD)

which calculates the SUM, arithmetic mean AVE, variance VAR, and standard deviation SD of the elements of a linear array A with N elements. (See Problem 6.6.)

7.26 Suppose A is a linear array with N elements. Write a SUBROUTINE subprogram:

(*a*) SORTUP(A, N) which sorts A so that its elements are increasing (see Problem 6.12).
(*b*) SORTDN(A, N) which sorts A so that its elements are decreasing.

7.27 Write a SUBROUTINE subprogram in the form

DEPR(COST, N, A)

where COST is to be depreciated by the sum-of-digits method (see Problem 5.37) over N years, and A is a linear array with N elements such that A(K) denotes the amount depreciated in the Kth year.

7.28 Suppose J and K are positive integers. Write FUNCTION subprograms:

(*a*) LGCD(J, K) which finds the greatest common divisor of J and K.
(*b*) LCM(J, K) which finds the least common multiple of J and K.

(Hint: LCM(J, K)·LGCD(J, K) = J·K.)

7.29 Suppose A is an M × N matrix array. Write a FUNCTION subprogram:

(*a*) MAXROW(A, M, N, K) which finds the position of the maximum element in the Kth row of A.
(*b*) MAXCOL(A, M, N, L) which finds the position of the maximum element in the Lth column of A.

7.30 Let A be an N × N square matrix array.

(*a*) Write a subroutine SYM which returns a value M = 1 if the matrix A is symmetric and returns M = 0 otherwise. (The matrix A is *symmetric* if $A_{ij} = A_{ji}$ for each *i*, *j*.)
(*b*) Write a subroutine TRANS which accepts A and returns with the transpose of A stored in A. (The *transpose* of A, denoted by A^T, is the N × N matrix B such that $B_{ij} = A_{ji}$ for each *i*, *j*.)

7.31 Suppose A is an N × N matrix array. It is possible to store the elements in the upper triangular part of A into a linear array B with N(N + 1)/2 elements as follows:

$$
\begin{array}{ccccc}
A(1, 1) & A(1, 2) & A(1, 3) & \ldots & A(1, N) \\
\downarrow & \downarrow & \downarrow & & \downarrow \\
B(1) & B(2) & B(3) & \ldots & B(N) \\
 & A(2, 2) & A(2, 3) & \ldots & A(2, N) \\
 & \downarrow & \downarrow & & \downarrow \\
 & B(N + 1) & B(N + 2) & \ldots & B(2N - 1)
\end{array}
$$

$$
\begin{array}{c}
A(N, N) \\
\downarrow \\
B(N(N + 1)/2)
\end{array}
$$

Write a SUBROUTINE subprogram to accomplish the above. (One may store a symmetric or an upper triangular matrix this way.)

Answers to Selected Supplementary Problems

7.13   (*a*)   There should not be a comma after FUNCTION or at the end of the statement.   2∗X cannot be
            a parameter.
      (*b*)   The FUNCTION subprogram has no name.
      (*c*)   M(K) cannot be a parameter, and there should not be a comma at the end of the statement.
      (*d*)   J(4) cannot be a parameter.

7.14   (*a*)   N − 1 cannot appear in the DIMENSION statement.
      (*b*)   K cannot appear in Y(M, K) since K is not a parameter.

7.15   (*a*)   DEP has not been assigned a value.
      (*b*)   REAL is meaningless since LOOK is not assigned a value.

7.16   The integers 65 and 37 are printed in fields of width 10.

7.17   (*a*)   Since ADD is to be integer valued, one needs a type statement:

```
            INTEGER FUNCTION ADD(M, N)
            ADD = 0
            DO 200 K = 1, N
                ADD = ADD + (M − 1) + K
        200 CONTINUE
            RETURN
            END
```

      (*b*)   The integers 14, 42, and 34 are printed on a line, each in a field of width 10.

7.18   (*a*)   No type statement is required since the name SUB is not assigned any value:

```
            SUBROUTINE SUB(J, K, JSUM, JPROD, JDIFF)
            JSUM = J + K
            JPROD = J∗K
            JDIFF = J − K
            RETURN
            END
```

      (*b*)   The integers 14, 2, 5, 8, 33 will be printed on a line.

7.19   The real numbers 1.08, 0.00, 0.45 are printed in fields of width 10.

7.20   F(R, S, T) = R∗R + S∗S − T∗T
       A = F(X, Y, 5.0)
       B = F(2.0∗X, 3.0∗Y, Z)
       C = SQRT(F(X, Y, 6.0))

Chapter 8

Programming Techniques and Numerical Calculations

8.1 INTRODUCTION

There will usually be several ways to write a program to compute the solution or solutions of a given problem. The preferable way will depend on a number of factors. First of all, one wants to minimize the effect of round-off errors so that the results are as accurate as possible. (See Section 2.10.) Secondly, one wants the program to be as efficient as possible, where the efficiency of a program mainly depends on two things:

1. the time required to run the program;
2. the number of memory locations used by the program.

In other words, one tries to write a program which minimizes the computing time and the number of memory locations used by the program.

One can usually write more efficient programs by adopting good programming habits. For example, an expression appearing many times should be assigned a name so that it is evaluated only once; a power such as X**2.0 should be written X*X or X**2; one should write

$$3.0*X**2 + 4.0*X + 5.0 \qquad \text{instead of} \qquad 3*X**2 + 4*X + 5$$

even though the computer may accept mixed-mode expressions; and so on.

Besides good programming habits, computing time can frequently be greatly reduced by using the proper algorithm. For example, if the polynomial

$$a_1X^N + a_2X^{N-1} + \cdots + a_NX + a_{N+1}$$

is evaluated as it is written, then $N(N + 1)/2$ multiplications and N additions would be required. On the other hand, using Horner's method (discussed in Section 8.6), it would require only N multiplications and N additions.

The amount of memory locations can also be greatly reduced by choosing the proper algorithm. For the sake of illustration, suppose we want to rearrange the N elements of a linear array A in reverse order, i.e., so that A(1) is last, A(2) is next to last, and so on, and to store the elements back in A. One way to do this is to first assign the elements of A to another array B (with N elements) by:

$$B(N) \leftarrow A(1), \quad B(N - 1) \leftarrow A(2), \quad \ldots, \quad B(1) \leftarrow A(N)$$

which can be accomplished by the DO loop:

```
      DO 99 J = 1, N
            B(N + 1 − J) = A(J)
   99 CONTINUE
```

In B, the elements are in the desired order. Hence, we next bring the elements back to A by assigning B(1) to A(1), B(2) to A(2), and so on. Observe that this method requires N new memory locations.

Actually, we can accomplish our task using only one additional memory location.   That is, we interchange A(1) and A(N), A(2) and A(N − 1), and so on:

```
      NN = N/2
      DO 88 J = 1, NN
            TEMP = A(J)
            A(J) = A(N + 1 − J)
            A(N + 1 − J) = TEMP
   88 CONTINUE
```

Thus the second method is more efficient than the first.   (Another such example can be found in our discussion in Section 6.8 on moving an array segment down one position.)

Finally, one must point out that there is a *human* factor in programming.   Although writing 2∗K as K + K may save a miniscule amount of computer time, it may make a program harder to understand and result in the loss of human time.   In other words, it is better to have a general, comprehensible, portable (machine independent) program than to have an incomprehensible, complicated program full of machine-dependent tricks.

The first part of this chapter treats various programming techniques for certain often-recurring problems, such as sorting, searching, and merging.   The second part of this chapter is devoted to various numerical calculations, such as the solution of linear equations, finding roots of polynomials, and multiplication of matrices.

8.2   SORTING

By sorting, we mean arranging elements in some order.   This process is familiar to everyday life.   The names in a telephone book are sorted into alphabetical order.   Student records may be sorted according to student ID numbers.   And so on.   Although sorting may seem to be a trivial task, sorting efficiently can be very difficult, both practically and theoretically.

Since sorting and searching are used in maintaining files in business data processing, we first introduce some terminology.   In data processing, one sorts a *file* of *records* according to a specific *key*.   For example, a university may maintain a *file* of its students.   For each student, the data appearing in the file is called a *record*.   The record may contain several *fields*; for example, name, social security number, student number, sex, class standing, cumulative average, and so on.   If we were to sort the file according to the alphabetical order of the names, then the name field is the *key*.   If we were to sort according to the social security number, then the social security number is the key.

For our purpose, we shall consider the problem of sorting an array of numbers A(1), A(2), . . . , A(N), say in increasing order, so that

$$A(1) < A(2) < A(3) < \cdots < A(N)$$

We will assume that we have instant access to the items and that they are stored in the main memory.   This is called *internal sort*.

Sometimes files are so large that they are kept on backup storage devices with limited access.   Sorting the files of this type—called *external sort*—is difficult and lies beyond the scope of this text.

(a) Bubble Sort

One way to sort A is by the algorithm called *Bubble Sort* discussed in Problem 6.12.   That is, first we compare A(1) and A(2) and arrange them in the desired order, in our case A(1) < A(2).   Then we compare A(2) and A(3) and arrange them so that A(2) < A(3).   Then we compare A(3) and A(4) and arrange them so that A(3) < A(4).   We continue until we compare A(N − 1) and

A(N) and arrange them so that A(N − 1) < A(N).   After this "sweeping" through the elements, the largest element is "bubbled up" to the top, i.e., to the Nth position.

We repeat the above process for the elements A(1), A(2), ..., A(N − 1).   After sweeping through these elements, the second largest element is bubbled up to the N − 1st position.   We continue this process, and after N − 1 sweeps, the array A will be sorted in increasing order.   The flowchart for the algorithm and the Fortran translation appear in Problem 6.12.

The efficiency of this algorithm can be improved as follows.   We note first that within each sweep (the outer DO loop), an interchange takes place only when there are elements which are not arranged in the desired order.   Accordingly, a counter can be added to count the number of interchanges in each sweep, and if no interchange takes place, then the array is sorted, and the job is done.

(b)   Selection Sort

The second sorting algorithm, called *Exchange Sort* or *Selection Sort*, works as follows.   We first find the smallest value in the array and put it in the first position.   Then we find the second smallest value and put it in the second position, and so on.   We state the algorithm more precisely as follows:

(1)   Find the position L of the smallest among the elements A(1), A(2), ..., A(N).   Interchange A(L) with A(1).

(2)   Find the position L of the smallest among A(2), A(3), ..., A(N).   Interchange A(L) with A(2).

....

(N − 1)   Find the position L of the smallest among A(N − 1), A(N).   Interchange A(L) with A(N − 1).

The array A will now be sorted in increasing order.

Observe that the steps are identical to one another; hence, we clearly can use a DO loop controlled by an index J ranging from 1 to N − 1.   Within this DO loop, we wish to find the position L of the smallest among A(J), ..., A(N), and then interchange A(L) with A(J).   The macro flowchart for the DO loop appears in Fig. 8-1(*a*), and the flowchart for finding the position L of the smallest among A(J), ..., A(N) appears in Fig. 8-1(*b*).   Combining these two flowcharts into one program gives us the following required sorting program:

```
C
C          SORTING PROGRAM FOR A(1), ... , A(N)
C
           NN = N − 1
           DO 100 J = 1, NN
C
C                 FIND LOCATION L OF SMALLEST
C
                  L = J
                  JJ = J + 1
                  DO 200 I = JJ, N
                        IF(A(L).LT.A(I)) GO TO 200
                        L = I
200               CONTINUE
C
C                 INTERCHANGE A(L) WITH A(J)
C
                  T = A(L)
                  A(L) = A(J)
                  A(J) = T
100        CONTINUE
```

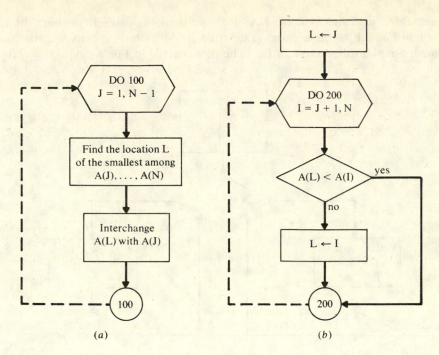

Fig. 8-1

Remark. The number of comparisons in the bubble sort method can be computed as follows. During the first sweep, there are $(N - 1)$ comparisons, during the second sweep there are $(N - 2)$ comparisons, and so on. Thus, the total number of comparisons is

$$(N - 1) + (N - 2) + \cdots + 2 + 1 = \frac{N(N - 1)}{2}$$

For the selection sort, one needs $(N - 1)$ comparisons to find the smallest element, $(N - 2)$ comparisons to find the second smallest element, and so on. Therefore, again a total of $N(N - 1)/2$ comparisons is required. We note that the average number of interchanges will be $N(N - 1)/4$, one-half the number of comparisons. By proper modification (cf. Problem 8.1), one can reduce the number of comparisons, but the average number of interchanges may be the same.

8.3   MERGING

Suppose A and B are sorted arrays (say, in increasing order) with M and N elements respectively. We wish to merge A and B into a sorted array C. One way to do this is to put A and B into C arbitrarily, say A at the beginning and B at the end, and then to sort C as in Section 8.2. Observe that this method does not use the fact that A and B are already sorted. A more efficient program is given below.

We first motivate our algorithm. Suppose we had two lines of students sorted by increasing heights, and suppose we want to merge them into one sorted line. One way to do this is to sequentially fill in the new line by the shorter of the two students who are at the head of the original lines until one of the lines has no more students. Then the remaining students line up at the end of the merged line.

In order to translate the above algorithm into Fortran, we must always keep track of the positions of the smallest elements of A and B which have not been placed in C. We will let NA and NB denote these positions, respectively. Thus, at each step we ask the question:

Is $A(NA) < B(NB)$?

If yes, we place A(NA) in C and increase NA by 1; and if no, we place B(NB) in C and increase NB by 1. If NA or NB reach its maximum value (that is, M or N respectively), then we place the remaining elements of the other array in C. The flowchart is in Fig. 8-2.

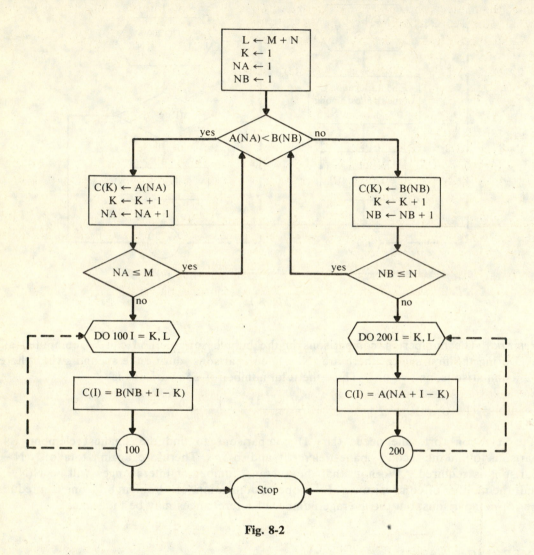

Fig. 8-2

8.4 SEARCHING

Suppose A is a linear array in memory, and we wish to find the position L of an element D in the array.

(a) Sequential Search (Linear Search)

Given no additional information about A, one can simply search for D by comparing it one by one with the elements of A. This method is called *sequential search* or *linear search* and is described in Problem 6.11. As can be easily seen, this method requires N comparisons to find D in the worst case and N/2 comparisons on the average.

(b) Binary Search

Suppose now A is a sorted array. Since the linear search method does not use the fact that A is sorted, a more efficient algorithm called *binary search*, can now be used to search for D.

We first motivate our algorithm.   Suppose we are searching for a name in a telephone directory where the names are listed alphabetically.   We do not search for the name sequentially from the first page on.   Rather, one opens the directory in the middle to decide which half of the directory contains the name.   Then one opens the half in the middle to decide which quarter of the directory contains the name, and so on until one finds the name.

We shall now formally describe the binary search algorithm.   First divide the array A into two parts:

$$A(1), A(2), \ldots, A(MID) \text{ and } A(MID), A(MID + 1), \ldots, A(N)$$

where   MID $= (1 + N)/2$.   That is,

(1)   IBEG $= 1$
(2)   IEND $= N$
(3)   MID $= (IBEG + IEND)/2$
(4)   If $D = A(MID)$, then L $=$ MID, and we are done.
(5)   If $D < A(MID)$, then D is in the first half of the array; otherwise D is in the second half of the array.

Observe that if D is in the first half of the array, then A(MID) is the end of the half; but, if D is in the second half of the array, then A(MID) is the beginning of the half.   We incorporate this idea in a loop by rewriting step 5 as follows:

(5)   If $D < A(MID)$, then reset IEND to MID and go to (3);
            or else reset IEND to IBEG and go to (3).

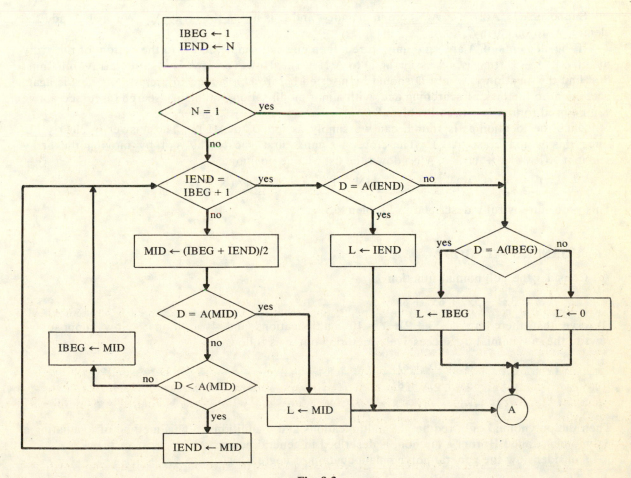

Fig. 8-3

The above procedure works fine as long as, at any given moment, the array segment A(IBEG),..., A(IEND) contains more than two elements. If the segment has two elements, i.e., if IEND = IBEG + 1, then MID will have the value

(IBEG + IBEG + 1)/2

which is again IBEG because of integer division. Accordingly, we would have an infinite loop if D > A(IBEG). To take care of this, we check to see if IBEG and IEND are consecutive integers.

One last point. If N = 1, that is, if the array originally began with only one element, then an infinite loop will also occur if D does not belong to the array. Thus, we must first test to see if N = 1. The flowchart of the algorithm appears in Fig. 8-3. Its Fortran translation is left as an exercise for the student (Problem 8.3).

Remark. We conclude this section by comparing the binary search method with the sequential search method. Using the binary search method, about half of the alternatives are eliminated each time around the loop. (See Fig. 8-3.) That is, given N original choices, there are N/2 choices left by the end of the first round, (N/2)/2 = N/4 choices left at the end of the second round, N/(2*2*2) = N/8 choices left at the end of the third round, and so on. The total number of comparisons in binary search in the worst case is $\log_2 N$, which is a great improvement over sequential search. In fact, $\log_2 N$ is much smaller than N/2, the average number of comparisons in sequential search. For example, if N = 10,000, then N/2 = 5000, but $\log_2 10,000 \approx 14$.

8.5 UPDATE

Suppose A(1), A(2),..., A(N) are in memory, and D is not in the array A. We wish to add the element D to this array.

If the elements of A are randomly stored, then one can simply add D to the bottom of the array by A(N + 1) ← D, that is, by assigning D to A(N + 1). However, if A is a sorted array, one must first find the location L where D should be inserted before D is added to the array. This is again equivalent to the task of searching and, with minor modification, the binary search discussed above can be used to find L. (See Problem 8.6.)

Once the location L is found, can we simply assign D to A(L)? The answer is clearly no, since this would erase A(L). Therefore, we must first vacate the slot by moving the array segment A(L), A(L + 1),..., A(N) down the list by one position:

A(L)   A(L + 1)   ...   A(N − 1)   A(N)   A(N + 1)

This procedure is fully described in Problem 6.10.

8.6 HORNER'S METHOD

Consider the polynomial function

$$f(x) = 3x^4 - 5x^3 + 6x^2 + 8x - 9$$

Observe that there are 4 + 3 + 2 + 1 = 10 multiplications and 4 additions. Now suppose we rewrite the polynomial by successively factoring out x as follows:

$$f(x) = (3x^3 - 5x^2 + 6x + 8)x - 9$$
$$= ((3x^2 - 5x + 6)x + 8)x - 9$$
$$= (((3x - 5)x + 6)x + 8)x - 9$$

Then the polynomial only requires 4 multiplications and 4 additions. This method of evaluating a polynomial, called Horner's method, is described in general below.

Consider now the general polynomial equation of degree *N*:

$$Y = F(X) = A_1X^N + A_2X^{N-1} + \cdots + A_NX + A_{N+1}$$

Evaluating the polynomial as it appears will require

$$N + (N - 1) + (N - 2) + \cdots + 2 + 1 = N(N + 1)/2$$

multiplications and N additions.   However, if one evaluates the polynomial using Horner's method:

$$Y = F(X) = ((\ldots((A_1X + A_2)X + A_3)X + \cdots)X + A_N)X + A_{N+1}$$

one would require only N multiplications and N additions.   Thus, this method is more efficient.

Horner's method has another important advantage.   Observe that at each step in evaluating Y, we multiply by X and add the next coefficient.   Thus, one can use a DO loop to evaluate Y as follows:

```
        Y = A(1)
        NN = N + 1
        DO 100 J = 2, NN
            Y = Y*X + A(J)
100  CONTINUE
```

In fact, one can write a subprogram to evaluate a polynomial of any degree.   (See Problem 8.13.)

Remark.   Suppose we let B(1), B(2), ..., B(N + 1) denote the partial results in Horner's method.   That is,

$$B(1) = A(1), \quad B(2) = B(1)*X + A(2), \quad \ldots, \quad B(N + 1) = B(N)*X + A(N + 1)$$

Then the value of the derivative $F'(X)$ can be shown to be

$$F'(X) = B_1X^{N-1} + B_2X^{N-2} + \cdots + B_{N-1}X + B_N$$

which can also be evaluated by Horner's method.   In fact, the following program segment gives $F(X)$ and $F'(X)$:

```
        B(1) = A(1)
        NN = N + 1
        DO 100 J = 2, NN
            B(J) = B(J - 1)*X + A(J)
100  CONTINUE
        C(1) = B(1)
        DO 200 K = 2, N
            C(K) = C(K - 1)*X + B(K)
200  CONTINUE
```

In this program segment, F(X) = B(N + 1) and F'(X) = C(N).

8.7 SOLUTIONS OF CERTAIN EQUATIONS

This section discusses finding real solutions of equations which come from polynomial, trigonometric, logarithmic, and exponential functions.   In general, there are two aspects to the problem:

1. Finding the vicinity of a root.
2. Approximating the root.

For pedagogical reasons, we first discuss methods of approximating a root if the vicinity is known.

Consider the polynomial equation

$$f(x) = x^3 - 4x^2 + 6x - 7 = 0$$

Note $f(2) = -3$ is negative and $f(3) = 2$ is positive. Since f is a polynomial function and its graph does not contain any breaks in its curve, the graph of f should cross the x axis between 2 and 3 as shown in Fig. 8-4. The point at which the graph crosses the x axis is a real solution of the equation. We give an algorithm, known as "interval halving", which finds an approximation of such a root, i.e., a number which is less than 0.001 from the actual root.

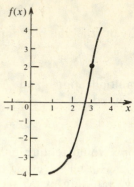

Fig. 8-4   Graph of $f(x)$.

(*a*)   Interval Halving

First set $XN = 2.0$ and $XP = 3.0$; that is, XN is the point at which f is negative, and XP is the point at which f is positive. The midpoint XM of XN and XP is given by the formula

$$XM = (XN + XP)/2$$

We find the midpoint XM and evaluate $f(XM)$:

$$XM = (XN + XP)/2 = 2.5 \quad \text{and} \quad f(XM) = f(2.5) = -1.375$$

Since $f(XM)$ is negative, reset $XN = 2.5$. Then find XM and $f(XM)$ again:

$$XM = 2.75 \quad \text{and} \quad f(XM) = f(2.75) = 0.046875$$

Since $f(XM)$ is positive, reset $XP = 2.75$. Note that the root now lies between 2.5 and 2.75.

We continue the above process. If at any step we obtain $f(XM) = 0$, then XM is a root; otherwise, XN and XP get closer and closer together. If

$$|XP - XN| < 0.001$$

the new XM will approximate an actual root to within 0.001.

The flowchart for this algorithm appears in Fig. 8-5.

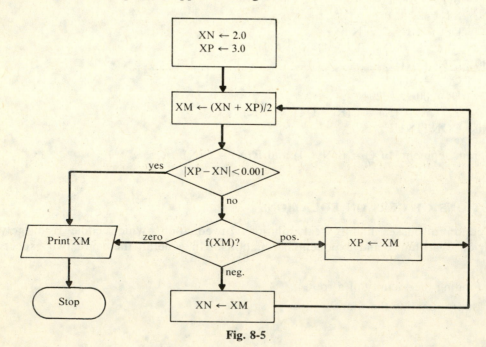

Fig. 8-5

(*b*)   Location of Roots

The above algorithm works fine if we are given the function $f(x)$ and the points A and B at which $f(A)$ and $f(B)$ have different signs.   The more difficult task is to find such points A and B.   This we shall discuss next.

Suppose we are given a function $f(x)$ and we seek a root between, say, $x = -5$ and $x = 5$.   We may evaluate $f(x)$ for $x = -5, -4, \ldots, 5$.   If f changes sign for any pair of values K and $K + 1$, then we know $f(x)$ has a root between K and $K + 1$, and we can proceed as in (*a*).   Specifically, we first set $XA = -5$ and $XB = XA + 1 = -4$ and test the product

F(XA)∗F(XB)

If the product is negative then $F(XA)$ and $F(XB)$ have different signs, and we can locate and print a root between XA and XB.   On the other hand, if the product is positive, then $F(XA)$ and $F(XB)$ have the same sign, and we do not know if there is a root between XA and XB.   In either case, we reset XA to be $XB = -4$ and then reset XB at $XA + 1 = -3$ and repeat the process.   The repetition ends after $XB = 5$.   Figure 8-6 gives a flowchart for such an algorithm.   The flowchart also takes into account the possibility that the product F(XA)∗F(XB) is zero, in which case XA may be a root.

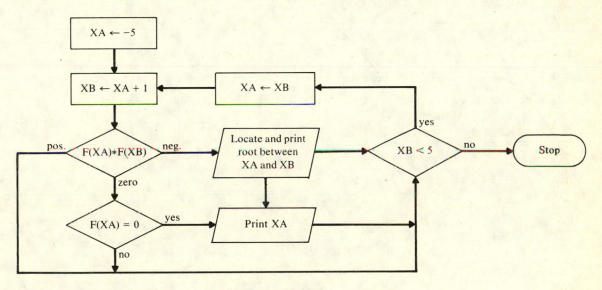

Fig. 8-6

The important thing to remember is that $f(x)$ may still have real roots even though it does not change signs at the points.   For example, the function

$$f(x) = 8x^2 - 26x + 21$$

has two roots between 1 and 2, and yet it is positive at all integral points.   Thus, one might want to evaluate $f(x)$ with smaller increments or in a larger interval before giving up on finding a solution. A deeper discussion of this problem lies beyond the scope of this text.

8.8 NUMERICAL INTEGRATION

Suppose a function f is positive in an interval $D = \{a \le x \le b\}$. We seek the area under the curve $y = f(x)$ between $x = a$ and $x = b$. This area is shaded in Fig. 8-7(a) and is equal to

$$\int_a^b f(x)\, dx$$

the integral of the function f from a to b.

We first divide D into n equal segments each with length $h = (a - b)/n$, by choosing the points

$$a_0 = a, \quad a_1 = a + h, \quad a_2 = a + 2h, \quad \ldots, \quad a_{n-1} = a + (n - 1)h, \quad a_n = a + nh = b$$

We claim that the following formula gives an approximation to the area:

$$\text{area} \approx \tfrac{1}{2}h[f(a_0) + 2f(a_1) + 2f(a_2) + \cdots + 2f(a_{n-1}) + f(a_n)]$$

This formula is called the "trapezoid rule" in view of its derivation which we describe below.

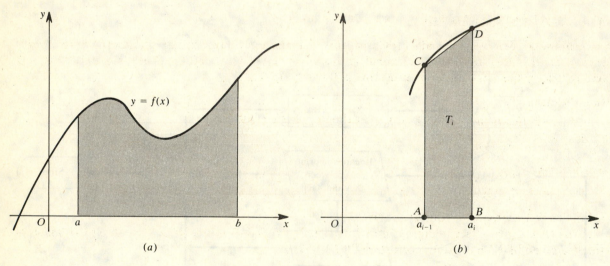

(a)   (b)

Fig. 8-7

Observe that when n is large and h is small, the curve $y = f(x)$ between $x = a_{i-1}$ and $x = a_i$ is almost linear as pictured in Fig. 8-7(b). Accordingly, the area under the curve is close to the area of the trapezoid T_i with vertices A, B, D, and C. Observe that

$$AC = f(a_{i-1}) \qquad \text{and} \qquad BD = f(a_i)$$

and that h is the distance between sides AC and BD. Hence,

$$\text{area}(T_i) = \tfrac{1}{2}h[f(a_{i-1}) + f(a_i)]$$

Consequently, the area under the curve is approximately equal to the sum of the areas of the trapezoids:

$$\text{area} \approx \text{area}(T_1) + \text{area}(T_2) + \cdots + \text{area}(T_n)$$

which gives the required formula.

The function $f(x) = 3x^3 - 4x^2 + 6x + 5$ is positive whenever x is positive. The following program reads A, B, N where $0 < A < B$, calculates the approximate area by the trapezoid rule, and prints A, B and the approximate area.

```
C         AREA BY TRAPEZOID RULE
          F(X) = ((3.0*X − 4.0)*X + 6.0)*X + 5.0
          READ(5, 10) A, B, N
10        FORMAT(2F8.2, I5)
          H = (B − A)/FLOAT(N)
          SUM = F(A) + F(B)
          NN = N − 1
          DO 200 K = 1, NN
                 SUM = SUM + 2*F(A + FLOAT(K)*H)
200       CONTINUE
          AREA = H*SUM/2.0
          WRITE(6, 20) A, B, AREA
20        FORMAT(1X, 2F10.2, F15.3)
          STOP
          END
```

8.9 VECTORS AND MATRICES

This section investigates algebraic operations on vectors and matrices.   Mathematically speaking, a vector is a linear array, and a matrix is a two-dimensional array.   (In the context of vectors and matrices, the term *scalar* is used for individual numbers.)

(*a*) Vectors

Mathematics usually denotes a vector (linear array) A by:

$$A = (A_1, A_2, \ldots, A_n)$$

For example,

$$A = (2, -3, 5, 7)$$

means A is a vector with four elements, 2, −3, 5, and 7.

Suppose A and B are vectors each with n elements, and X is a scalar.   The sum of A and B is the vector obtained by adding corresponding elements:

$$A + B = (A_1 + B_1, A_2 + B_2, \ldots, A_n + B_n)$$

The product of the vector A by a scalar X is the vector obtained by multiplying each element of A by X:

$$X \cdot A = (XA_1, XA_2, \ldots, XA_n)$$

The *inner* (*dot, scalar*) product of A and B, written $A \cdot B$, is the scalar

$$A \cdot B = A_1 B_1 + A_2 B_2 + \cdots + A_n B_n = \sum_{k=1}^{n} A_k B_k$$

The length (or: norm) of A, written $\|A\|$, is the scalar

$$\|A\| = \sqrt{A \cdot A} = \sqrt{A_1^2 + A_2^2 + \cdots + A_n^2}$$

For example, suppose $A = (2, -3, 5, 7)$ and $B = (4, 2, -1, 3)$.   Then

$$A + B = (2 + 4, -3 + 2, 5 - 1, 7 + 3) = (6, -1, 4, 10)$$
$$3A = (3 \cdot 2, 3 \cdot (-3), 3 \cdot 5, 3 \cdot 7) = (6, -9, 15, 21)$$
$$A \cdot B = 2 \cdot 4 + (-3) \cdot 2 + 5 \cdot (-1) + 7 \cdot 3 = 8 - 6 - 5 + 21 = 18$$
$$\|A\|^2 = 2^2 + (-3)^2 + 5^2 + 7^2 = 4 + 9 + 25 + 49 = 87, \text{ and so } \|A\| = \sqrt{87}$$
$$\|B\| = \sqrt{16 + 4 + 1 + 9} = \sqrt{30}$$

Suppose A, B, C, D are linear arrays with N elements, and X is a scalar.   The following is a program segment which stores in C the sum of A and B, stores in D the scalar product of X and A, and stores in DOT, ANORM, BNORM the scalars A·B, $\|A\|$, $\|B\|$, respectively.

```
        DOT = 0.0
        SUMA = 0.0
        SUMB = 0.0
        DO 100 K = 1, N
                C(K) = A(K) + B(K)
                D(K) = X*A(K)
                SUMA = SUMA + A(K)**2
                SUMB = SUMB + B(K)**2
                DOT = DOT + A(K)*B(K)
   100  CONTINUE
        ANORM = SQRT(SUMA)
        BNORM = SQRT(SUMB)
```

(b)   Matrix Addition and Scalar Multiplication

Recall first that a matrix is a two-dimensional array whose elements are usually written in the form of a rectangle where the first subscript denotes the row and the second subscript the column of the matrix.

Suppose $A = (a_{ij})$ and $B = (b_{ij})$ are $m \times n$ matrices.   The sum of A and B, written $A + B$, is the $m \times n$ matrix whose ijth element is $a_{ij} + b_{ij}$, i.e., obtained by adding the corresponding elements of A and B.   The product of the matrix A and a scalar k, written $k \cdot A$, is the $m \times n$ matrix whose ijth element is ka_{ij}, i.e., obtained by multiplying each element of A by k.

For example, suppose A and B are the following 2×3 matrices:

$$A = \begin{pmatrix} 1 & -3 & 5 \\ 2 & 0 & -6 \end{pmatrix} \quad \text{and} \quad B = \begin{pmatrix} 4 & 1 & -2 \\ 1 & -5 & -3 \end{pmatrix}$$

Then

$$A + B = \begin{pmatrix} 1+4 & -3+1 & 5-2 \\ 2+1 & 0-5 & -6-3 \end{pmatrix} = \begin{pmatrix} 5 & -2 & 3 \\ 3 & -5 & -9 \end{pmatrix}$$

$$-3A = \begin{pmatrix} -3\cdot1 & -3\cdot(-3) & -3\cdot5 \\ -3\cdot2 & -3\cdot0 & -3\cdot(-6) \end{pmatrix} = \begin{pmatrix} -3 & 9 & -15 \\ -6 & 0 & 18 \end{pmatrix}$$

As in ordinary algebra, $2A - 4B = 2A + (-4B)$.   Hence,

$$2A - 4B = \begin{pmatrix} 2 & -6 & 10 \\ 4 & 0 & -12 \end{pmatrix} + \begin{pmatrix} -16 & -4 & 8 \\ -4 & 20 & 12 \end{pmatrix} = \begin{pmatrix} -14 & -10 & 18 \\ 0 & 20 & 0 \end{pmatrix}$$

Now suppose A, B, C, D are M × N matrix arrays, and X and Y are scalars.   The following is a Fortran program segment which stores in C the sum of A and B and stores in D the matrix X*A + Y*B:

```
        DO 100 L = 1, M
                DO 200 J = 1, N
                        C(I, J) = A(I, J) + B(I, J)
                        D(I, J) = X*A(I, J) + Y*B(I, J)
   200          CONTINUE
   100  CONTINUE
```

Observe that nested DO loops are used in view of the two subscripts.

(c) Summation Symbol

Before we define matrix multiplication, it will be convenient to first introduce the *summation symbol* Σ (the Greek letter sigma).

Suppose $f(k)$ is an algebraic expression involving the variable k.   Then the expression

$$\sum_{k=1}^{n} f(k) \qquad \text{or equivalently} \qquad \sum_{k=1}^{n} f(k)$$

has the following meaning.   First we let $k = 1$ in $f(k)$, obtaining

$$f(1)$$

Then we let $k = 2$ in $f(k)$, obtaining $f(2)$, and add this to $f(1)$, obtaining

$$f(1) + f(2)$$

Next we let $k = 3$ in $f(k)$, obtaining $f(3)$, and add this to the previous sum, obtaining

$$f(1) + f(2) + f(3)$$

We continue this process until we obtain the sum

$$f(1) + f(2) + f(3) + \cdots + f(n - 1) + f(n)$$

Observe that at each step we increase the value of k by 1 until k is equal to n.   (We note that any other symbol, such as i or j, could have been used in place of the k.)

We also generalize our definition by allowing the sum to range from any integer n_1 to any integer n_2 where $n_1 \leq n_2$; that is, we define

$$\sum_{k=n_1}^{n_2} f(k) = f(n_1) + f(n_1 + 1) + f(n_1 + 2) + \cdots + f(n_2)$$

For example,

for $f(k) = x_k$, we have $\displaystyle\sum_{k=1}^{5} x_k = x_1 + x_2 + x_3 + x_4 + x_5$

for $f(i) = a_i b_i$, we have $\displaystyle\sum_{i=1}^{n} a_i b_i = a_1 b_1 + a_2 b_2 + \cdots + a_n b_n$

for $f(j) = j^2$, we have $\displaystyle\sum_{j=3}^{5} j^2 = 3^2 + 4^2 + 5^2 = 9 + 16 + 25 = 50$

Also, we have:

$$\sum_{k=1}^{5} (-1)^{k+1}(1/k) = 1 - 1/2 + 1/3 - 1/4 + 1/5$$

$$\sum_{k=1}^{p} a_{ik} b_{kj} = a_{i1} b_{1j} + a_{i2} b_{2j} + a_{i3} b_{3j} + \cdots + a_{ip} b_{pj}$$

$$\sum_{k=1}^{n+1} a_k x^{n+1-k} = a_1 x^n + a_2 x^{n-1} + \cdots + a_n x + a_{n+1}$$

(d) Matrix Multiplication

Suppose $A = (a_{ij})$ is an $m \times p$ matrix, and $B = (b_{ij})$ is a $p \times n$ matrix.   The product of A and B, written AB, is the $m \times n$ matrix $C = (c_{ij})$ whose ijth element c_{ij} is given by

$$c_{ij} = a_{i1} b_{1j} + a_{i2} b_{2j} + \cdots + a_{ip} b_{pj} = \sum_{k=1}^{p} a_{ik} b_{kj}$$

[We may view c_{ij} as the scalar obtained by the inner (dot) product of the ith row of A and the jth column of B.]

For example, suppose A and B are the following 2×3 and 3×4 matrices respectively:

$$A = \begin{pmatrix} 1 & 2 & 3 \\ 4 & 5 & 6 \end{pmatrix} \quad \text{and} \quad B = \begin{pmatrix} 5 & 6 & 7 & 8 \\ -1 & -2 & -3 & -4 \\ 0 & 9 & 0 & 9 \end{pmatrix}$$

To obtain the product $C = AB$, we note that C will be a 2×4 matrix. The element c_{11} is the inner product of the first row of A and the first column of B:

$$c_{11} = (1, 2, 3) \cdot (5, -1, 0) = 5 - 2 + 0 = 3$$

The element c_{12} is the inner product of the first row of A and the second column of B:

$$c_{12} = (1, 2, 3) \cdot (6, -2, 9) = 6 - 4 + 27 = 29$$

Similarly,

$$c_{13} = 7 - 6 + 0 = 1$$
$$c_{14} = 8 - 8 + 27 = 27$$

The second row of C is obtained by multiplying the second row of A by each of the columns of B:

$$c_{21} = 20 - 5 + 0 = 15$$
$$c_{22} = 24 - 10 + 54 = 68$$
$$c_{23} = 28 - 15 + 0 = 13$$
$$c_{24} = 32 - 20 + 54 = 66$$

Accordingly,

$$C = \begin{pmatrix} 3 & 29 & 1 & 27 \\ 15 & 68 & 13 & 66 \end{pmatrix}$$

Observe that the product BA is not defined since the number of columns of B (which is 4) is not equal to the number of rows of A (which is 2).

Generally speaking, if A is an M × L matrix and B is an L × N matrix, then the element c_{ij} in the product matrix C = AB can be calculated by

```
      C(I, J) = 0.0
      DO 100 INDEX = 1, L
            C(I, J) = C(I, J) + A(I, INDEX)*B(INDEX, J)
100   CONTINUE
```

In fact, the following is a complete SUBROUTINE subprogram which finds C:

```
      SUBROUTINE MATMUL(A, B, M, L, N, C)
      DIMENSION A(M, L), B(L, N), C(M, N)
      DO 300 I = 1, M
            DO 200 J = 1, N
                  C(I, J) = 0.0
                  DO 100 INDEX = 1, L
                        C(I, J) = C(I, J) + A(I, INDEX)*B(INDEX, J)
100               CONTINUE
200         CONTINUE
300   CONTINUE
      RETURN
      END
```

8.10   LINEAR EQUATIONS

This section is devoted to the solution of a system of n linear equations in n unknowns. We first consider the special case of a triangular system, and then we consider the general case using Gaussian elimination.

(*a*)   Triangular System

The following system of linear equations is said to be in triangular form ·

$$a_{11}x_1 + a_{12}x_2 + \cdots\cdots\cdots\cdots + a_{1,n-1}x_{n-1} + a_{1n}x_n = b_1$$
$$a_{22}x_2 + \cdots\cdots\cdots\cdots + a_{2,n-1}x_{n-1} + a_{2n}x_n = b_2$$
$$\cdots\cdots\cdots\cdots\cdots\cdots\cdots\cdots\cdots$$
$$a_{n-2,n-2}x_{n-2} + a_{n-2,n-1}x_{n-1} + a_{n-2,n}x_n = b_{n-2}$$
$$a_{n-1,n-1}x_{n-1} + a_{n-1,n}x_n = b_{n-1}$$
$$a_{nn}x_n = b_n$$

Here $x_1, x_2, \ldots, x_n$ are the n unknowns, and the $a_{11}, a_{12}, \ldots, a_{1n}, \ldots, a_{nn}$ are the coefficients. We assume that since none of the diagonal entries $a_{11}, a_{22}, \ldots, a_{nn}$ are zero, the system has a unique solution. We will also refer to the equations by $L_1, L_2, \ldots, L_n$ respectively.

Solving for x_n in the last equation L_n, we obtain

$$x_n = b_n/a_{nn}$$

We now solve for the rest of the unknowns by the process known as *back-substitution*. Specifically, we substitute for x_n in the next-to-last equation L_{n-1} and solve for x_{n-1} obtaining

$$x_{n-1} = (b_{n-1} - a_{n-1,n}x_n)/a_{n-1,n-1}$$

We next substitute for x_n and x_{n-1} in the third-from-last equation L_{n-2} and solve for x_{n-2} obtaining

$$x_{n-2} = (b_{n-2} - a_{n-2,n-1}x_{n-1} - a_{n-2,n}x_n)/a_{n-2,n-2}$$

and so on. That is, for each $k < n$, we substitute for $x_n, \ldots, x_{k+1}$ in L_k and solve for x_k obtaining

$$x_k = (b_k - a_{k,k+1}x_{k+1} - \cdots - a_{kn}x_n)/a_{kk} = \left(b_k - \sum_{m=k+1}^{n} a_{km}x_m\right)\Big/ a_{kk}$$

(The name *back-substitution* comes from the fact that the x_k are obtained in reverse order.)

Suppose the above triangular system is stored in the computer by an $N \times (N+1)$ array. The subroutine BKSUB, which follows, will store the solution in an array X:

```
            SUBROUTINE BKSUB(A, N, L, X)
            DIMENSION A(N, L), X(N)
            X(N) = A(N, N + 1)/A(N, N)
            NN = N - 1
            DO 100 J = 1, NN
                K = N - J
C               CALCULATING SUM FOR X(K)
                SUM = 0.0
                NNN = N - K
                DO 200 JJ = 1, NNN
                    M = K + JJ
                    SUM = SUM + A(K, M)*X(M)
200             CONTINUE
C               SOLVING FOR X(K)
                X(K) = (A(K, N + 1) - SUM)/A(K, K)
100         CONTINUE
            RETURN
            END
```

Observe the nested DO loops in the subroutine. The outer DO loop refers to the variable x_k in equation L_k, and the inner DO loop refers to the summation in the formula for x_k. We must also take into account that the x_k are obtained in reverse order, and that the summation for x_k is from $k + 1$ to n.

Observe also that L denotes the number of columns in A, and, hence, should always be equal to N + 1.

(*b*) General System

A general system of n linear equations $E_1, E_2, \ldots, E_n$ in n unknowns $x_1, x_2, \ldots, x_n$ can be denoted by:

$$a_{11}x_1 + a_{12}x_2 + \cdots + a_{1n}x_n = b_1$$
$$a_{21}x_1 + a_{22}x_2 + \cdots + a_{2n}x_n = b_2$$
$$\cdots\cdots\cdots\cdots\cdots\cdots\cdots\cdots\cdots\cdots$$
$$a_{n1}x_1 + a_{n2}x_2 + \cdots + a_{nn}x_n = b_n$$

We will assume that the system has a unique solution. Note that one can always interchange two equations or add a multiple of one equation to another without changing the solution. We shall now discuss the method of Gaussian elimination which uses these steps to transform the system into an equivalent system in triangular form. Once in triangular form, one uses back-substitution to find its solution.

First we eliminate x_1 from equations $E_2, E_3, \ldots, E_n$ by the following two steps:

1. Find the equation E_k such that the coefficient a_{k1} of x_1 has the largest absolute value among all the coefficients of x_1, and interchange E_k with E_1. In other words, interchange equations so that a_{11} has the largest absolute value among the coefficients of x_1. (This guarantees that $a_{11} \neq 0$ and also leads to better accuracy.)

2. Use the first equation E_1 and, in particular, the coefficient a_{11} of x_1 to eliminate the x_1 from the remaining equations as follows. For $k > 1$, multiply E_1 by $m_{k1} = -a_{k1}/a_{11}$ and add the equation to E_k. (The coefficient a_{11} is called the *pivot* in this step.)

The above steps transform the system into the form

$$a_{11}x_1 + a_{12}x_2 + a_{13}x_3 + \cdots + a_{1n}x_n = b_1$$
$$a_{22}x_2 + a_{23}x_3 + \cdots + a_{2n}x_n = b_2$$
$$\cdots\cdots\cdots\cdots\cdots\cdots\cdots\cdots\cdots\cdots$$
$$a_{n2}x_2 + a_{n3}x_3 + \cdots + a_{nn}x_n = b_n$$

(Naturally, the a_{ij}, b_i in the new system need not be the same as the a_{ij}, b_i in the original system.)

We repeat the above process with the subsystem $E_2, \ldots, E_n$; that is, we eliminate x_2 from equations $E_3, \ldots, E_n$ by the analogous two steps:

1. Interchange equations (excluding E_1) so that the pivoting element a_{22} has the largest absolute value among the coefficients of x_2 in the subsystem.

2. For $k > 2$, multiply E_2 by $m_{k2} = -a_{k2}/a_{22}$ and add it to E_k.

These steps transform the system into the form

$$a_{11}x_1 + a_{12}x_2 + a_{13}x_3 + a_{14}x_4 + \cdots + a_{1n}x_n = b_1$$
$$a_{22}x_2 + a_{23}x_3 + a_{24}x_4 + \cdots + a_{2n}x_n = b_2$$
$$a_{33}x_3 + a_{34}x_4 + \cdots + a_{3n}x_n = b_3$$
$$\cdots\cdots\cdots\cdots\cdots\cdots\cdots\cdots\cdots$$
$$a_{n3}x_3 + a_{n4}x_4 + \cdots + a_{nn}x_n = b_n$$

After repeating the above process $n - 1$ times, the system will be transformed into triangular form which can then be solved by back-substitution.

We now wish to translate the above algorithm into a SUBROUTINE subprogram called GAUSS. We shall assume that the system of linear equations is stored in memory by its *augmented matrix*, i.e., the N × (N + 1) array

$$\begin{pmatrix} A_{11} & A_{12} & \ldots & A_{1N} & A_{1,N+1} \\ A_{21} & A_{22} & \ldots & A_{2N} & A_{2,N+1} \\ \cdots & \cdots & \cdots & \cdots & \cdots \\ A_{N1} & A_{N2} & \ldots & A_{NN} & A_{N,N+1} \end{pmatrix}$$

where the N + 1st column of the matrix is the column of constants of the equations. Our subroutine GAUSS will use the following three subroutines which are given in Problem 7.14:

1. SUBROUTINE FIND(A, N, L, K, J)

    which finds the row J such that A(J, K) contains the largest absolute value among A(K, K), A(K + 1, K), . . . , A(N, K).

2. SUBROUTINE CHANGE(A, N, L, K, J)

    which interchanges the elements of the Kth row of A with the corresponding elements of the Jth row.

3. SUBROUTINE ROWMUL(A, N, L, K, J, D)

    which adds D times the Kth row to the Jth row.

(In these subroutines, A is an N × L matrix array.)

We can eliminate x_1 from equations $E_2, \ldots, E_n$ using the program segment

```
        CALL FIND(A, N, N + 1, 1, J)
        CALL CHANGE(A, N, N + 1, 1, J)
        DO 100 I = 2, N
            CALL ROWMUL(A, N, N + 1, 1, I, −A(I, 1)/A(1, 1))
100 CONTINUE
```

Similarly, we can eliminate x_2 from equations $E_3, \ldots, E_n$ with the program segment.

```
        CALL FIND(A, N, N + 1, 2, J)
        CALL CHANGE(A, N, N + 1, 2, J)
        DO 200 I = 3, N
            CALL ROWMUL(A, N, N + 1, 2, I, −A(I, 2)/A(2, 2))
200 CONTINUE
```

And so on. The complete subprogram uses a DO loop for each of the above steps, and then uses the subroutine BKSUB to find the solution after the system is in triangular form.

```
        SUBROUTINE GAUSS(A, N, L, X)
C
C       SOLUTION BY GAUSSIAN ELIMINATION
C
        DIMENSION A(N, L), X(N)
        NN = N - 1
        DO 99 K = 1, NN
            CALL FIND(A, N, N + 1, K, J)
            CALL CHANGE(A, N, N + 1, K, J)
            KK = K + 1
            DO 88 I = KK, N
                CALL ROWMUL(A, N, N + 1, K, I, -A(I, K)/A(K, K))
88          CONTINUE
99      CONTINUE
        CALL BKSUB(A, N, N + 1, X)
        RETURN
        END
```

Problems

PROGRAMMING TECHNIQUES

8.1   Modify the bubble sort program in Problem 6.12 to include a counter which counts the number of interchanges.   If in any sweep no exchange takes place, terminate the program.

8.2   Translate into Fortran the flowchart in Fig. 8-2 which merges two sorted arrays A and B into a sorted array C.   Test the program with the data:

A: 1, 5, 6, 12, 14, 21;   B: 2, 3, 9, 16, 18, 19, 24, 28

8.3   Translate into Fortran the flowchart in Fig. 8-3 which gives the binary search algorithm.

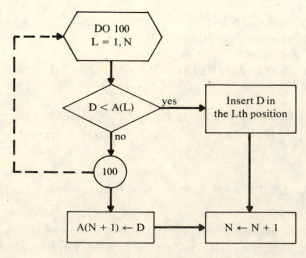

Fig. 8-8

8.4   (*Update*)   Suppose A(1), A(2), . . . , A(N) are in increasing order, and suppose D is not in the array A.   The flowchart in Fig. 8-8 updates A by using a linear search to find the position L where D should be inserted.   Translate the flowchart into Fortran.

8.5   (*Update*)   Modify the program in Problem 8.4 so that a binary search is used to find the position L where D should be inserted.

8.6   (*Search and Update*)   Suppose A(1), A(2), . . . , A(N) are in increasing order, and an item D is given.   If D belongs to the array A, we wish to find its position; but if D does not belong to A, then we wish to update A by finding the position L where D should be inserted.

    (*a*)   Write such a program using sequential search.
    (*b*)   Write such a program using binary search.

8.7   (*Insertion Sort*)   Another sorting algorithm called insertion sort is described below.   The main idea is to insert an item into its proper position relative to an already sorted portion of the file.   Namely, sort the first two items A(1), A(2).   Insert the third item so that A(1), A(2), A(3) are properly ordered.   In general, A(K) is inserted into the sorted array segment A(1), . . . , A(K − 1) so that A(1), . . . , A(K) is properly sorted.

    Write a program for insertion sort.   Observe that the position into which A(K) should be placed can be found by sequential search or binary search.   Discuss the maximum number of comparisons that may be required in each case.   Discuss the drawback of insertion sort.

8.8   (*Merge-Sort*)   Another well-known and efficient sorting algorithm is called *merge-sort*.   The algorithm is outlined below.   In the first sweep, sort the first pair, the second pair, the third pair, and so on until all pairs are sorted, i.e., so that each of

$$\{A_1, A_2\}, \{A_3, A_4\}, \{A_5, A_6\}, \{A_7, A_8\}, \{A_9, A_{10}\}, \ldots$$

are sorted.   In the second sweep, the first pair of sorted array segments of two elements are merged, then the second pair of sorted array segments of two elements are merged, and so on.   At the end of the second sweep, each of the quadruplets

$$\{A_1, A_2, A_3, A_4\}, \{A_5, A_6, A_7, A_8\}, \{A_9, A_{10}, A_{11}, A_{12}\}, \ldots$$

is sorted.   Pairs of quadruplets are then merged in the third sweep, and so on until the entire array is sorted.   Write a program to implement this idea.   Show that this algorithm requires approximately $n \log_2 n$ comparisons.

8.9   (*a*)   Write a subroutine DELETE which deletes a given array segment A(IN), A(IN + 1), . . . , A(LAST) from an array A.   [Hint: Move the array segment A(LAST + 1), . . . , A(N) up an appropriate number of slots.]
    (*b*)   Suppose the array ID(1), ID(2), . . . , ID(N) is in memory, but some of the entries are zero.   Write a program to compress the array ID by using DELETE.

8.10   Suppose each salesperson in a department store is assigned an ID number.   For each sale made, a card is punched with the salesperson's ID and the amount of the sale.   At the end of a day, these cards are collected, but they are not in any order.   Write a program to calculate the total sales made by each salesperson.

8.11   Suppose the Computing Activities Center of a university charges its user at the rate of $600.00 per hour.   Each user is assigned a user's ID.   For each job run by the computer, a card is punched with the user's ID and the time in seconds the job required.   These cards are not sorted.   Assuming a flat handling charge of $5.00 is also added to each run, write a program to calculate the total bill for each user.   Use a trailer card to terminate.

8.12   In the master file of Adler Telephone Company, each record consists of a customer's account number and his/her basic monthly charge. These records are punched on cards, one record per card, and the master file is sorted according to account number. When a long distance telephone call is made, a card is punched with the customer's account number and the long distance charge. These cards are not sorted in any way.

Suppose telephone bills are prepared at the end of each month. Assuming that the Adler Telephone Company serves no more than 100 customers, and that the long distance cards are separated from the master file by a blank card, and the deck is terminated by a trailer card, write a program to calculate the bills for each customer.

NUMERICAL CALCULATIONS

8.13   Write a function subprogram HORNER(A, N, X) which calculates the value of the $N - 1$st degree polynomial

$$A_1 X^{N-1} + A_2 X^{N-2} + \cdots + A_{N-1} X + A_N$$

8.14   Find a root of $f(x) = x^3 - 4x^2 + 6x + 7$ between $x = 2$ and $x = 3$ by translating into Fortran the flowchart on interval halving in Fig. 8-5.

8.15   Locate and find the three real roots of $f(x) = x^3 + x^2 - 37x + 33$ between $x = -10$ and $x = 10$ using the algorithm described in Fig. 8-6 for locating the roots and the algorithm of interval halving for finding the roots.

8.16   Find two real roots of $f(x) = x^2 - \sin x$.

8.17   Find the area under the curve $y = x^2 - 3x + 4$ between $x = 3$ and $x = 5$.

8.18   Find the area under the curve $y = x^2 + \sin x$ between $x = 0$ and $x = 2$.

8.19   Write a subroutine subprogram NEWTON(A, N, X, Y, Z) which calculates $Y = F(X)$ and $Z = F'(X)$ where

$$F(X) = A_1 X^{N-1} + A_2 X^{N-2} + \cdots + A_{N-1} X + A_N$$

and $F'(X)$ is the derivative of $F(X)$. Compare with Problem 8.13. (Hint: See discussion at the end of Section 8.6.)

8.20   (*Newton-Raphson*)   Consider the functional equation

$$F(X) = 0$$

Let X_0 denote a value in the vicinity of a solution of the equation. We form the sequence

$$X_1 = X_0 - F(X_0)/F'(X_0), \quad X_2 = X_1 - F(X_1)/F'(X_1), \quad \ldots$$

that is,

$$X_{N+1} = X_N - F(X_N)/F'(X_N)$$

[Here $F'(X)$ denotes the derivative of $F(X)$.] Under certain conditions, whose discussion lies beyond the scope of this text, the sequence $X_0, X_1, X_2, \ldots$ converges to a root of $F(X)$. (This process is called the Newton–Raphson method.) Write a program using this method to calculate $\sqrt{5}$, that is, to find a solution of

$$X^2 - 5 = 0$$

Choose $X_0 = 3$ and terminate the program when $|X_{N+1} - X_N| \leq 0.001$.

8.21 Use the Newton–Raphson method to find to three decimal places the roots of $x^2 + x - 11 = 0$. First choose $x_0 = -5$ and then $x_0 = 5$.

VECTORS, MATRICES, LINEAR EQUATIONS

8.22 Suppose $A = (2, -1, 0, -3)$, $B = (1, -4, -4, 3)$, $C = (1, 3, -2, 5)$.

(a) Find: (i) $2A - 3B$; (ii) $5A - 3B - 4C$; (iii) $A \cdot B$, $A \cdot C$, and $B \cdot C$; (iv) $\|A\|$, $\|B\|$, and $\|C\|$.

(b) Write a Fortran program to calculate the above.

8.23 Suppose

$$A = \begin{pmatrix} 1 & -1 & 2 \\ 0 & 3 & 4 \end{pmatrix}, \qquad B = \begin{pmatrix} 4 & 0 & -3 \\ -1 & -2 & 3 \end{pmatrix}, \qquad C = \begin{pmatrix} 2 & -3 & 0 & 1 \\ 5 & -1 & -4 & 2 \\ -1 & 0 & 0 & 3 \end{pmatrix},$$

and $D = \begin{pmatrix} 2 & 2 \\ 3 & -1 \end{pmatrix}$

Find: (a) $A + B$ (d) AC (g) D^3
        (b) $3A - 4B$ (e) BC (h) DA
        (c) $2A + 3B$ (f) D^2 (i) DB

8.24 Suppose six cards each contain three real numbers. Write a program which reads these numbers into the rows of two 3×3 matrix arrays A and B, and calculates and prints: (a) $5A + 2B$, (b) $3A - 7B$, (c) AB, (d) BA, (e) A^2.

8.25 Consider the 6×6 matrix A with 0 on the main diagonal, 1 above the main diagonal, and -1 below the main diagonal:

$$A = \begin{pmatrix} 0 & 1 & 1 & 1 & 1 & 1 \\ -1 & 0 & 1 & 1 & 1 & 1 \\ -1 & -1 & 0 & 1 & 1 & 1 \\ -1 & -1 & -1 & 0 & 1 & 1 \\ -1 & -1 & -1 & -1 & 0 & 1 \\ -1 & -1 & -1 & -1 & -1 & 0 \end{pmatrix}$$

Write a program which stores A in the computer and calculates and prints A, A^2, and A^3.

8.26 Find the solution of the system:

$$\begin{aligned}
3x + 4y - 5z + 2s + 6t &= 10 \\
5y + 7z - 4s - 6t &= -1 \\
2z + 6s - 3t &= -35 \\
8s + 3t &= -11 \\
5t &= 35
\end{aligned}$$

8.27 Find the solution of the system:

$$\begin{aligned}
2x + 3y + 4z - 5s + 7t &= -35 \\
8x - 2y - 3z + 9s + 3t &= 53 \\
4y + 6z - 3s - 2t &= -33 \\
5x - 7y + 8z + 3s - 9t &= -19 \\
3x + 5y - 2z + 4s + 6t &= 27
\end{aligned}$$

8.28 (*Gauss–Jordan*) Suppose a system of N equations in N unknowns is stored in the computer by an N × (N + 1) matrix array A. One can modify the Gaussian method and transform the matrix into the form

$$\begin{pmatrix} A_{11} & 0 & \dots & 0 & A_{1,N+1} \\ 0 & A_{22} & \dots & 0 & A_{2,N+1} \\ \dots\dots\dots\dots\dots\dots\dots\dots\dots \\ 0 & 0 & \dots & A_{NN} & A_{N,N+1} \end{pmatrix}$$

rather than into triangular form. The solution of the system is then:

$$X_1 = A_{1,N+1}/A_{11}, \quad X_2 = A_{2,N+1}/A_{22}, \quad \dots, \quad X_N = A_{N,N+1}/A_{NN}$$

(This process is called the Gauss–Jordan method.) Write a program to implement this algorithm and test the program with the system in Problem 8.24.

8.29 Let A be an N × N square matrix. An N × N matrix B is called the *inverse* of A if AB = BA = I, where I is the identity matrix, the matrix with 1's on the main diagonal and 0's elsewhere. The inverse of A, if it exists, is unique and denoted by A^{-1}. One algorithm for finding A^{-1} follows. First form the N × 2N matrix

$$(A, I) = \begin{pmatrix} A_{11} & A_{12} & \dots & A_{1N} & 1 & 0 & \dots & 0 \\ A_{21} & A_{22} & \dots & A_{2N} & 0 & 1 & \dots & 0 \\ \dots\dots\dots\dots\dots\dots\dots\dots\dots\dots\dots\dots \\ A_{N1} & A_{N2} & \dots & A_{NN} & 0 & 0 & \dots & 1 \end{pmatrix}$$

i.e., the left half of the matrix is A and the right half is I. Using a modification of the Gaussian method, one transforms the above matrix into a matrix of the form

$$(I, B) = \begin{pmatrix} 1 & 0 & \dots & 0 & B_{11} & B_{12} & \dots & B_{1N} \\ 0 & 1 & \dots & 0 & B_{21} & B_{22} & \dots & B_{2N} \\ \dots\dots\dots\dots\dots\dots\dots\dots\dots\dots\dots\dots \\ 0 & 0 & \dots & 1 & B_{N1} & B_{N2} & \dots & B_{NN} \end{pmatrix}$$

i.e., where the left half is now I. The right half B is then the inverse of A. Write a program to implement this algorithm.

Answers to Selected Problems

8.22   (*i*) (1, 10, 12, −15)   (*ii*) (3, −5, 20, −44)   (*iii*) −3, −16, 12   (*iv*) $\sqrt{14}, \sqrt{42},$ and $\sqrt{39}$

8.23

(*a*) $\begin{pmatrix} 5 & -1 & -1 \\ -1 & 1 & 7 \end{pmatrix}$ (*d*) $\begin{pmatrix} -5 & -2 & 4 & 5 \\ 11 & -3 & -12 & 18 \end{pmatrix}$ (*g*) $\begin{pmatrix} 26 & 18 \\ 27 & -1 \end{pmatrix}$

(*b*) $\begin{pmatrix} -13 & -3 & 18 \\ 4 & 17 & 0 \end{pmatrix}$ (*e*) $\begin{pmatrix} 11 & -12 & 0 & -5 \\ -15 & 5 & 8 & 4 \end{pmatrix}$ (*h*) $\begin{pmatrix} 2 & 4 & 12 \\ 3 & -6 & 2 \end{pmatrix}$

(*c*) $\begin{pmatrix} 14 & -2 & -5 \\ -3 & 0 & 17 \end{pmatrix}$ (*f*) $\begin{pmatrix} 10 & 2 \\ 3 & 7 \end{pmatrix}$ (*i*) $\begin{pmatrix} 6 & -4 & 0 \\ 13 & 2 & -12 \end{pmatrix}$

8.26 $x = 3, y = -2, z = 5, s = -4, t = 7$

8.27 $x = 2, y = 1, z = -5, s = 3, t = -1$

Chapter 9

Character Information.
Logical Variables and Operations

9.1 INTRODUCTION

Fortran was mainly developed for FORmula TRANslation. However, Fortran can also manipulate character information. Recall that we were able to print out messages by placing the message between a pair of apostrophes in the FORMAT statement. For example,

        WRITE(6, 10)
    10 FORMAT(1X, 'THE END')

will cause the message

    THE END

to be printed. This message has seven characters, T, H, E, a blank space (which we subsequently denote by $_b$), E, N, and D. Fortran also allows us to read and store such character strings and to manipulate them, e.g., to alphabetize a list of names. In this chapter, we will discuss symbol manipulation using Fortran.

Fortran can also be used to perform logical operations and evaluate logical expressions. This will also be discussed in this chapter.

9.2 STORING CHARACTERS

When characters are stored in computer memory, they are stored in codes. In a binary machine, characters are stored as a sequence of 0's and 1's. Clearly, such a sequence may be interpreted as a binary number. This number is termed the numeric equivalent of the character information. One point needs to be emphasized. The internal representation of

    1234

stored as a character string is completely different from the internal representation of 1234 stored as an integer.

There is a limit on the maximum number of characters that can be stored in any given memory location. This number, which varies from machine to machine, will be called the *character capacity* (or simply *capacity*) of the machine and will be denoted by the letter M. For machines in the IBM 360/370 series, M = 4, and in the CDC 6000 series, M = 10. (To make programs portable, it is advisable that one assumes M = 4.)

Theoretically, one may use either real or integer locations to store character information. However, it is safer to use only integer locations as this avoids any round-off error that may occur if the character information is manipulated.

One way to store character information is by the nonexecutable DATA statement. (The DATA statement is discussed in detail in Section 10.2.) For example, the statement

        DATA NAME/'PAT'/

placed before any executable statement in the program, will store the character string PAT in a location called NAME. The apostrophes signal to the computer that PAT will be stored as characters.   The slashes are used to enclose the input item, thus separating it from the variable name.   Assuming the character capacity M = 4, PAT will be stored in memory as follows:

NAME | P | A | T | b |

i.e., the character string will be stored left-justified in the memory location and padded with blank spaces on the right.

On the other hand, suppose the statement

DATA ID/'JOHNSON'/

is given; i.e., the character string JOHNSON is to be stored in the memory location called ID. Again the character string will be stored left-justified in memory.   However, assuming M = 4 is the capacity, the excess characters on the right will be chopped off, and only JOHN will be stored:

ID | J | O | H | N |

Namely, only the M = 4 left-most characters will be stored in memory.

The following comments are in order.

1. Some compilers do allow character constants to appear in executable statements.   In that case, one may store character information by an assignment statement. For example, the statement

NAME = 'PAT'

will have the same effect as

DATA NAME/'PAT'/

That is, the character string PAT between the apostrophes will be stored in a memory location called NAME.

2. With M = 4, one would require at least two locations to store the character string JOHNSON.   For example, any one of the following,

DATA IDA/'JOHN'/
DATA IDB/'SON'/

or

DATA IDA/'JOHN'/, IDB/'SON'/

or

DATA IDA, IDB/'JOHN', 'SON'/

will store JOHN in IDA and SON_b in IDB:

IDA | J | O | H | N | IDB | S | O | N | b |

3. One can also use H-field instead of apostrophes in the DATA statement; e.g.,

DATA NAME/3HPAT/

also stores the character string PAT in NAME. (See Section 9.5.)

CHAP. 9]   CHARACTER INFORMATION. LOGICAL VARIABLES, OPERATIONS   219

4. Although some compilers do not allow character constants to appear in executable statements as in (1), one can always copy the content of one location into another by an assignment statement.   For example, assuming M = 4, the program segment

        DATA NAME/'PAT'/
        NEXT = NAME

will store PAT$_b$, the content of NAME, in a memory location called NEXT:

NEXT | P | A | T | $_b$ |

Observe that NEXT and NAME are both integer variables.   It is advisable not to mix types in such assignment statements.

Warning.   When the length l of a character constant in a DATA statement exceeds the character capacity M, some compilers may give an error message.   There are other possibilities which are discussed in Problem 10.3.   However, all compilers give the same result when $l \leq$ M.

9.3   A-FIELD

Another way to store character information is by having the information read in, say, by a READ statement.   When character information is to be read in or printed out, one uses the A-field, whose specification has the form

        Aw

where w is the field width.   (One can also use *rAw*, where r is the repetition factor.)

(*a*) Input

Suppose the capacity M = 4 and a data card is punched as follows:

```
                      1                 2
          1 2 3 4 5 6 7 8 9 0 1 2 3 4 5 6 7 8 9 0 1 2 3 4 5

          L O N G F E L L O W
```

Furthermore, suppose the input instruction is

        READ(5, 10) NAME
    10 FORMAT(A3)

This tells the computer that the character string in columns 1–3 is to be stored in the location called NAME.   Here the field width $w = 3$ does not exceed the character capacity M, and so the character string will be stored left-justified in memory with blanks padded on the right:

NAME | L | O | N | $_b$ |

On the other hand, suppose the input instruction were

        READ(5, 20) NAME
    20 FORMAT(A10)

Here the field width $w = 10$ exceeds M.   In this case, only the M = 4 right-most characters in the field will be stored in memory:

NAME | L | L | O | W |

Observe that the DATA statement

> DATA NAME/'LONGFELLOW'/

will have a different result. Namely, the DATA statement will input only the M = 4 left-most characters in memory:

NAME | L | O | N | G |

The above results can be summarized as follows:

Rules on character input using A-field. Suppose M is the character capacity and w is the field width given in the input FORMAT statement.

1. If $w \leq M$, then the w characters in the field will be stored left-justified in memory with $M - w$ blanks on the right.

2. If $w > M$, then only the M right-most characters in the field will be stored in memory.

Accordingly, to read in the name LONGFELLOW using the above data card and with M = 4, we require at least three memory locations.   For example,

> READ(5, 10) L1, L2, L3
> 10   FORMAT(3A4)

will store the first four characters LONG in L1, the second four characters FELL in L2, and the third four characters OW_{bb} in L3:

L1 | L | O | N | G | L2 | F | E | L | L | L3 | O | W | b | b |

In case the Format statement is changed to

> 10   FORMAT(2A4, A2)

only 10 columns are read.   However, the final result will be identical since the characters OW will be stored left-justified in L3 with two blanks padded on the right.

Obviously, one can also use an array to store the name LONGFELLOW as follows:

> DIMENSION L(3)
> READ(5, 10) L
> 10   FORMAT(3A4)

Lastly, we emphasize that blanks are understood as blank characters when read using A-field, although they are understood as zeros when read using numerical fields.

(*b*)   Output

First, we emphasize that if a storage location contains character information, then it must contain exactly M characters (i.e., blank spaces are padded on the left if the original character string has less than M characters).   Before we formally state the rules on using the A-field in output, we give an example.

Suppose the capacity M = 4 and NAME contains

NAME | P | A | T | b |

Then

          WRITE(6, 20) NAME
    20   FORMAT(1X, A4)

will print the content of NAME

          PAT$_b$

Here, the given field width w is the same as the capacity M = 4. However, if the FORMAT statement is

    20   FORMAT(1X, 2A)

where the given field width $w = 2$ is less than M = 4, then only the two left-most characters in storage are printed; namely, only

          PA

is printed.

On the other hand, if the FORMAT statement is

    20   FORMAT(1X, A7)

where the given field width $w = 7$ is greater than M = 4, then the M = 4 characters in storage will be printed right-justified in the field as follows:

          $_{bbb}$PAT$_b$

In other words, the output consists of $w - $ M = 3 blanks followed by the content of NAME.

The above results can be summarized as follows.

Rules on character output using A-field.   Suppose M is the character capacity and w is the field width given in the output FORMAT statement.

1. If $w \leq $ M, then the output result will be the w left-most characters in storage; i.e., the M $- w$ right-most characters will be truncated.

2. If $w > $ M, then the output result will be $w - $ M blanks followed by the M characters in storage.

EXAMPLE 9.1

We wish to punch cards and store and print 200 names so that the output looks like:

```
BROWN         ERIC
EVERLING      MICHAEL
LIPSON        AUDREY
. . . . . . . .     . . . . . . .
```

Assuming no name (first or last) exceeds 15 characters, we punch the last name left-justified in columns 1–15 and the first name left-justified in columns 17–31.   (Thus, at least one blank space separates the last name from the first name.)

Assuming the capacity M = 4, each name requires at least eight memory locations to store the possible 31 characters.   Accordingly, we use a two-dimensional 200×8 array called NAME.   To store and print the array row by row, we must use implied DO loops.   The program segment follows:

```
          DIMENSION NAME(200, 8)
          DO 99 K = 1, 200
              READ(5, 15) (NAME(K, I), I = 1, 8)
    15        FORMAT(8A4)
              WRITE(6, 25) (NAME(K, I), I = 1, 8)
    25        FORMAT(1X, 8A4)
    99   CONTINUE
```

9.4 MANIPULATING CHARACTER INFORMATION

As noted in Section 9.2, the content of any memory location is a sequence of 0's and 1's (assuming we have a binary machine). Hence relational operations can also be performed on the numerical equivalents of character strings. Thus character information can be manipulated as seen in the following discussion.

(*a*) Sorting

Frequently, one wants to sort items by their character names, i.e., to list names alphabetically. To order character strings alphabetically, one must first know how the alphabetic characters are coded internally. Fortunately, most compilers do code alphabetic characters in increasing order. That is, the numerical equivalent of the character A is less than that of B, and so on. For example, suppose IA and IB contain the following character information:

IA | A | L | A | N | IB | D | A | L | E |

Then the numerical equivalent of ALAN stored in IA is less than the numerical equivalent of DALE stored in IB. Accordingly, the relational expression

       IA.LT.IB

is true. Thus, the various methods for sorting numerical values can also be used to sort character strings. Problem 9.8 uses the bubble sort method to sort a list of names.

(*b*) Text Analysis

Suppose a sentence S is punched into a data card. (Recall that a data card has 80 columns.) Consider the problem of writing a program segment which

    1. Prints the sentence S.
    2. Counts the number of times the letter E appears in S.

Had we only wanted to print S, we could store four characters per location using a linear array with 20 elements as follows:

```
        DIMENSION L(20)
        READ(5, 15) L
   15   FORMAT(20A4)
        WRITE(6, 25) L
   25   FORMAT(1X, 20A4)
```

However, with such a program we could not count the number of times the letter E appears. In order to do this, we must store one character per location using a linear array with 80 elements. Such a program follows:

```
        DIMENSION L(80)
        DATA JJ/'E'/
        READ(5, 15) L
   15   FORMAT(80A1)
        WRITE(6, 25) L
   25   FORMAT(1X, 80A1)
        N = 0
        DO 99 K = 1, 80
            IF(L(K).EQ.JJ) N = N + 1
   99   CONTINUE
        WRITE(6, 35) N
   35   FORMAT(1X, 'THE LETTER E APPEARS', 1X, I2, 1X, 'TIMES')
```

Observe that we use a DATA statement to store the letter E in a location called JJ, and then we use a DO loop to compare JJ with each element of L, i.e., with each letter of the sentence S.

9.5 H-FIELD

Recall from Section 3.8 that we can print messages in our output by enclosing the character string within apostrophes in the output FORMAT statement. For example, suppose X contains 123.45. Then the WRITE-FORMAT pair

        WRITE(6, 10) X
   10   FORMAT(1X, 'THE BALANCE IS $', F8.2)

will produce

        THE$_b$BALANCE$_b$IS$_b$$\$_{bb}$123.45

Similarly,

        WRITE(6, 20)
   20   FORMAT('1', 'ACCOUNT NUMBER', 10X, 'BALANCE')

will print the following heading on top of a new page:

        ACCOUNT NUMBER$_{bbbbbbbbbb}$BALANCE

One can also print messages using the H-field (Hollerith field). The field specification has the form

   wH   followed by *w* characters to be printed

In particular, the previous FORMAT statements could have been equivalently punched as follows:

   10   FORMAT(1X, 16HTHE BALANCE IS $, F8.2)
   20   FORMAT(1H1, 14HACCOUNT NUMBER, 10X, 7HBALANCE)

We emphasize that the *w* characters are not enclosed in apostrophes (unless the apostrophes are to be printed). The following gives a list of H-field specifications and their equivalent literal-field specifications:

H-field	Literal field
8HSEQUENCE	'SEQUENCE'
7HTHE END	'THE END'
15HNOW IS THE TIME	'NOW IS THE TIME'

The disadvantage of the H-field specification is that spaces must be counted accurately. We note that blanks within the H-field are not ignored since a blank is a character.

H-field can also be used for input. In particular, one can use the H-field to specify a character string in a DATA statement. For example,

        DATA I/3HPAT/, J/4HMARK/

has the same effect as

        DATA I/'PAT'/, J/'MARK'/

One can also use the H-field in an input FORMAT statement. In such a case, dummy characters (or: blank spaces) must appear in the FORMAT statement. We illustrate this case with the following example.

EXAMPLE 9.2

Suppose the first two data cards are punched as follows:

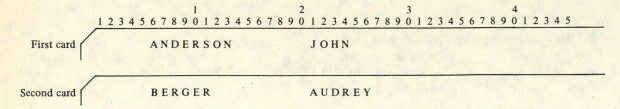

and the following program segment is executed:

```
        DO 100 K = 1, 2
              READ(5, 10)
   10         FORMAT(5X, 15HAAAAABBBBBCCCCC, 15HXXXXXYYYYYZZZZZ)
              WRITE(6, 10)
  100   CONTINUE
```

When the READ statement is first executed, the character strings in columns 6–20 and columns 21–35 are substituted for the characters in the H-field specifications in the FORMAT statement; i.e., the FORMAT statement effectively becomes

```
   10   FORMAT(5X, 15HANDERSON           , 15HJOHN                  )
```

Hence, when the WRITE statement is executed, the name on the data card is printed.   Similarly, when the READ statement is executed a second time, the name on the second card is read into the FORMAT statement and will be printed when the WRITE statement is executed.   Consequently, the output will look like the following:

```
ANDERSON     JOHN
BERGER       AUDREY
```

9.6   LOGICAL CONSTANTS AND LOGICAL VARIABLES

While discussing the logical IF statement in Chapter 4, we introduced the simplest form of a logical expression, the relational expression.   These are expressions relating two arithmetic expressions by one of the following six relational operators:

.EQ.   .NE.   .LT.   .LE.   .GT.   .GE.

Relational expressions are also called *logical expressions* because each assumes a logical value TRUE or FALSE.   In Fortran, these two logical constants are represented by

.TRUE.   and   .FALSE.

respectively.   We emphasize that the words TRUE and FALSE are preceded and followed by periods.

Storage locations (variables) which are used to store logical constants are called *logical variables*.   Like all variable names, a logical variable name consists of one to six alphanumeric characters with the first character being alphabetic.   Logical variable names must be declared by the type statement LOGICAL.   For example,

LOGICAL I, A45X, CAR

declares I, A45X, and CAR to be logical variables.   Logical arrays can also be declared by the LOGICAL statement.   For example,

LOGICAL A(15)

not only declares A to be a logical array, but also allocates A with 15 memory locations. A LOGICAL statement is nonexecutable, and so it must appear before any executable statement in the program.

9.7 LOGICAL OPERATORS AND LOGICAL EXPRESSIONS

Logical expressions more complex than the relational expressions can be constructed from the following three Fortran logical operations (connectives):

> .AND.
> .OR.
> .NOT.

Again we emphasize that the words AND, OR, and NOT are preceded and followed by periods.

Given any two logical expressions *lexp*1 and *lexp*2, we can form the compound logical expressions:

> *lexp*1.AND.*lexp*2
>
> *lexp*1.OR.*lexp*2
>
> .NOT.*lexp*1

The logical values of these compound expressions depend on the logical values of *lexp*1 and *lexp*2 and are shown in Tables 9-1 and 9-2 (where T means true, and F means false).   Note that

1. The operator .AND. is true only when *lexp*1 and *lexp*2 are *both true*.
2. The operator .OR. is false only when *lexp*1 and *lexp*2 are *both false*.
3. The operator .NOT. is a *unary operator* that changes the logical value of any logical expression from T to F or from F to T.

These operators are the same as the connectives used in English in forming compound sentences.

Table 9-1

*lexp*1	*lexp*2	*lexp*1.AND.*lexp*2	*lexp*1.OR.*lexp*2
T	T	T	T
T	F	F	T
F	T	F	T
F	F	F	F

Table 9-2

*lexp*1	.NOT.*lexp*1
T	F
F	T

EXAMPLE 9.3

(*a*) Consider the following logical expressions:

(*i*) (I.LT.J).OR.(K.GT.10)

(*ii*) (X.GT.1.0).AND.(K.LT.(I + 10))

(*iii*) .NOT.(X.GT.0.0)

We have

    (*i*)   is true if I < J or if K > 10.

    (*ii*) is true if both X > 1 and K < I + 10.

    (*iii*) is true if "X > 0" is false, that is, if X ≤ 0.

(*b*) One common mistake beginning students make is to translate $1 \le x \le 2$ into Fortran by writing

    1.0.LE.X.LE.2.0

One must realize that $1 \le x \le 2$ means $1 \le x$ and $x \le 2$. Hence, the correct Fortran equivalent is

    (1.0.LE.X).AND.(X.LE.2.0)

Although logical expressions are used frequently in logical IF statements, problems in Boolean algebra and propositional logic can also be programmed and solved using these expressions.

9.8 ASSIGNING LOGICAL VALUES

One may store a logical constant in a logical variable by an assignment statement. For example,

    LOGICAL A
    A = .TRUE.

assigns the constant .TRUE. to the location named A.   In general, the logical assignment statement has the form

    Logical variable = logical expression

Therefore,

    LOGICAL B, C
    B = X.LT.Y
    C = B

assigns to B the value .TRUE. or .FALSE. according to whether X < Y is true or false, and this value of B is then assigned to C.   Likewise,

    LOGICAL D
    D = (R.GT.S).OR.(X.LE.Y)

assigns the value .TRUE. to D if either R > S is true or X ≤ Y is true (or both are true), and the value .FALSE. is assigned to D otherwise.   (Note that parentheses can be used in the conventional way.)

A DATA statement may also be used to assign logical values.   For example,

    LOGICAL A, B
    DATA A/.TRUE./, B/.FALSE./

assigns the value .TRUE. to location A and .FALSE. to B during compilation. (The DATA statement is discussed in detail in Section 10.2.)

The value associated with the name of a FUNCTION subprogram can be logical.   The following FUNCTION subprogram returns the value .TRUE. only if X is an element of array A.

```
          LOGICAL FUNCTION CHECK(A, N, X)
          DIMENSION A(N)
          CHECK = .TRUE.
          DO 99 I = 1, N
                  IF(X.EQ.A(I)) RETURN
      99  CONTINUE
          CHECK = .FALSE.
          RETURN
          END
```

Observe the type declaration in the FUNCTION defining statement which tells the computer that CHECK is a logical variable and not a real variable.

9.9 L-FIELD

Logical variables can be stored or printed by READ and WRITE statements.   This is done via the L-field, whose format specification has the form

   Lw

where *w* denotes the field width.   (One may also use *rLw*, where *r* is the repetition factor.)   The use of the L-field is given as follows.

(*a*) Input

Suppose the format code *Lw* corresponds to the logical variable A.   Then A is assigned the value .TRUE. if the leading nonblank character in the designated field is the letter T.   If the leading nonblank character is F or the entire field consists of blanks, then .FALSE. is assigned to A.   (Some Fortran compilers consider any leading symbol other than T or F as .FALSE., whereas other compilers will give an error message.)

(*b*) Output

In output, the letter T or F will be printed right-justified in its field according as the corresponding logical variable has the value .TRUE. or .FALSE.   For example, suppose A and B are logical variables containing .TRUE. and .FALSE. respectively; then the output instruction

```
          WRITE(6, 10) A, B
      10  FORMAT(1X, L5, 2X, L3)
```

will print T in column 5 and F in column 10.   Thus the format code *Lw* will output $w - 1$ blanks before printing the letter T or F.

EXAMPLE 9.4

(*a*) Suppose a data card is punched as follows:

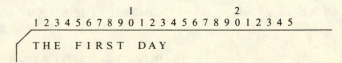

```
                     1                   2
          1 2 3 4 5 6 7 8 9 0 1 2 3 4 5 6 7 8 9 0 1 2 3 4 5
          ─────────────────────────────────────────────────
          THE  FIRST  DAY
```

Furthermore, suppose the input instruction is:

```
          LOGICAL A, B, C
          READ(5, 10) A, B, C
      10  FORMAT(L3, 2L5)
```

The field widths are 3, 5, 5 respectively.   The first nonblank character in columns 1–3 is T, in columns 4–8 is F, and in columns 9–13 is T.   Hence, .TRUE. is assigned to the logical variables A and C, and .FALSE. is assigned to B.

    (*b*)   Suppose the FORMAT statement in part (*a*) is changed to

        10   FORMAT(3L5)

Here T, I, and D are the first nonblank characters in the three fields.   Hence, some compilers will assign .TRUE. to A and .FALSE. to B and C, but other compilers will give an error message.

    (*c*)   Find the output of the program segment:

```
         LOGICAL X, Y, Z
         J = 5
         X = .FALSE.
         Y = 3*J.GT.12
         Z = Y.AND.X
         WRITE(6, 20) X, Y, Z
  20     FORMAT(1X, 3L10)
```

By line three, .FALSE. is assigned to X.   Since 3*J = 5 > 12 is true, .TRUE. is assigned to Y by line four.   Although Y is true, X is false; so Z is assigned .FALSE. by line five.   Accordingly, F, T, and F are printed in columns 10, 20, and 30 respectively.

9.10 HIERARCHY OF OPERATIONS

Since the logical operators involve relational expressions which in turn involve arithmetic expressions and arithmetic operators, it is important to understand the complete hierarchy of operations.   The order in which the operations are carried out is given below:

    1. Arithmetic operations
      (*a*) Exponentiation (**)
      (*b*) Multiplication and division (* and /)
      (*c*) Addition and subtraction (+ and −)

    2. Relational operators

    3. Logical operators
      (*a*) .NOT.
      (*b*) .AND.
      (*c*) .OR.

(As noted in Section 2.6, we will treat unary plus and minus on the same level as binary addition and subtraction.)

We note that the arithmetic operations are performed first.   Relational operations are then carried out before the logical operations.   Among the six relational operations, there is no priority.   Namely, the relational operators are carried out in the order as they appear from left to right.   As in the arithmetic expressions, it is possible to change this hierarchy by the use of parentheses.   Furthermore, it is highly advisable to use parentheses whenever such usage enhances understanding of the ordering of the operations.   For example, it is advisable to write

    (M.GE.1).OR.(X.NE.Y)   and   (K.GT.10).OR.((X.GE.0.2).AND.(Y.EQ.3.0))

instead of

    M.GE.1.OR.X.NE.Y   and   K.GT.10.OR.X.GE.0.2.AND.Y.EQ.3.0

although they are equivalent.

Solved Problems

CHARACTER DATA

9.1 Assuming the character capacity is M = 4, find the data assigned to I and J following the statement

DATA I/'NO'/, J/'THE END'/

The string NO is stored left-justified in I with 4 − 2 = 2 blanks padded on the right, but only the M = 4 left-most characters (including blanks) of the string THE END are stored in J:

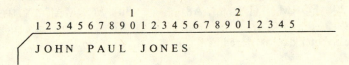

9.2 Assume M = 4 and a data card is punched as follows:

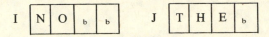

```
              1                 2
1 2 3 4 5 6 7 8 9 0 1 2 3 4 5 6 7 8 9 0 1 2 3 4 5
```
JOHN PAUL JONES

Find the data in storage if the input instruction is

(a)   READ(5, 10) I   (c)   DIMENSION K(4)
     10 FORMAT(A3)   READ(5, 30) K
                                  30 FORMAT(4A4)

(b)   READ(5, 20) L   (d)   DIMENSION J(3)
     20 FORMAT(A7)   READ(5, 40) J
                                  40 FORMAT(3A5)

(a) Since the field width is 3, the character string JOH in columns 1–3 is assigned to I. It will be stored left-justified in I with one blank padded on the right, as in Fig. 9-1(a).

(b) Since the field width is 7, the character string 'JOHN PA' in columns 1–7 is assigned to L. It will be truncated on the left, and only the four right-most characters will be stored in I, as in Fig. 9-1(b).

(c) Since each field width is 4, the data is stored as in Fig. 9-1(c).

(d) Since each field width is 5, the strings 'JOHN_b', 'PAUL_b', and 'JONES' are assigned to the elements of J. However, since only the four right-most characters are put in storage, the data is stored as in Fig. 9-1(d).

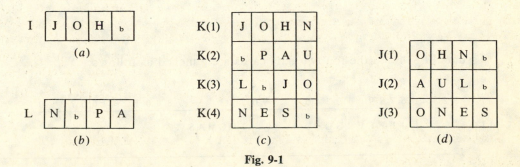

Fig. 9-1

9.3   Suppose M = 4 and a card is punched as

```
              1                   2
 1 2 3 4 5 6 7 8 9 0 1 2 3 4 5 6 7 8 9 0 1 2 3 4 5
 E R I C S O N   M O R T Y
```

(a)   Find data in storage if the input instruction is

        INTEGER A, B, C, D
        READ(5, 10) A, B, C, D
    10 FORMAT(4A4)

(b)   Find the output if the output instruction is

(i)   WRITE(6, 20) A, B   (ii)   WRITE(6, 30) C, D, B, A
    20 FORMAT(1X, A8, A8)   30 FORMAT(1X, 2A1, 1X, 2A4)

(a)   The character data is stored as

A	E	R	I	C
B	S	O	N	b
C	M	O	R	T
D	Y	b	b	b

(b)   (i) Excluding the carriage-control signal 1X, the field widths for A, B are 8 and 8.   The contents in storage are printed right-justified in their fields as follows:

        bbbbERIC$_{bbbb}$SON$_b$

Observe that $w - M = 8 - 4 = 4$ blanks precede ERIC and SON$_b$.

(ii) The field widths for C, D, B, A are respectively 1, 1, 4, 4.   The character strings in C, D are truncated on the right; hence,

        MY$_b$SON$_b$ERIC

is printed.

9.4   Assume M = 4 and the top two data cards are punched as follows:

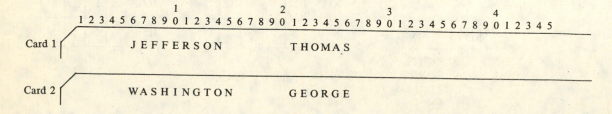

```
                  1                 2                 3                 4
   1 2 3 4 5 6 7 8 9 0 1 2 3 4 5 6 7 8 9 0 1 2 3 4 5 6 7 8 9 0 1 2 3 4 5 6 7 8 9 0 1 2 3 4 5
Card 1      J E F F E R S O N          T H O M A S

Card 2       W A S H I N G T O N          G E O R G E
```

Find the output for each program segment:

(a)
```
      DIMENSION NAME(30)
      DO 100 I = 1, 2
         READ(5, 60) NAME
60       FORMAT(5X, 30A1)
         WRITE(6, 60) NAME
100   CONTINUE
```

(b)
```
      DIMENSION NAME(10)
      DO 100 I = 1, 2
         READ(5, 35) NAME
35       FORMAT(5X, 10A4)
         WRITE(6, 45)
45       FORMAT(5X, 10A3)
100   CONTINUE
```

(c)
```
      DO 100 I = 1, 2
         READ(5, 25)
25       FORMAT(5X, 30HAAAAAAAAAABBBBBBBBBBCCCCCCCCCC)
         WRITE(6, 25)
100   CONTINUE
```

(a) Each character is stored in an element of NAME, and then the character is printed.   Hence, the output appears as on the data card:

```
JEFFERSON      THOMAS
WASHINGTON     GEORGE
```

(b) Note that four characters are assigned to each element of NAME, but only three characters, the first three, are printed.   Hence, the output will appear as follows:

```
JEFERSN     HOMS
WASINGON    EORE
```

(c) The 30 characters in columns 6–35 replace the characters following 30H in the FORMAT statement, and then the characters are printed.   Hence, the output will appear as on the data card:

```
JEFFERSON      THOMAS
WASHINGTON     GEORGE
```

9.5 Suppose a complete sentence S is punched on one card starting with column 1.   Count the number N of words in S.

Assuming that words are separated by one blank and that the sentence ends in a period, N is equal to one more than the number of blanks preceding the period.   Since a card contains 80 columns, we store our sentence in a linear array STRING with 80 elements.   The program follows:

```
      INTEGER STRING(80), BLANK, PERIOD
      DATA BLANK/' '/, PERIOD/'.'/
      READ(5, 10) STRING
10    FORMAT(80A1)
      N = 0
      DO 100 K = 1, 80
C        TEST IF IT IS A BLANK CHARACTER
         IF(STRING(K).EQ.BLANK) N = N + 1
C        TEST IF IT IS THE END OF THE SENTENCE
         IF(STRING(K).EQ.PERIOD) GO TO 55
100   CONTINUE
55    N = N + 1
      WRITE(6, 20) N
20    FORMAT(1X, 'THE NUMBER OF WORDS = ', I3)
      STOP
      END
```

9.6 A list of no more than 500 names is punched on cards, one name per card.   The last names are punched in columns 1–15, and the first names are punched in columns 17–32, and a trailer card is added with XXX punched in columns 1–3.   Assuming M = 4, write a Fortran program segment to count the number N of names and to store the names in an array.

Since the capacity M = 4, each name requires at least 32/4 = 8 storage locations to store the possible 32 characters.   Hence, we will store the names in a 500 × 8 array NAME with one name in each row of the array.   Furthermore, each time we read a card, we check to see if XXX appears in the first storage location.   The program follows:

```
        DIMENSION NAME(500, 8)
        DATA JJ/'XXX'/
        N = 0
        DO 100 K = 1, 500
            READ(5, 10) (NAME(K, L), L = 1, 8)
10          FORMAT(8A4)
            IF(NAME(K, 1).EQ.JJ) GO TO 88
            N = N + 1
100     CONTINUE
88      ...................
```

9.7 Suppose M = 4 and an I × J array NAME contains one name per row. Write a SUBROUTINE subprogram

ALPHA(NAME, I, J, K, L)

which interchanges the Kth and Lth names if they are not in alphabetical order.

We alphabetize the names as we would sort their numerical equivalents, except that if the two names have the same first four characters, i.e.,

NAME(K, 1) = NAME(L, 1)

then we have to compare the second four characters, and so on.   The program follows:

```
        SUBROUTINE ALPHA(NAME, I, J, K, L)
        DIMENSION NAME(I, J)
        DO 99 N = 1, J
            IF(NAME(K, N).GT.NAME(L, N)) GO TO 50
            IF(NAME(K, N).LT.NAME(L, N)) GO TO 40
99      CONTINUE
40      RETURN
50      DO 88 M = N, J
            JSAVE = NAME(K, M)
            NAME(K, M) = NAME(L, M)
            NAME(L, M) = JSAVE
88      CONTINUE
        RETURN
        END
```

We note that the effect of the statement labeled 50 is equivalent to

50   DO 88 M = 1, J

We let the reader give the reason for this.

9.8   Suppose N names are in memory in a 500 × 8 array NAME with one name per row.   Write a program segment to sort NAME alphabetically.

Suppose $A_1, A_2, \ldots, A_N$ are the N names.   We will use the bubble sort algorithm discussed in Problem 6.2 and Section 8.2, except that here we alphabetize names rather than order numbers.   Using the subroutine ALPHA from Problem 9.7, we alphabetize A_1 and A_2, then A_2 and A_3, and so on until A_{N-1} and A_N.   After this "sweeping" through the elements, the correct name is in the last position.   We repeat with the names $A_1, A_2, \ldots, A_{N-1}$.   After sweeping through these names, the correct name is in the next to last position.   We continue, and after N − 1 sweeps, the names will be in alphabetical order.

To translate the algorithm into Fortran, we use a nested DO loop.   The outer index I will range from 1 to N − 1 and the inner index J from 1 to N − I.   The program follows:

```
          NN = N − 1
          DO 99 I = 1, NN
               JJ = N − I
               DO 88 J = 1, JJ
                    CALL ALPHA(NAME, 500, 8, J, J + 1)
     88        CONTINUE
     99   CONTINUE
```

LOGICAL VARIABLES AND CONNECTIVES

9.9   Suppose a data card is punched as follows:

```
                    1                   2                   3
     1 2 3 4 5 6 7 8 9 0 1 2 3 4 5 6 7 8 9 0 1 2 3 4 5 6 7 8 9 0 1 2 3 4 5
     NOW  IS  THE  TIME  TO  RETURN
```

Assuming that any nonblank character in a field, other than T, will be accepted as .FALSE. (see p. 227), find the values of I, J, K, X, Y if the instruction is

```
          LOGICAL I, J, K, X, Y
          READ(5, 10) I, J, K, X, Y
     10   FORMAT(L6, L3, 3L6)
```

The field widths are 6, 3, 6, 6, 6 respectively.   The first nonblank character in columns 1–6 is N, in columns 7–9 is T, in columns 10–15 is E, in columns 16–21 is T, and in columns 22–27 is T.   Hence, .FALSE. is read into I and K, and .TRUE. is read into J, X, and Y.

9.10   Write the following in Fortran:
(a)   If J = K and N > 15, stop.
(b)   If $X \geq Y^2$ or A + B < C, go to the statement labeled 71.
(c)   If A is not greater than B, go to the statement labeled 72.
(d)   If it is false that A < B and C ≥ D, stop.

Recall that "and", "or", and "not" are denoted in Fortran by ".AND.", ".OR.", and ".NOT.", respectively.

(a)   IF(J.EQ.K.AND.N.GT.15) STOP   (c)   IF(.NOT.A.GT.B) GO TO 72
(b)   IF(X.GE.Y**2.OR.(A + B).LT.C) GO TO 71   (d)   IF(.NOT.(A.LT.B.AND.C.GE.D)) STOP

9.11 Suppose K contains 5 and A and B have been declared LOGICAL variables.   Find the final value of A after each Fortran program segment:

(*a*)   A = .FALSE.   (*b*)   B = .TRUE.   (*c*)   B = 10.LT.3*K
      B = 2*K.LT.15   A = 5.NE.K   A = K**2.GT.4*K
      A = A.OR.B   A = A.AND.B   IF(B) A = .NOT.A

(*a*) By line one, A is false; but by line two, B is true.   Hence, A.OR.B, the final value of A, is true.
(*b*) B is true by line one, and A is false by line two.   Hence, A.AND.B, the final value of A, is false.
(*c*) By line one, B is true. By line two, A is true. Since B is true, A = .NOT.A is executed; hence the value of A is changed to false.

9.12 Suppose A, B, C are logical variables containing .TRUE., .FALSE., and .TRUE. respectively.   Find the output of each instruction:

(*a*)   WRITE(6, 10) A, B, C   (*b*)   WRITE(6, 20), A, B, C
   10   FORMAT(1X, 3L8)   20   FORMAT(1X, L4, 3X, L4, 3X, L4)

    In output, the format code *Lw* prints *w* − 1 blanks followed by T or F according to whether the corresponding logical variable is true or false. Hence:

(*a*) T, F, and T are printed in columns 8, 16, and 24 respectively.
(*b*) T, F, and T are printed in columns 4, 11, and 18 respectively.

Supplementary Problems

CHARACTER DATA

9.13 Assuming the character capacity is M = 4, find the data in storage following:

      DATA I/'YES'/, J/'GO NOW'/

9.14 Assume M = 4 and a data card is punched as follows:

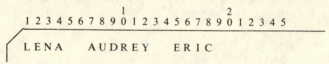

Find the data in storage if the input instruction is

(*a*)   READ(5, 10) J   (*c*)   DIMENSION K(5)
   10   FORMAT(A2)   READ(5, 30) K
                          30   FORMAT(5A4)

(*b*)   READ(5, 20) J   (*d*)   DIMENSION L(4)
   20   FORMAT(A7)   READ(5, 40) L
                          40   FORMAT(4A5)

9.15 Suppose M = 4 and LONDON is stored in IA and IB as follows:

    IA | L | O | N | D | IB | O | N | b | b |

Find the output if the WRITE statement is

    WRITE(6, 55) IA, IB

and the accompanying FORMAT statement is

(*a*) 55 FORMAT(1X, 2A4)   (*c*) 55 FORMAT(1X, A2, A3)
(*b*) 55 FORMAT(1X, 2A7)   (*d*) 55 FORMAT(1X, A3, A2)

9.16   Assume M = 4 and the top two data cards are punched as follows:

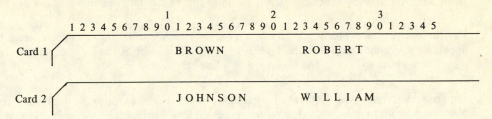

Find the output for each program segment:

(*a*)   DIMENSION NAME(6)
             DO 99 K = 1, 2
                      READ(5, 15) NAME
         15   FORMAT(10X, 6A4)
                      WRITE(6, 15) NAME
         99 CONTINUE

(*b*)   DIMENSION NLAST(3), NFIRST(3)
             DO 99 K = 1, 2
                      READ(5, 15) NLAST, NFIRST
         15   FORMAT(10X, 6A4)
                      WRITE(6, 15) NLAST, NFIRST
         99 CONTINUE

(*c*)   DO 99 K = 1, 2
                      READ(5, 15)
         15   FORMAT(10X, 24HAAAAAAAABBBBBBBBCCCCCCCC)
                      WRITE(6, 15)
         99 CONTINUE

(*d*)   DIMENSION NAME(6)
             DO 99 K = 1, 2
                      READ(5, 15) NAME
         15   FORMAT(10X, 6A4)
                      WRITE(5, 25) NAME
         25   FORMAT(10X, 6A2)
         99 CONTINUE

9.17   Do Problem 9.5, except now the words of the sentence are separated by one or more blanks.

9.18   Suppose a deck of no more than 80 cards is given.   Each card contains a student name in columns 1–32 and a letter grade in column 34.   The valid letter grades are A, B, C, D, F, and I (for incomplete).   Assuming a trailer card is added with XXX punched in columns 1–3, write a program to

(*a*) Count the number of students in each grade.
(*b*) Print the student names in each grade category.

9.19   Suppose a poem P is punched into a deck of cards with one line of the poem to a card, and suppose the deck has a trailer card with XXX punched into columns 1–3.   (Assume the poem P does not have more than 20 lines.)   Write a program which prints the poem P and the number of cards in the deck, i.e., the number of lines in P.

9.20   For the poem P in Problem 9.19, write a program which counts the number of times the letters A, E, I, O, U appear in P.

9.21   For the poem P in Problem 9.19, write a program which counts the number of lines beginning with the word THE. (Assume every line of the poem begins in column 1 of the data card.)

9.22   For the poem P in Problem 9.19, write a program which counts the number of times the word THE appears. (Assume that the word THE is always followed by a blank space and is always preceded by a blank space except at the beginning of a line.)

9.23   Suppose a short story SS is punched into a deck of cards, and suppose the deck has a trailer card with XXX punched into columns 1–3. Write a program which prints the short story SS and the number of lines in SS. (Assume that the story does not have more than 400 lines excluding the title punched on the first card and the author's name punched on the second card.)

9.24   For the short story SS in Problem 9.23, write a program which counts the number of paragraphs in SS. (Assume each paragraph is punched beginning on a new card in column 6; otherwise, all cards are punched using column 1.)

9.25   Suppose a title of less than 80 characters is punched on a card beginning in column 1. Write a program which prints the title so that it is centered in columns 1–80.

9.26   Suppose a list of N names (with $N \leq 500$) is stored in a 500×8 array called NAME with one name per row. Suppose a linear integer array PERSON(1), . . . , PERSON(8) contains another name. Write a program segment to determine if PERSON is in NAME. If yes, find the position L of the name; otherwise, set $L = 0$.

9.27   Suppose N names (with $N < 500$) are stored in a 500×8 array called NAME. A name stored in the integer array PERSON(1), . . . , PERSON(8) is to be inserted into the Lth row of the array NAME by having the names in rows L, $L + 1$, . . . , N move down one position. Write a program segment to accomplish this task.

9.28   Suppose N names (with $N \leq 500$) are stored in a 500×8 array called NAME in alphabetical order. Use the binary search method to determine if the name stored in the integer array PERSON(1), . . . , PERSON(8) is in the array NAME. If so, set logical variable IN to .TRUE., and find its row position L. If not, set IN to .FALSE., find the row position L into which this name should be inserted, and insert the name as in Problem 9.27.

LOGICAL VARIABLES AND CONNECTIVES

9.29   Suppose the only LOGICAL variables in a program are A, B, C, D. Find errors, if any, in each statement.

(*a*) A = FALSE   (*c*) C = R.GT.(A + 2.0)   (*e*) F = C.AND.D
(*b*) B = Y.GT.X   (*d*) D = A.OR.B   (*f*) A = A.AND..TRUE.

9.30   Suppose a data card is punched as follows:

```
                              1                   2
          1 2 3 4 5 6 7 8 9 0 1 2 3 4 5 6 7 8 9 0 1 2 3 4 5
      ┌───────────────────────────────────────────────────
      │   T O M   L E F T   I N   T H E   N I G H T
```

Assuming the compiler considers any leading symbol other than T as false, find the output of each program segment:

(*a*)　　LOGICAL A(6)　　　　　(*b*)　　LOGICAL X, Y, Z
　　　　　READ(5, 15) A　　　　　　　　　READ(5, 15) X, Y, Z
　　15　FORMAT(5L4)　　　　　　　15　FORMAT(3X, 3L4)
　　　　　WRITE(6, 25) A　　　　　　　　　WRITE(6, 25) X, Y, Z
　　25　FORMAT(1X, 5L4)　　　　　25　FORMAT(1X, 3L4)

9.31　　Write the following in Fortran:

(*a*)　If A > B and C ≤ 10, stop.
(*b*)　If J ≠ L or A is positive, go to the statement labeled 100.
(*c*)　If 7 < X < 10, go to the statement labeled 200.
(*d*)　If it is false that A ≤ B and X ≥ Y, stop.

9.32　　Suppose A, B, C have been declared logical variables and have values .FALSE., .FALSE., and .TRUE., respectively.　Find the value of each logical expression.

(*a*)　A.OR.C　　　　　(*d*)　.NOT.A.AND.B　　　　(*g*)　A.OR.B.AND.C
(*b*)　B.AND.C　　　　(*e*)　.NOT.(A.AND.B)　　　(*h*)　.NOT.(.NOT.B.OR.A)
(*c*)　A.OR..NOT.C　　(*f*)　A.AND.B.OR..NOT.C　(*i*)　A.OR.C.AND.B.OR.C

9.33　　Suppose J contains 10 and A and B have been declared LOGICAL variables.　Find the final value of A after each program segment.

(*a*)　A = .TRUE.　　　　　　(*c*)　A = J + 10.EQ.2*J
　　　　B = J.LT.5　　　　　　　　　B = .TRUE.
　　　　A = A.AND.B　　　　　　　　IF(A.OR..NOT.B) J = J + 10
　　　　　　　　　　　　　　　　　　　A = J.GT.15

(*b*)　B = .TRUE.　　　　　　(*d*)　A = .TRUE.
　　　　A = .FALSE.　　　　　　　　B = .NOT.A
　　　　IF(.NOT.A) B = .FALSE.　　A = B.OR.J**2.EQ.100
　　　　A = A.OR.B

9.34　　Suppose J, K, and L contain 10, 20, and 30 respectively.　Find the value of each logical expression.

(*a*)　2*J.EQ.K.AND.K.LE.L　　　　(*c*)　K.EQ.10.AND..NOT.J.LT.L − 15
(*b*)　.NOT.J.GT.K.OR.L.LT.5　　　(*d*)　.NOT.(5.EQ.J − 5.AND.2*K.EQ.J + L)

9.35　　Write a logical Fortran expression for each condition:

(*a*)　A is less than each of X, Y, Z.
(*b*)　A is less than at least one of X, Y, Z.
(*c*)　X > 2, but Y ≤ 3.
(*d*)　A and B are both positive, or one of them is greater than 100.
(*e*)　0 < X < 1 and Y ≥ Z.

Answers to Selected Supplementary Problems

9.13   YES_b in I and GO_bN in J.

9.14   (*a*) LE_bb in J.   (*b*) A_bbA in J.   (*c*) LENA in K(1), _bbAU in K(2), DREY in K(3), _bbER in K(4), and IC_bb in K(5).   (*d*) ENA_b in L(1), AUDR in L(2), Y_bbE in L(3), and IC_bb in L(4).

9.15   (*a*) LONDON_bb   (*b*) _bbbLOND_bbbON_bb   (*c*) LOON_b   (*d*) LONON

9.16   (*a*),(*b*), and (*c*) Output appears as on the data cards.
           (*d*) BRN_bbbRORT_bb and JOSO_bbWIIA_bb

9.29   (*a*) A = .FALSE.   (*b*) No error.   (*c*) A + 2.0 is unacceptable since A is a logical variable.   (*d*) No error.   (*e*) Unacceptable since F is not a logical variable.   (*f*) No error.

9.30   (*a*) T, F, F, T, F, T   (*b*) F, T, T

9.31   (*a*) IF(A.GT.B.AND.C.LE.10.0) STOP
           (*b*) IF(J.NE.L.OR.A.GT.0.0) GO TO 100
           (*c*) IF(7.0.LT.X.AND,X.LT.10.0) GO TO 200
           (*d*) IF(.NOT.(A.LE.B.AND.X.GE.Y)) STOP

9.32   (*a*) T   (*b*) F   (*c*) F   (*d*) F   (*e*) T   (*f*) F   (*g*) F   (*h*) F   (*i*) T

9.33   (*a*) F   (*b*) F   (*c*) T   (*d*) T

9.34   (*a*) T   (*b*) T   (*c*) F   (*d*) F

9.35   (*a*) A.LT.X.AND.A.LT.Y.AND.A.LT.Z
           (*b*) A.LT.X.OR.A.LT.Y.OR.A.LT.Z
           (*c*) X.GT.2.0.AND.Y.LE.3.0
           (*d*) A.GT.0.0.AND.B.GT.0.0.OR.(A.GT.100.0.OR.B.GT.100.0)
           (*e*) (0.0.LT.X.AND.X.LT.1.0).AND.(Y.GE.Z)

Chapter 10

Additional Features of Input/Output

10.1 INTRODUCTION

There are other features of input/output that have not been discussed. In Chapter 3, we discussed the I-field, F-field, E-field, and X-field specifications and, in Chapter 9, the A-field, H-field, and L-field specifications. This chapter will introduce several new features. In addition, we discuss how to output (print) the graph of a function.

First, we want to remind the reader that the first character in any output stream (record) is not printed by the line printer but is used for carriage control. This and other material on input/output can be found in Chapters 3 and 9.

10.2 DATA STATEMENT

Consider the constant π. To store this value, one may use the assignment statement

PI = 3.14159

As this is an executable statement, the constant 3.14159 will be assigned to PI whenever the statement is executed. Since π is unaltered (constant) throughout the program, one may wish to set the value 3.14159 to PI once and for all. This can be accomplished by the DATA statement as

DATA PI/3.14159/

That is, the word DATA is followed by the variable name, and then by its value enclosed in slashes. A DATA statement is nonexecutable, and so it must be placed before any executable statement in the program.

One may also use DATA statements to initialize the values of certain variables; e.g., we may wish to initialize the counter KOUNT by 1 and the cumulative sum SUM by 0.0. This can be done as

DATA KOUNT/1/
DATA SUM/0.0/

One may use a single DATA statement to set several values, for example,

DATA KOUNT/1/, SUM/0.0/

or alternately,

DATA KOUNT, SUM/1, 0.0/

The last statement has the general form:

DATA *List of variables/List of constants/*

Here the variables are separated by commas, the constants are separated by commas, and there is a one-to-one correspondence between the variables and the constants.

Although the DATA statement has the same effect as the assignment statements, there is a distinct difference. The DATA statement is a declaration and is nonexecutable, so that the values

239

of the variables are specified during the compilation.   On the other hand, the assignment statements are executable and, hence, will be carried out during execution.

Remark.   We emphasize the word "initialize" in our discussion.   Although we may initialize a
counter KOUNT by

     DATA KOUNT/1/

the variable KOUNT can be changed during the execution.   However, since the DATA statement
is nonexecutable, it *cannot* be called during execution to reinitialize the variable.   Namely,
KOUNT will have the value 1 as long as KOUNT is not assigned another value during execution,
but once KOUNT is assigned another value, the DATA statement cannot be executed to reinitialize KOUNT to 1.

One may also initialize array elements using the DATA statement.   In particular, one may
always initialize an entire array by writing only its name, for example,

     DIMENSION GRADE(4)
     DATA GRADE/92.0, 78.0, 43.5, 88.0/

stores 92.0, 78.0, 43.5, 88.0 in GRADE(1), . . . , GRADE(4), respectively.   We emphasize that if an
array is listed by name only, then the entire array is initialized in the order that the array is stored;
i.e., the first subscript varies fastest, etc.   (See Section 6.6.)   Some compilers also permit the use
of an implied-DO in a DATA statement to initialize part of an array.   For example, the statements

     INTEGER A(10)
     DATA A(2)/5/, (A(I), I = 4, 7)/1, 2, 3, 4/

store the value 5 in A(2) and the values 1, 2, 3, 4 in A(4), A(5), A(6), A(7), respectively.

Fortran also allows a repetition factor to be used in DATA statements.   Specifically, the
notation

     $n*$

written before a constant, where n is an unsigned positive integer, indicates that that constant is
repeated n times.   For example,

     DIMENSION X(100)
     DATA X/100*0.0/

indicates that 0.0 is repeated 100 times, and so 0.0 is assigned to all 100 elements of the array X.

DATA statements can also be used to store character string constants and logical constants.   (By a character string constant, we mean a character string enclosed in apostrophes, e.g.,
'AVERAGE' and 'THE END'.)

Standard Fortran does not allow character string constants to appear in assignment statements.   Accordingly, to store characters other than using a READ statement, one must use the
DATA statement.   This was discussed in Section 9.2.   We summarize as follows.

The maximum number M of characters that can be stored in any memory location (called the
character capacity) varies from machine to machine.   Suppose M = 4.   Then

     DATA NAME/'PAT'/

stores the character string PAT left-justified in location NAME as

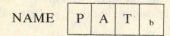

with one blank padded on the right.   In case M = 2, only the two left-most characters PA will be stored in memory:

NAME | P | A |

Some compilers such as WATFOR-WATFIV will regard as error whenever the character string length *l* exceeds the capacity M.   Some compilers may store the excess characters in the next location of the array if an array name is used to input the characters.   (See Problem 10.3.)

To store logical values using DATA statements, one simply writes

> LOGICAL A, B
> DATA A, B/.TRUE., .FALSE./

as discussed in Section 9.8.

EXAMPLE 10.1

    (*a*)   Consider the program segment

> DIMENSION B(100)
> LOGICAL L(5)
> DATA B/40*0.0, 30*1.0, 20*2.0, 10*3.0/, L/3*.TRUE., .FALSE., .TRUE./

Then B(1) to B(40) are assigned 0.0, and B(41) to B(70) are assigned 1.0, and so on.   Also L(1) through L(3) and L(5) are assigned .TRUE., but .FALSE. is assigned to L(4).

    (*b*)   The statements

> DIMENSION A(3, 2)
> DATA A, B, C, D/1., 2., 3., 4., 5., 6., 3*9.9/

will set

> A(1, 1) = 1., A(2, 1) = 2., A(3, 1) = 3., A(1, 2) = 4.,
> A(2, 2) = 5., A(3, 2) = 6.   and   B = 9.9, C = 9.9, D = 9.9

10.3   T-FIELD

In the same way we use the tab key on a typewriter, we may inform the computer of the column position for reading or writing.   This can be done by using T-field.   The general form of the field specification is

> *Tp*

where *p* is an unsigned integer constant.   The *p* specifies the *starting column position* where the information is to be read or printed.

Suppose, for example, we want to store in locations I and X the values punched in columns 13–15 and in columns 21–28, respectively.   We can accomplish this by

> READ(5, 80) I, X
> 80   FORMAT(12X, I3, 5X, F8.2)

Using T-fields, we may use the following equivalent FORMAT statement:

> 80   FORMAT(T13, I3, T21, F8.2)

Observe that the T-field specifies the *starting position* for the next field specification.

Sometimes, one finds the use of T-field simpler since it eliminates the need for counting column positions.

Since all field specifications refer to contiguous fields, the READ-FORMAT pair

        READ(5, 22) A, B
    22 FORMAT(T20, F8.2, 12X, F8.2)

implies that the value for A will be found in columns 20–27, and the value for B will be in columns 40–47.

Using T-fields, values may be read in any order.   For example,

        READ(5, 23) X, Y
    23 FORMAT(T31, F8.2, T11, F8.2)

will assign to X the number in columns 31–38 and assign to T the number in columns 11–18.

We may even read in an item several times.   For example,

        READ(5, 24) M, N, N1, N2, N3
    24 FORMAT(T21, A3, T21, I3, T21, 3I1)

will store the information in columns 21–23 as a character string (i.e., in alphanumeric form) into location M, as an integer value (in numerical form) in location N, and the digits in locations N1, N2, N3 respectively.

On output, the T-field specification gives the starting position in the output record (stream), not on the print paper.   Since the first character in an output record is used for carriage control, the starting position on the print paper will be one less than the number appearing in the T-field specification.   For example,

        WRITE(6, 28) I, J, K
    28 FORMAT(15X, I7, T28, I5, T42, I9)

instructs the computer to print I right-justified in columns 14–20, to print J right-justified in columns 27–31, and print K right-justified in columns 41–49.   This is equivalent to

        WRITE(6, 28) I, J, K
    28 FORMAT(T15, I7, 6X, I5, 9X, I9)

Naturally, values may be printed in any order.   For example,

        WRITE(6, 39) X, Y
    39 FORMAT(T31, F8.2, T11, F8.2)

will print Y in columns 10–17 and X in columns 30–37.

10.4 G-FIELD

Generalized format, G-field, can be used to input/output either integer, real, logical, or complex data.   (Complex data is discussed in Chapter 11.)   The general form of the field specification is

$Gw.d$

where w denotes the field width and d is an unsigned integer constant.   (One can also use $rGw.d$, where r denotes the repetition number.)

The meaning of $Gw.d$ is determined by the type of the corresponding variable as follows:

Integer Variable

$Gw.d$ has the same meaning as Iw in both input and output.

Logical Variable

Gw.d has the same meaning as Lw in both input and output.

Real Variable

There are two cases.

1. *Input.*   Gw.d has the same meaning as Ew.d or Fw.d according to whether the input value does or does not have an E punched in its field.

2. *Output.*   Here the d will always denote the number of significant digits.   The output will be in F-form if the value can be printed in a field of width $w - 4$.   In this case, the value will be printed with exactly 4 blanks at the right end of the field (i.e., right-justified to the fifth column from the right side of the field).   The output will be in E-form if the value cannot be printed in a field of width $w - 4$.   In this case, the value will be printed right-justified in its field.

Complex Variable

Discussed in Chapter 11.

EXAMPLE 10.2

(*a*)   Suppose I, J, A, B are stored using

```
    LOGICAL J
    READ(5, 30) I, J, A, B
30  FORMAT(3G10.3, G12.3)
```

where the data card is punched as follows:

```
          1               2               3               4
  1 2 3 4 5 6 7 8 9 0 1 2 3 4 5 6 7 8 9 0 1 2 3 4 5 6 7 8 9 0 1 2 3 4 5 6 7 8 9 0 1 2 3 4 5
 /          1 2 3       T H E   E N D       4 . 5 6 7 8 9   - 1 2 . 3 4 5 6 E - 0 6
```

Since G10.3 has the repetition factor 3, the field specifications are G10.3, G10.3, G10.3, G12.3 with field widths 10, 10, 10, 12 respectively.

(*i*)   The first G10.3 corresponds to the integer variable I, so that it is interpreted as I10.   Hence, I is assigned 123, the integer punched in the first field, columns 1–10.

(*ii*)   The second G10.3 corresponds to the logical variable J, and so it is interpreted as L10.   The first nonblank character in the second field, columns 11–20, is T; hence, .TRUE. is stored in J.

(*iii*)   The third G10.3 corresponds to the real variable A.   No E is punched in its field, columns 21–30; so it has the same meaning as F10.3.   Hence, 4.56789 is assigned to A.

(*iv*)   G12.3 corresponds to the real variable B.   There is an E punched in its field, columns 31–42, so that it becomes E12.3.   Hence, $-12.3456E - 06$, or equivalently -0.0000123456, is stored in B.

(*b*)   Suppose the output instruction is

```
    DO 100 K = 1, 6
        WRITE(6, 30) A(K)
30      FORMAT(6X, G12.4)
100 CONTINUE
```

where A is a linear array with six elements containing, respectively,

77.777, 0.333×10^{-5}, 2.2222×10^{2}, 666.66×10^{7},   12.3, 8.88×10^{-3}

The code G12.4 rounds-off each number to four significant digits:

77.78,   0.00000333,   222.2,   6667000000.,   12.30,   0.00888

The output field (columns 6–17) has width 12.   Those numbers which cannot be printed with four blank spaces on the right, i.e., require more than $w - 4 = 8$ columns, are printed in exponential form.   Thus, A(2) and A(4) are printed in exponential form, and the output appears as in Fig. 10-1.   Observe that one can tell immediately those numbers in exponential form.

```
     77.78
  0.3330E−05
     222.2
  0.6667E+10
     12.30
  0.00888
```

Fig. 10-1

10.5 SCALE FACTOR

When dealing with large data sets, sometimes it is useful to incorporate a scale factor in E or F fields.   A scale factor has the form

sP

where s (called the scale factor) is an unsigned integer constant or a negative integer constant.   It is written to the left of the first field to which it is to be applied, for example,

3PF8.2   or   −4PE14.4

However, the effect of the scale factor on F-field is different from the effect on E-field.

(*a*)   Scale Factor Used with F-field

When used with F-field, the effect of sP is as follows:

External value = internal value $\times 10^s$

or, equivalently,

Internal value = external value $\times 10^{-s}$

This is true in both output and input.

EXAMPLE 10.3

(*a*)   Suppose X contains 0.325, and we wish to print X in percent.   We may write

WRITE(6, 10) X
10   FORMAT(1X, 2PF8.2, 1X, 'PERCENT')

The internal value is multiplied by 10^2, and so the output will be

32.50 PERCENT

(*b*)   Suppose the number punched in columns 1–8 of a data card is 7.50, and

READ(5, 20) RATE
20   FORMAT(2PF8.2)

is executed.   Then the number assigned to RATE will be 0.075.

In other words, when sP is used with F-field in input, the number stored will be the number punched multiplied by a factor 10^{-s}; but when used with output, the number printed will be the internal number multiplied by a factor 10^s.

(*b*) Scale Factor Used with E-field

When scale factors are used with E-fields in input, they are ignored.   On output, the magnitude of the number printed is not changed, but the mantissa is multiplied by a factor of 10^s, and the exponent is reduced by s.   (Recall that the mantissa is a number between 0.1 and 1.0 or -0.1 and -1.0.)

For example, suppose the internal value of X is 0.0004321.   If we print X using the field specification E12.4, then X will appear in the form

  0.4321E $-$ 03

On the other hand, if we print X using the field specification 1PE12.4, then X will appear in the form

  4.321E $-$ 04

(Now the value of X appears in *scientific notation*; i.e., as a number between 1.0 and 10.0 or -1.0 and -10.0 followed by a power of 10.)

Warning.   Once a scale factor is used in an E or F-field, then it is automatically *applied to all succeeding E and F-fields* in the program until another scale factor is encountered.   Therefore, one must use the scale factor

  0P   (zeroP)

when one wants to offset the effect of a preceding scale factor.   For example, suppose the internal values of A, B, C, D are 0.0111, 0.0222, 0.0333, and 0.0444, respectively, and output instructions are as follows:

        WRITE(6, 10) A, B
    10 FORMAT(1X, 1PE12.4, 5X, E12.4)
        WRITE(6, 20) C, D
    20 FORMAT(1X, E12.4, 5X, 0PE12.4)

Then the scale factor 1P applies to printing A, B, C but not to D or any real value in any succeeding WRITE statement.   Thus, the output will appear in the form

    1.110E$-$02   2.220E$-$02
    3.330E$-$02   0.4440E$-$01

10.6   LEFT-PARENTHESIS RULE

Recall that if the variable list in a READ or WRITE statement contains more elements than there are field specifications in the accompanying FORMAT statement, then the FORMAT statement is repeated over and over again (reading a new data card or printing a new line each time) until all the variables are accommodated.   For example, suppose the following is executed.

        READ(5, 10) A, B, C, D, E, F, G, H
    10 FORMAT(F6.2, F8.3, F5.1)

Then the FORMAT statement is used to read in values for A, B, C (on the first data card); and then the FORMAT statement is repeated for D, E, F (on the second data card); and then it is repeated for G, H (on the third data card).

Sometimes we may want only part of a FORMAT statement repeated.   The rule is that the FORMAT statement is repeated beginning at the right-most left parenthesis and continuing to the end of the FORMAT statement.   For example, suppose the above FORMAT statement is modified as follows:

> READ(5, 20) A, B, C, D, E, F, G, H
> 20   FORMAT(F6.2, (F8.3, F5.1))

After the FORMAT statement is used for A, B, C, the FORMAT statement is repeated but only beginning at the right-most left parenthesis, i.e., beginning with the field specification F8.3.   Hence, D, E are read in from the second data card; F, G from the third data card; and H from the fourth data card, each time using the specifications F8.3 and F5.1.

   The above rule also applies to a parenthesis which is preceded by a repetition factor.   Consider, for example,

> READ(5, 30) A, B, C, D, E, F, G, H
> 30   FORMAT(F6.2, 2(F8.3, 3X), F5.1)

The FORMAT statement is equivalent to the statement

> 30   FORMAT(F6.2, (F8.3, 3X, F8.3, 3X), F5.1)

After the FORMAT statement is used for A, B, C, D, the FORMAT statement is repeated at the right-most left parenthesis, i.e., at F8.3, and continued until the end of the statement (not to the end of the inner parenthesis).   Thus, E, F, G are assigned values from the second data card using F8.3, 3X, F8.3, 3X, F5.1; and H is assigned a value from the third data card using F8.3.

   The above rule also applies to FORMAT statements which accompany WRITE statements.

10.7   EXECUTION-TIME FORMAT

   According to features discussed so far, once a program is written, all FORMAT statements are specified and, therefore, fixed.   It would be very convenient if FORMAT statements could be modified during execution to fit the data; e.g., one might want to enlarge field widths if the values are larger than normally anticipated.   This section discusses such ability using the so-called *execution-time* (*user specified*) FORMAT statements.

   As the name suggests, a FORMAT statement which is given (specified) during execution is called an execution-time FORMAT statement.   The general idea behind execution-time FORMAT is to store (input) the format field specifications as a character string in an array. The READ/WRITE statement then calls the array when the field specifications of the array are to be used for the input/output.

   Consider the READ-FORMAT pair

> READ(5, 10) A, B, I, J
> 10   FORMAT(2(F10.2, 2X), I5, 2X, I8)

Assuming that the character capacity M = 4, we show how we can accomplish the same result using execution-time FORMAT.   First we punch

> (2(F10.2, 2X), I5, 2X, I8)

on a data card, and then we read in the character string (using A-field) in an array.   Say

> INTEGER FORM(6)
> ⋮
> READ(5, 20) FORM
> 20   FORMAT(6A4)

The characters stored in the array FORM are as follows:

FORM(1)	(	2	(	F
FORM(2)	1	0	.	2
FORM(3)	,	2	X	)
FORM(4)	,	I	5	,
FORM(5)	2	X	,	I
FORM(6)	8	)		

To use this execution-time FORMAT, we write

> READ(5, FORM) A, B, I, J

Observe that the name of the array FORM (where the field specifications are stored) is written instead of the label of a FORMAT statement.

The array used for format specifications may have any number of elements—as long as it is large enough to contain the anticipated specifications.   For full flexibility, one frequently uses

>   INTEGER FORM(80)
>   READ(5, 40) FORM
> 40 FORMAT(80A1)

This accommodates any specifications punched on one data card and any capacity M.

We summarize by listing important points to remember.

1. User specified FORMAT must be stored in an array even if it can be stored in one location.   For example, even though

    > (1X, I8)

    can be stored in one location INFOR when the character capacity M = 9, one must still declare INFOR to be an array.

2. When preparing the data card for format codes, the word FORMAT is not punched, but the field specifications are punched within parentheses.

3. When using the user specified FORMAT, the name of the array containing the format specifications appears in the READ/WRITE statement.   For example,

    > WRITE(6, INFOR) A, B, C, J, K

    tells the computer that the format specifications are contained in the array INFOR.

Instead of reading the format specifications into an array as above, we could also initialize an execution-time FORMAT using a DATA statement:

>   INTEGER FORM(3)
>   DATA FORM/'(F8.', '3,I8', ')'/

If the compiler allows character string constants to appear in assignment statements, then one could use

>   INTEGER FORM(3)
>   FORM(1) = '(F8.'
>   FORM(2) = '3,I8'
>   FORM(3) = ')'

(Naturally, Hollerith field could also be used.)

Once the format specification is stored in an array as above, one can also modify format specifications depending on data generated.   We illustrate this technique with examples.

1. Suppose the format is prespecified by

```
DIMENSION INFOR(3), X(100)
DATA INFOR/'(I3,', '2X,F', '6.2)'/, IBIG/'8.2)'/, ISMALL/'6.2)'/
```

That is, (I3, 2X, F6.2) is stored in INFOR.   The program segment

```
      DO 100 K = 1, 100
            IF(ABS(X(K)).GT.100.0) INFOR(3) = IBIG
100   CONTINUE
      WRITE(6, INFOR) (N, X(N), N = 1, 100)
```

will first check if the magnitude of any element in the array X exceeds 100.   If so, the format specification F6.2 is changed to F8.2 to allow more space to accommodate the data.   Alternately,

```
      DO 200 K = 1, 100
            IF(ABS(X(K)).GT.100.0) INFOR(3) = IBIG
            WRITE(6, INFOR) K, X(K)
            INFOR(3) = ISMALL
200   CONTINUE
```

changes F6.2 to F8.2 only for those individual elements in the array which have magnitude greater than 100.   For all other elements, F6.2 is retained.

2. Suppose F-field is preferred in printing the array A, and F12.4 is used.   However, whenever the magnitude of A(K) is too large to fit into 12 columns, then printout in E-form is also acceptable.   The following program segment does exactly this.

```
      INTEGER XFORM, EFORM, FFORM
      DIMENSION A(100), XFORM(4)
      DATA XFORM/'(1X,', 'I3,2', 'X,F1', '2.4)'/, EFORM/'X,E1'/, FFORM/'X,F1'/
            ⋮
      DO 300 K = 1, 100
            IF(ABS(A(K)).GT.1.0E6) XFORM(3) = EFORM
            WRITE(6, XFORM) K, A(K)
            XFORM(3) = FFORM
300   CONTINUE
```

Note that the original format specification is (1X, I3, 2X, F12.4), but the F is changed to E whenever A(K) is too large; i.e., its magnitude is greater than 10^6.

10.8   GRAPHING

Besides using the computer to compute lists of values, one can also use the computer to plot the values in graphical form.   The graph will consist of lines of dots "........." for the axes and a cross "X" for each computed point (x, y) of the graph.   By plotting a sufficient number of points of the graph, we obtain a picture of the graph.   This technique is illustrated below.

Suppose, for example, we wish to plot the function

$$y = 2x^3 - x^2 - 22x + 21$$

for $-4 \leq x \leq 4$.   We must first choose values of x between -4 and 4 to calculate y, say

$$x = -4, -3.9, -3.8, \ldots, 3.9, 4$$

Observe that there are 81 values of x and that they have an increment of 0.1. We also require the range of y for these values. Suppose we are given that for $-4 \leq x \leq 4$, we have $-50 \leq y \leq 50$. We then let each position along the y axis denote incremental values of y. If we choose the increment 1.0, then the positions along the y axis represent the values

$$y = -50, -49, -48, \ldots, 49, 50$$

Observe that there are 101 such values of y.

There are two ways to proceed from here.

Method 1

We choose the horizontal axis (across the print page) as the x axis, and the vertical axis (down the print page) as the y axis. In this case, one must compute all the values (x, y) and store the entire graph in a matrix G before the graph can be plotted. The reason for this is that the line printer prints one line at a time, and it is possible that two different values of x will have the same (horizontal) value y. (It is not feasible to move the carriage up and down the print page.) Thus, G will have 101 rows corresponding to the 101 y positions, and 81 columns corresponding to the 81 values of x. That is, G will be a 101×81 matrix. The most severe drawback of this method is that the graph requires a matrix with $101 \times 81 = 8181$ memory cells. For this reason, one usually plots graphs using Method 2.

Method 2

We choose the horizontal axis as the y axis, and the vertical axis as the x axis. (The reader can turn the page for normal viewing.) Since each value of x gives a unique value of y, we can calculate and plot our graph one line at a time. Consequently, we would require only a linear array with 101 cells.

Specifically, we have the following steps:

1. Set x equal to its minimal value.
2. Find the corresponding value of y.
3. Scale the value of y to an integer J between 1 and 101.
4. Print a line with a cross (X) in column J of the graph.
5. Increment the value of x and repeat steps 1–4 as long as x does not exceed its maximum value.

The above steps are straightforward. In step 4, we also want to print a dot (.) for the column which represents the x axis (when $y = 0$), and we also want to print a whole line of dots (....) when the line represents the y axis (when $x = 0$). These tasks are detailed but not difficult.

The scaling function in step 3 is obtained as follows. We are given that y lies between -50 and 50. Adding 51 to y gives a positive real number between 1 and 101. Since we want to round off y to an integer between 1 and 101, rather than truncate, we must also add 0.5 to y. This yields the scaling function

$$\text{JSCALE}(Y) = \text{INT}(Y + 51.0 + 0.5)$$

Observe that $\text{JSCALE}(0) = 51$; i.e., column 51 of the graph is the x axis.

The program which plots our function follows:

```
          INTEGER BLANK, DOT, CROSS, LINE(101), LINEY(101)
          DATA BLANK, DOT, CROSS, LINE, LINEY/' ', '.', 'X', 101*' ', 101*'.'/
C
C         BEGIN NEW PAGE AND SKIP LINES
C
          WRITE(6, 10)
  10      FORMAT('1', 10X, 'GRAPH OF A FUNCTION'//3X, 'X', 6X, 'Y'//)
C
C         BEGIN GIVING VALUES TO X
C
          X = -4.0
  50      Y = ((2.0*X - 1.0)*X - 22.0)*X + 21.0
          J = INT(Y + 51.5)
C               TEST IF Y AXIS
          IF(ABS(X).LT.0.001) GO TO 100
          LINE(51) = DOT
          LINE(J) = CROSS
          WRITE(6, 20) X, Y, LINE
  20      FORMAT(1X, 2(F6.2, 1X), 101A1)
          LINE(J) = BLANK
          GO TO 200
  100     LINEY(J) = CROSS
          WRITE(6, 20) X, Y, LINEY
  200     X = X + 0.1
          IF(X.LE.4.0) GO TO 50
          STOP
          END
```

Observe that we use a DATA statement to store the characters ♭ (blank), . (dot), and X (cross) in BLANK, DOT, and CROSS respectively. We use LINE to print every line of the graph except when the line represents the y axis, in which case we use LINEY. Hence, LINE is initialized with blanks, but LINEY with dots. (We could have used only one array, but then the array would have to be reset with blanks or dots after each increment of X.) The line

          LINE(J) = BLANK

is crucial; it erases the cross in LINE(J) after it is printed. We note that one could have used a DO loop for the different values of X. The output of the program appears in Fig. 10-2. Observe that the values of X and Y appear on the left side of the graph.

Remark. The scaling function JSCALE(Y) discussed above and in Problem 10.16, requires one to know beforehand the range of values of y. In case one does not have this information, one can proceed as follows: (1) Calculate all values of y and store them in an array Y (before any plotting is done). (2) Find the maximum and minimum values in the array Y. (3) Use these values to obtain the scaling function JSCALE as in Problem 10.16. (4) Plot the graph using the function JSCALE and the array Y. (This procedure is also described in Problems 10.36 and 10.37.)

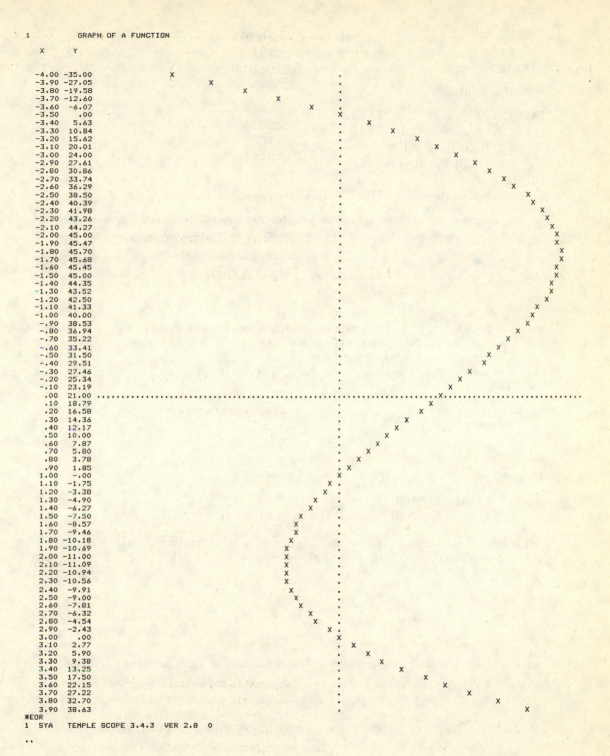

```
1          GRAPH OF A FUNCTION

      X      Y

   -4.00 -35.00
   -3.90 -27.05
   -3.80 -19.58
   -3.70 -12.60
   -3.60  -6.07
   -3.50    .00
   -3.40   5.63
   -3.30  10.84
   -3.20  15.62
   -3.10  20.01
   -3.00  24.00
   -2.90  27.61
   -2.80  30.86
   -2.70  33.74
   -2.60  36.29
   -2.50  38.50
   -2.40  40.39
   -2.30  41.98
   -2.20  43.26
   -2.10  44.27
   -2.00  45.00
   -1.90  45.47
   -1.80  45.70
   -1.70  45.68
   -1.60  45.45
   -1.50  45.00
   -1.40  44.35
   -1.30  43.52
   -1.20  42.50
   -1.10  41.33
   -1.00  40.00
    -.90  38.53
    -.80  36.94
    -.70  35.22
    -.60  33.41
    -.50  31.50
    -.40  29.51
    -.30  27.46
    -.20  25.34
    -.10  23.19
     .00  21.00
     .10  18.79
     .20  16.58
     .30  14.36
     .40  12.17
     .50  10.00
     .60   7.87
     .70   5.80
     .80   3.78
     .90   1.85
    1.00   -.00
    1.10  -1.75
    1.20  -3.38
    1.30  -4.90
    1.40  -6.27
    1.50  -7.50
    1.60  -8.57
    1.70  -9.46
    1.80 -10.18
    1.90 -10.69
    2.00 -11.00
    2.10 -11.09
    2.20 -10.94
    2.30 -10.56
    2.40  -9.91
    2.50  -9.00
    2.60  -7.81
    2.70  -6.32
    2.80  -4.54
    2.90  -2.43
    3.00    .00
    3.10   2.77
    3.20   5.90
    3.30   9.38
    3.40  13.25
    3.50  17.50
    3.60  22.15
    3.70  27.22
    3.80  32.70
    3.90  38.63
  *EOR
  1  SYA   TEMPLE SCOPE 3.4.3  VER 2.8  0

  ..
```

Fig. 10-2

Solved Problems

DATA STATEMENT

10.1   Find the input:

(*a*)   DATA A, B, C /2.4, '2.4', 1.5/
(*b*)   DATA A, B /2*2.4/, C/1.5/
(*c*)   DIMENSION A(10)
　　　DATA A, B, C/6*1.0, 6*2.0/
(*d*)   LOGICAL C
　　　DATA A, B, C /2.4, 'TRUE', .TRUE./

(*a*)   A, B, and C are assigned the values between the slashes. Hence, 2.4 is assigned to A, 1.5 is assigned to C, and B is assigned a character string as follows:

B | 2 | · | 4 | b |

(We assume the character capacity M = 4.)

(*b*)   The 2* is a repetition factor. Hence, 2.4 is assigned to both A and B, and 1.5 is assigned to C.

(*c*)   The 6* is a repetition factor. The first six elements of A are assigned 1.0; B, C, and the last four elements of A are assigned 2.0.

(*d*)   A is assigned 2.4, B is assigned the character string TRUE, and C is assigned the logical value .TRUE..

10.2   Find the input:

　　　LOGICAL A(3, 2)
　　　DATA A/2*.TRUE., 3*.FALSE., .TRUE./

　　The array A is ordered so that the first subscript (row subscript) varies fastest. Hence, .TRUE. is assigned to A(1, 1) and A(2, 1); .FALSE. is assigned to A(3, 1), A(1, 2) and A(2, 2); and .TRUE. is assigned to A(3, 2).

10.3   Assuming the character capacity M = 4, find the data in storage in the following:

　　　DIMENSION L(2)
　　　DATA L/'SLEEP', 'IN'/

　　Since the length *l* of the first character string exceeds the capacity M, any one of the following may happen:

(*i*)   Each character string is stored left-justified in memory with excess characters chopped off or extra blanks added on the right:

L(1) | S | L | E | E | L(2) | I | N | b | b |

(*ii*) An error message is given.

(*iii*) Since the array name L is used in the DATA statement, SLEEP is stored left-justified in L(1), and any excess characters are moved to the next location L(2) as follows:

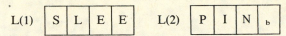

L(1) | S | L | E | E | L(2) | P | I | N | ♭ |

(We emphasize that all compilers give the same result if no character string length exceeds the capacity M.)

T-FIELD

10.4   Suppose a data card is punched as follows:

```
                    1                   2                   3
   1 2 3 4 5 6 7 8 9 0 1 2 3 4 5 6 7 8 9 0 1 2 3 4 5 6 7 8 9 0 1 2 3 4 5
   ─────────────────────────────────────────────────────────────────────
     1 1 1 1    2 2 2 2    T H E   E N D         3 3 3 3
```

Find the input if the following is executed:

(*a*)   READ(5, 10) I, J
       10 FORMAT(T6, I4, T3, I6)
(*b*)   LOGICAL J
           READ(5, 20) I, J, X, Y
       20 FORMAT(T11, A4, T11, L4, T21, F5.2, T3, F6.3)

(*a*) I is assigned the integer in columns 6–9, that is, in the field of width 4 beginning in column 6. Hence, I is assigned 2222.; J is assigned the integer in columns 3–8, that is, in the field of width 6 beginning in column 3. Since blanks are interpreted as zeros in numerical fields, J is assigned 110222.

(*b*) I is assigned the character string 'THE♭', the characters in the field of width 4 beginning in column 11. J is assigned .TRUE. since J is a logical variable, and T is the first nonblank character in the field of width 4 beginning in column 11. (Observe that I and J both use the data punched in columns 11–14.) Since T21 and T3 instruct the card reader to go to columns 21 and 3, respectively, X is assigned 333.30, and Y is assigned 110.222.

10.5   Find the output if the following program is executed:

                   I = 111
                   J = 222
                   K = 333
                   WRITE(5, 30) I, J, K
              30   FORMAT(T15, I3, T6, I6, T20, I8)

In output Tp refers to the pth position in the output stream (record); hence, Tp refers to column $p - 1$ on the print page since the first character on record is not printed. Accordingly, I is printed right-justified in the field of width 3 beginning in column 14 on the print page, i.e., columns 14–16; J is printed right-justified in the field of width 6 beginning in column 5, i.e., columns 5–10; and K is printed right-justified in the field of width 8 beginning in column 19, i.e., columns 19–26. See Fig. 10-3.

```
         1         2         3
123456789012345678901234567890123456789012345
```

Fig. 10-3

G-FIELD

10.6   Suppose a data card is punched as follows:

```
                 1                   2
1 2 3 4 5 6 7 8 9 0 1 2 3 4 5 6 7 8 9 0 1 2 3 4 5
  1 1 1     2 2 2     3 3 E 3   T H E N
```

Find the input if the following is executed:

```
      LOGICAL Z
      READ(5, 10) J, A, B, Z
   10 FORMAT(4G5.1)
```

There are four G5.1 entries, one for each variable.   So there are four fields, each of width 5.

(*a*) J is an integer variable, and so G5.1 is interpreted as I5.   Hence J is assigned 1110, the integer appearing in columns 1–5. (The blank space in column 5 is viewed as a zero.)

(*b*) A is a real variable, and there is no E punched in columns 6–10.   Hence, G5.1 is interpreted as F5.1.   There is no decimal point in the field, and so a decimal is embedded one place from the right side of the field.   Thus, 222.0 is assigned to A.

(*c*) B is a real variable, and there is an E punched in columns 11–15.   Hence, G5.1 is interpreted as E5.1.   There is no decimal point in the field, and so a decimal is embedded one place to the left of the letter E.   Thus, 3.3E3 or, equivalently, 3300. is assigned to B.

(*d*) Z is a logical variable, and so G5.1 is interpreted as L5.   The first nonblank character in columns 16–20 is T.   Thus, .TRUE. is assigned to Z.

10.7   Suppose J contains 2345 and K is a logical variable containing .FALSE.   Find the output following

```
      WRITE(6, 20) J, K
   20 FORMAT(1X, 2G10.3)
```

Excluding the carriage control instruction 1X, the field widths for J and K are ten each.   Since J is an integer variable, G10.3 becomes I10, and so 2345 is printed right-justified in columns 1–10. Since K is a logical variable, G10.3 becomes L10, and so F is printed in column 20.

10.8   Suppose a linear array A with seven elements contains, respectively,

$$111.18, \quad -22227000.0, \quad -6.15, \quad 0.0000033333, \quad 44.4, \quad -0.023, \quad 888.88$$

Find the following output:

```
      DO 100 K = 1, 7
         WRITE(6, 40) A(K)
   40    FORMAT(1X, G12.4)
  100 CONTINUE
```

The G12.4 rounds off each number to four significant places as follows:

$$111.2, \quad -22230000.0, \quad -6.150, \quad 0.000003333, \quad 44.40, \quad -0.02300, \quad 888.9$$

Those numbers which cannot be printed in fields of width $w - 4 = 12 - 4 = 8$ (i.e., which are relatively large or small in absolute value) will be printed in exponential form. The other numbers are printed in F-form right-justified but ending with 4 blanks as follows:

```
     111.2
 -0.2223E 08
    -6.150
  0.3333E-05
     44.40
  -0.02300
     888.9
```

SCALE FACTOR

10.9 Find the internal value given the following format code and external number as input:

	Format code	External number as input
(a)	3PF6.1	123.45
(b)	−4PF6.1	123.45
(c)	4PE6.1	123.45
(d)	−3PE8.1	123.45E1
(e)	1PF6.2	12345.
(f)	−1PE9.2	12345E − 2

The scale factor sP has the following effect on external numbers as input written without an exponent:

$$\text{Internal number} = \text{external number} \times 10^{-s}$$

The scale factor does not effect numbers written with an exponent as in (d) and (f). Hence,

(a) 0.12345   (b) 1234500.   (c) 0.012345   (d) 123.45E1 or 1234.5   (e) 1234.5
(f) A decimal point is embedded between 3 and 4 to yield 123.45E − 2 or 1.2345. The scale factor has no effect on the number.

10.10 Suppose 12345.6 is the internal number. Find the output if the field specification is

(a) 2PF12.1   (c) −1PF12.2   (e) −1PE15.6
(b) −3PF12.2   (d) 2PE12.4   (f) 1PE15.3

Recall first that $Fw.d$ rounds off the number to d decimal places whereas $Ew.d$ rounds off the number to d significant digits.

For F-field, the scale factor sP multiplies the internal value by 10^s. Hence, we have

(a) 1234560.0   (b) 12.35   (c) 1234.56

With E-field, the scale factor sP does not change the value of the number, as it did with F-field, but it only changes the exponential form. Specifically, the decimal point is moved by multiplying the mantissa by 10^s, and then $-s$ is added to the exponent. Thus,

(d) 12.35E + 03   (e) 0.0123456E + 06   (f) 1.23E + 04

10.11 Suppose A contains 111.888. Find the output if the instruction is

```
     WRITE(6, 10) A, A, A, A, A
  10 FORMAT(1X, F10.2, E12.4, 1PF10.2, E12.4, F10.2)
```

The scale factor sP applies to each succeeding field specification until another scale factor is encountered.   Hence, the output is

111.89   0.1119E + 03   1118.88   1.119E + 02   1118.88

where the numbers are printed right-justified in fields of widths 10, 12, 10, 12, 10 respectively.

10.12 Suppose in the preceding Problem 10.11, one only wanted the scale factor to apply to the third A and not to the fourth and fifth.   How would one write the FORMAT statement?

One writes 0P when one does not want the scale factor to apply any more.   Hence, the FORMAT statement would be written:

10   FORMAT(1X, F10.2, E12.4, 1PF10.2, 0PE12.4, F10.2)

EXECUTION-TIME FORMAT

10.13 Assuming the character capacity is M = 4, describe the input

```
INTEGER FORM(6)
DATA FORM/'(1X,', 'I2,', '5X,', 'F6.', '2)', ' '/
```

The array FORM is stored as follows:

FORM(1)	(	1	X	,
FORM(2)	I	2	,	
FORM(3)	5	X	,	
FORM(4)	F	6	.	
FORM(5)	2	)		
FORM(6)				

Note that FORM(6) has only blanks.

10.14 Suppose J and R are each linear arrays with four elements and are assigned

11, 2222, 77, 666   and   3333.33, 44.44, 5.555, 88888.888

respectively.   Find the output if the following is executed using the array FORM in the preceding Problem 10.15.

```
DATA K1/'I4,'/, K2/'F9.'/
DO 100 I = 1, 4
      IF(J(I).GE.100) FORM(2) = K1
      IF(R(I).GE.1.0E3) FORM(4) = K2
      WRITE(6, FORM) J(I), R(I)
100   CONTINUE
```

If J(I) $\geq$ 100, then its field width is extended from 2 to 4, and if R(I) $\geq$ 1000, then its field width is extended from 6 to 9.   Hence, the output will appear as in Fig. 10-4.   In all cases, the R value is rounded off to two decimal places.

```
123456789012345678901232345
```

○	11	3333.33
	2222	44.44
	77	5.56
○	666	88888.89

Fig. 10-4

GRAPHING

10.15   Suppose we want to use a DO loop to obtain the values of x from an integer J to an integer K with increment 1/N, where N is a positive integer.   Find (*a*) the number of values of x; (*b*) the value of x in terms of the index INDEX of the DO loop; (*c*) the value of INDEX, if any, which gives the y axis.   Test the results for the case J = -2, K = 8, and N = 4, that is, where x takes on the values from -2 to -8 with increment 1/4 = 0.25.

(*a*)   There are K $-$ J unit intervals between J and K and N values of x corresponding to each unit.   Also there is a starting value of x.   Thus, there is a total of

$$N*(K - J) + 1$$

values of x.   In the example, x takes on the values

$$-2, -1.75, -1.50, \ldots, 0, \ldots, 7.75, 8$$

Altogether there are $4(8 + 2) + 1 = 41$ values of x.

(*b*)   The relationship between the INDEX and x follows:

$$x: \quad \text{J} \quad \text{J} + 1/\text{N} \quad \text{J} + 2/\text{N} \quad \text{J} + 3/\text{N} \quad \ldots \quad \text{K}$$
$$\text{INDEX:} \quad 1 \quad 2 \quad 3 \quad 4 \quad \ldots \quad \text{N}*(\text{K} - \text{J}) + 1$$

Observe that

$$x = \text{J} + (\text{INDEX} - 1)/\text{N}$$

In the example,

$$x = -2 + (\text{INDEX} - 1)/4$$

(*c*)   The y axis occurs when $x = 0$.   But x can equal zero only if J $\leq 0 \leq$ K.   In this case, there are $N*(-\text{J})$ values of x preceding $x = 0$.   Thus, the y axis occurs when INDEX = $N*(-\text{J}) + 1$.   In the example, the y axis occurs when INDEX = $4(2) + 1 = 9$.

10.16   Suppose we are given that all values of y lie between the integers L and M (where L < M).   Find the scaling function which scales each value of y to an integer J between 1 and 101.   (We are assuming that the graph will have 101 columns.)   Test the scaling function for the case that L = -10 and M = 30, that is, that the values of y lie between -10 and 30.

Adding $-$L to y gives values between 0 and M $-$ L.   Multiplying by 100/(M $-$ L) gives values between 0 and 100.   Adding 1 gives values between 1 and 101.   Since we want to round off y to an integer J between 1 and 101, rather than truncate, we must also add 0.5.   Thus, the scaling function is as follows:

$$JSCALE(Y) = INT((Y + FLOAT(-L))*(100.0/FLOAT(M - L)) + 1.5)$$

In the example,

$$JSCALE(Y) = INT((Y + 10.0)*(100.0/40.0) + 1.5)$$

10.17 Write a program which graphs the parabola

$$y = 3x^2 - x - 8$$

from $x = -3$ to $x = 3$.   Assume y lies between -10 and 30, and calculate y for values of x which differ by 0.1.

We use a DO loop (with index I) for the different values of x.   The relationship between I and x follows:

x:	-3	-2.9	-2.8	...	0	...	2.9	3
I:	1	2	3	...	31	...	60	61

Observe that there are 61 values of x, the y axis occurs when I = 31, and x can be obtained from I by

$$x = -3.0 + FLOAT(I - 1)*0.1$$

(See Problem 10.15.)

Assuming our graph will contain 101 columns, each value of y can be scaled to an integer J between 1 and 101 using the scaling function

$$JSCALE(Y) = INT((Y + 10.0)*(100.0/40.0) + 1.5)$$

as discussed in the preceding Problem 10.16.   Observe that JSCALE(0.0) = 26; so column 26 of the graph is the x axis.

The Fortran program which graphs the parabola follows.   The procedure is the same as that discussed in Section 10.8.   Specifically, there will be a line of dots (. . . . .) for each axis, and a cross (X) for each point of the graph.

```
C        GRAPH OF A PARABOLA
         INTEGER DOT, CROSS, BLANK, LINE(101), LINEY(101)
         DATA DOT, CROSS, BLANK, LINE, LINEY/'.', 'X', ' ', 101*' ', 101*'.'/
C        BEGIN NEW PAGE
         WRITE(6, 10)
     10  FORMAT(1H1, 10X, 'GRAPH OF A PARABOLA'///3X, 'X', 6X, 'Y'//)
         DO 100 I = 1, 61
             X = -3.0 + FLOAT(I - 1)*0.1
             Y = 3.0*X*X - X - 8.0
             J = INT((Y + 10.0)*(100.0/40.0) + 1.5)
             IF(I.EQ.31) GO TO 50
             LINE(26) = DOT
             LINE(J) = CROSS
             WRITE(6, 20) X, Y, LINE
     20      FORMAT(1X, 2(F4.2, 2X), 101A1)
             LINE(J) = BLANK
             GO TO 100
     50      LINEY(J) = CROSS
             WRITE(6, 20) X, Y, LINEY
    100  CONTINUE
         STOP
         END
```

10.18 Write a program which reads an integer N and prints N^2 asterisks so that there are N lines with N asterisks on a line in columns 1, 3, 5, ..., 2N − 1.   The picture should begin on the fifth line of a new page.

We first set up a linear array LINE with 132 elements (each element corresponding to a column on the print page), and then we store a blank in each element of LINE.   After reading N, we then store an asterisk in the elements LINE(1), LINE(3), . . . , LINE(2N − 1).   The program follows:

```
C          PROGRAM PRINTING A SQUARE OF ASTERISKS
           DIMENSION LINE(132)
           INTEGER AST
           DATA LINE/132*' '/, AST/'*'/
           READ(5, 10) N
    10     FORMAT(I5)
           NN = 2*N − 1
           DO 100 K = 1, NN, 2
                LINE(K) = AST
   100     CONTINUE
C          SKIP 5 LINES ON NEW PAGE
           WRITE(6, 20)
    20     FORMAT('1'/////)
C          PRINT THE ARRAY N TIMES USING A-FIELD
           DO 200 K = 1, N
                WRITE(6, 30) LINE
    30          FORMAT(1X, 132A1)
   200     CONTINUE
           STOP
           END
```

Supplementary Problems

DATA STATEMENTS

10.19   Write a DATA statement to initialize:

(a)   J = 5, K = 5, L = 5, M = .TRUE. (where M is a logical variable)
(b)   A(I, J) = 0 for every element of a 4×5 array A

10.20   Find the input:

(a)   DATA L, M, N/2*2, '2*2'/, X, Y, Z/2.5, 2*3.5/
(b)   DIMENSION X(6)
       DATA X, Y, Z/5*2.22, 2*3.3, 4.4/
(c)   LOGICAL K(4)
       DATA J, K, L/ 555, 3*.FALSE., .TRUE., 'TRUE'/

T-FIELD

10.21   Suppose a data card is punched as follows:

```
              1              2              3
1 2 3 4 5 6 7 8 9 0 1 2 3 4 5 6 7 8 9 0 1 2 3 4 5 6 7 8 9 0 1 2 3 4 5
_____
  NOW  AND  THEN        4 4 4 4 4 5 5 5 5 5
```

Find the input if the following is executed:

(a)   READ(5, 10) A, B   (c)   LOGICAL J, K
    10   FORMAT(T16, 2F5.2)   READ(5, 30) I, J, K, C, D
(b)   READ(5, 20) X, J, K   30   FORMAT(T16, I3, T4, 2L4, T16, 2F3.1)
    20   FORMAT(T14, F4.2, 2I3)

10.22 Find the output for each program segment:

(a)   J = 1111   (b)   A = 22.22
             K = 5555   B = 77.77
             L = 8888   C = 11.11
             WRITE(5, 10) J, K, L   WRITE(5, 20) A, B, C
      10   FORMAT(T16, I5, T6, I5, T26, I5)   20   FORMAT(T16, F5.1, 5X, F5.1, T1, F5.1)

G-FIELD

10.23 Suppose a data card is punched as follows:

```
1 2 3 4 5 6 7 8 9 0 1 2 3 4 5 6 7 8 9 0 1 2 3 4 5
1 1 1 1   4 4 4 4   6 6 6 E 2   T H A T
```

Find the input if the following is executed:

(a)   LOGICAL J, K   (b)   LOGICAL J, K
             READ(5, 10) N, X, Y, J, K   READ(5, 20) X, N, Y, J, K
      10   FORMAT(5G5.2)   20   FORMAT(G7.1, 4G4.2)

10.24 Find the output if the values of N, J, K, X, Y in the preceding Problem 10.23 are printed using

             WRITE(6, 30) N, J, K, X, Y
      30   FORMAT(1X, 5G10.3)

10.25 Suppose a linear array A with five elements contains respectively

$$44.444, \; 0.66666 \times 10^{-6}, \; 33.3 \times 10^{2}, \; 22.2 \times 10^{8}, \; 333.3 \times 10^{-2}$$

Find the output if the instruction is

             DO 100 K = 1, 5
                   WRITE(6, 50) A(K)
      50   FORMAT(11X, G12.4)
     100   CONTINUE

SCALE FACTOR

10.26 Find the internal value given the following format code (field specification) and external number as input:

	(a)	(b)	(c)	(d)	(e)
Format code:	2PF5.1	−3PF5.1	3PE5.1	−4PE10.1	−1PE10.1
Input:	77.77	77.77	77.77	77.77E + 2	7777E + 2

10.27 Suppose 444.888 is the internal number. Find the output if the field specification is

(a) 3PF10.2   (c) −PF10.3   (e) −1PE15.5
(b) −2PF10.1   (d) 4PE15.3   (f) 2PE15.4

10.28 Suppose X contains 444.777. Find the output if the instruction is

             WRITE(6, 10) X, X, X, X, X, X
      10   FORMAT(1X, F12.2, 3X, E12.4, 3X, 2PF12.2, 3X, E12.4, 3X, 0PF12.2, 3X, E12.4)

LEFT-PARENTHESIS RULE

10.29 Consider the program segment

        DIMENSION K(6)
        DATA K/4*33, 2*66/
        WRITE(6, 10) K

Find the output if the accompanying FORMAT statement is

(*a*) 10 FORMAT(1X, I2, (I4, I6))   (*b*) 10 FORMAT(1X, I2, 2(3X, I2), 8X, I2)

10.30 Consider the READ statement

        READ(5, 20) A, B, C, X, Y, Z

Write a FORMAT statement so that

        A is read from the first card using F10.2;
        B, C, and X are read from the second card using F10.3, F10.2, and F10.4;
        Y, Z are read from the third card using F10.3, F10.2.

EXECUTION-TIME FORMAT

10.31 Assuming the character capacity M = 4, describe the input:

        INTEGER FORM(5)
        DATA FORM/'(1X,', 'I3,', '3X,', 'F6', '.3)'/

10.32 Suppose J and X are linear arrays with five elements each, and suppose J and X are assigned

        333, 33333, 33, 333333, 3   and   4.4, 66666.66, 1.1, 88.88888, 2222.2

respectively. Find the output if the following is executed using the array FORM in the preceding Problem 10.31:

        DATA IA, IB/'I7,', 'F10'/
        DO 100 K = 1, 5
            IF(J(K).GE.1000) FORM(2) = IA
            IF(X(K).GE.100.0) FORM(4) = IB
            WRITE(6, FORM) J(K), X(K)
        100 CONTINUE

10.33 Suppose a linear array J contains 75 positive integers less than 10,000. Write a program segment which prints the numbers in a column so that they are left-justified, for example,

        28
        111
        5
        3344
        62
        ⋮

GRAPHING

10.34   Write a program which graphs the function $y = \sin x$ for $-10 \le x \le 10$.   (Recall that $-1 \le y \le 1$ for any value of x.)

10.35   Suppose the values $y_1, y_2, \ldots, y_N$ are stored in a linear array Y with N elements.   Write a SUBROUTINE subprogram

ENDS(Y, N, YMIN, YMAX)

which finds the minimum value YMIN and the maximum value YMAX of the elements in the array Y.

10.36   Write a program which plots the function

$$y = x^3 + 2x^2 - 15x - 8$$

from $x = -5$ to $x = 4$, where the values of x differ by 0.2.   In particular, first store all the values of y in a linear array Y, and then use the subroutine ENDS of Problem 10.35 and scaling function similar to the one in Problem 10.16 to scale y to an integer J between 1 and 101.

10.37   Write a program which accepts two positive integers J and K and prints a rectangle of J*K asterisks so that there are J lines with K asterisks appearing in columns $1, 3, 5, \ldots, 2K - 1$.   (The picture should begin on the third line of a new page.)

Answers to Selected Supplementary Problems

10.19   (a)   DATA J, K, L, M/3*5, .TRUE./   (b)   DATA A/20*0.0/

10.20   (a)   L and M contain 2, N contains the four characters 2*2$_b$ (assuming M = 4), X contains 2.5, and Y and Z contain 3.5.
(b)   X(1), . . . , X(5) contain 2.22, X(6) and Y contain 3.3, and Z contains 4.4.
(c)   J contains 555; K(1), K(2), K(3) contain .FALSE.; K(4) contains .TRUE.; and L contains the character string TRUE (assuming M = 4).

10.21   (a)   A contains 444.44, and B contains 555.55.
(b)   X contains 0.44, J contains 444, and K contains 555.
(c)   I contains 444; J contains .FALSE.; K contains .TRUE.; C contains 44.4; D contains 44.5.

10.22   (a) $_{bbbbbb}$5555$_{bbbbbb}$1111$_{bbbbbb}$8888   (b)   11.1$_{bbbbbbbbbbb}$22.2$_{bbbbbb}$77.8

10.23   (a)   11110, 444.40, 6.66E2(or: 666.0), .TRUE., .FALSE.
(b)   111104.4, 4406, 0.66E2(or: 66.0), .TRUE., .TRUE.

10.24   Right-justified in their fields:
(a)   11110, T, F, 444.$_{bbbb}$, 666.$_{bbbb}$ (b)   4406, T, T, 0.111E$_b$06, 66.0$_{bbbb}$

10.25   See Fig. 10-5.

```
    44.44
    0.6667E−06
    3330.
    0.2220E 10
    3.333
```

Fig. 10-5

10.26   0.7777; 77770.; 0.07777; 77.77E + 2, i.e., 7777.0 (no effect); 777.7E + 2, i.e., 77770.0 (no effect)

10.27   (*a*)   444888.00   (*c*)   44.489   (*e*)   0.044489E 04
        (*b*)   4.4   (*d*)   4450.E − 01   (*f*)   44.49E 01

10.28   bbbbbb444.78bbbbb0.4448E$_b$03bbbbbbb44477.70bbbbbb44.48E$_b$01bbbbbbbbb444.78bbbbb0.4448E$_b$03

10.29   (*a*)   33bb33bbbb33 on a line, b33bbbb66 on the next line, and b66 on the third line.
        (*b*)   33bbb33bbb33bbbbbbbb33 on line, and bb66bbb66 on the next line.

10.30   20   FORMAT(F10.2/(F10.3, F10.2, F10.4/))

10.31   The array FORM is stored as follows:

FORM(1)	(	1	X	,
FORM(2)	I	3	,	
FORM(3)	3	X	,	
FORM(4)	F	6		
FORM(5)	.	3	)	

10.32   See Fig. 10-6.

```
333      4.400
  33333      66666.660
  33       1.100
  333333      88.889
   3       2222.200
```

Fig. 10-6

10.33   Hint: Use execution-time format with format code I1, I2, I3, or I4 according as J contains one, two, three, or four digits.

Chapter 11

Miscellaneous Features of Fortran

11.1 INTRODUCTION

This chapter treats various additional features of the Fortran programming language. In particular, we consider type statements in general and the IMPLICIT statement, DOUBLE PRECISION and COMPLEX variables, and the COMMON and EQUIVALENCE statements.

11.2 TYPE STATEMENTS

There are various types of variables: REAL, INTEGER, LOGICAL, DOUBLE PRECISION, and COMPLEX. The REAL and INTEGER variables were discussed in Chapter 2, the LOGICAL variables were discussed in Chapter 9, and the DOUBLE PRECISION and COMPLEX variables will be discussed in Sections 11.4 and 11.5.

Fortran allows us to use the "first letter" type convention to imply the type of a variable. Namely, any variable whose name begins with the letter I, J, K, L, M, or N is an integer variable, and any other is a real variable. However, this convention can be overruled by using a type statement.

A type statement has the form

    TYPE *variable list*

where the variable names are separated by commas. The type statement declares the variables in the list to be of the given type. For example,

```
REAL MONEY, RATE, NEW
INTEGER X, Y, NEXT
LOGICAL A, B
DOUBLE PRECISION S, T
COMPLEX ROOT, COEF
```

declares MONEY, RATE, and NEW to be real variables; X, Y, and NEXT to be integer variables; and so on. Observe that RATE did not have to be included in the first statement or NEXT in the second statement. In fact, some programmers feel it is a worthwhile practice to list in a type statement every variable regardless of its first letter.

Array names can also appear in type statements. In fact, one can avoid the use of a separate DIMENSION statement by including the size of the array in the type statement. For example,

```
INTEGER COUNT(30)
REAL NUMBER(4, 5), LAST
```

declares COUNT to be a linear integer array with 30 elements, and NUMBER to be a 4×5 real array.

Type statements are nonexecutable statements. They should appear at the beginning of the program before the DATA statement and before any variables are used.

11.3 IMPLICIT STATEMENT

The implicit "first letter" type convention can be expanded by the use of the IMPLICIT statement. We illustrate with an example. Consider the IMPLICIT statement

IMPLICIT INTEGER(B, D, W − Z), LOGICAL(A, N − P), COMPLEX(F − H)

This informs the compiler that, unless explicitly stated by a type statement, all variable names beginning with the letters B, D, W, X, Y, Z are integer variables, A, N, O, P are logical variables, and F, G, H are complex variables. Observe that a range of letters is indicated by writing the first and last letters separated by a minus sign. Observe also that the letters and range of letters follow the TYPE name, and they are separated by commas and enclosed in parentheses.

We note the following in the use of the IMPLICIT statement.

1. Usually only one IMPLICIT statement can appear in any program or subprogram, and it should be the first possible statement. That is, it should be the first statement in a main program, and it should come immediately after the subprogram defining statement in a subprogram.

2. One can override an IMPLICIT statement with a type statement. Moreover, the usual "first letter" type convention holds for any variables which are not covered by the IMPLICIT statement or type statements. For example, suppose a program has the statements

IMPLICIT DOUBLE PRECISION (A − D, S), INTEGER(F − G)
COMPLEX ALPHA, BETA
INTEGER SET, CLASS

Then ALPHA, BETA are COMPLEX variables, and SET and CLASS are integer variables in view of the type statements. ANSWER and SUM are DOUBLE PRECISION variables in view of the IMPLICIT statement. On the other hand, RATE and KOUNT are not covered by any of the statements; so they are REAL and INTEGER variables respectively.

3. The parameters of a subprogram and also the name of a FUNCTION subprogram are covered by an IMPLICIT statement in the subprogram.

11.4 DOUBLE PRECISION

Normally a computer may store seven to eight significant digits in any one memory location, and its arithmetic (also called *single precision arithmetic*) will retain a similar number of significant digits. However, Fortran permits us to obtain more accurate results by using the so-called *double precision values and arithmetic*. In this case, each value is stored in two (2) memory locations; so the number of significant digits is approximately doubled. (For example, the IBM 360/370 series retains seven significant digits under ordinary arithmetic but 16 significant digits under double precision arithmetic.) In this section, we shall discuss the rules concerning double precision arithmetic.

Remark. Since double precision values occupy twice as many memory locations, and since the arithmetic may take 2 to 10 times as long to execute, double precision should be used only when extreme accuracy is required.

Variables

Double precision variables and arrays are declared by using the DOUBLE PRECISION statement as discussed in Section 11.2.

Constants

Double precision constants are written in ways similar to single precision real constants. In particular, a *decimal point* must be present in any double precision constant.

1. *Without exponent.* A real constant written without an exponent is interpreted as a single precision constant, unless the number of significant digits exceeds the maximum allowable number for a single precision real constant. For example, for IBM 360/370 machines which allow seven significant digits, the constant 123.456 will be assumed to be single precision while 123.456000000 will be assumed to be double precision.

2. *With exponent.* Single precision constants are represented in exponential form using the character E; for example, 46.8086E7 is a single precision constant. Double precision constants are represented in exponential form using the letter D in place of the letter E. Thus, 46.8086D7 represents the same number in double precision; however, it is stored internally with a full 16 significant digits as

$$0.4680860000000000 \times 10^9$$

(That is, trailing zeros are added to obtain the required 16 significant digit number.)

We note that there are no such things as double precision integers.

Input/Output

The D-field is used to input/output double precision values. Aside from the fact that D-fields allow longer decimal digits to be handled, the use of the D-field is entirely similar to the E-field; e.g., the field specification has the form

   Dw.d

where w is the field width, and d in the number of decimal digits. Therefore, readers are advised to review Chapter 3 on E-fields for a comprehensive discussion.

Arithmetic Operations

Double precision arithmetic takes place when both operands are of double precision type. Most compilers allow the mixture of single precision and double precision terms. In such a case, the single precision term is first converted to double precision (by adding trailing 0's), and then double precision arithmetic is carried out. On the other hand, most compilers do not allow the mixture of integer and double precision types; except, a double precision value can always be raised to an integer exponent. We also note here that a negative double precision value cannot be raised to a real or double precision power as was the case with negative real numbers. (See page 28.)

Assignment Statements

As in the single precision case, the types on two sides of the = sign may be different. The value that is to be stored is always converted to the type of the storage location. Furthermore, double precision values are truncated, not rounded off, when converted to single precision. Consider, for example, the segment

```
DOUBLE PRECISION A
A = 1.0
B = 123.456789098
J = 123.456789098
K = 3.4444D3
```

Then,

    1. The constant is converted to double precision and stored in A.

    2. Only 123.4567 is stored in B; that is, the constant is truncated after seven significant digits.

    3. Only 123 is stored in J; that is, the constant is truncated at the decimal point.

    4. Although 3.4444D3 equals 3444.4, only 3 is assigned to K since the constant is truncated at the decimal point.

Library Functions

The library functions DFLOAT and DBLE convert, respectively, integer and single precision values to double precision, and the function SNGL converts a double precision value to single precision. There are also library functions which provide double precision calculations for most of the frequently used functions. For example, if DX is a double precision argument, then

    DSQRT(DX)

will give the square root of DX using double precision arithmetic. Similarly, DABS(DX), DLOG(DX), DSIN(DX) give the double precision absolute value, logarithm, and sine of DX. Generally speaking, the letter D in front of a function denotes double precision calculations. A list of many other functions is given in Appendix A. We note that one would have to use

    DLOG(DBLE(X))

to obtain the double precision natural logarithm of a single precision real value X since the argument of the function DLOG has to be double precision.

Subprograms

Double precision values may be transmitted to and from a subprogram via the arguments (just like any other types of values); however, the names of these arguments and the corresponding parameters must be declared double precision both in the calling program and in the subprogram. A FUNCTION subprogram, itself, can be declared double precision by writing DOUBLE PRECISION at the beginning of the FUNCTION defining statement or by declaring the NAME to be double precision in the subprogram. For example, the following are equivalent subprograms:

```
DOUBLE PRECISION FUNCTION SUM(A, B)
DOUBLE PRECISION A, B
SUM = A + B
RETURN
END
```

and

```
FUNCTION SUM(A, B)
DOUBLE PRECISION SUM, A, B
SUM = A + B
RETURN
END
```

Furthermore, most compilers require that the NAME of a double precision FUNCTION subprogram be so declared in the calling program. That is, the statement

    DOUBLE PRECISION SUM

or its equivalent must appear in the calling program using the above subprogram SUM. (This requirement is not universal; so a programmer should find out the exact requirements for the particular compiler that is used.) On the other hand, there is no such thing as a DOUBLE PRECISION SUBROUTINE subprogram since no value is assigned to the NAME of the subroutine.

EXAMPLE 11.1

Assuming we are using IBM 360/370 machines, the program segment

```
      DOUBLE PRECISION DA, DB
      DA = 2./3.
      DB = 2.0D0/3.0D0
      WRITE(6, 10) DA, DA
      WRITE(6, 10) DB, DB
   10 FORMAT(1X, D23.16, 10X, D12.4)
```

will produce

0.6666666000000000D 00	0.6667D 00
0.6666666666666666D 00	0.6667D 00

The difference occurs because 2./3. is calculated in single precision and is truncated after seven significant digits, i.e., has the value 0.6666666. When 2./3. is stored in DA, it is converted to double precision by adding 0's. On the other hand, 2.0D0/3.0D0 is calculated in double precision and is truncated after 16 significant digits, i.e., has the value 0.6666666666666666. (There is no rounding off in these calculations.) However, when the values are printed, they are rounded off to four significant digits as specified by the format codes.

11.5 COMPLEX NUMBERS

Fortran compilers provide the arithmetical operations to handle complex numbers. We first review the arithmetic of complex numbers and then discuss the way Fortran handles them.

A complex number z is usually written in the form

$$z = a + bi$$

where a, b are ordinary real numbers and $i = \sqrt{-1}$. The a is called the *real part* of z, and the b is called the *imaginary part* of z. (A real number a can be identified as the complex number $a + 0i$.)

The sum and product of complex numbers can be obtained by using the usual commutative and distributive laws of algebra and that $i^2 = -1$:

$$(a + bi) + (c + di) = a + c + bi + di = (a + c) + (b + d)i$$
$$(a + bi)(c + di) = ac + bci + adi + bdi^2 = (ac - bd) + (bc + ad)i$$

The *conjugate* of the complex number $z = a + bi$ is denoted and defined by

$$\bar{z} = a - bi$$

(Notice that $z\bar{z} = a^2 + b^2$.) If $z \neq 0$; i.e., if $a \neq 0$ or $b \neq 0$, then the inverse z^{-1} of z and division by z are given by

$$z^{-1} = \frac{\bar{z}}{z\bar{z}} = \frac{a}{a^2 + b^2} + \frac{-b}{a^2 + b^2} i \quad \text{and} \quad \frac{w}{z} = wz^{-1}$$

where w is also a complex number. We also define

$$-z = -1z \quad \text{and} \quad w - z = w + (-z)$$

The *absolute value* or *magnitude* of $z = a + bi$, written $|z|$, is defined by

$$|z| = \sqrt{a^2 + b^2} = \sqrt{z\bar{z}}$$

EXAMPLE 11.2

Suppose $z = 2 + 3i$ and $w = 5 - 2i$. Then

$$z + w = (2 + 3i) + (5 - 2i) = 2 + 5 + 3i - 2i = 7 + i$$
$$zw = (2 + 3i)(5 - 2i) = 10 + 15i - 4i - 6i^2 = 16 + 11i$$
$$\bar{z} = \overline{2 + 3i} = 2 - 3i \quad \text{and} \quad \bar{w} = \overline{5 - 2i} = 5 + 2i$$
$$\frac{w}{z} = \frac{5 - 2i}{2 + 3i} = \frac{(5 - 2i)(2 - 3i)}{(2 + 3i)(2 - 3i)} = \frac{4 - 19i}{13} = \frac{4}{13} - \frac{19}{13}i$$
$$|z| = \sqrt{4 + 9} = \sqrt{13} \quad \text{and} \quad |w| = \sqrt{25 + 4} = \sqrt{29}$$

Since a complex number consists of two parts, the real part and the imaginary part, two memory locations are required to store a complex number. The rules concerning the complex constants and variables and their arithmetic follow.

Variables

Complex variables and arrays are declared by using the COMPLEX statement as discussed in Section 11.2.

Constants

Fortran represents a complex constant by an ordered pair of *real* constants, separated by a comma and enclosed in parentheses. The first real number denotes the real part of the complex number and the second, the imaginary part. Each of the two numbers can be written with or without exponent but *cannot* be an integer. Thus,

$$1 + 2i$$

may be written in Fortran by any of the following:

(1.0, 2.0)
(0.1E1, 2.0)
(1.0, 2.0E0)
(0.1E1, 0.2E1)

But it cannot be represented by

(1, 2)

On the other hand, an ordered pair of real variables or expressions is not acceptable to define a complex value. For example, given that X is real, we cannot use

(X, 2.0)

to define a complex value. However, Fortran provides us with a complex library function CMPLX which converts an ordered pair of *real expressions* into its complex-valued constant. Thus,

CMPLX(X, 2.0)   and   CMPLX(X + 2.0, X − 2.0)

are the Fortran ways of writing the complex numbers $x + 2i$ and $(x + 2) + (x - 2)i$.

Input/Output

There is no special field for the input/output of complex numbers. However, since two real numbers will correspond to each complex number, two field specifications must be given for each complex variable. For example,

```
      COMPLEX Z
      READ(5, 10) Z
   10 FORMAT(F10.2, 10X, F10.2)
```

will assign the value in columns 1–10 as the real part of Z and the value in columns 21–30 as the imaginary part of Z. Thus, if the data card is prepared as

```
          1         2         3
 1234567890123456789012345678901234 5

     12.34     333.33     13.579
```

then Z will have the value $12.34 + 13.579i$. Naturally, the field specifications could be E-field, F-field, or G-field, or a combination of them.

Arithmetic Operations

Complex arithmetic takes place when both operands are complex, or when one is real and the other is complex. In the latter case, the real value, say a, is converted to its complex equivalent $(a, 0.0)$, and then complex arithmetic is performed. For example, if X is real and C is complex, then

$$X + (1.0, 2.0), \qquad X + C, \qquad C - X, \qquad X/C, \qquad C*X, \qquad C + 1.0$$

are acceptable Fortran expressions. In case the compiler accepts the mixture of integer and real values, then integer values can also be used with the complex values; for example, C + 1 would be acceptable, and complex arithmetic will be performed. However, there is one special restriction that holds for complex numbers but not for reals: a complex number cannot be raised to a real power. In other words, a complex number can only be raised to an integer power.

Assignment Statements

Real, integer, and complex values can be assigned to complex variables. For example, if A, B are complex variables and X, Y are real variables, then the following assignment statements are valid:

```
A = (1.0, 0.2E1)
A = A + B**2
A = 25
A = 3*X
A = 3*B + Y − 8.0
A = CMPLX(X, Y + 2.0)
```

Specifically, the real and integer values are converted to complex values before they are stored in the complex variable A. On the other hand, complex values cannot be assigned to real or integer variables. Thus, for example,

```
X = A + B
K = B**2
```

are not valid.

Complex Library Functions

The function CMPLX(X, Y), discussed before, takes two real arguments X, Y and converts them into a complex number $X + Yi$. The real and imaginary parts and the magnitude (or: absolute value) of a complex variable can be obtained by the functions REAL, AIMAG, and CABS respectively. That is, if $C = X + Yi$, then

```
REAL(C)     will give the value X
AIMAG(C)    will give the value Y
CABS(C)     will give the value
```
$\sqrt{X^2 + Y^2}$

There are other complex library functions which are analogous to real functions.   For example, if C is a complex variable or expression, then

     CSQRT(C)

will give the complex square root of C.   Similarly, CSIN(C), CCOS(C), CLOG(C), and CEXP(C) evaluate the complex sine, cosine, logarithm, and exponential, respectively, of C.   Generally speaking, the letter C in front of a function denotes a complex function.   A list of many such functions is given in Appendix A.

Subprograms

Complex values are used in subprograms in the same way double precision values are used.   Specifically, complex values are transmitted to and from a subprogram via the arguments, and the names of these arguments and the corresponding parameters must be declared to be complex in both the calling program and the subprogram.   Also, a FUNCTION subprogram can be declared complex by writing COMPLEX at the beginning of the FUNCTION defining statement or by declaring the NAME to be complex in the subprogram.   For example, the following are equivalent:

    COMPLEX FUNCTION XYZ(A, B, C)   or   FUNCTION XYZ(A, B, C)
    COMPLEX A, B   COMPLEX XYZ, A, B

Each declares that XYZ is a complex-valued function and A, B are complex variables.   Furthermore, as with double precision functions, most compilers require that the NAME of a complex FUNCTION subprogram be declared complex in the calling program.   That is, the statement

    COMPLEX XYZ

should appear in the calling program using the above complex subprogram XYZ.

11.6 ASSIGNED GO TO STATEMENT, ASSIGN STATEMENT

Some compilers provide another transfer of control statement called the assigned GO TO statement.   The assigned GO TO statement and a corresponding ASSIGN statement have the following form:

    ASSIGN n TO J
         ⋮
    GO TO J, $(n_1, n_2, \ldots, n_k)$

Here, $n, n_1, n_2, \ldots, n_k$ are unsigned integer constants standing for statement numbers (labels), and J is an integer variable.   The ASSIGN statement assigns the constant n to the variable J.   When the assigned GO TO statement is executed, control is transferred to the statement labeled n, the current value of J.

We summarize rules for the ASSIGN statement and the assigned GO TO statement as follows:

1. The variable J must be an integer (unsubscripted) variable.

2. The variable J cannot be changed except by another ASSIGN statement.   For example, the segment

        ASSIGN 25 to LAST
        LAST = LAST + 5
        GO TO LAST, (20, 25, 30, 35)

  is not valid.

3. The value of J must appear in the list of statement numbers following J in the assigned GO TO statement.

11.7 MULTIPLE ENTRIES AND RETURNS TO A SUBPROGRAM

(a) Multiple Entry

Normally, when a subprogram (FUNCTION or SUBROUTINE) name appears in a calling program, entry into the subprogram is at the first executable statement following the subprogram defining statement.   Some compilers provide instructions to enter a subprogram at different entry points. To indicate alternative entry points, one uses the ENTRY statement in the subprogram.   This statement has the form

> ENTRY NAME(parameter list)

where the NAME of the entry point is different from the name of the subprogram.   The ENTRY statement is nonexecutable and is placed in the subprogram at the point where the entry will be made.   The statement will have no effect on the logic of the subprogram.

There may be several ENTRY declarations in a subprogram, each defining a different entry point.   Clearly, each entry point must have its own name.   Furthermore, the parameters associated with an entry point need not agree with the parameters of the subprogram, nor do they need to agree with the parameters of any other entry points.   However, when a particular entry point NAME is used in the calling program, the argument list of the calling statement must agree with the parameters of the ENTRY statement.

The form of the calling statement for an entry point in a subprogram follows analogously as that for a SUBROUTINE or FUNCTION subprogram.   In either case, when the entry NAME is used by a calling program, execution will begin at the first executable statement following the ENTRY declaration in the subprogram.

The following program skeleton illustrates the above concepts:

Main program	*Subprogram*
. . . .	SUBROUTINE ABC(X, Y, Z)
CALL ABC(P, Q, R)	. . . .
. . . .	GO TO 10
CALL TWOA(E, F)	ENTRY ONEA(W, K)
. . . .	. . . .
CALL ONEA(S, M)	GO TO 10
. . . .	ENTRY TWOA(U, V)
STOP	. . . .
END	10 RETURN
	END

(b) Multiple Return (for SUBROUTINE Only)

Normally, when a RETURN statement is encountered in a SUBROUTINE, control is transferred to the first executable statement following the CALL statement in the calling program.   Fortran also allows us to return to different points of the calling program.   We illustrate this facility using the following program skeleton:

Main program	*Subroutine*
DIMENSION TEST(100)	SUBROUTINE GRADE(R, *, S, T, *, W)
. . . .	DIMENSION W(100)
CALL GRADE(A, 30, B, C, 20, TEST)	. . . .
. . . .	RETURN 2
END	. . . .
	RETURN
	. . . .
	RETURN 1
	END

Observe that there are two asterisks in the parameter list in the SUBROUTINE defining statement.   Also observe that the statement labels 30 and 20 in the argument list correspond, respectively, to these two asterisks.   Accordingly, the statements RETURN 1 and RETURN 2 will correspond to the statement labels 30 and 20 respectively in the following way.   If RETURN 1 is encountered in the subprogram, then control is transferred to the statement labeled 30 in the calling program; and if RETURN 2 is encountered, then control is transferred to the statement labeled 20 in the calling program.   On the other hand, when RETURN is encountered, control is returned to the first executable statement following the CALL statement.

Generally speaking, the multiple RETURN statement has the form

    RETURN *n*

where *n* is an unsigned integer constant.   This statement can only appear in a subroutine which has at least *n* asterisks in its parameter list and where each asterisk corresponds to a statement number in the argument list.   Then when RETURN *n* is encountered in the subroutine, control is transferred to the statement in the calling program whose label is the same as the *n*th label in the argument list.

11.8   UNLABELED COMMON STATEMENTS

Recall that the variables, other than the parameters, in a subprogram are local to that subprogram.   Consequently, the only way to pass information between a calling program and a subprogram is to specify them in the argument list of the programs.   However, this arrangement could be complicated if large numbers of memory locations are to be shared by several subprograms.   Fortran provides us with an alternate way for subprograms to share common memory spaces.   Specifically, a common storage area can be defined using a COMMON statement, and subprograms with proper declaration and description will have access to any data stored there.

There are two kinds of COMMON statements: labeled COMMON and unlabeled (blank) COMMON.   Both kinds are nonexecutable and must be placed at the beginning of any program before any executable statement.   In this section, we shall discuss unlabeled COMMON statements, and in the next section we shall discuss labeled COMMON statements.

A typical unlabeled (blank) COMMON statement follows:

    DIMENSION Y(2, 3), W(2)
    COMMON X, Y, Z, W

Observe that the COMMON statement begins with the word COMMON and is followed by a list of variable names, including array names separated by commas.   One can also avoid the use of a separate DIMENSION statement for arrays in a COMMON statement by including the size of the array in the COMMON statement itself.   For example, each of the following arrangements,

    COMMON X, Y(2, 3), Z, W(2)   or   DIMENSION Y(2, 3)
                                          COMMON X, Y, Z, W(2)

is equivalent to the above declaration.

Any one of the above COMMON statements sets up a common block of 10 memory locations $(1 + 6 + 1 + 2)$, where the memory locations are allocated according to the order of the variable list.   Specifically, in our example, the memory locations are named as in Fig. 11-1.

We illustrate how the COMMON statement is used and how common storage area is shared by way of the program skeleton given in Fig. 11-2.   (For simplicity, the subprograms use precisely the same common statement, although this is not generally necessary.   See *Remark A* on page 275.) Observe that the main program defines a common storage area of 20 locations and calls 3 subroutines

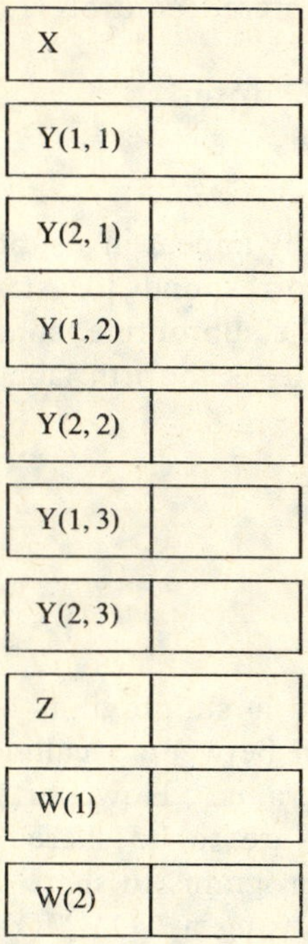

```
Main program
COMMON A(10), B, X(2, 4), Q
..............................
CALL XXX(S, I)
..............................
CALL WWW(P1, P2, P3)
..............................
T = TAX + ZZZ(U, V)
..............................
CALL YYY
..............................
END

Subprogram 1
SUBROUTINE XXX(F, K)
COMMON A(10), B, X(2, 4), Q
..............................
RETURN
END

Subprogram 2
SUBROUTINE YYY
COMMON A(10), B, X(2, 4), Q
..............................
RETURN
END

Subprogram 3
FUNCTION ZZZ(G, H)
COMMON A(10), B, X(2, 4), Q
..............................
ZZZ = ..........
RETURN
END

Subprogram 4
SUBROUTINE WWW(F, G, H)
B = 0.0
..............................
RETURN
END
```

X	
Y(1, 1)	
Y(2, 1)	
Y(1, 2)	
Y(2, 2)	
Y(1, 3)	
Y(2, 3)	
Z	
W(1)	
W(2)	

Fig. 11-1   Fig. 11-2

and 1 function subprogram.   The subroutines XXX, YYY, and the function subprogram ZZZ contain the COMMON statement and, hence, will have access to the common storage area.   In particular, each of the programs can use or alter any of the values stored there.   On the other hand, the subroutine WWW does not have a COMMON statement and, consequently, does not have access to the common storage area.

There is one other point we want to emphasize.   The statement

B = 0.0

in the subroutine WWW has no effect on the common storage area since B is local to the subprogram WWW.   However, if this statement appeared in any of the other subprograms, then when it is executed, it will alter the value of B in the common storage area to 0.0.   Furthermore, this value of B would then be available afterward to any of the other programs.

Remark A.   The use of unlabeled (blank) COMMON statements creates only *one* common storage area that is accessible to different subprograms.   However, the memory locations in this common area may be called different names in different subprograms.   For example, suppose the subprogram XXX above has the following form:

        SUBROUTINE XXX(F, K)
        COMMON AA(4, 2), BB, CC(11)
        . . . .
        RETURN
        END

Although the COMMON statement refers to the same common storage area, the memory locations in this common storage are called by different names in the different programs as indicated in Fig. 11-3.   Thus, if the statement

        CC(2) = 5.5

appears in the subroutine XXX and is executed in the subroutine, then the value of B in the subprograms YYY and ZZZ and in the main program is also changed to 5.5.

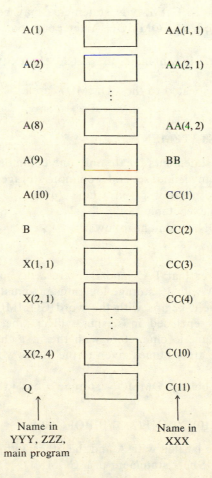

Fig. 11-3

Remark B. The number of memory cells defined in the COMMON area in a subprogram may be smaller than the COMMON area defined in the main program. For example, the following is permitted:

        Main program: COMMON X, A(5), Y
        Subprogram: COMMON B(2, 2)

Furthermore, the variables will share memory cells in the COMMON area as follows:

Name in main program:	X	A(1)	A(2)	A(3)	A(4)	A(5)	Y
Name in subprogram:	B(1, 1)	B(2, 1)	B(1, 2)	B(2, 2)			

Observe that the first elements in the COMMON statements, X and B(1, 1), share the same location. On the other hand, the number of memory cells in the COMMON area of a subprogram can never exceed that in the main program. For example,

        Main program: COMMON C(2, 3)
        Subprogram: COMMON D(8)

is not permitted.

Remark C. Several unlabeled COMMON statements may be used in a program. However, this is equivalent to writing one long COMMON statement. For example,

    COMMON A(10), T
    COMMON C(2)   is equivalent to   COMMON A(10), T, C(2)

and 13 memory locations are allocated to the COMMON area.

11.9 LABELED COMMON STATEMENTS

The unlabeled COMMON statements create only one common storage area. By using labeled COMMON statements, one can define several common storage areas. As the name suggests, each of these common storage areas is given a label (name). These statements, like unlabeled COMMON statements, are nonexecutable.

A typical labeled COMMON statement follows:

    COMMON /A/ TAX(10), X, INF(2, 4)

This statement not only declares that TAX and INF are array names but also defines a common storage area labeled (named) A with 19 storage locations, as illustrated in Fig. 11-4. Observe that the labeled COMMON statement begins with the word COMMON and is followed by the label (name) of the common block enclosed in slashes. (The label, like any other variable name, consists of one to six alphanumeric characters with the first character being alphabetic.) Next follows the list of variable and array names given to the memory locations in this common storage area.

One may define several labeled COMMON storage areas in one COMMON statement. For example,

    COMMON /A/ TAX(10), X, INF(2, 4)/B/POP(100)

defines two common areas, one labeled with A and the other with B. We note that the arrays may be declared in either a DIMENSION statement or a COMMON statement, but not in both. Thus, any one of the following arrangements is equivalent to the above statement:

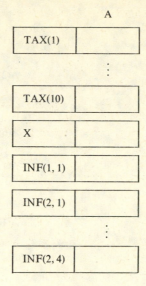

Fig. 11-4

        DIMENSION TAX(10), INF(2, 4), POP(100)
        COMMON /A/TAX, X, INF /B/POP

or

        DIMENSION TAX(10)
        COMMON /A/TAX, X, INF(2, 4)
        COMMON/B/POP(100)

We emphasize that there is no comma separating the different labeled common areas in one COMMON statement (e.g., there is no comma preceding /B/ in any of the above statements).

One main advantage of labeled common areas is that different subprograms may have access to different common areas. It is most important to remember that it is the *label* which must be communicated from one subprogram to another. The names of the memory cells within a particular common block are local to that subprogram and, hence, may be different, as discussed in the unlabeled case. We illustrate this with an example.

EXAMPLE 11.2

Consider the program skeleton in Fig. 11-5. Observe that two common areas are defined and their labels are AX and AY. Subroutine SUB1 has access to common area AY containing eight memory locations, and the names of these locations in the subroutine are the same names as in the main program, that is, X(1, 1), X(2, 1), ..., X(2, 4). Subroutine SUB2 shares with the main program the common area labeled AX with 11 memory locations. These locations are called A(1), ..., A(10), B in the main program, but are called T(1, 1), ..., T(2, 3), S(1), ..., S(5) in the subroutine as shown in Fig. 11-6.

We conclude with a few other things about labeled COMMON statements.

    1. If two common area names are identical in a subprogram, such as in

        COMMON /A/T(2, 4)/B/X, Y, Z /A/Q(10)
        COMMON /B/W(10)

    then the effect is cumulative; i.e., the above is the same as

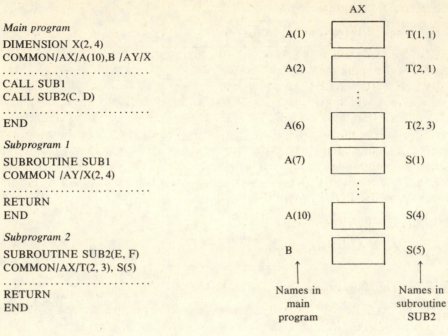

Main program
DIMENSION X(2, 4)
COMMON/AX/A(10),B /AY/X
. . . .
CALL SUB1
CALL SUB2(C, D)
. . . .
END

Subprogram 1
SUBROUTINE SUB1
COMMON /AY/X(2, 4)
. . . .
RETURN
END

Subprogram 2
SUBROUTINE SUB2(E, F)
COMMON/AX/T(2, 3), S(5)
. . . .
RETURN
END

Fig. 11-5   **Fig. 11-6**

COMMON /A/T(2, 4), Q(10) /B/X, Y, Z, W(10)

2. The total number of memory locations in a labeled common area must be the same in all subprograms that have access to it. Observe that this is different from the unlabeled area.

3. The labeled and unlabeled common areas may be defined in the same program using the same COMMON statement. For example, the statement

    COMMON TAX(100), A, B /Q/X(25, 10)

creates an unlabeled common area with 102 locations and a labeled common area called Q with 250 locations. Equivalently, we could use

    COMMON /Q/X(25, 10)//TAX(100), A, B

Observe that no label appears between the slashes for the second storage area; hence, it creates an unlabeled common area as above. This is the reason why an unlabeled COMMON statement is also called a blank COMMON statement.

The most general use of labeled and unlabeled COMMON statements can be extremely complicated and confusing; therefore, we consider further discussion beyond the scope of this text.

11.10 EQUIVALENCE STATEMENTS

Suppose after writing and punching a long program, a programmer realizes that different names, say MAX, LARGE, and JBIG were used for the same quantity. Instead of changing all the names and repunching the cards, the programmer may simply insert the EQUIVALENCE statement

EQUIVALENCE (MAX, LARGE, JBIG)

at the beginning of the program. This card informs the computer that the names MAX, LARGE, and JBIG all refer to the same memory location.

Observe that the EQUIVALENCE statement begins with the word EQUIVALENCE and is followed by parentheses which enclose those variables which refer to the same memory location.

The EQUIVALENCE statement can also be used to save memory locations by assigning different names to the same memory locations, provided the different variables are used in different parts of the program. For example, suppose the average AVE, the median XMED, and the largest BIG of 100 numbers are computed and printed by a program. If the variables AVE, XMED, and BIG are never needed at the same time, then one can conserve storage space by assigning the three variables to the same location by the EQUIVALENCE statement

EQUIVALENCE(AVE, XMED, BIG)

As usual, one EQUIVALENCE statement can be used to denote different equivalences. For example,

EQUIVALENCE(A, X, Z), (NEXT, LAST), (C, D, E, F)

tells the compiler that A, X, Z will share the same storage location, NEXT and LAST will share the same storage location, and C, D, E, F will share the same storage location.

The main application of the EQUIVALENCE statement occurs with arrays since thousands of storage locations could possibly be saved. However, the way arrays share storage space can be tricky; so the EQUIVALENCE statements involving arrays is not as simple as that for the unsubscripted variables discussed above.

For example, suppose A, B, C are arrays in a program declared by

DIMENSION A(50, 100), B(25, 50), C(3750)

Suppose, further, that we know that array A is required only at the beginning part of the program and is not used in the calculation of arrays B and C. We can save memory locations by storing arrays B and C in the memory locations allocated for A. Specifically, we indicate that the first element of A and the first element of B will have the same memory by

EQUIVALENCE(A1, 1), B(1, 1))

Since array elements are contiguous, this statement also informs the computer that the first 1250 locations of A will have the same locations as the 1250 locations of B. (Can you give the correspondence?) We may use the remaining 3750 locations of A for the array C by the statement

EQUIVALENCE(A(1, 26), C(1))

These two statements may be combined into the one statement

EQUIVALENCE(A(1, 1), B(1, 1)), (A(1, 26), C(1))

The storage areas now overlap, and only 5000 locations, instead of 10,000 locations, will be allocated.

The crucial thing to remember about arrays is that

1. The elements of a given array are always next to each other in a given linear order, and this cannot be changed by any other EQUIVALENCE statement.

2. Only array elements can appear in an EQUIVALENCE statement, not the array name itself.

Remark. Recall that arrays are stored linearly in memory even though the arrays may be multidimensional. Some compilers allow one to use the linear position of the elements of an array in an EQUIVALENCE statement.   For example, A(1, 1) occupies the first position in the above array A, and A(1, 26) occupies the 1251st position in A.   Also, B(1, 1) occupies the first position in B.   Accordingly,

> EQUIVALENCE(A(1, 1), B(1, 1)), (A(1, 26), C(1))

can be replaced by

> EQUIVALENCE(A(1), B(1)), (A(1251), C(1))

The advantage of using linear position is its ease of computing the position.

In either of the above forms, it is important to note that the subscripts must be constants as the EQUIVALENCE statement is nonexecutable, and memory locations are allocated during compilation.

We next give some other examples involving arrays with EQUIVALENCE statements.

EXAMPLE 11.3

(a)   Consider the statements

> DIMENSION A(2, 3)
> EQUIVALENCE(A(2), X, Y), (A(5), C)

The variables share storage as follows:

A(1, 1)	A(2, 1) X Y	A(1, 2)	A(2, 2)	A(1, 3) C	A(2, 3)

That is, A(2, 1), X, Y are assigned the same storage location, and A(1, 3), C are assigned the same storage location.

(b)   Suppose the linear position of an array may be used.   Consider the statements

> DIMENSION A(2, 3), B(2, 2), C(5)
> EQUIVALENCE(A(1), B(1), C(1))

The arrays share storage space as follows:

A(1, 1) B(1, 1) C(1)	A(2, 1) B(2, 1) C(2)	A(1, 2) B(1, 2) C(3)	A(2, 2) B(2, 2) C(4)	A(1, 3) C(5)	A(2, 3)

Observe that C(4) is forced to share a location with A(2, 2) and B(2, 2) since we originally assigned the first elements in each array to the same location.

(c)   Consider the statements

> DIMENSION A(2, 3), C(7)
> EQUIVALENCE(A(3), C(1))

Then the arrays appear in storage as follows:

A(1, 1)	A(2, 1)	A(1, 2) C(1)	A(2, 2) C(2)	A(1, 3) C(3)	A(2, 3) C(4)	C(5)	C(6)	C(7)

Observe that the array C extends out on the right hand side.

One can also use an EQUIVALENCE statement with a COMMON statement; however, the EQUIVALENCE statement can only lengthen the common storage, it cannot change the original locations of the variables.   We illustrate with examples:

EXAMPLE 11.4

(*a*) Consider the statements

        DIMENSION A(4), C(2), D(8)
        COMMON A, B, C
        EQUIVALENCE(A(3), D(1))

The common storage area will appear as follows:

        A(1)   A(2)   A(3)   A(4)   B   C(1)   C(2)
                      D(1)   D(2)   D(3)   D(4)   D(5)   D(6)   D(7)   D(8)

(For notational convenience, we have not drawn boxes with the variable names as we did in Example 11.3.)   The original COMMON statement set up seven locations in common storage.   The EQUIVALENCE statement extended the common storage to 10 locations.

(*b*) The following FORTRAN statements are not allowed.

        DIMENSION A(4), C(2), D(8)
        COMMON A, B, C
        EQUIVALENCE(A(1), D(3))

By previous reasoning, the sharing of common storage should look as follows:

                       A(1)   A(2)   A(3)   A(4)   B   C(1)   C(2)
        D(1)   D(2)   D(3)   D(4)   D(5)   D(6)   D(7)   D(8)

Here A(1) occupies the third location, yet by the COMMON statement A(1) should occupy the first location.   Since Fortran does not allow us to change the original positions of the variables in common storage, these statements are not allowed.

Other uses of the EQUIVALENCE statement, especially involving COMMON statements, can be very complicated and may be machine dependent; hence, we consider further discussion beyond the scope of this text.   Furthermore, since it is entirely possible to do without the EQUIVALENCE statement, we advise the beginning programmer to avoid use of the EQUIVALENCE statement whenever possible.

11.11 BLOCK DATA

Some compilers do not allow the use of the DATA statement to initialize values of variables in labeled COMMON areas, and some do not allow initialization on any COMMON areas.   However, a subprogram called BLOCK DATA may be used for this purpose.

A BLOCK DATA subprogram may consist only of the following nonexecutable statements:

        DATA
        COMMON
        DIMENSION
        EQUIVALENCE

and any type declarations.   We illustrate how such a program works with an example.
Suppose in a main program we have

        DIMENSION X(20), Y(15)
        COMMON /A/X, U, V /B/Y
                        :

        END

Suppose we want each element of X and Y to be initialized at 0.0.   The use of a DATA statement is not permitted since X and Y are in labeled COMMON areas.   Clearly, one can use assignment statements for the initialization which would require execution time.   On the other hand, the following BLOCK DATA subprogram can be used:

```
BLOCK DATA
DIMENSION X(20), Y(15)
COMMON /A/X, U, V /B/Y
DATA X/20*0.0/, Y/15*0.0/
END
```

We summarize the use of the BLOCK DATA subprogram:

1. The subprogram always begins with the statement BLOCK DATA.
2. All variables in the COMMON area must be listed in the subprogram even though one might want to initialize only some of the variables.
3. Only one BLOCK DATA subprogram can be used to initialize variables in any one COMMON area.

11.12   EXTERNAL

Recall that the only communication between a calling program and a subprogram (besides COMMON and EQUIVALENCE) is via the argument list.   Sometimes it may be desirable to use a subprogram name as an actual argument in the calling statement for another subprogram.   The following program skeleton illustrates this situation:

```
            Main program

            . . . . . . . . . . .
            EXTERNAL TOTAL
            X = BAL(ASSET, PAY, TOTAL)
            . . . . . . . . . . .
Subprogram { END
            FUNCTION BAL(A, B, C)
            T = C(A)
            . . . . . . . . .
            RETURN
Subprogram { END
            FUNCTION TOTAL(Z)
            . . . . . . . . . . .
            RETURN
            END
```

As indicated by one of the arrows, the subprogram name TOTAL is being transferred to the subprogram BAL using the parameter C.   Therefore, C(A) is calculated in BAL using the subprogram TOTAL as indicated by the other arrow.

However, without special declaration, the compiler will not be able to distinguish a subprogram name from a simple variable name which carries a value.   To avoid confusion, an EXTERNAL declaration is used in the calling program to indicate that the subprogram name used in the argument is external to that program.

Problems

TYPE, IMPLICIT STATEMENTS

11.1   Find errors, if any, in each segment:

(a)   INTEGER, RATE, TIME, DISTANCE

(b)   DIMENSION R(4), S(5, 3)
      DOUBLE PRECISION A(7), B, R(8), S,

(c)   IMPLICIT, COMPLEX (A – D, F, G) LOGICAL(C, X – Z)

(d)   IMPLICIT REAL M, N, COMPLEX P – R

(e)   DOUBLE PRECISION NUMBER(4, 7) X, Y, TEST(8, 15) L, M

11.2   Consider the following segment:

      IMPLICIT COMPLEX(H – K) LOGICAL(P, R)
      REAL COEF, KAPPA, LAMBDA
      INTEGER RATE, TIME

Indicate the type of each variable:

(a)	ALPHA	(d)	KOUNT	(g)	LAST	(j)	ROOM
(b)	INDEX	(e)	PARTY	(h)	LAMBDA	(k)	TIME
(c)	KAPPA	(f)	QUEUE	(i)	RATE	(l)	TARGET

DOUBLE PRECISION

11.3   Indicate if each represents a real (single precision) or a double precision constant (assuming seven significant digits for real constants):

(a)	$1.45D + 03$	(d)	12345678	(g)	$123.123123 + 0.E0$
(b)	$5.9321E – 7$	(e)	$23.4 + 0.D0$	(h)	$5.55E – 26 + 58.4$
(c)	3456.765432	(f)	$111.222333E – 5$	(i)	$6.7 + 4.5D1 – 7.8E3$

11.4   Determine the output of each program segment:

(a)
```
      DOUBLE PRECISION DA
      A = 0.555666777888999
      DA = 0.555666777888999
      WRITE(6, 10) A, A
   10 FORMAT(1X, E25.3, 5X, E25.9)
      WRITE(6, 20) DA, DA
   20 FORMAT(1X, D25.3, 5X, E25.9)
      STOP
      END
```

(b)
```
      DOUBLE PRECISION X, Y, Z
      X = 70/9
      Y = 70.0/9.0
      Z = 70.0D0/9.0D0
      WRITE(6, 30) X, Y, Z
   30 FORMAT(1X, D20.12)
```

11.5   Suppose A = 9999999.0, B = 125.0, and C = 9999998.0.   Observe that

$$X = A + B - C = 126.0$$

(which can be obtained using double precision arithmetic).

(a)   Calculate X using single precision arithmetic (assuming seven significant digits).

(b)   Find the error and percent error.

11.6   Write a program which calculates $n!$ for $n = 1, 2, \ldots, 15$.   (Double precision arithmetic must be used since neither integer arithmetic nor single precision arithmetic is accurate enough.)

11.7   Recall that the area of a triangle whose sides have lengths a, b, c is given by

$$AREA = \sqrt{s(s-a)(s-b)(s-c)}$$

where

$$s = (a + b + c)/2$$

Write a program which reads values for a, b, c and calculates and prints the AREA using double precision arithmetic.

COMPLEX NUMBERS

11.8   Let $z = 2 - 3i$ and $w = 4 + 5i$.   Find algebraically

    (*a*) $z + w$ (*b*) zw (*c*) z/w (*d*) $\bar{z}$ and $\bar{w}$ (*e*) $|z|$ and $|w|$

    Verify the results on a computer using a Fortran program.

11.9   Assuming X, Y, Z are complex variables and A, B, C are real variables, find errors, if any, in each statement.

    (*a*) X = (3, 4.5)   (*c*) Z = 3.6 + (5.0, 7.6)

    (*b*) Y = (A, B + C)   (*d*) A = COMPLEX(B, C)

11.10   Suppose the first two data cards are punched as follows:

```
                        1               2
              12345678901234567890012345

First card        1.1  2.2  3.3  4.4


Second card       5.5  6.6  7.7  8.8
```

Find the output of each program segment:

    (*a*)   COMPLEX A, B, C   (*b*)   COMPLEX A, B, C

            READ(5, 10) A, B   READ(5, 50) A, B

      10   FORMAT(2F5.1)   50   FORMAT(3F5.1)

            C = A*B   C = A*B

            WRITE(6, 20) C   WRITE(6, 60) C

      20   FORMAT(1X, F10.2)   60   FORMAT(1X, 'REAL PART IS', 7X, F10.2/1X,

                                1   'IMAGINARY PART IS', 2X, F10.2)

11.11   Write a program which reads three complex numbers and prints the three numbers on one line, and their sum and product on a second line.

11.12   Write a program which reads real numbers a, b, c and solves the quadratic equation

$$ax^2 + bx + c = 0$$

Use the formula

$$x = \frac{-b \pm \sqrt{b^2 - 4ac}}{2a}$$

(Note that the roots are complex if the discriminant $D = b^2 - 4ac$ is less than zero.)

ASSIGNED GO TO STATEMENTS, MULTIPLE ENTRIES AND RETURNS

11.13   Find errors, if any, in each Fortran statement:

(a)   ASSIGN +45 TO NUMBER   (c)   GO TO NUMBER (5, 78, 6, −43)

(b)   ASSIGN N TO NUMBER   (d)   GO TO 200, (75, 25, 200, 50)

11.14   Find errors, if any, in each Fortran program segment:

(a)   ASSIGN 25 TO NEXT   (b)   ASSIGN 25 TO NEXT
     GO TO NEXT, (50, 75, 300)   NEXT = 50
                                          GO TO NEXT, (25, 40, 50, 70)

11.15   Find errors, if any, in the following program skeleton:

Main program	*Subprogram*
....	SUBROUTINE BIG(A, B, C)
CALL BIG(X, Y, Z)	....
....	ENTRY MIDDLE(X, Y, Z)
CALL MIDDLE(P, A + B)	....
....	ENTRY RATE(C, D, K)
CALL RATE(X + Y, J, N + 4)	....
....	END
STOP	
END	

11.16   Consider the following CALL statement and corresponding SUBROUTINE statement:

        CALL UPDATE(A, 88, B, 36, C, N, 44)
        SUBROUTINE UPDATE(X, *, Y, *, Z, NUMBER, *)

Find the point to which control is transferred if the following statement is encountered in the subprogram UPDATE:

(a)   RETURN 1   (b)   RETURN 2   (c)   RETURN 3   (d)   RETURN

COMMON, EQUIVALENCE

11.17   Find errors, if any, in each Fortran statement:

(a)   COMMON (X, Y, Z)
(b)   EQUIVALENCE X, Y, Z
(c)   COMMON X, Y(2, 4), Z(8), W,
(d)   EQUIVALENCE (X, Y) (A(1), B(4), Z)
(e)   COMMON /A/ NUM(5), X, /B/ INDEX(4, 5)

11.18   Sketch the storage layout which results from the following program skeleton:

Main program	*Subprogram*
COMMON Y(4), A, B, C(2)	SUBROUTINE NNN(P1, P2, P3)
....	COMMON D, X(2), E(2), F(2)
CALL NNN(P, Q, R)	....
....	END
END	

11.19   Determine the storage layout which results from the following program segments:

(a)   DIMENSION A(5), B(4), C(7)   (b)   DIMENSION X(2, 3), Y(3, 2)
     EQUIVALENCE (A(1), B(1), C(2))   EQUIVALENCE(X(3), Y(1))

11.20 Suppose A is an 3×3 matrix array. We want DIAG to be a linear array with three elements denoting the diagonal entries of A. Discuss the error in the following program segment:

```
DIMENSION A(3, 3), DIAG(3)
EQUIVALENCE (A(1), DIAG(1)), (A(5), DIAG(2)), (A(9), DIAG(3))
```

Answers to Selected Problems

11.1 (a) There should not be a comma after INTEGER.
       (b) R is declared twice with different sizes.   There should not be a comma after S.
       (c) There should not be a comma after IMPLICIT.   There should be a comma before LOGICAL.
       (d) IMPLICIT REAL(M, N), COMPLEX(P − R)
       (e) There should be commas before X and L.

11.2 (a) real   (b) complex   (c) real   (d) complex   (e) logical   (f) real
       (g) integer   (h) real   (i) integer   (j) logical   (k) integer   (l) real

11.3 (a) double   (b) real   (c) double   (d) Neither, since it is an integer.   (e) double
       (f) double   (g) double   (h) real   (i) double

11.4 (a) 0.556E 00   0.555666700E 00   (b) 0.700000000000D 01
            0.556D 00   0.555666778D 00   0.777777700000D 01
                                                      0.777777777778D 01

11.5 (a) 122.0   (b) Error = 4, which is 3 percent.

11.7 All variables should be declared DOUBLE PRECISION, and the double precision square root function DSQRT should be used:

```
      DOUBLE PRECISION A, B, C, S, AREA
      READ(5, 10) A, B, C
   10 FORMAT(3D20.10)
      S = (A + B + C)/2.0
      AREA = DSQRT(S*(S − A)*(S − B)*(S − C))
      WRITE(6, 20) AREA
   20 FORMAT(1X, 'AREA IS', 3X, D20.12)
      STOP
      END
```

11.8 (a) $6 + 2i$ (b) $23 − 2i$ (c) $−7/41 − 22i/41$ (d) $2 + 3i, 4 − 5i$ (e) $\sqrt{13}, \sqrt{41}$

11.9 (a) The 3 should be written 3.0.
       (b) CMPLX(A, B + C), not (A, B + C).
       (c) Correct.
       (d) CMPLX(B, C), not COMPLEX(B, C).

11.10 (a) −8.47   (b) REAL PART IS   −8.47
             19.36   IMAGINARY PART IS   13.31

11.13   (*a*)   43 must be unsigned since it must be a statement number.
      (*b*)   The N must be an actual statement number, not an integer variable.
      (*c*)   There should be a comma after NUMBER.   Also −43 is not permitted.
      (*d*)   The first 200 must be an integer variable, not an integer constant.

11.14   (*a*)   The value 25 of NEXT must appear in the list following NEXT in the GO TO statement.
      (*b*)   The value of NEXT can only be changed by another ASSIGN statement, for example,

          ASSIGN 30 TO NEXT

     It cannot be changed by an arithmetic assignment statement.

11.15   MIDDLE in main program has only two arguments, but MIDDLE has three parameters in the subprogram. The second argument J in RATE should be real since it corresponds to the real parameter D.

11.16   (*a*)   To the statement labeled 88 in the calling program.
      (*b*)   To the statement labeled 36 in the calling program.
      (*c*)   To the statement labeled 44 in the calling program.
      (*d*)   To the first executable statement following the CALL statement.

11.17   (*a*)   The variables should not be enclosed in parentheses.
      (*b*)   The variables should be enclosed in parentheses.
      (*c*)   There should not be a comma after W.
      (*d*)   There should be a comma after (X, Y).
      (*e*)   There should not be a comma after X.

11.18   Name in main program: Y(1) Y(2) Y(3) Y(4)   A   B   C(1) C(2)
       Name in subprogram: D   X(1) X(2) E(1) E(2) F(1) F(2)

11.19   (*a*)   A(1) A(2) A(3) A(4) A(5)
                B(1) B(2) B(3) B(4)
        C(1) C(2) C(3) C(4) C(5) C(6) C(7)
      (*b*) X(1, 1) X(2, 1) X(1, 2) X(2, 2) X(1, 3) X(2, 3)
                   Y(1, 1) Y(2, 1) Y(3, 1) Y(1, 2) Y(2, 2) Y(3, 2)

11.20   The three equivalences indicate that DIAG(1) should share a location with A(1, 1), DIAG(2) with A(2, 2), and DIAG(3) with A(3, 3) as follows:

        A(1, 1)   A(2, 1) A(3, 1) A(1, 2) A(2, 2)   A(3, 2) A(1, 3) A(2, 3) A(3, 3)
        DIAG(1)   DIAG(2)   DIAG(3)

However, the above violates the condition that the elements of an array must appear next to each other in storage; that is, we cannot separate the elements of DIAG.

Chapter 12

Structured Fortran

Even with many years of practice and experience, it is very difficult to master the art of programming. Beginners sometimes become very confused and discouraged because their programs often turn out to be mere collections of statements without apparent organization and logic.

The primary source of confusion and error in Fortran programming can be traced to: (1) the confusing control structures in the Fortran language itself, and (2) the undisciplined use of some of the Fortran constructs, notably the GO TO statements.

Over the years, certain principles for good programming practice have evolved, and this has given rise to the notion of structured programming. Accordingly, many nicely structured control mechanisms were incorporated into many Fortran preprocessors. These structured Fortran constructs seem to help reduce beginners' confusions and reduce errors, and programs written with them are more readable and can be more easily understood and modified.

This chapter discusses some of these popular control structures, their use, and their relationship to unstructured Fortran. In fact, those readers with access to structured Fortran processors can study the IF-structures after Chapter 4 and the DO structures after Chapter 5.

12.1 IF-STRUCTURES

The IF-structures in structured Fortran have several variations. However, each IF-structure always begins with a *block* IF *statement* which has the form

    IF(*logexp*) THEN

(where *logexp* is a logical expression) and ends with the

    ENDIF

statement. These two statements serve as delimiters enclosing the body of the structure. We discuss some of these variations.

Single Alternative

One form of an IF-structure and its flowchart equivalent are shown in Fig. 12-1.

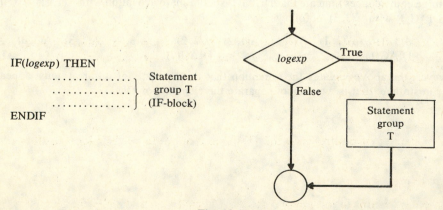

Fig. 12-1

As indicated by the flowchart, the logical expression *logexp* is evaluated first.   If *logexp* is true, then the entire statement group T (called an IF-block) is executed.   If *logexp* is false, then the statement group T is skipped, and control is transferred to the first statement following the ENDIF statement.

The above IF-structure is equivalent to either of the following unstructured Fortran program segments which use the logical IF statement:

```
     IF(.NOT.logexp) GO TO 10                          IF(logexp) GO TO 20
                                                        GO TO 10
           ................  }  Statement         20
           ................  }  group T                      ...........   }  Statement
           ................  }                                ...........   }  group T
  10  ...............                                         ...........   }
                                                        10  ...............
```

Observe that the first segment uses the complement of *logexp* in the logical IF statement; this avoids the use of an extra GO TO statement as in the second segment. The complement of a logical expression can be obtained by simply putting .NOT. before the expression.   However, for single relational operators, the complements are shown as:

Operator	.EQ.	.NE.	.GT.	.GE.	.LT.	.LE.
Complement	.NE.	.EQ.	.LE.	.LT.	.GE.	.GT.

We note that the complement of the complement of a logical expression *logexp* is *logexp* itself; namely, .NOT.(.NOT.*logexp*) is equivalent to *logexp*.

EXAMPLE 12.1

The following Fortran segments are equivalent:

```
(a)   IF(A.GT.B) THEN        (b)      IF(A.LE.B) GO TO 10
          TEMP = A                        TEMP = A
          A = B                           A = B
          B = TEMP                        B = TEMP
      ENDIF                        10  ....................
```

A single alternative IF-structure containing only a single statement in its statement group is equivalent to a logical IF statement, and vice versa.   For example, the following are equivalent:

```
(a)   IF(BIG.LT.A) THEN      (b)   IF(BIG.LT.A) BIG = A
          BIG = A
      ENDIF
```

Remark.   Transfer of control into the IF-block from outside the block itself is not allowed.

Double Alternatives

To implement decisions involving two distinct alternatives, an ELSE clause may be inserted in the above IF-structure.   The general form of such a structure and its flowchart equivalent are shown in Fig. 12-2.

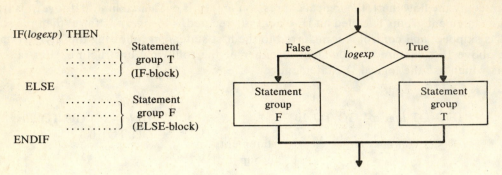

```
IF(logexp) THEN
         .........  ⎫ Statement
         .........  ⎬ group T
         .........  ⎭ (IF-block)
     ELSE
         .........  ⎫ Statement
         .........  ⎬ group F
         .........  ⎭ (ELSE-block)
ENDIF
```

Fig. 12-2

As indicated by the flowchart, the logical expression *logexp* is evaluated first. If *logexp* is true, then the entire IF-block (statement group T) is executed. If *logexp* is false, then the statement group F (called the ELSE-block) is executed instead. In either case, after the execution of either the group T or the group F, control is transferred to the first executable statement after the terminator statement ENDIF.

The above IF-structure is equivalent to either of the following Fortran segments using the logical IF statement:

(*a*)   IF(.NOT.*logexp*) GO TO 10   (*b*)   IF(*logexp*) GO TO 20

```
            .........  ⎫ Statement              .........  ⎫ Statement
            .........  ⎬ group T                .........  ⎬ group F
            .........  ⎭                        .........  ⎭
        GO TO 99                            GO TO 99
10          .........  ⎫ Statement       20      .........  ⎫ Statement
            .........  ⎬ group F                .........  ⎬ group T
            .........  ⎭                        .........  ⎭
99      .................                  99  .................
```

Observe that if the complement of *logexp* is not used, as in (*b*), then the positions of the statement groups are reversed; i.e., group F appears first and then group T, whereas in the IF-structure, group T appears first and then group F.

EXAMPLE 12.2

The following are equivalent; each calculates the GROSS wage of an employee who receives time and a half for overtime:

```
(a)     IF(HOUR.LE.40.0) THEN
                GROSS = HOUR*RATE
        ELSE
                GROSS = 40.0*RATE + (HOUR − 40.0)*1.5*RATE
        ENDIF
(b)     IF(HOUR.GT.40.0) GO TO 10
                GROSS = HOUR*RATE
        GO TO 99
    10          GROSS = 40.0*RATE + (HOUR − 40.0)*1.5*RATE
    99  .............................
```

Remark. As before, transfer of control into an IF-block or an ELSE-block from outside the block itself is not permitted.

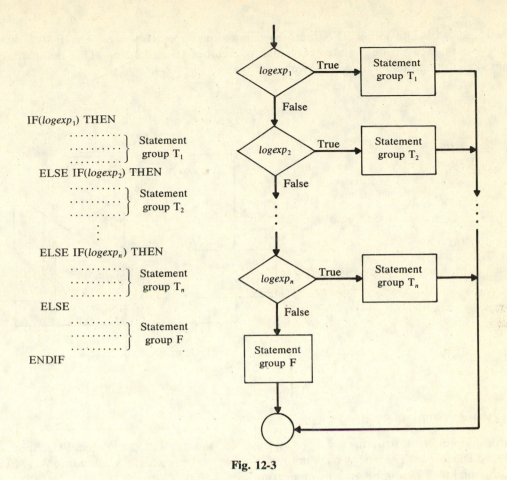

IF(*logexp₁*) THEN

................⎫ Statement
................⎬ group T₁
................⎭

ELSE IF(*logexp₂*) THEN

................⎫ Statement
................⎬ group T₂
................⎭

      ⋮

ELSE IF(*logexpₙ*) THEN

................⎫ Statement
................⎬ group Tₙ
................⎭

ELSE

................⎫ Statement
................⎬ group F
................⎭

ENDIF

Fig. 12-3

Multiple Alternatives

A number of ELSE IF clauses may also be inserted into the basic IF-structure to implement certain decisions involving more than two alternatives. Such a multiple-alternative structure and its equivalent flowchart have the form shown in Fig. 12-3.

As indicated by the flowchart, the logical expressions $logexp_1$, $logexp_2$, ... are evaluated one by one. If $logexp_k$ is the first expression that is true, then the statement group T_k is executed. If all the expressions are false, then the statement group F is evaluated. In any event, after one of the statement groups is executed, control is then transferred to the first instruction following the ENDIF statement.

The use of ELSE is optional. Namely, if there is no statement group F, then the key word ELSE is also omitted.

EXAMPLE 12.3

The following is a structured Fortran segment which calculates the BONUS of a salesman. Many GO TO statements would be required if the program were written in unstructured Fortran.

```
IF(SALES.LE.200.0) THEN
     BONUS = 0.0
ELSE IF(SALES.LE.1000.0) THEN
     BONUS = SALES*0.05
ELSE
     BONUS = 50.0 + SALES*0.02
ENDIF
```

Lastly, as with DO loops, IF-structures cannot overlap. However, an IF-structure can be completely contained inside a statement block of another IF-structure. This is illustrated in the program skeleton and its equivalent flowchart shown in Fig. 12-4.

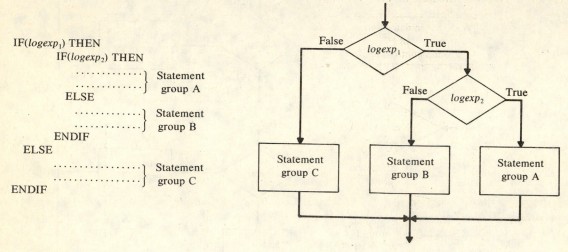

IF(*logexp$_1$*) THEN
    IF(*logexp$_2$*) THEN
        ⋯⋯⋯⋯⋯} Statement
        ⋯⋯⋯⋯⋯} group A
    ELSE
        ⋯⋯⋯⋯⋯} Statement
        ⋯⋯⋯⋯⋯} group B
    ENDIF
ELSE
        ⋯⋯⋯⋯⋯} Statement
        ⋯⋯⋯⋯⋯} group C
ENDIF

Fig. 12-4

12.2 LOOP-CONTROL STRUCTURES

Three loop-control structures will be discussed: the WHILE loop, the FOR loop, and the generalized DO loop. The first two are implemented on many processors, including WATFIV-S, and the third is included in some versions of Fortran 77.

The DO loop in unstructured Fortran discussed in Chapter 5 has been a useful and convenient loop-control structure. However, there are several inconvenient restrictions; namely, the loop-control variable (the index) must be of integer type, the loop parameters cannot be arithmetic expressions, and one cannot decrement the index. These drawbacks prompted the construction of many other loop structures. The WHILE-structure and the FOR-structure, which we discuss next, are two of the most popular ones.

WHILE-Structure

Many iterative processes cannot be easily controlled by a counter. Frequently, in such cases, the WHILE-structure may be conveniently used. This structure has the following general form:

WHILE(*logexp*) DO
    ⋯⋯⋯⋯⋯
    ⋯⋯⋯⋯⋯} Body of the loop
    ⋯⋯⋯⋯⋯
ENDWHILE

The logical expression *logexp* is evaluated first. If it is true, then the body of the loop is executed. Furthermore, the body of the loop will be repeated as long as *logexp* is true. When *logexp* is false, the body of the loop is skipped, and control is transferred to the first statement after the ENDWHILE statement. Observe that the WHILE and the ENDWHILE statements serve as delimiters enclosing the iterative structure.

It is most important to remember that the logical expression *logexp* is always evaluated first before the loop is executed.

Normally, one or more variables may be involved in the logical expression *logexp* of the WHILE-structure. These variables, called loop-control variables, must be initialized prior to the execution of the WHILE-structure. To avoid having an infinite loop, the values of the variables must also be updated with each loop iteration. The update is usually done just before the ENDWHILE statement. This is indicated in the flowchart in Fig. 12-5 which represents the WHILE-structure.

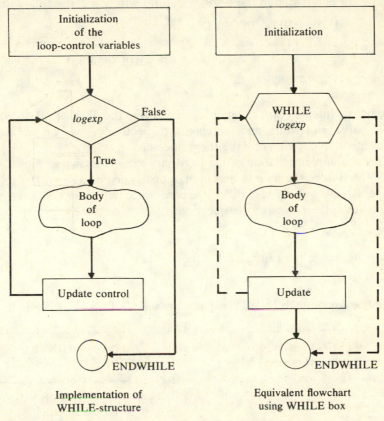

Implementation of
WHILE-structure

Equivalent flowchart
using WHILE box

Fig. 12-5

EXAMPLE 12.4

Consider the quadratic polynomial $y = 2x^2 - 3x - 5$. The following Fortran program using the WHILE-structure finds y for values of x from -4 to 4 in steps of 0.5.

```
        X = -4.0
        WHILE(X.LE.4.0) DO
                Y = 2.0*X**2 - 3.0*X - 5.0
                WRITE(6, 10) X, Y
10              FORMAT(2(3X, F10.3))
                X = X + 0.5
        ENDWHILE
```

Compare the simplicity of the above program with the program in Problem 5.11(*a*), which does the same thing but uses the basic indexed DO loop. There it was necessary to count the number of iterations and also to write X in terms of the index I.

FOR-Structure

As mentioned before, one severe restriction of the unstructured DO loop is its inability to decrement the index. Another drawback is that the index is not tested for the end value until after the first iteration.   Thus even though M > N, the basic (unstructured) DO loop headed by the DO statement

$$DO\ 50\ K = M, N$$

will be executed once.

These drawbacks are eliminated in the FOR-structure, which has the following form:

$$FOR(INDEX = INV, ENDV, INCR)\ DO$$

> ....
> .... } Body of the loop
> ....

ENDFOR

The INDEX must be an integer variable name.   However, the INV, ENDV, and INCR, which represent the *initial value*, *end value*, and *increment*, respectively, may be any integer expression except that the increment INCR cannot have the value zero.

The flowchart for the implementation of the FOR-structure is shown in Fig. 12-6.   The INDEX is initially set to INV.   Before the loop is executed, a test is given to see if the INDEX has passed the given end value ENDV.   This test differs according to whether INCR is positive or negative.   If INCR is positive, the test asks the question:

$$Is\ INDEX \leq ENDV?$$

However, if INCR is negative, the test asks the question:

$$Is\ INDEX \geq ENDV?$$

The loop is executed as long as the INDEX has not passed ENDV, i.e., as long as the result of the

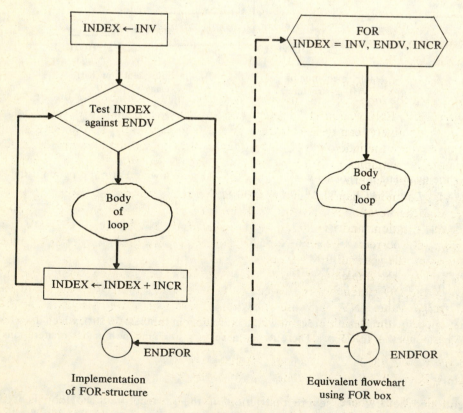

Fig. 12-6

test is "yes". After the loop is executed, the value of the INDEX is incremented by INCR before the next iteration.

As the increment INCR may be negative, the INDEX is able to decrease in value. This advantage is illustrated in the next example.

EXAMPLE 12.5

Suppose we want to print the integers $100, 99, 98, \ldots, 1$, in this order. We do this in two ways: (1) with the basic (unstructured) DO loop (see Example 5.5) and (2) with the FOR-structure:

```
(a)         DO 500 K = 1, 100      (b)         FOR(K = 100, 1, −1) DO
                J = 101 − K                        WRITE(6, 30) K
                WRITE(6, 30) J          30         FORMAT(1X, I5)
        30      FORMAT(1X, 5I)                  ENDFOR
        500 CONTINUE
```

Note in (b) that the loop terminates when K has the value 0, i.e., has passed the end value 1.

Generalized DO Loop (Structured DO Loop)

The WHILE-structures and the FOR-structures eliminate some of the drawbacks of the basic (unstructured) DO loop discussed in Chapter 5. The new Fortran 77 contains a generalized DO loop construct which combines the features of both the WHILE-structure and the FOR-structure into one construction.

This generalized DO loop has the same basic appearance as the indexed DO loop introduced in Sections 5.3 and 5.4. Namely, it will have the following form:

DO n VAR = INV, ENDV, INCR

```
        ........................
        ........................  }  Body of the DO loop
        ........................
    n   CONTINUE
```

Again, the DO-CONTINUE pair encompasses the body of the loop to be repeated.

The VAR, called the *loop-control variable*, may be the name of an integer or a real variable; the *loop parameters* INV, ENDV, and INCR, representing the *initial value, end value* (or *test value*), and *increment*, respectively, can be any integer or real expressions. (This contrasts with the DO loop in Chapter 5 where the index had to be an integer variable and the parameters positive integer constants or integer variables.) If INCR is not present, the increment is assumed to be 1; however, INCR cannot be zero.

From the discussion in Chapter 5 and on the FOR-structure above, the above DO-CONTINUE form suggests that the iteration starts with VAR initially set to INV, then VAR is incremented by INCR with each iteration, and the iteration is repeated until VAR passes ENDV. This interpretation is basically correct. However, it is essential that we give the precise meaning of this important construct, the generalized DO loop.

The flowchart for the implementation of the generalized DO loop appears in Fig. 12-7. With the execution of the DO statement, the values of INV, ENDV, and INCR are evaluated, VAR is assigned the initial value INV, and the *iteration count*, which we designate by KOUNT, is evaluated. Normally, the iteration count KOUNT can be calculated as the result of the integer value of $(\text{ENDV} − \text{INV} + \text{INCR})/\text{INCR}$. For example,

DO 100 K = 2, 13, 3 ·   yields   KOUNT = 4
DO 200 K = 2.0, 1.0, −0.05   yields   KOUNT = 21

To account for situations where INV > ENDV and INCR is positive, or where INV < ENDV and INCR is negative (i.e., where VAR has initially passed the end value ENDV), KOUNT is assigned

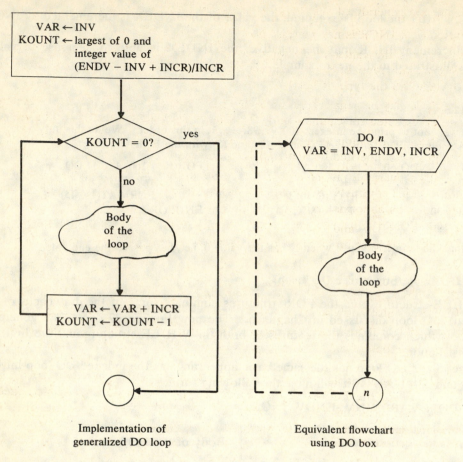

Implementation of
generalized DO loop

Equivalent flowchart
using DO box

Fig. 12-7

the larger of zero and the integer value of (ENDV − INV + INCR)/INCR. We emphasize that this
number KOUNT gives the number of times the loop is to be executed.

As indicated by Fig. 12-7, before the loop is executed, KOUNT is tested for zero. If
KOUNT ≠ 0, the loop is executed, and VAR is incremented by INCR and the iteration count
KOUNT is decreased by one. When KOUNT = 0, control is transferred to the first executable
statement following the CONTINUE statement.

EXAMPLE 12.6

(*a*) Suppose we want to print the integers 100, 99, . . . , 1, in this order. Using the generalized DO loop,
we simply have

```
        DO 500 K = 100, 1, −1
              WRITE(6, 30) K
   30         FORMAT(1X, I5)
  500   CONTINUE
```

(*b*) Using the generalized DO loop for the problem in Example 12.4, we have

```
        DO 999 X = −4.0, 4.0, 0.5
              Y = 2.0*X**2 − 3.0*X − 5.0
              WRITE(6, 10) X, Y
   10         FORMAT(2(3X, F10.3))
  999   CONTINUE
```

Properties of the generalized DO loop can be summarized as follows:

1. As usual, if INCR is not present, it is assumed to be 1.

2. The type of the values of the loop parameters INV, ENDV, and INCR need not be the same as the type of VAR. In such a case, the values of the parameters are first converted to the type of VAR.

3. As INCR may be negative, it is possible for VAR to decrease in value. In any case, the loop is executed for each value of VAR until VAR passes the end value ENDV.

4. The value of the loop variable VAR may not be altered within the body of the DO loop except by its inherited incrementing mechanism.

5. The loop variable is always defined when control is transferred from the DO loop. [This contrasts with the index of the basic (unstructured) DO loop, which is only defined in an abnormal exit from the loop.]

6. If INV > ENDV and INCR is positive, or if INV < ENDV and INCR is negative, KOUNT will have an initial value of zero and the body of the loop will not be executed at all.

7. Transfer of control into the middle of a generalized DO loop from the outside is not allowed (as with the basic indexed DO loop). Rules for nested DO loops discussed in Section 5.9 also apply here.

8. DO loops and IF-structures cannot overlap. However, a DO loop can be contained in a statement block of an IF-structure, and an IF-structure can be contained in a DO loop.

Remark. If the loop variable VAR is an integer variable, then the execution of the generalized DO loop is exactly like the FOR-structure discussed above. In fact, the generalized DO loop behaves much like the basic indexed DO loop except that (*a*) INCR may be negative; (*b*) the loop parameters INV, ENDV, and INCR may be expressions; and (*c*) testing is done before execution of the loop.

Solved Problems

IF-STRUCTURES

12.1 Suppose the RATE of interest on a loan AMT is 7% if AMT ≤ $10,000.00, but is 6% if AMT exceeds $10,000.00. Assuming INT is a real variable and AMT is in memory, write a program segment which finds the interest INT on the loan.

Figure 12-8 contains such a program. (Compare it with the unstructured program on page 84.)

```
IF(AMT.LE.10000.0) THEN
       RATE = 0.07
   ELSE
       RATE = 0.06
ENDIF
INT = AMT*RATE
WRITE(6, 10) AMT, RATE, INT
10   FORMAT(3(5X, F10.2))
```

Fig. 12-8

```
IF(TYPE.EQ.1) THEN
       NET = PAY − 9.75
   ELSE IF(TYPE.EQ.2) THEN
       NET = PAY − 16.25
   ELSE IF(TYPE.EQ.3) THEN
       NET = PAY − 24.50
ENDIF
WRITE(6, 20) ID, NET
20   FORMAT(1X, I5, 3X, F12.2)
```

Fig. 12-9

12.2   Suppose the health insurance premium is deducted from an employee's salary according to the following plan (where TYPE is an integer variable):

$$\text{Premium} = \begin{cases} 9.75 & \text{if TYPE} = 1 \quad \text{(single)} \\ 16.25 & \text{if TYPE} = 2 \quad \text{(married without children)} \\ 24.50 & \text{if TYPE} = 3 \quad \text{(married with children)} \end{cases}$$

Write a program segment deducting the premium from an employee's salary assuming his PAY, TYPE, and ID are in memory (and NET is a real variable).

The flowchart for such a program and an unstructured Fortran translation appear on page 89. Figure 12-9 contains a structured Fortran translation using the multiple-alternative IF-structure.

12.3   Write a program segment which reads an integer M and prints whether the integer is positive, negative, or zero.

Figure 12-10 contains such a program using the multiple-alternative IF-structure.

```
      READ(5, 10) M
10    FORMAT(I5)
      WRITE(6, 20) M
20    FORMAT(1X, I5, 2X, 'IS')
      IF(M.GT.0) THEN
            WRITE(6, 30)
30          FORMAT(1X, 'POSITIVE')
      ELSE IF(M.EQ.0) THEN
            WRITE(6, 40)
40          FORMAT(1X, 'ZERO')
      ELSE
            WRITE(6, 50)
50          FORMAT(1X, 'NEGATIVE')
      ENDIF
```
Fig. 12-10

```
      READ(5, 10) A, B, C
10    FORMAT(3F10.2)
      WRITE(6, 20) A, B, C
20    FORMAT(1X, 'SIDES', 3(2X, F10.2))
      IF(A.EQ.B.AND.B.EQ.C) THEN
            WRITE(6, 30)
30          FORMAT(1X, 'EQUILATERAL')
      ELSE IF(A.EQ.B.OR.A.EQ.C.OR.B.EQ.C) THEN
            WRITE(6, 40)
40          FORMAT(1X, 'ISOSCELES')
      ENDIF
```
Fig. 12-11

12.4   Write a program segment which reads the lengths A, B, C of a triangle T and prints if T is equilateral or isosceles.

T is equilateral if $A = B$ and $B = C$. Otherwise, T is isosceles if $A = B$ or $A = C$ or $B = C$. Figure 12-11 contains such a program. (We use the logical connectives .AND. and .OR. discussed in Chapter 9.)

DO-STRUCTURES

12.5   Find the iteration count KOUNT for each DO statement.

(*a*)   DO 100 K = 4, 20, 3   (*c*)   DO 300 K = 4, −9, −2
(*b*)   DO 200 X = −4, 4, 0.6   (*d*)   DO 400 X = 5, −2, 0.2

First find the quotient Q = (ENDV − INV + INCR)/INCR. Let J denote the integer value of Q. Then KOUNT is J or 0, whichever is larger.

(*a*)   Q = (20 − 4 + 3)/3 = 19/3; so J = 6.   Hence KOUNT = 6.
(*b*)   Q = (4 + 4 + 0.6)/0.6 = 8.6/0.6; so J = 14.   Hence KOUNT = 14.
(*c*)   Q = (−9 − 4 − 2)/−2 = −15/−2; so J = 7.   Hence KOUNT = 7.
(*d*)   Q = (−2 − 5 + 0.2)/0.2 = −6.8/0.2; so J = −34.   Hence KOUNT = 0.

12.6 Find the final value of K and L.

(a)
```
        DO 100 K = 1, 5
            L = K**2
100     CONTINUE
        K = 2*K
```

(b)
```
        DO 200 K = 5, 1
            L = K**2
200     CONTINUE
        K = 2*K
```

(a) The DO loop is executed for K = 1, 2, 3, 4, and then 5. Hence the final value of L is $5^2 = 25$. However, when control is transferred from the loop, K was incremented to 6. Hence 12 is the final value of K.

(b) The DO loop is not executed at all since the iteration count KOUNT = 0; hence L is not defined. However, K is assigned the initial value 5 when the DO statement is executed. Hence 10 is the final value of K.

12.7 Suppose $z = x^3 - y^2$. Write a program segment which finds z for values of x and y where x and y vary from -4 to 4 in steps of 0.5.

Figure 12-12 contains such a program which uses nested generalized DO loops. [Compare this program with a similar program in Problem 5.11(b).]

```
        DO 200 X = -4, 4, 0.5
            DO 100 Y = -4, 4, 0.5
                Z = X**3 - Y**2
                WRITE(6, 10) X, Y, Z
10              FORMAT(3(2X, F10.2))
100         CONTINUE
200     CONTINUE
```

```
        FOR(J = N, K, -1) DO
            A(J + 1) = A(J)
        ENDFOR
        A(K) = D
```

Fig. 12-12   **Fig. 12-13**

12.8 Write a program segment using a FOR-structure which inserts an element D in the Kth position of an array A(1), A(2), ..., A(N).

As discussed in Problem 6.10, we must move the array segment A(K),...,A(N) down one position before assigning D to A(K). This is accomplished by first assigning A(N) to A(N + 1), then A(N − 1) to A(N), and so on until A(K) to A(K + 1). Figure 12-13 contains such a program.

12.9 Write a program using a WHILE-structure which prints all odd positive integers less than 100 omitting multiples of 7:

$$1, 3, 5, 9, 11, 15, 17, 19, 23, \ldots, 97, 99$$

Figure 12-14 contains such a program. Observe how N is initialized before the loop and updated at the end of the loop.

```
        N = 1
        WHILE(N.LT.100) DO
            K = (N*7)/7
            IF(K.EQ.N) GO TO 5
            WRITE(6, 10)
10          FORMAT(10X, I2)
5           N = N + 2
        ENDWHILE
```

```
        DIMENSION SCORE(300)
        N = 1
        READ(5, 10) GRADE
10      FORMAT(F8.0)
        WHILE(GRADE.GE.0.0) DO
            SCORE(N) = GRADE
            N = N + 1
            READ(5, 10)GRADE
        ENDWHILE
        N = N - 1
```

Fig. 12-14   **Fig. 12-15**

12.10   Student test scores are punched one to a card, and the deck has a trailer card punched with a negative number. Assuming there are less than 300 scores, write a program segment using a WHILE-structure which counts the number N of scores and stores them in an array SCORE.

Figure 12-15 contains such a program. Observe that N is decreased by one after control is transferred from the loop. (Why?)

Supplementary Problems

IF- AND DO-STRUCTURES

12.11   Suppose J = 5 and K = 10. Find the final value of J and K if each of the following is executed:

```
(a)   IF(J.LE.10) THEN        (c)   IF(J.GT.10) THEN
            K = K + 5                      K = K + 5
            J = J + K                      J = J + K
      ENDIF                         ENDIF
      J = J + K                     J = J + K
      J = 2*J                       J = 2*J

(b)   IF(J.LE.10) THEN        (d)   IF(J.GT.10) THEN
            K = K + 5                      K = K + 5
            J = J + K                      J = J + K
        ELSE                          ELSE
            J = J + K                      J = J + K
      ENDIF                         ENDIF
      J = 2*J                       J = 2*J
```

12.12   Consider the following program segments:

```
(i)   M = 5                   (ii)  M = 5
      IF(J.LT.K) THEN               IF(J.LT.K) THEN
            J = J + 5                      J = J + 5
            M = M + 3                      M = M + 3
      IF(J.LT.8) THEN               ELSE IF(J.LT.8) THEN
            M = M + 10                    M = M + 10
        ELSE                          ELSE
            M = M + 20                    M = M + 20
      ENDIF                         ENDIF
```

Find the final value of M for each program if:

(a)   J = 2, K = 5   (b)   J = 2, K = 1   (c)   J = 10, K = 15   (d)   J = 10, K = 1

12.13   Find the iteration count KOUNT for each DO statement.

(a)   DO 100 K = −3, 19, 4   (c)   DO 300 K = 2, 25, −6
(b)   DO 200 X = 4, −6, −0.3   (d)   DO 400 X = 1, −3, −0.2

12.14   Find the final value of J and M:

```
(a)         DO 100 J = 2, 9, 3      (c)         DO 300 J = 9, 2, 3
                  M = J + 5                            M = J + 5
      100   CONTINUE                 300   CONTINUE

(b)         DO 200 J = 9, 2, −5     (d)         DO 400 J = 2, 3, 9
                  M = J + 5                            M = J + 5
      200   CONTINUE                 400   CONTINUE
```

12.15   Find the final value of J, K, and L:

(a)   DO 100 J = 2, 6, 3   (b)   J = 3
                 DO 200 K = J, 4   WHILE(J.LT.6) DO
                      L = J + K   K = 2*J
         200   CONTINUE   L = 3*J
         100   CONTINUE   J = J + 2
                                              ENDWHILE

PROGRAMS

12.16   A test score T is assigned the letter grade A, B, C, D, or F according as:

$$T \geq 90, \quad 80 \leq T < 90, \quad 70 \leq T < 80, \quad 60 \leq T < 70, \quad \text{or} \quad T < 60$$

Write a program which reads a test score T and prints its letter grade.

12.17   Each card in a deck contains a student's test score, and the deck has a trailer card with a negative number. Write a program which finds the number N of students who took the exam, the number M of students who had perfect papers (i.e., who scored 100), and the number L of students who failed (i.e., who scored <60).

12.18   Write a program which computes the real roots of the quadratic equation

$$ax^2 + bx + c = 0$$

given the coefficients A, B, C with A $\neq$ 0.   (Compare it with the program on page 90.)

12.19   Write a program which reads three positive numbers A, B, C and determines whether A, B, C can be the lengths of the sides of a triangle. If yes, compute the perimeter of the triangle; if no, print the message 'NOT A TRIANGLE'. (Hint: A, B, C cannot form a triangle if and only if one side is greater than or equal to the sum of the other two sides.)   Test the program with the data:
(a)   A = 3.0, B = 4.0, C = 5.0   (b)   A = 3.0, B = 12.0, C = 5.0

12.20   Write a program segment using a generalized DO loop which inserts an element D in the Kth position of an array A(1), A(2), ..., A(n).   (Compare with Problems 12.8 and 6.10.)

12.21   Find the number of points with integer coordinates which lie inside:
(a)   the circle $x^2 + y^2 = 50$ (b)   the ellipse $2x^2 + 3y^2 = 100$
(Compare with Problem 5.12.)

12.22   Write a program which prints the number 20 twenty times, the number 19 nineteen times, the number 18 eighteen times, and so on.

12.23   Each card in a deck contains a positive integer, and the deck has a blank trailer card.   Write a program which finds the number of the integers which are even and the number which are odd.

12.24   Consider the equation $y = x^2 - 4x + 6$.   Write a program which finds y for values of x from I to J in increments D, where I, J, and D are on a card and I < J and D > 0.

12.25   Suppose \$2,000.00 is deposited in a savings account at 7% interest compounded annually.   Write a program using a WHILE-structure to determine the number of years it takes for the account to reach \$5,000.00.

12.26 A department store decides to give a discount on the PRICE of a color television set according to the SIZE in inches of the TV as follows:

$$\text{Discount} = \begin{cases} \$\ \ 40.00 & \text{if SIZE} = 12 \text{ or } 15 \\ \$\ \ 70.00 & \text{if SIZE} = 17 \text{ or } 19 \\ \$110.00 & \text{if SIZE} = 21 \text{ or } 23 \\ \$140.00 & \text{if SIZE} = 25 \end{cases}$$

There is an additional discount of 3% of the PRICE if $300 \le \text{PRICE} < 400$, and 4% if $\text{PRICE} > 400$. Write a program which reads the ID number of a TV and its SIZE and PRICE, and finds the NET cost of the TV. (Assume SIZE is an integer variable and NET is a real variable.)

12.27 There are four candidates for a position on the school board. A person votes by punching 1, 2, 3, or 4 on a card. The deck of cards will have a trailer card on which -1 is punched. Write a program which counts the number N of people who vote and the number of votes for each candidate.

12.28 Redo Problem 12.27, except now the program also finds the winner of the election.

12.29 Redo Problem 12.27, except now there are five candidates for two positions, and the program also finds the two winners.

Answers to Selected Problems

12.11 (*a*) 70, 15   (*b*) 40, 15   (*c*) 30, 10   (*d*) 30, 10

12.12 (*a*) (*i*) 18   (*ii*) 8   (*c*) (*i*) 28   (*ii*) 8
      (*b*) (*i*) 15   (*ii*) 15   (*d*) (*i*) 25   (*ii*) 25

12.13 (*a*) 5   (*b*) 33   (*c*) 0   (*d*) 20

12.14 (*a*) J = 11, M = 13   (*c*) J = 9, M not defined
      (*b*) J = −1, M = 9   (*d*) J = 11, M = 7

12.15 (*a*) J = 8, K = 5, L = 4   (*b*) J = 7, K = 10, L = 15

Appendix A

Library Functions

This appendix gives a list of library (built-in) functions which are available to most Fortran systems. The arguments of the functions in Table A-1 are denoted by the following symbols, which also tell their type:

J, K   integer type   DX, DY   double precision type

X, Y   real type   C   complex type

The word *double* will be used for double precision. The sign of an argument a, denoted by sgn(a), is defined as:

$$\text{sgn}(a) = \begin{cases} 1 & \text{if } a \geq 0 \\ -1 & \text{if } a < 0 \end{cases}$$

The largest integer function, denoted by $[a]$, gives the largest integer $\leq a$.

Table A-1

Verbal description	Definition	Function name with arguments	Function type
Square root	$\sqrt{a}$	SQRT(X) DSQRT(DX) CSQRT(C)	Real Double Complex
Exponential	e^a	EXP(X) DEXP(DX) CEXP(C)	Real Double Complex
Natural logarithm	$\log_e(a)$	ALOG(X) DLOG(DX) CLOG(C)	Real Double Complex
Common logarithm	$\log_{10}(a)$	ALOG10(X) DLOG10(DX)	Real Double
Absolute value	$\lvert a \rvert$	IABS(J) ABS(X) DABS(DX)	Integer Real Double
Functions of a complex argument $C = x + iy$: 　Magnitude 　Complex conjugate 　Real part 　Imaginary part	 $\sqrt{x^2 + y^2}$ $x - iy$ x y	 CABS(C) CONJG(C) REAL(C) AIMAG(C)	 Real Complex Real Real

Table A-1 (*Continued*)

Verbal description	Definition	Function name with arguments	Function type
Complex form of two real values x, y	$x + iy$	CMPLX(X, Y)	Complex
Type conversion	Convert integer to real	FLOAT(J)	Real
	Convert integer to double precision	DFLOAT(J)	Double
	Convert real to double precision	DBLE(X)	Double
	Convert double precision to real by truncation	SNGL(DX)	Real
	Convert real to integer by truncation	IFIX(X)	Integer
Largest value	$\text{Max}(a_1, a_2, \ldots)$	MAX0(J, K, ...)	Integer
		MAX1(X, Y, ...)	Integer
		AMAX0(J, K, ...)	Real
		AMAX1(X, Y, ...)	Real
		DMAX1(DX, DY, ...)	Double
Smallest value	$\text{Min}(a_1, a_2, \ldots)$	MIN0(J, K, ...)	Integer
		MIN1(X, Y, ...)	Integer
		AMIN0(J, K, ...)	Real
		AMIN1(X, Y, ...)	Real
		DMIN1(DX, DY, ...)	Double
Positive difference or zero of (a_1, a_2)	$a_1 - \min(a_1, a_2)$	IDIM(J, K)	Integer
		DIM(X, Y)	Real
Trigonometric functions with argument in radian measure	$\sin(a)$	SIN(X)	Real
		DSIN(DX)	Double
		CSIN(C)	Complex
	$\cos(a)$	COS(X)	Real
		DCOS(DX)	Double
		CCOS(C)	Complex
	$\tan(a)$	TAN(X)	Real
		DTAN(DX)	Double
Transfer of sign of (a_1, a_2)	$|a_1| \cdot \text{sgn}(a_2)$	ISIGN(J, K)	Integer
		SIGN(X, Y)	Real
		DSIGN(DX, DY)	Double
Modulus truncation	$\text{sgn}(a) \cdot [|a|]$	INT(X)	Integer
		AINT(X)	Real
		IDINT(DX)	Integer
Find the representative with the smallest absolute value in the residue class of a_1 (modulo a_2)	$a_1 - \text{sgn}(b)[|b|] \cdot a_2$, where $b = a_1/a_2$	MOD(J, K)	Integer
		AMOD(X, Y)	Real
		DMOD(DX, DY)	Double

Appendix B

Internal Representation of Data

INTRODUCTION

Each memory cell is composed of devices which are bistable in nature, i.e., devices which can be in either of two states. Since these states can be represented by the binary digits 0 and 1, each bistable device is capable of storing one *bit* (short for *b*inary dig*it*) of information. Usually, a collection or sequence of bits is used to represent a unit of information.

Since sequences of binary digits may be viewed as binary numbers, the representation of numbers in the binary system is important in computer science. Table B-1 lists the binary representation of the first sixteen positive integers. Sometimes, one uses the subscript 2 to distinguish a binary number from a decimal number; for example,

$(101101)_2$ means the binary number 101101

which has the decimal representation 45. A general discussion of the conversion of decimal numbers to binary numbers and vice versa lies beyond the scope of this appendix.

Table B-1

Decimal number	Binary number
1	1
2	10
3	11
4	100
5	101
6	110
7	111
8	1000
9	1001
10	1010
11	1011
12	1100
13	1101
14	1110
15	1111
16	10000

WORDS AND BYTES

The basic unit of information that is stored or retrieved from a memory cell is called a *word*. Some popular word sizes are 24, 30, 32, 36, 48, and 60 bits. There are computers with words of fixed length, and computers with words of variable length. However, each word in memory must have its own address. Furthermore, whenever we input/output a word from memory, all its bits are transmitted simultaneously.

Some computers also allow part of a word to be stored or retrieved from memory. Such a subunit of a word is called a *byte*. A byte usually consists of 6 or 8 bits and may be addressed individually. Machines with such features are said to be *byte-addressable*. The CDC 6000–7000 series has words composed of ten 6-bit bytes, giving a 60-bit word. For illustration purposes, we will assume that our machine is similar to the IBM 360/370 series, which has words composed of four 8-bit bytes, giving a 32-bit word as follows:

Word

Byte 0	Byte 1	Byte 2	Byte 3

Even in these byte-addressable machines, the word is still an important unit of information, its address being the address of its left-most byte.

CHARACTER DATA

Normally, the characters recognizable by any Fortran compiler include the 48 characters mentioned in Chapter 2; namely, the 10 digits, 26 alphabetical characters, and the 12 special characters. Since

$$2^5 < 48 < 2^6$$

a minimum of 6 bits is required to represent these characters. Any 6-bit character code can represent up to 64 distinct characters allowing for a maximum of $64 - 36 = 28$ special characters. Most third generation computers use 8-bit character codes. This would allow up to 256 characters, which is more than adequate.

The alphabetic characters are usually coded in their alphabetical order; i.e., the character code of A is smaller than the code for B, and so on. This coding forms a collating sequence that can be used for sorting alphabetical data. (See Chapter 9.)

The 8-bit (6-bit) code corresponding to a given character is usually arranged into a zoned portion, usually the four (three) left-most bits, and a numeric portion, usually the four (three) right-most bits. (See Fig. B-1.) The character code used by the IBM 360/370 machines is called

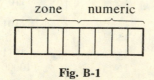

Fig. B-1

EBCDIC (Extended Binary Coded Decimal Interchange Code). Table B-2 gives the EBCDIC code for the 26 alphabetical characters and the 10 digits. Observe that the code for each digit contains 1111 in its zoned portion and its binary representation in its numeric portion. Since no more than four 8-bit characters may be stored in a 32-bit word, this explains the reason the character capacity of the IBM 360/370 series is M = 4.

Table B-2   EBCDIC Codes

Char	EBCDIC	Char	EBCDIC	Char	EBCDIC	Char	EBCDIC
	zone numeric		zone numeric		zone numeric		zone numeric
						0	1111 0000
A	1100 0001	J	1101 0001			1	0001
B	0010	K	0010	S	1110 0010	2	0010
C	0011	L	0011	T	0011	3	0011
D	0100	M	0100	U	0100	4	0100
E	0101	N	0101	V	0101	5	0101
F	0110	O	0110	W	0110	6	0110
G	0111	P	0111	X	0111	7	0111
H	1000	Q	1000	Y	1000	8	1000
I	1100 1001	R	1101 1001	Z	1110 1001	9	1111 1001

NUMERICAL DATA

There are essentially two different ways to code numerical data, coding the quantity or coding the individual digit.   We first discuss coding the quantity.

Coding the Quantity

Fortran provides both integer and floating point arithmetics for computation.   The internal representation of these two types of numerical data are different.

(a)   Integers

One straightforward way of representing an integer in a memory cell is to use its binary representation.   Assuming memory cells with 32 bits, with the first bit reserved for the sign, the integers 327 and -327 will be stored as follows:

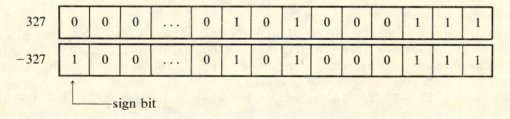

Accordingly, the largest integer that can be stored in a 32-bit word is

$$0\underbrace{(111\ldots 1111)_2}_{31 \text{ ones}}$$

representing $2^{31} - 1$.   Any attempt to store integers larger than the capacity will cause overflow, and the most significant digits will probably be lost.

For computational reasons, negative numbers are sometimes stored in memory using the so-called *radix-minus-one* complement or the *radix* complement representations.   We shall first discuss these representations in the decimal system where they are called the *nine*'s complement and the *ten*'s complement, respectively.   The nine's complement of a decimal number is obtained by subtracting each decimal digit from 9, and the ten's complement of a number is its nine's complement plus one.   For example,

Decimal number:	327	123	320
Nine's complement:	672	876	679
Ten's complement:	673	877	680

The corresponding complements for binary numbers are called the *one's* complement and *two's* complement, respectively.   Analogously, the one's complement of a binary number is obtained by subtracting each binary digit from 1 (i.e., converting each 0 to 1 and each 1 to 0), and the two's complement of a binary number is its one's complement plus one.   For example,

Binary number:	11001	10111	10100
One's complement:	00110	01000	01011
Two's complement:	00111	01001	01100

Representing negative numbers by complements enables us to perform subtraction using addition.   (Since multiplication is repeated addition and division is repeated subtraction, all integer arithmetic can thus be performed using addition.)   We indicate how this arithmetic works with an example:

Ordinary arithmetic	Decimal system using nine's complement	Binary system using one's complement with 32-bit word
705	705	$00000\ldots0001011000001$
-327	$+672$	$+11111\ldots1111010111000$
378	①377	①$00000\ldots0000101111001$
	→1	→1
	378	$00000\ldots0000101111010$

Observe that the left-most 1 is deleted and then added to the sum, as indicated by the arrows.   This is called "end-around carry".   The details of this arithmetic lies beyond the purpose of this appendix and so will not be discussed further.

(*b*)   Floating Point Numbers

Integer addition, subtraction, and multiplication always yield exact integer results.   However, integer division also yields an integer result, but then its fractional part is not stored.   Furthermore, no number with absolute value exceeding 2^{31} can be stored in a 32-bit word.   These limitations are the main reason why floating point numbers are used.

Consider the number -32.75.   Using normalized exponential notation, it can be written as

$$-0.3275 \times 10^2 \quad \text{with} \begin{cases} \text{sign} - \\ \text{fraction } 0.3275 \\ \text{exponent 2 (base 10)} \end{cases}$$

A similar representation can be used for binary numbers.   For example, the decimal number -32.75 can be written as the binary number $(-100000.11)_2$ and is normalized as

$$-0.10000011 \times 2^6 \quad \text{with} \begin{cases} \text{sign} - \\ \text{fraction } 0.10000011 \\ \text{exponent 6 (base 2)} \end{cases}$$

Clearly every real number can be so normalized to yield a unique sign, a unique binary fraction, and a unique binary exponent.   Thus, it can be stored internally as follows:

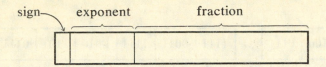

In our 32-bit word, we assume 1 bit for the sign, 7 bits for the exponent, and, hence, $32 - 8 = 24$ bits for the binary fraction. We note here that any real number, whether stored using E-field or F-field, will have the same internal representation as above.

Since an exponent may be negative, some arrangement must be made for its sign within its 7-bit field. Rather than using one bit to denote the sign of the exponent, we convert the true exponent to its so-called *characteristic* by adding $(100000)_2 = 2^6 = 64$, and then the characteristic is stored instead of the true exponent. The following shows the relationship between the true exponent and its characteristic:

True exponent:	−64	−63	−62	−61	...	−1	0	1	...	63
Characteristic:	0	1	2	3	...	63	64	65	...	127

(In case we use an 8-bit field for the exponent, we add $2^7 = 128$ to the true exponent to obtain its characteristic, and so on.)

Consider again the number -32.75, whose normalized binary representation is

$$-0.10000011 \times 2^6$$

Here the true exponent is 6, and so the characteristic is

$$6 + 64 = 70 = (100110)_2$$

Thus, -32.75 is stored internally as

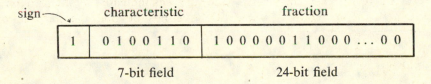

It can be seen that the largest floating point number that can be stored in a 32-bit word (using binary floating point form) is 2^{63}, and the smallest number is 2^{-64}. Any attempt to store numbers larger than 2^{63} (or smaller than 2^{-64}) will cause floating point overflow (or underflow). Because of the finite word length, floating point numbers may have inexact internal representations.

Lastly, we remark that in floating point form, complement notation is not used for negative fractions.

Coding Individual Digits

Another way to code numeric data is to use the zoned-format character code for each of its digits. In such a case, the sign is assigned to the zone field of the right-most digit as follows:

zone	digit	zone	digit	...	zone	digit	sign	digit

In EBCDIC, the plus and minus signs are represented by 1100 and 1101, respectively. Using Table B-2 for the EBCDIC codes of digits, the numbers 327 and −327 are coded as

3		2	+	7	
1111	0011	1111	0010	1100	0111

3		2	−	7	
1111	0011	1111	0010	1101	0111

The above is the way that numerical data are represented in input and output. However, when numerical data are used in computation, they are converted to a different form for easy processing. One such form is the binary coded decimal (BCD) system.

The BCD coding of numbers is similar to the above coding except that the zone fields are not used, and the sign code appears in the right-most field. In other words, one uses a 4-bit binary representation of each decimal digit in the number with the sign code on the end. Accordingly, 327 and −327 are coded in BCD as

3	2	7	+
0011	0010	0111	1100

3	2	7	−
0011	0010	0111	1101

Addition in BCD uses binary addition for the individual decimal digits. However, when a sum exceeds nine, a unit is carried to the next place as in ordinary decimal arithmetic. Any further discussion of this arithmetic lies beyond the scope of this appendix.

Index